Critical theory and human rights

Manchester University Press

Critical theory and contemporary society

Series editors:

David M. Berry, Professor of Digital Humanities, University of Sussex

Darrow Schecter, Professor of Critical Theory and Modern European History, University of Sussex

The *Critical Theory and Contemporary Society* series aims to demonstrate the ongoing relevance of multi-disciplinary research in explaining the causes of pressing social problems today and in indicating the possible paths towards a libertarian transformation of twenty-first century society. It builds upon some of the main ideas of first generation critical theorists, including Horkheimer, Adorno, Benjamin, Marcuse, and Fromm, but it does not aim to provide systematic guides to the work of those thinkers. Rather, each volume focuses on ways of thinking about the political dimensions of a particular topic, which include political economy, law, popular culture, globalisation, feminism, theology, and terrorism. Authors are encouraged to build on the legacy of first-generation Frankfurt School theorists and their influences (Kant, Hegel, Kierkegaard, Marx, Nietzsche, Weber, and Freud) in a manner that is distinct from, though not necessarily hostile to, the broad lines of second-generation critical theory. The series sets ambitious theoretical standards, aiming to engage and challenge an interdisciplinary readership of students and scholars across political theory, philosophy, sociology, history, media studies, and literary studies.

Previously published by Bloomsbury

Critical theory in the twenty-first century   Darrow Schecter
Critical theory and the critique of political economy   Werner Bonefeld
Critical theory and contemporary Europe   William Outhwaite
Critical theory of legal revolutions   Hauke Brunkhorst
Critical theory of libertarian socialism   Charles Masquelier
Critical theory and film   Fabio Vighi
Critical theory and the digital   David Berry
Critical theory and disability   Teodor Mladenov
Critical theory and the crisis of contemporary capitalism   Heiko Feldner and
   Fabio Vighi

Previously published by Manchester University Press

Critical theory and demagogic populism   Paul K. Jones
Critical theory and epistemology   Anastasia Marinopoulou
Critical theory and feeling   Simon Mussell
Critical theory and legal autopoiesis   Gunther Teubner
Critical theory and sociological theory   Darrow Schecter

Critical theory and human rights

From compassion to coercion

David McGrogan

MANCHESTER UNIVERSITY PRESS

Published by Manchester University Press
Oxford Road, Manchester M13 9PL

www.manchesteruniversitypress.co.uk

British Library Cataloguing-in-Publication Data

A catalogue record for this book is available from the British
Library

ISBN 978 1 5261 3182 9 hardback
ISBN 978 1 5261 7464 2 paperback

First published 2021
Paperback published 2023

Typeset by
Deanta Global Publishing Services

For my girls, M and E, and with thanks to Al Di Meola, Zoltan Kocsis, Ivo Pogorelich, and Glenn Gould for sanity-saving musical accompaniment.

Contents

Preface

This book would not have come into being were it not for the kindness of the series editors, Darrow Schecter and David Berry. I owe them my thanks for providing the opportunity to write it. The impetus to begin writing would also not have come about save for a period as a Research Fellow at Sussex Law School, and I would like to thank Alex Conte, Elizabeth Craig, and Stephanie Berry for making that possible.

Eric Heinze, Conall Mallory, Adam Ramshaw, Richard Mullender, and Eleni Frantziou all read parts of this book during its formation, and provided invaluable help in doing so. William Ralston, Birju Kotecha, Siobhan McConnell, Jaqueline Smart, James Gray, Helen Rutherford, and other colleagues at Northumbria Law School were perhaps of more hindrance than help in providing relentless friendly distraction, but the process of writing the book would not have been the same without them.

Any idiosyncrasy and eccentricity in the book's contents are attributable to me alone – as are any errors.

David McGrogan, 2020

Abbreviations

CEDAW	Committee on the Elimination of Discrimination Against Women/Convention on the Elimination of All Forms of Discrimination Against Women
CERD	Committee on the Elimination of Racial Discrimination/Convention on the Elimination of All Forms of Racial Discrimination
CESCR	Committee on Economic, Social and Cultural Rights
CRPD	Convention on the Rights of Persons with Disabilities
CRC	Children's Rights Committee/Convention on the Rights of the Child
ECOSOC	United Nations Economic and Social Council
EHRC	Equality and Human Rights Commission [UK]
FAO	Food and Agriculture Organization
FCO	Foreign & Commonwealth Office [UK]
HRC	Human Rights Committee
ICCPR	International Covenant on Civil and Political Rights
ICESCR	International Covenant on Economic, Social and Cultural Rights
IMF	International Monetary Fund
JCHR	Parliamentary Joint Committee on Human Rights [UK]
NHRI	National Human Rights Institution
OHCHR	Office of the United Nations High Commissioner for Human Rights
SHRC	Scottish Human Rights Commission
UDHR	Universal Declaration of Human Rights
UNESCO	United Nations Educational, Scientific and Cultural Organization
UNICEF	United Nations International Children's Fund
WHO	World Health Organization

Introduction

Moral realism

Lionel Trilling once called for a "moral realism" to alert those concerned with social injustice that there was a danger in the "moral life" – that to choose to act did not settle all moral problems, but simply displaced them.[1] The "moral passions," as he called them, were "wilful and imperious and impatient" – and their tendency was not to liberate, but to restrict. "Some paradox in our natures leads us," as he put it, "when once we have made our fellow men the objects of our enlightened interest, to go on and make them the objects of our pity, then of our wisdom, ultimately of our coercion."[2]

The subject matter of this book is how that paradox finds expression in modern international human rights law and practice. The core of its argument is that the chief concern of the human rights movement has become the deployment of political and economic power through the State, international organisation, and private enterprise in order to improve human well-being. This makes its character increasingly managerial, concerned above all with the technical and programmatic implementation of policies designed to achieve that broad aim. It is a project which is motivated by compassion, or "pity," but which gives rise to a vision of an all-knowing and all-encompassing form of governance whose final consequences, if fully realised, would be antithetical to individual freedom properly understood. The way in which the international human rights system has developed, in other words, traces precisely the path which Trilling described. The end result of this is an alienating discourse, about which ordinary rights-holders are, at best, unenthusiastic: "a set of reforms," as Orwell once described a movement of a not altogether dissimilar kind, "which 'we,' the clever ones, are going to impose upon 'them,' the Lower Orders."[3] This book argues that it should hardly be surprising if this has failed to capture the popular imagination.

The individual in the international human rights system

In making this argument, it is necessary to add nuance to a truism which has become ingrained in how human rights are understood to work – by advocates and critics alike. A story is told about human rights. In it, a world of sovereign States, governing themselves *inter se* by rules to which they and they alone are subject, suddenly finds the human individual thrust into its midst. For hundreds of years, "international law and the law governing individual life did not come together."[4] But the creation of the United Nations (UN) Charter and Universal Declaration of Human Rights (UDHR) brought about the recognition that "the individual, by dint of the acknowledgement of his fundamental rights and freedoms, [is] the ultimate subject of international law."[5]

This story has been criticised more or less since its inception, being described as ahistorical,[6] simplistic,[7] Whiggish, facile and triumphalist,[8] dismissive of the roles played by actors in the developing world during the Cold War,[9] and so on. But what these criticisms do not dispute is the basic essence of the human rights story: that it represents a reification of the entitlements of the *human individual* where hitherto there was simply a humanitarian charitable concern for individual people where it existed at all.

This has, accordingly, led critics of human rights of all stripes to predicate their critiques on the fact that human rights purportedly rely upon and buttress the primacy of the individual. The oldest iteration of this argument is, of course, that which has the finest pedigree, having been advanced by Marx: in it, individual rights find their "very Eden" in capitalist markets,[10] where they produce the individual as the stuff of commerce and the (un)emancipated citizen of the nation state.[11] In its more modern form, the Marxian critique finds expression in exposing a purported relationship between human rights and the "market fundamentalism" of neoliberalism, with these two movements seemingly having taken prominence in tandem beginning in the 1970s and reaching a shared apogee in the period 1993–2000. Here, human rights are described as a means to an end of globalising neoliberal democracy,[12] sharing with that agenda a suspicion of the State and a placement of the individual above all collective endeavours.[13] They do not so much provide a corrective to the excesses of "market fundamentalism" as they operationalise it, privileging private individual rights to facilitate the free movement of capital and the erosion of sovereignty.[14] Perhaps more subtly, scholars influenced by Foucault have described human rights as a form of neoliberal governmentality – a mechanism by which liberalism "self-limits" in order to produce the freedom on which it is predicated, and to manage and organise that freedom.[15] In this account, human rights are part of the "social frame" by which a market is "actively and ceaselessly created."[16]

The left critique of human rights, in other words, has always rested, and continues to rest, on rights' purported inherence in the individual. But the same is equally true of other critiques. There are those, for instance, which portray the individualism of human rights as an instantiation of the "European colonial project"[17] – an imposition of individualistic Western values on a world which primarily organises itself on communitarian and religious principles. Here, Western values, of which human rights are a part, do not merely undermine collectivist endeavours of the welfarist or statist stripe; they attack the foundations of societies – particularly Asian societies – which privilege the community over the individual and harmony over freedom.[18] And bearing a family resemblance to this argument is the view from the traditional conservative right in the West, which is that the language of individual rights crowds out notions of duty and responsibility, whether to one's self or others; this misses the "dimension of sociality" in solving political problems[19] and, at worst, cultivates a victim mentality that prevents people from marginalised groups thinking of themselves as citizens owing civic duties.[20]

Critiques of rights are diverse, then, but, they all tend to take rights' purported reification of the individual as their locus of attack. Yet this preoccupation with the relationship between rights and the individual, I will argue, has led both critics and supporters of human rights astray. It has caused them to overlook the fact that, quietly and almost unnoticed, the individual tends to disappear from view in the modern practice of international human rights law. In fact, as this book will argue, in the modern field of human rights practice, the individual has become a relatively minor concern – pertinent, as Foucault once put it, "only to the extent that, properly managed, maintained and encouraged, it will make possible what one wants to obtain at the level that is pertinent" – namely, the population.[21] Modern international human rights practice has become interested, in other words, chiefly in human rights in the abstract. Above all, its concern is with the concept of *human rights performance*.

An example will serve to demonstrate. In June 2014, the UK submitted its sixth periodic report to the Committee on Economic, Social and Cultural Rights (CESCR).[22] The List of Issues provided by the CESCR in response requests information, amongst other things, on the following: measures taken to ensure that corporations respect economic, social, and cultural rights throughout their operations; the UK's strategy to overcome gender inequality, including the gender pay gap; the impact of measures taken to address unemployment and provide access to work among marginalised groups; whether the minimum wage provides workers and their families with a "decent living"; concrete measures to make childcare services available; measures adopted to reduce poverty; how the UK ensures that the entire population has access to affordable food; to what extent measures taken by the UK have reduced homelessness; measures taken to ensure that higher education is accessible for all; the UK's strategy for protecting and enhancing development of the Irish language; and steps taken to ensure that "everyone benefits from scientific progress and its application."[23]

This is by no means unusual, or viewed as controversial within modern human rights practice. Rights are increasingly understood not as Dworkin's "trump against the state"[24] held by the individual citizen against public authority, but as the legal justification for a programmatic interest in abstract social goals. And the State, as a result, is understood not merely or indeed primarily as a potential violator of individual rights, but rather the means by which rights are protected or find expression and "enjoyment" (with the failure to provide such enjoyment itself being a violation). Even in the arena of so-called negative rights – the classical field of civil and political "freedoms from" – we find it being expressed. The List of Issues the Human Rights Committee (HRC) gave in response to the UK's seventh periodic report under the International Covenant on Civil and Political Rights in 2014, for instance, might have been expected to have chiefly addressed topics under the rubric of "negative" restraints on public power. And, indeed, it does raise concerns about the scope of anti-terrorism legislation, measures to prevent deaths in police custody, and the use of physical restraint in young offender institutions.[25] Yet the List of Issues also addresses matters of much broader and more aspirational scope. Among them are what the UK is doing to combat racial and religious hatred and negative stereotyping of minorities in the media, racism on the internet and in sport, and racist bullying and name-calling in schools; what it is doing to increase representation of ethnic minorities in the civil service and judiciary; what it is doing to eliminate the wage gap between men and women; what it is doing to address suicide rates, particularly in Scotland; and what it is doing to explicitly prohibit corporal punishment of children in the home.[26]

In other words, an instrumental understanding of rights as being the justifications and rationales for the achievement of certain goals has come to prominence, whether they be reducing the suicide rate, protecting and enhancing development of the Irish language, ensuring that the entire population has access to affordable food, and so on. This, in effect, derives from the operationalising of a relationship of care between powerful actors and those over whom they exercise that power. In the first instance this is the State vis-à-vis the population, but it also increasingly includes the international organisation and population(s), and the business and its stakeholders. The bearer of duties must act to improve conditions for the rights-holders, who are its beneficiaries, in view of certain goals, and its record in doing so must be held to account. The State must reduce the suicide rate, or promote the Irish language, for example, and must submit its performance record in that respect to scrutiny. This shifts the focus of human rights practice from the individual to the abstraction of the performance of the "duty-bearer."[27] In other words, the core of modern international human rights law and practice can hardly be said to be the human individual and how he or she exercises his or her rights. It is what duty-bearers (chiefly, but not only, the State) are doing to make measurable progress towards social goals at the level of the population and sub-groups within it.

From "L'État-Leviathan" to the power of care

This way of conceiving of human rights calls for an explanation, and an exploration of its consequences, because it is so striking when viewed against its historical background. The drafters of the UDHR shared a sense that their immediate task was to find a way to limit the capacity of what Cassin had termed – even before the Nazi seizure of power in 1933 – "L'État-Leviathan."[28] This was for reasons entirely natural and obvious. The fear of "Leviathan States" and the necessity of curbing their capacity to reduce individuals to mere pawns had grown during the 1930s, and those fears had, of course, been realised in the most compelling terms over the course of the Second World War. Ameliorating them and providing the individual with legal recourse against the abuses of an all-powerful State had been the consistent interest of the network of international jurists who had worked to promote the cause of human rights during the war and its immediate aftermath on both sides of the Atlantic, and who would go on to form the core of the Commission on Human Rights in the UN Economic and Social Council (ECOSOC).[29] Set against this background, it would have been unusual indeed if the focus of the drafters of the UDHR had not been on limiting what Malik had called "statism."[30] This is by no means to suggest that the drafters had no interest in the social or communal aspects of human life. The international human rights movement has never been monolithically interested in solely protecting the human individual against the excesses of State power. Yet undoubtedly, a significant shift in emphasis has taken place. "Doing human rights"[31] in the current era means not so much protecting the individual from the Leviathan State, or indeed other powerful actors, but shaping and controlling the means by which authority is deployed so that it achieves apparently benevolent ends.

So we are required to look at the phenomenon of human rights in a fresh light. That is the project of this book. It portrays international human rights law in the modern context as being *managerial* in character – an instrument for the technical implementation of particular interests, purposes, and values.[32] These values, in the case of human rights, hardly concern the separation of State and market that "neoliberalism" is said to amount to, let alone the self-limitation of a governmentalised liberal State achieved through the reification of individual rights. Quite the contrary – they concern a much more direct and purposive attempt to constitute a mode of governance which is best described, above all, as pastoral, and which is primarily enacted not through an insistence on the autonomy of the individual but through manipulation at the level of the population and sub-populations within it. In this mode of governance the powerful – primarily organs of States, but also, increasingly, international organisations and private actors – are produced as duty-bearers, whose responsibilities are not so much to refrain from interfering with the rights of individuals, but rather to "govern men."[33] What is "governmentalized" by the modern discourses of human rights, to borrow Foucault's "ugly" word,[34] is not neoliberalism, but rather a high-modernist mode of benevolent rule which imagines the role of the powerful as governing the population for its own good. International human rights law has a "structural bias,"[35] that is, but it is a bias towards a "power of care,"[36] not towards the primacy of the individual.

The background of this picture has been sketched before, primarily by the prominent historian of human rights, Samuel Moyn.[37] In this thesis, during the pivotal decade of the 1970s, ideology "died" and the "dream of revolution" was left behind. The movement of Soviet and Eastern European dissidents to the West, the Vietnam War, the end of colonialism and the appearance of the Failed State all contributed to a general malaise of internationalism. Into the void stepped human rights, a new and more "hardy" form of utopianism, which involved smaller-scale and less overtly political projects – a minimalist approach to achieving social goals. It was a "post-revolutionary" form of idealism for what Eckel calls a "post"-age.[38] Internationalists, activists, leftists, and former revolutionaries shifted their focus from the bloody and/or muddy and unsatisfactory world of political change to the apparently moral sphere of human rights, which was "unsullied by compromise."[39] There the focus remains to this day – insistent, disappointingly to some, not on genuine engagement with how to "think the state"[40] or perform real structural critique,[41] but rather on securing only a minimal taming of market fundamentalism's worst excesses.[42]

This sketch is broadly persuasive, but it is this final claim which needs to be both challenged and explored. It might well be the case that human rights now occupies the territory once held by "other political possibilities."[43] But that does not mean it is a territory that is devoid of political vision or values – a wilderness of ideology from which the genuinely compassionate can merely cast moral aspersions in the hope of achieving some limited reversals against the prevailing dominance of the neoliberal machine. Such a description could not be further from the truth: the territory occupied by human rights is strongly shaped by a vision of governance and rule, and those who occupy it are themselves frequently staunch advocates of that vision. That vision, as this book will reveal, is, first, pastoral: a vision of the shepherd and his flock, something akin to the "wise minority in the saddle" guiding the herd,[44] of global governance as the "benign policeman or doctor."[45] It is also, secondly, international: a global vision which sees pastoralism not merely as a relationship between the State and its citizens but as a mode of rule which permeates all relationships of governance, and which constitutes entirely new ones. It is a political vision that is altogether different from the old "possibilities" of the Cold War, but a political one nonetheless: "[a] strange fusion of empire, liberal internationalism, and moral self-righteousness ... entirely at ease with the idea of world leadership [and] capable of seeing the exercise of power as a burden undertaken for the general good."[46] That is, just as human rights in the 1990s was a post-revolutionary movement for a "post"-age, it was also "about constructing new political causes, meanings, and futures."[47] Those new political causes, meanings, and futures hinge around the pastoral. They envisage human rights as the legal justification for the deployment of a globalised "power of care," operationalising a vision of powerful benevolent actors bestowing blessings on the powerless in the name of improving human well-being. This vision is rooted in compassion. But it associates human rights not so much with freedom but with *governing*.

Oakeshott's critique

Describing this phenomenon and analysing its effects require us to look beyond the traditional sphere of critique. In particular, since Trilling's form of moral realism has frequently been lacking from academic writing on human rights (whether critical or advocatory), we have to search for it elsewhere.[48] This book finds it in the political and moral philosophy of Michael Oakeshott, a thinker who is generally associated with conservatism or "old-fashioned" liberalism, but who is also widely acknowledged to be a fish either "too big or too slippery" to categorise.[49] As we shall see, Oakeshott's critique (for it must be called that) of the modern understanding of the relationship between law, morality, and the State is a rich seam to mine for analytical tools for conceptualising developments in the field of human rights. Particularly when read in sympathetic counterbalance to Foucault's later lectures, it allows us to go beyond both existing critiques of the international human rights movement and its advocacy. It casts international human rights law as being utilised as declaratory justifications for a new form of managerialism, purposive and programmatic, which attempts to achieve implementation of human rights laws not so much as laws *per se*, but as intermediate goals on the road to universal human well-being. Human rights laws do retain their character as rules, but they are imbued with a *telos* which produces them not merely as conditions specifying just conduct, but as the specifications of outcomes and the means of getting there.

This ultimately allows us to describe human rights law in the modern age as ambiguous: vacillating between a "nostalgia" for civil rights as constraints on the State's power to infringe on liberty, and a utopian dream of equality and welfare achieved through bestowing "positive" freedoms on populations.[50] The conclusion is that the more international human rights law becomes oriented towards the latter, the more it undermines the former, and the more restrictive and even coercive it appears. The result is that it begins to seem deeply unattractive to those who are supposed to be its beneficiaries – the ordinary men and women who are the rights-holders in the first place.

Chapter synopses

Chapter 1 describes the modern field of international human rights practice. It portrays it, borrowing from Koskenniemi, as managerial – a solipsistic and imperialistic regime which seeks to expand into every corner of human life with the aim of realising an overarching purpose. The chapter explains the most significant legal developments making this possible, from teleological interpretation of treaty texts, to the expansion of positive obligations through the "respect, protect, fulfil" framework, to the imposition of duties on non-State actors. It shows that the result is an ever-increasing range of obligations being imposed upon an ever-widening scope of actors, and a preoccupation with how to achieve compliance and hence implement the overarching purpose of the regime.

Chapter 2 provides a summary of Oakeshott's thinking with respect to law and the State. It observes that the crucial element in this is the ambiguity of both phenomena. Law is sometimes conceived as general conditions of just or moral conduct and sometimes as a "rule-book" for achieving particular purposes; and the State is sometimes conceived as a purposeless relationship between autonomous *cives* related only in their shared acknowledgement of a system of neutral laws, and sometimes as a purposive association for the achievement of nebulous goals such as the "common good." The chapter then considers international law and international association in the same terms, particularly with respect to human rights, and notes that international law and international community are likewise ambivalent concepts vacillating between opposing poles roughly similar to those appearing in the context of the State. I suggest in particular that international human rights law is situated between two opposing ideals, as the conditions of just conduct on the part of States (*nomocracy*), or as a set of rules specifying ends and the means of achieving them (*teleocracy*), and that it will orient itself in one direction or another under the influence of both circumstance and prevailing ideas.

Chapter 3 argues that international human rights law has come to orient itself towards *teleocracy* under the influence of what, borrowing from the French constitutional theorist Maurice Hauriou, I call a "directing idea." This directing idea is that human rights are the legal mechanism for achieving the overriding objective of improving universal well-being, and that this is to be brought about by assigning obligations to the powerful in order to make them act benevolently towards the powerless. The chapter locates this in a broader trend among international lawyers, which understands international law itself as, ultimately, a project of improving universal human welfare. The chapter then demonstrates that this directing idea is rooted in compassion, the hatred of looking on while others suffer, which imbues the human rights movement with a species of what Kundera described as "kitsch." This causes human rights advocates to seek to give effect to their shared sense of compassion through law, which has the capacity to give effect to this feeling across time.

Chapter 4 unites the work of Oakeshott and Foucault on the nature of the relationship between *teleocratic* law and governance. It argues that what Foucault labelled "governmentality" is chiefly the result of purposive social action. In the modern State such social action tends to take place within the complex of law, discipline, and security, producing a regulatory or managerial approach which derives from law but achieves its purposes through what Foucault called "tactics" rather than laws. That is, while law is able to declare purposes and also specify intermediary objectives on the way to achieving those ends, it is unable, in itself, to realise them: it cannot in itself affect change at the desired level of the population. Instead, it must give rise to more indirect means for manipulating conditions within the population so as to "conduct conduct" more subtly. While, in other words, law becomes oriented to *teleocracy*, it retains elements of *nomos* which prevent it from bringing about social change on its own. Governmentality is understood, therefore, as the means of circumventing this problem. The chapter ends by arguing that just as the State was "governmentalised" by imagining the State as having the purpose of improving well-being – declared in law but achieved through regulatory "tactics" – so a sphere of global human rights governance is now being "governmentalised" by imagining

---

the international community as having the purpose of improving well-being universally. Here, human rights law declares the relevant ends, and gives rise to the deployment of regulatory "tactics" for achieving them.

Chapter 5 describes these regulatory "tactics" and maps the contours of what I call the "governmentalisation of global human rights governance." It draws on the work of Miller and Rose to describe this as a phenomenon of "governing human rights at a distance." I demonstrate that this consists of three broad and overlapping categories of tactics: auditing and other methods borrowed from financial management and accounting; the pluralisation and atomisation of governing functions; and the specification of new subjectivities. Taken together, these result in the creation of a regulatory sphere in which actors are continually enjoined to monitor themselves and others in light of human rights obligations or "responsibilities"; in which the governing of human rights is dispersed between public authorities, nongovernmental organisations and other civil society actors, businesses, and international organisations; and in which this entire range of actors, and even human individuals themselves, are re-conceived as being "human rights governors" in their own right.

Chapter 6 critiques the "governmentalisation of global human rights governance." It argues that the phenomenon causes international law to have unpredictable effects for individuals; that it removes the conditions of international law from the realm of politics properly understood; and that it brings about a mode of rule which sees concern with the individual as an end in him- or herself replaced with an understanding that the individual is simply part of an abstract whole, which is the true field of action. The result is that human rights are set in opposition to the way in which freedom was conceptualised by both Oakeshott and Foucault – the necessary conditions within which self-enactment can take place, and hence the necessary conditions of a moral or ethical life. On the one hand, this produces a kind of benevolent coercion – a pastoral power which is pervasive and potent for all that it is kind. But on the other, it produces a distaste for the human rights movement in the very rights-holders themselves, setting them at odds with its aims and tactics, and resulting in a counter-conduct of basic refusal.

Notes

1 L. Trilling, "Manners, Morals and the Novel," in *The Liberal Imagination: Essays on Literature and Society* (Secker & Warburg, 1951), 205, p. 219.
2 *Ibid.*, p. 221.
3 G. Orwell, *The Road to Wigan Pier* [1937] (Secker & Warburg, 1980), p. 179.
4 L. Henkin, "International Law: Politics, Values and Functions," 216, Collected Courses of The Hague Academy of International Law (Brill, 1989), 208.

5 H. Lauterpacht, *International Law and Human Rights* (Stevens & Sons, 1950), p. 61.

6 L. Hunt, *Inventing Human Rights: A History* (W.W. Norton & Company, 2007).

7 J. Eckel and S. Moyn (eds), *The Breakthrough: Human Rights in the 1970s* (University of Pennsylvania Press, 2014).

8 R. Afshari, "On Historiography of Human Rights: Reflections on Paul Gordon Lauren's *The Evolution of International Human Rights: Visions Seen*," 29, *Human Rights Quarterly* (2007) 1.

9 V. Prashad, *The Darker Nations: A People's History of the Third World* (New Press, 2007).

10 K. Marx, *Capital: A Critique of Political Economy: Vol I* (Penguin, 1976; trans. B. Fowkes), p. 280.

11 K. Marx, *On the Jewish Question* [1844], in J. Waldron (ed.), *Nonsense Upon Stilts: Bentham, Burke and Marx on the Rights of Man* (Routledge, 1987), 137.

12 S. Hopgood, *The Endtimes of Human Rights* (Cornell University Press, 2013), p. 95.

13 S. Moyn, "A Powerless Companion: Human Rights in the Age of Neoliberalism," 77, *Law & Contemporary Problems* (2014) 147, p. 156.

14 B. S. Chimni, "International Institutions Today: An Imperial Global State in the Making," 15 (1), *European Journal of International Law* (2004) 1, esp. pp. 11–12.

15 R. Nigro, "From Reason of State to Liberalism: The *Coup d'État* as a Form of Government," in V. Lemm and M. Vatter (eds), *The Government of Life: Foucault, Biopolitics and Neoliberalism* (Fordham University Press, 2014), 127.

16 P. Chevallier, "Michel Foucault and the Question of Right," in B. Golder (ed.), *Re-Reading Foucault: On Law, Power and Rights* (Routledge, 2013), 171, pp. 181–183.

17 M. Mutua, "The Complexity of Universalism in Human Rights," in A. Sajo (ed.), *Human Rights with Modesty: The Problem of Universalism* (Springer, 2004), 51.

18 There is a vast literature on this topic. The most concise and well-known statement is B. Kausikan, "Asia's Different Standard," 92, *Foreign Policy* (1993) 24.

19 M. A. Glendon, *Rights Talk: The Impoverishment of Political Discourse* (Free Press, 1991).

20 C. Thomas, "The Rights Revolution and America's Urban Poor: Victims or Beneficiaries?" Address Before the Federalist Society and the Manhattan Institute (16th May 1994), in 60 Vital Speeches of the Day (1994), 514, pp. 514–517.

21 M. Foucault, *Security, Territory, Population: Lectures at the Collège de France, 1977–1978* (Palgrave Macmillan, 2008; ed. M. Senellart, trans. G. Burchell), p. 42.

22 CESCR, Consideration of reports submitted by States Parties under articles 16 and 17 of the International Covenant on Economic, Social and Cultural Rights – Sixth periodic report of States Parties due in 2014: United Kingdom of Great Britain and Northern Ireland, UN Doc. E/C.12/GBR/6 (2014).

23 CESCR, List of issues in relation to the sixth periodic report of the United Kingdom of Great Britain and Northern Ireland, UN Doc. E/C.12/GBR/Q/6 (2015), paras 2, 7–8, 9, 10, 16, 21, 22, 24, 30, 31, and 32, respectively.

24 R. Dworkin, "Is There a Right to Pornography?" 1, *Oxford Journal of Legal Studies* (1981) 177.

25 HRC, List of issues in relation to the seventh periodic report of the United Kingdom of Great Britain and Northern Ireland, UN Doc. CCPR/C/GBR/Q/7 (2014), paras 11, 12, and 16, respectively.

26 *Ibid.*, paras 5, 6, 9, 10, 12, and 19, respectively.

27 W. Vandenhole (ed.), *Challenging Territoriality in Human Rights Law: Building Blocks for a Plural and Diverse Duty-Bearer Regime* (Routledge, 2015).

28 R. Cassin, "L'État-Leviathan," in *La Pensée et l'Action* (F. Lalou, 1972), 63, pp. 63–71.

29 J. Winter and A. Prost, *Rene Cassin and Human Rights: From the Great War to the Universal Declaration* (2nd edition, Cambridge University Press, 2013), pp. 227–236.

30 C. Malik, cited in J. Morsink, *The Universal Declaration of Human Rights: Origins, Drafting and Intent* (University of Pennsylvania Press, 2000), p. 242.

31 I borrow this phrase from B. Sokhi-Bulley, *Governing (Through) Rights: Human Rights Law in Perspective* (Hart, 2016).

32 M. Koskenniemi, "International Law: Constitutionalism, Managerialism and the Ethos of Legal Education," 1, *European Journal of Legal Studies* (2007) 1.

33 Foucault, *Security, Territory, Population*, p. 123.

34 *Ibid.*, p. 115.

35 M. Koskenniemi, *From Apology to Utopia: The Structure of International Legal Argument* (reissue with new epilogue) (Cambridge University Press, 2005), pp. 603–607.

36 Foucault, *Security, Territory, Population*, p. 127.

37 In, most notably, S. Moyn, *The Last Utopia: Human Rights in History* (Harvard University Press, 2010).

38 J. Eckel, "Explaining the Human Rights Revolution of the 1970s," in J. Eckel and S. Moyn, *The Breakthrough*, p. 259.

39 See T. Judt, *Ill Fares the Land* (Penguin, 2010), esp. pp. 162–164.

40 *Ibid.*

41 S. Marks, "Human Rights and Root Causes," 74, *Modern Law Review* (2011) 57.

42 See, e.g., W. Brown, "'The Most We Can Hope For …': Human Rights and the Politics of Fatalism," 103, *South Atlantic Quarterly* (2004) 451.

43 *Ibid.*, p. 462.

44 E. A. Ross, *Social Control: A Survey of the Foundations of Order* (Macmillan, 1901), p. 74.

45 K. Annan, 35th Annual Ditchley Foundation Lecture, UN Doc. SG/SM/6613, 26th June 1998.

46 M. Mazower, *No Enchanted Palace: The End of Empire and the Ideological Origins of the United Nations* (Princeton University Press, 2013), p. 66.

47 J. Eckel, "Explaining the Human Rights Revolution."

48 In the interest of maintaining a coherent and comprehensible argument in as concise a form as possible, this book does not make extensive reference to existing critical scholarship on human rights. This is by no means to suggest that this work is unimportant or uninteresting – rather that this book stakes out an orthogonal approach.

49 L. Armour, "Michael Oakeshott – A Fish Too Big or Too Slippery?" 13 (4), *British Journal for the History of Philosophy* (2005) 779. Maurice Cranston summed Oakeshott up as "a traditionalist with few traditional beliefs, an 'idealist' who is more skeptical than many positivists, a lover of liberty who repudiates liberalism, an individualist who prefers Hegel to Locke, a philosopher who disapproves of philosophisme [and] a romantic perhaps (if Hume could possibly be called one)." M. Cranston, "Michael Oakeshott's Politics," 28, *Encounter* (1967) 82, p. 82.

50 On its "nostalgia," see O. de Schutter, *International Human Rights Law: Cases, Materials and Commentary* (3rd edition, Cambridge University Press, 2019), p. 1.

1

Solipsism and imperialism

> [R]ights are public goods: Taxpayer-funded and government-managed social services designed to improve collective and individual well-being. All rights are positive rights.
>
> (Holmes and Sunstein, *The Cost of Rights*)[1]

Introduction

Providing an explanation for the development and an account of the consequences of human rights in its managerial mode is the project of this book. First of all, however, the phenomenon requires definition and description. In this chapter I give that definition and description, showing how it has become not only possible to think of human rights as the rationale and justification for purposive social action carried out by the State or other powerful actors, but the predominant way in which they are understood by human rights advocates and institutions. As we shall see, this has resulted from an overriding sense that "human rights" is a purposive regime. This causes an inexorable growth in the scope of its purview, the range of rights it encompasses, and the number of actors upon which it imposes obligations. The consequence of this is that bodies engaged in human rights discourses – particularly courts and the United Nations (UN) treaty- and charter-based mechanisms – have become characterised by a vaunting ambition which sees human rights as the means by which the world can be shaped for the better. Here, I provide an overview of the scene. In the chapters which follow, I shall lay out the reasons for why it takes on this tenor.

Managerialism

There exist sizeable literatures in various fields on the meanings, effects, and origins of "managerialism." In addition, the word is often used in lay terms as a shorthand for the deployment of techniques developed in the context of business management in other fields – or, alternatively, simply hierarchical or "top-down" organisation in general.[2] The purpose of this section is not to provide a survey of those existing usages or to provide a definition of general applicability. Rather, it is to outline the core elements of what I will refer to subsequently as "managerialism" within the context of human rights for the purposes of this volume, drawing primarily on the work of the most prominent thinker in the field of international law to have written extensively on the topic – Martti Koskenniemi. This may produce an idiosyncratic understanding of that term, but it is the one which will be used in the remainder of this chapter and the rest of this book.

In Koskenniemi's usage of the term, managerialism originates, most simply, in two things: "each [legal] regime understood as a purposive association and each institution assumed to have jurisdiction wide enough for realising it."[3] That is to say – speaking in particular about international law – managerialism is the phenomenon by which a particular field or regime (trade law, criminal law, investment law, human rights law, EU law, environmental law, etc.) becomes understood as having a purpose distinct from mere settlement of disputes, and an unlimited and unrestricted purview vis-à-vis other legal regimes in which to realise that purpose. The relevant purpose, of course, varies from regime to regime. For trade law, it is unrestricted trade; for investment law, protection of investments; for EU law, European integration; for environmental law, environmental protection, and so on. But for each the mindset or underlying approach is the same – the purpose, having been identified, is to be realised through process, and is not to be hedged or hindered by the kind of constitutional or institutional barriers which exist in a domestic legal framework and help to keep different legal regimes distinct and circumscribed.

The result is a prevailing tendency within such regimes to what Koskenniemi (borrowing from Kelsen) refers to as "solipsism and imperialism."[4] Any international event – we might extend this to any event *per se* – can be conceived of as being significant in the eyes of any international legal regime in that regime's own perspective. And this means that, unrestricted by constitutional or institutional barriers, any international legal regime is capable of perceiving any event as coming under its own purview. To use Koskenniemi's own example to illustrate, in 2006 the European Court of Justice (ECJ) gave its decision in the MOX Plant case, which had originated in a dispute between Ireland and the UK over the operation of the nuclear processing plant at Sellafield in Cumbria.[5] Ireland had brought claims against the UK to international dispute settlement under the OSPAR Treaty, concerning the protection of the natural environment in the Irish Sea, and the United Nations Convention on the Law of the Sea 1982. As a result, the European Commission raised a claim against Ireland because it had taken the UK (a fellow EU Member State) to international arbitration rather than raising the dispute in the relevant EU bodies applying EU rules. The ECJ ruled in the Commission's favour. Here, an event – a dispute over nuclear processing on the Irish Sea coast – capable of being resolved under a variety of different legal regimes (environmental law, the law of the sea, and also most probably trade law, the law of maritime transport, human rights, etc.) became understood as being a problem of relevance to the purpose of EU law – European integration. EU law and the institutions of the Union thus quickly extended themselves in order to advance that project, and ruled accordingly, so as to prevent the dispute being resolved under a different set of rules.[6] To the legal regime of EU law, nuclear processing on the Irish Sea was an event capable of being its own subject matter, and hence, absent any external constraint, EU law brought it within its purview in order to be resolved.

Hence, international legal regimes are both solipsistic (because they are only capable of seeing a given problem or event through the lens of their own respective projects) and imperialistic (because they know of no bounds to their self-perceived authority to make rulings with respect to anything they conceive as being relevant to said projects). The consequence is a continual struggle between such regimes, resolved purely through power: "every purpose is hegemonic in the sense of seeking to describe the social world through its own vocabulary so that its own expertise would apply and its structural bias would become the rule."[7] In the MOX Plant case, the project of European integration prevailed over other legal regimes because of the comparative strength and vigour of the relevant institutions, and for no other reason than that.

But for Koskenniemi this is not the end of the story as far as managerialism is concerned, and this is where his account finds its relationship to other more mainstream understandings of that term. Because international legal regimes have purposes or projects which are to be realised, and because the realisation of such a purpose or project is not automatic but subject to constant challenges and difficulties thrown up by the randomness of events, the project has to be able to react, and in order to undertake this, "there have to be experts."[8] There must be a class of people whose role is to pursue implementation – to see the project through. From the existence of such experts there are, then, two necessary consequences. First, a complex array of technical processes flow: monitoring bodies, committees, compliance groups, and so on – followed by the policies which they enact. And, second, law as such becomes seen as a mere instrument to justify and fulfil whatever purpose it is that the experts are implementing – and hence to be ignored or circumvented (replaced by concepts such as "regulation," "governance," and "compliance") if they appear to contravene such purposes. The result is an absence of critical reflection or contestation of anything other than how the technical processes in question contribute to the overall project.[9]

For Koskenniemi, then, managerialism might be described as the combination of solipsism and imperialism, producing in that combination an interest, above all, in process. Because the purpose of a given regime, whatever it might be, is known, and because that purpose is overriding, the only matters to be resolved concern how that purpose is to be achieved. And this, fundamentally, is a matter of technical expertise, not political contestation or legal principle. This transforms legal regimes into fundamentally programmatic enterprises where the dominant interest is merely in developing the techniques necessary to achieve identified goals. This causes them, indeed, to cease to resemble bodies of law *per se*, with their character becoming increasingly regulatory or policy-oriented in tenor.

There are certain lacunae in Koskenniemi's account, which was only ever, after all, provided in the spirit of a spur to further investigation. The first of these will be evident to anybody reading it, and indeed was perfectly evident to Koskenniemi himself: a legal regime might have a "purpose," but that purpose will itself always be contestable and contested – and, indeed, can be understood to mean more or less anything with the right amount of "ingenuity."[10] The purpose of environmental law might be protection of the environment, for instance, but careful argumentation can turn that broad principle in many different directions in any given circumstance. This means that international legal regimes are not so much settled domains but sites of "controversy and compromise where prevailing 'mainstreams' constantly clash with minority challengers."[11] By extension, this means that despite their "solipsism," such regimes are by no means monolithic – far from it. They are the battleground of competing narratives, "divided as regards their point and purpose and the right strategic choices to be made."[12] Yet Koskenniemi does not aim to provide an explanation for how one narrative comes to prevail in a given context so as to become "mainstream," nor how one strategic choice becomes preferred over others.

The second, related lacuna – more accurately, a series of lacunae – is that his sketch does not contain a full explanation for where competing narratives concerning the central project or purpose of an international legal regime come from, nor what or who generates them, nor why. They are postulated not so much as givens, but as the products of technical idioms or "functional vocabularies."[13] But the task of elucidating what in turn produces and shapes those vocabularies is left, in effect, to others.[14]

In particular, the ideals, values, and beliefs of the participants in the formation of the purposes he discusses are not considered in any depth – though, again, this is in large part because he deliberately left this task to others.

The third is the specificity of what takes place within the context of the different legal regimes he identifies. His explanation for why public international law has fragmented in the fashion that it has is, in essence, that there is a lack of a unifying constitutional framework in international law to impose limits on the ambitions of legal regimes (resulting in their solipsism)[15] and a lack of a general cosmopolitan ethos or "mindset" to provide them with modesty (resulting in their imperialism).[16] Lacking a clear hierarchy of norms and a set of meta-rules to govern regime conflicts, as a domestic constitution provides, international law is structurally incapable of resolving norm conflict and expansion,[17] and vulnerable to hubristic and ultimately imperial impulses to put in place "blueprints for perpetual peace, *civitas maxima*, and world government."[18] This, on its face, is perfectly plausible. But it does very little to shed light on what takes place within each given legal regime, whether international environmental law, criminal law, trade law, human rights law, or otherwise; that is, what the mechanisms and underlying values and ideals are which drive the solipsism and imperialism of a given functional regime in particular.

This book will fill these lacunae, whether directly or indirectly, at least with respect to international human rights law. Indeed, that might be thought of as the spine of its central inquiry: how it is that international human rights law, as a functional regime, developed and continues to develop its central purpose or project in the presence of competing narratives; where that project itself comes from; and why it takes the particular form that it does. For the purposes of this chapter and the next, however, we focus on the descriptive aptness of Koskenniemi's sketch of managerialism, and use it as a conceptual framework for understanding the modern form which the human rights movement takes – a programmatic endeavour produced by the solipsism and imperialism of the overarching international legal regime from which it derives. In the remainder of this chapter, I begin by identifying the characteristics and developments within the field of international human rights law which give it its own particular blend of solipsistic and imperialistic impulses. Then, in the one which follows, I describe how this blend of impulses results in an overwhelming preoccupation with process. This account will necessarily be incomplete at this stage, because – as will become clear – it raises further questions requiring more detailed and thoroughgoing answers. For the time being, I focus on simply elucidating why Koskenniemi's particular description of managerialism is so suitable for explaining the way international human rights law is developing.

The solipsism and imperialism of international human rights law

The language of solipsism and imperialism was originally Kelsen's.[19] Given as a critique of a particular strand of monism, it need not detain us in detail, except in one crucial respect. For Kelsen, solipsism and imperialism were intertwined: the latter was fundamentally an expression of the former. For the solipsist, there is no reality outside of his or her own thoughts and feelings – the external world is merely an expression or extension of the internal. This is, in effect, the epistemology of what Kelsen called imperialism:[20] if the interpretation or perception of the object is simply an extension of the internal world of the subject, then ultimately the act of interpretation can be nothing other than the unending expansion of the subject's own values, purposes, and ideals. This is must needs "imperialistic" (it could hardly be anything different) because it means that interpretation can only, in effect, be an enlargement of the self – provided, of course, it meets no stronger barrier or opposition. That is to say, bluntly, that a solipsistic perception will almost inevitably be an imperialist one. The one follows the other.

Therefore, it is useful to think of these two tendencies as linked, rather than separate, phenomena, and to examine how they manifest themselves in relationship with each other. In the following three subsections I do this across three of the different characteristic approaches of modern human rights practice, all of which, as we shall see, are related to one another. First, we examine the interpretation of human rights treaties, and how a doctrine of so-called dynamic or evolutive interpretation has developed. Second, we consider the expansion of the scope of human rights obligations in their "positive" dimensions, which have resulted in recent decades in a vast proliferation of circumstances in which duties are said to exist where they would previously have been considered absent. Third, and finally, we turn to the related broadening of the scope of human rights duties beyond the mere State and its organs to include, for example, corporations and international organisations and how they "respect" rights.

The evolutive interpretation of treaty texts

Origins and main characteristics

Faced with the task of interpreting the meaning of a given treaty provision, any prospective "interpreter" is called upon by the Vienna Convention on the Law of Treaties 1969 (VCLT) to take into account the ordinary meaning of the words in their context (meaning any other relevant treaties or instruments) and the object and purpose of the treaty itself.[21] This poses several questions. The first is how that "object and purpose" is to be established:

does it mean the object and purpose of the original drafters, or of those currently carrying out the act of interpretation? And the second is how "ordinary meaning" and "object and purpose" are to be balanced where they conflict. Within modern global human rights practice the answers to those questions are, emphatically, that "object and purpose" refers to that of those currently carrying out the act of interpretation, and that where there is a conflict between "ordinary meaning" and "object and purpose," the latter must prevail. These two principles combine to produce an interpretive approach which suggests that the role of the interpreter – whether a court, quasi-judicial body, or any other authoritative person or body – is to read the text in light of its own perspective on what the object and purpose of the treaty is.

This state of affairs originated as a technical matter in the early jurisprudence of the European Court of Human Rights (ECtHR). In a series of decisions beginning with *Golder v. United Kingdom,*[22] the Court took the opportunity to set out a number of interpretive techniques which would largely serve as its model, and those of other courts and quasi-judicial bodies, through to the present day. In *Golder*, the applicant, a prisoner, wished to commence libel proceedings against a prison officer but had been prevented from consulting a solicitor by the prison authorities. He argued that this was a violation of his right to a fair trial under Article 6 of the Convention because it, in effect, denied him access to court. The respondent State argued that there was no right *per se* to access to court under the ECHR. Once a trial commences it must be fair, but there is no obligation for the State to ensure that anybody and everybody can have a case heard. In support of this argument, it pointed out that the drafters had mentioned the right of access to court in Articles 5 and 13 of the Convention but not in Article 6, and this, it followed, clearly suggested that they had omitted it from the text of Article 6 deliberately. Hence, the right to a fair trial could not be read so as to include a right to access to court.

The Court, however, found in favour of the applicant. Under the Article 31 (2) of the VCLT, it said, it was called on to interpret Article 6 in light of the "object and purpose" of the Convention and this, in its view, drew it to the preamble, which referred to the "common heritage of political traditions, ideals, freedom and the rule of law" in European countries. Since "one can scarcely conceive of the rule of law without there being a possibility of having access to courts,"[23] the right of access to court was "inherent"[24] within Article 6 and must therefore be included within any reading of it.

In other words, in the eyes of the Court, the intention of the drafters was irrelevant in determining the correct interpretation of the treaty text. Where the "object and purpose" of the treaty was capable of being dispositive of the issue, it should be. Moreover – and although this was implicit in *Golder*

– the Court did not view the matter of "object and purpose" through what in American jurisprudence might be called a textualist approach of determining that purpose through examining the context in which drafting took place. Rather, the "object and purpose" of the treaty was that as it was understood by the Court when the decision was taken. It could hardly have been otherwise: having been given the opportunity by the respondent State's arguments to consider the intentions of the drafters (which would necessarily have involved analysis of what their object and purpose was), the Court did not take it. The preamble was read as it was understood by the particular judges sitting in 1975 – not as those writing the text would have understood its object and purpose in 1950.

It is important to be clear about this point, because the idea that a human rights treaty should be thought of as a "living instrument," as the concept is generally known, is often misunderstood or mischaracterised as being merely a matter of keeping human rights treaty texts current in the light of changing circumstances. This is in large part due to the phrasing of the judgment in a case decided shortly after *Golder* – *Tyrer v. United Kingdom*.[25] Here, the Court was required to rule on the matter of whether the birching of a 15-year-old boy on the Isle of Man for the offence of assault occasioning actual bodily harm was in breach of Article 3, prohibiting torture and inhuman or degrading treatment or punishment. Having decided that Tyrer's punishment could not have been described as torture, nor inhuman, it was then simply to determine whether it would qualify as having been degrading. Recalling that the Convention was a "living instrument" which must be interpreted in light of "present-day conditions," the Court felt that it had to be influenced by what were now the commonly accepted standards within the other Member States of the Council of Europe.[26] The Court seemed in essence to be basing its decision at least in part on the fact that contemporary penal policy in other Member States had generally turned its face against corporal punishment, and, by extension, while it did not spell this out, such punishment was therefore to be viewed as degrading *per se*. As the judgment put it, judicial corporal punishment was not used among other European States, and "if nothing else, this [cast] doubt on whether the availability of this penalty is a requirement for the maintenance of law and order in a European country."[27] This brought the Court back to the preamble to the ECHR itself, and its common heritage of "political traditions, ideals, freedom and the rule of law," which, in its view, the Isle of Man must be regarded as sharing. While it stopped short of saying so in as many words, the Court's implication was clear: present-day conditions reveal that in modern Europe, reading the Convention in light of its object and purpose (that is, by referring to its preamble) indicates that judicial corporal punishment is inherently degrading and hence prohibited under Article 3.

The *Tyrer* judgment, then, seemed to suggest that the approach which the Court would take to interpretation would be to view the text in light of prevailing circumstances and help thereby refresh it or keep it up to date as those circumstances change. This, indeed, crystallised in a number of subsequent decisions, with the position being best summarised by the judgment in *Goodwin v. United Kingdom*: the Court, that is, "must have regard to the changing conditions within the respondent State and within Contracting States generally and respond, for example, to any evolving convergence as to the standards to be achieved."[28] And this is very often the way in which "dynamic" or "evolutive" interpretation is described.[29]

Clearly, the Court's approach to interpretation does allow it to respond to changing circumstances. Perhaps the best example of this is the creation of the European Parliament, a body which could hardly have been envisaged by the original drafters of the Convention but which nonetheless was held to be within its scope as regards the right to vote.[30] But there is clearly much more to the doctrine than it simply being a method for allowing the Convention to be interpreted flexibly in circumstances the drafters could not have envisaged. As Sir Gerald Fitzmaurice noted in his dissenting opinion in *Tyrer*, the fact that modern opinion had generally come to regard corporal punishment as undesirable could not automatically be said to make it degrading, which was the term on which the case turned.[31] The former is an empirical observation; the latter is a normative statement. And a close reading of the judgment in *Tyrer* reveals that the real basis for the Court's decision cannot justifiably be said to have been currency. The Court appears to have conducted no survey of other Member States' criminal law, nor any exercise to establish that the abolition of corporal punishment had taken place in general in Council of Europe countries, and it even explicitly rejected the argument that judicial corporal punishment could not be considered degrading in the Isle of Man because public opinion there was currently in favour of it.[32] On the contrary, in its view, in order to establish that a punishment was degrading, one would have to inquire "in particular [into] the nature and context of the punishment itself and manner and method of its execution."[33] While the Court set out its "living instrument" approach apparently on the basis of drawing comparisons with what was commonly accepted across Member States, its decision was in fact entirely based on substantive considerations: "the very nature of judicial corporal punishment" was degrading because it involved the infliction of physical violence, constituted an institutionalised assault on a person's dignity and physical integrity, and involved total strangers and the baring of the convict's posterior.[34] In the final analysis, then, responding to current or changing circumstances had nothing to do with the Court's reasoning in reaching a decision on whether Tyrer's treatment had been "degrading." The fact that the ECHR was a "living instrument" was much more to do with, as Letsas put it, finding a "better understanding" of the rights contained in the Convention[35] – namely, in this case, that judicial corporal punishment is degrading *per se.*

The full import of this interpretive stance was made explicit in *Young, James and Webster v. United Kingdom.*[36] Here, the three applicants were former employees of British Rail who had refused to join one of the three trade unions which all employees were required to join under a so-called closed shop agreement, and been dismissed as a result. They brought their claim against the respondent on the basis of Article 11, arguing that their right to freedom of association had a negative aspect which guaranteed that they would not be compelled to join a union. The respondent State argued that not only did the text of Article 11 fail to permit such a reading – it provides only that everybody has the right to "form and to join trade unions" – the drafters had deliberately excluded it. It cited the *travaux préparatoires*:

> On account of the difficulties raised by the "closed shop system" in certain countries, the Conference in this connection considered that it was undesirable to introduce into the Convention a rule under which "no one may be compelled to belong to an association."[37]

This was ultimately deemed irrelevant by the Court. The reasoning here is particularly instructive: "[t]o construe Article 11 as permitting every kind of compulsion in the field of trade union membership," the judgment puts it, "would strike at the very substance of the freedom it is *designed to guarantee* [emphasis added]."[38] In other words, what the Convention was "designed to guarantee" is most decidedly not, in the Court's view, what the drafters *actually* designed it to guarantee, which was the right to form and join trade unions excluding the right not to be compelled to join one or face dismissal. Rather, it was what the Convention was designed to guarantee (its object and purpose) assessed by the Court at the time that it was sitting.

While no judge on the Court itself has rationalised its approach in these terms, others have seen in this a fidelity to intentions of principle rather than intentions of detail.[39] In such accounts, the Court is adhering to the designs of the drafters in the abstract – namely, the intention to protect a list of fundamental freedoms, whatever they might be – rather than the specific and concrete freedoms which they believed to be important when they were writing the text. That is, its interpretation of the treaty is based on an attempt to get to the "moral truth" of the rights contained in the ECHR.[40] While the drafters may have deliberately excluded a negative right not to be compelled to join a trade union from the text of Article 11, there was a greater moral purpose at stake. As the judgment itself put it, "to construe Article 11 as permitting every kind of compulsion in the field of trade union membership would strike at the very substance of the freedom it is designed to guarantee"[41] – which is to say, freedom of association.

Some would see in the Court's approach to interpretation a commitment to the role of constitutionalist actor, developing the Convention into a pan-European framework for realising particular principles in such a way that they apply across all States parties in an integrated way.[42] One could, of course, just as well argue that that the doctrine of the "living instrument" is merely a "banner under which the Strasbourg Court has assumed power to legislate."[43] Irrespective of the view one takes, however, the conclusion must be that the Court's evolutive or dynamic approach is ultimately a teleological one: its reading of the EHCR rights is a product of its own understanding of the overarching purpose of the Convention and the provision in question. It is not merely a means by which the Convention's text can be refreshed or kept up to date as the social environment changes. Rather, it is a "first-order moral reading" which gives effect to the judges' own understanding of the moral principles underpinning the Convention rights.[44] This is necessarily current in the sense that the judges apply their own existing understanding rather than that which may have prevailed at some time in the past, but currency is by no means the main consideration. Perhaps the most straightforward evidence for this observation is that one cannot realistically envisage the ECtHR giving a retrogressive ruling, to the effect that a given human rights obligation must be narrowed in scope, merely because of a change in the prevailing political or legal climate in a majority of Council of Europe countries.

The ECtHR's living instrument approach, initially confined to its own jurisprudence, began rapidly to spread in other spheres of international human rights law during the decades after *Golder*. The Inter-American Court of Human Rights (IACtHR) has developed a broadly similar doctrine. In *Velasquez Rodriguez v. Honduras*, the very first case in which the Court sat, this was expressed in the language of effectiveness – "[t]he object and purpose of the American Convention is the effective protection of human rights" – the effects being those that are "appropriate."[45] But by the late 1990s it was being expressed in broadly similar terms as those used by the ECtHR, and indeed the *Tyrer* decision, among others, was cited with approval as the "proper approach" in the IACtHR's *Advisory Opinion on Consular Assistance in the Framework of the Guarantees of the Due Process of Law* in 1999.[46] And there is an echo of the European Commission on Human Rights' desire to "establish a common public order of the free democracies of Europe"[47] present in the rhetoric of the judges of the IACtHR, as for instance when Judge Trindade described the creation of an "international *ordre public* based upon the respect for human rights in all circumstances."[48] The Court's role, in other words, is not to give voice to the intentions of the drafters in detail, but to interpret the American Convention through the much broader lens of what is necessary to achieve that international *ordre public*.

Unlike in the context of the ECtHR and IACtHR (what might be called judicial systems proper), the interpretive stances taken by the UN treaty bodies have never been made explicit. Yet a teleological approach is readily apparent in much of their work. An interesting illustration of how such an approach has crystallised can be found in the Human Rights Committee's (HRC's) interpretation in its jurisprudence of Article 6 of the International Covenant on Civil and Political Rights (ICCPR) – protecting the right to life – as including an obligation for States which have abolished the death penalty not to extradite or deport prisoners to States which do practice it. This issue first arose in the complaint of *Kindler v. Canada*.[49] Kindler, who had been convicted of first-degree murder and kidnapping in Pennsylvania and sentenced to death on the recommendation of the jury, fled to Quebec, whereupon the United States requested his extradition. The Supreme Court of Quebec then ordered extradition accordingly. Kindler complained, among other things, that this violated his right to life under Article 6 of the ICCPR. The text of Article 6 (2) is as follows:

> In countries which have not abolished the death penalty, sentence of death may be imposed only for the most serious crimes in accordance with the law in force at the time of the commission of the crime and not contrary to the provision of the present Covenant [...]. This penalty can only be carried out pursuant to a final judgement rendered by a competent court.

In the views of Kindler's counsel, this meant that Article 6 (2) applied only in countries "which have not abolished the death penalty," and hence it was implicit in the Covenant that the death penalty was to be abolished by default. In countries which had done this, there was no permission within the Covenant to have it re-imposed. Moreover, one ought not to be able to "do indirectly what one cannot do directly" and extradite a prisoner where there was a real possibility that he or she might face the death penalty.[50] In effect, in other words, there was an obligation on Canada as a non-death penalty State not to subject a person in its jurisdiction to the risk of having the death penalty imposed through extradition, without seeking assurances that no execution would be carried out.

The Committee rejected this argument. While it had in its General Comment No. 6 expressed the view that abolition of the death penalty was desirable and that States were obliged to limit its use,[51] it was unwilling to take the step of holding that non-death penalty States had a strict obligation under the Covenant to seek assurances before extradition or not to extradite at all. Canada had not itself imposed the death penalty on Kindler, and

Kindler did not face a risk in the United States of a violation of his rights under Article 6 (2) of the Covenant, because the death sentence had been imposed on him for serious crimes in accordance with law after a final judgment of a competent court.[52] That is, the majority in the HRC applied an essentially objective reading of the relevant provisions.

However, five of the members of the HRC dissented from this decision, all broadly on the same grounds. These were, in effect, those stated by Bertil Wennergren, whose position was that Article 6 (2) of the Covenant should be interpreted narrowly. In his view, that Article provided a special dispensation for States parties that had not abolished the death penalty to continue practising it in limited circumstances. But only that. The rest of the text of Article 6 was to be interpreted broadly, and its object and purpose was to protect human life, which was of "immeasurable" value to any human being and the supreme right under the Covenant. The effect was that there was an absolute obligation on States to protect the right to life within their jurisdictions, and for a non-death penalty State such as Canada, this included an obligation not to extradite somebody within its jurisdiction to face a death sentence. To rule otherwise was to "defeat the purpose of Article 6."[53] While Wennergren did also look to the intentions of the drafters as expressed in the *travaux* for the Covenant, the decisive factor is clear: "the right to life … is the supreme human right [and] it is an obligation of States parties to the Covenant to protect the lives of all human beings in their territory and under their jurisdiction."[54] The interest, in other words, ought to be the Committee's own understanding of the "moral truth" underpinning the text.

These arguments were repeated shortly afterwards in very similar circumstances in *Ng v. Canada*[55] and *Cox v. Canada*.[56] However, the next time the issue arose, in *Judge v. Canada*, the Committee effectively reversed its stance.[57] Roger Judge had been convicted of two counts of first-degree murder in Pennsylvania and sentenced to death, but escaped from prison shortly afterwards and fled to Canada. He was later convicted of two robberies in Vancouver and sentenced to 10 years' imprisonment; on release, he was ordered deported to the United States. The HRC was again asked to consider the question of whether this violated Judge's rights under Article 6 of the Covenant, and here it openly departed from its previous jurisprudence. The Covenant, in its view, had to be interpreted as a "living instrument" and, hence, in light of present-day conditions. These conditions suggested that there was a broadening international consensus in favour of abolition of the death penalty, and hence it was proper to review the scope of application of "that most fundamental of rights," the right to life.[58] And here it adopted the hitherto dissenting views of Bertil Wennergren in *Kindler* almost *verbatim*: Article 6 imposed a wide obligation on States parties to protect life in their jurisdiction – this was its object. For a State such as Canada, which did not practice the death penalty, this meant there was an obligation not to expose those within its jurisdiction to a "real risk" of its application. Otherwise it would become the "crucial link in the causal chain" making execution of the complainant possible.[59]

While the HRC did not express its doctrine of interpretation with as much clarity as the ECtHR, then, it did set out in this case a similarly teleological approach. The provisions of the Covenant, it said, had to be interpreted in light of their object and purpose (in the case of Article 6, to secure life) in consideration of current conditions. But as with the ECtHR, it would be misleading to take currency as the decisive, or even a major, factor in the final outcome. While the decision in *Judge* was said to have been based on a changing international consensus on the desirability of the death penalty, this apparently empirical observation was, for the most part, divorced from the much stronger overriding normative concerns. As Francisco Urbina, in his own dissenting view in *Kindler*, had put it, "the spirit of [Article 6] is to eliminate the death penalty as a punishment."[60] The HRC's interpretation of the treaty text is a matter of the Committee discerning its own understanding of the "moral truth" within it, not only keeping it up to date and certainly not giving effect to the intentions of the drafters.

It would not be an exaggeration to say that the view that human rights treaties ought to be read teleologically or programmatically has now become not only the orthodox position, but the only acceptable one within human rights practice. At the time of the decisions in *Golder* and *Tyrer*, it was possible for Sir Gerald Fitzmaurice, sitting on the ECtHR, to issue separate opinions clearly and openly rooted in textualism. In *Golder*, he put his point with typical clarity: it was "not whether the Convention ought to provide for such a right [i.e., the right of access to the courts] but whether it *actually does* [emphasis added]" which mattered.[61] This position has now been well and truly ruled out: if the Convention *ought* to provide for a given right, then, in current interpretive practice in human rights courts and quasi-judicial bodies, it *actually does* by definition. This is because what it "actually does" provide is based not on a strict reading of its text or the views of the drafters, but on its object and purpose, as identified and elucidated by the Court. Exactly the same pattern has played out in the jurisprudence of the HRC and other human rights treaty bodies, as the *Judge* decision aptly demonstrates. The current position is perhaps summarised best of all by Magdalena Sepulveda, former Special Rapporteur (SR) on Extreme Poverty and Human Rights, speaking about the role of the Committee on Economic, Social and Cultural Rights (CESCR) in a manner which could easily be applied across the piece: it is to "[promote] changes in perception, [and] creatively interpret the Covenant by incorporating such changes in perception into the protection afforded by the Covenant."[62] It should be perfectly evident that this is, in effect, a euphemism for teleological interpretation based on the individual court or quasi-judicial body's own conception of "object and purpose" at the time the interpretation is made.

The effects of the teleological approach

The result of the widespread adoption of a teleological approach to interpretation of human rights treaty texts is that there exists no realistic legal restriction on the scope and purview of international human rights law – except for those which are self-imposed by the judges or constituent members of a given quasi-judicial body in a given circumstance. Theoretically, with the appropriate amount of "ingenuity" (to return us to Koskenniemi), any event is capable of being conceptualised as being of relevance to the object and purpose of a given human rights treaty, given that those objects and purposes are generally couched in exceptionally broad and amorphous terms. And, unconstrained by constitutional norm hierarchy or rules of procedure (again to return us to Koskenniemi), there is therefore no legal barrier to a court or quasi-judicial body doing so.

This is not to suggest that there exist no other barriers in practice, whether self-imposed or otherwise.[63] The ECtHR has shown itself to be particularly alive to the need for human rights protections to be realistically achievable (both practically and conceptually) in, for example, refusing to recognise that sleep disturbance from night flights could be read as a violation of the right to a private life under Article 8 of the ECHR,[64] and in developing an extensive and detailed doctrine of a "margin of appreciation." But it is to suggest that the tendencies of quasi-judicial bodies in particular frequently lean towards expanding the scope and extent of human rights obligations in the name of their own conceptions of what the object and purpose of their own particular treaties or human rights in general are. Put another way, the judicial "style" of human rights courts and quasi-judicial bodies tends towards a form of solipsism (the temptation to view any and all events as being of relevance to the purpose of the treaty in question) and a concomitant imperialism (the temptation to issue a ruling or recommendation accordingly). The result is a proliferation in duties.

Three examples will illustrate. The first is the CESCR's General Comment No. 4 on the right to adequate housing.[65] Here, the Committee examined Article 11 (1) of the Covenant on the right to an adequate standard of living, which includes, in the text of the Article, adequate food, clothing, and housing. The Committee began with the premise that the right to housing should not be interpreted only in the narrow sense of shelter or even housing *per se*, but must be seen as the right to "live somewhere in security, peace and dignity." This was because the right was "integrally linked ... to the fundamental principles on which the Covenant is premised" (namely protecting the inherent dignity of the human person).[66] In other words, the right to "housing" must be considered in light of the object and purpose of the ICESCR – or, put more technically, it must be given an interpretation which would in turn give effect to protecting the inherent dignity of the human person. The result was an interpretation of the obligation to provide adequate housing in the Covenant as including, among other things, legal security of tenure; the availability of services and infrastructure such as refuse disposal and emergency services; affordability including subsidies and rent controls; and locations allowing access to places to work and childcare.[67] That is, the Committee's approach to interpreting the text of the treaty is that which gives effect to its own understanding of the meaning of the object and purpose of the Covenant – and from this, in turn, flows an extensive and detailed list of purported obligations covering a wide and expansionary range of circumstances.

The second example is the development by the CESCR of a right to water. Water is not mentioned in the International Covenant on Economic, Social and Cultural Rights (ICESCR). Yet, in its general comments, the Committee has identified such a right as existing under Article 11, paragraph (1) (the right to an adequate standard of living, "including adequate food, clothing and housing"), and under Article 12, paragraph (1), which contains the right to the highest attainable standard of health.[68] While the Committee did make some effort to base its reasoning in this respect on the text of the treaty (the use of the word "including" in Article 11 meaning that it had wider scope than just food, clothing, and housing and could therefore include water), almost all of the justifications given for reading the right to water into these Articles were purposive. Water is a "public good fundamental for life and health" and "indispensable for leading a life in human dignity"; it is necessary to produce food, to prevent death, and to reduce the risk of disease.[69] The logic is clear: the right to water is necessary for the achievement of certain goods connected with the ICESCR's purpose, and hence it must exist. And, as with the right to housing, from this a list of obligations flow, including to make water available, to ensure the supply is of sufficiently good quality, to ensure that is accessible, to ensure that there is no discrimination in the enjoyment of the right, and so on.[70]

The third example is the Committee on the Elimination of Discrimination Against Women (CEDAW Committee)'s interpretation of the Convention on the Elimination of All Forms of Discrimination Against Women (CEDAW) as including a "due diligence" obligation to prevent domestic violence against women, arising from the requirements to eliminate discrimination against women and to eliminate prejudices and stereotypes. This was initially expressed in its General Recommendation No. 12,[71] but it achieved its full elaboration in General Recommendation No. 19.[72] In this Recommendation, the Committee set out a comprehensive statement on its understanding of the meaning of discrimination against women as defined in Article 1 of the Convention ("any distinction, exclusion or restriction made on the basis of sex which has the effect or purpose of impairing or nullifying the recognition, enjoyment or exercise by women ... of human rights and fundamental freedoms"). This definition, it declared, "includes gender-based violence, that is, violence that is directed against a woman because she is a woman or that affects women disproportionately." It also included acts inflicting mental or sexual harm, threats of such acts, and coercion and other deprivations of liberty.[73] The Convention therefore applied to violence perpetrated by public authorities, but it also required States to act with due diligence to prevent violence when perpetrated by private actors, and to investigate and punish such acts and provide compensation.[74]

This obligation, the Committee stated, came from "general international law and specific human rights covenants."[75] What the Committee was referring to were some recent comments made by the HRC, and two recent decisions of the IACtHR, in *Velasquez Rodriguez*, mentioned briefly earlier in this chapter, and *Godinez Cruz v. Honduras*,[76] decided shortly afterwards. The effect of these decisions was that, in the words of the IACtHR in *Velasquez Rodriguez*, "an illegal act which violates human rights and which is initially not directly imputable to a State (for example, because it is the act of a private person or because the person responsible has not been identified) can lead to international responsibility of the State, not because of the act itself, but because of the lack of due diligence to prevent the violation or respond to it as required by the Convention."[77] This chimed with what the HRC had said in its General Comment No. 7 in 1982, to the effect that there was an obligation under Article 7 of the ICCPR (prohibiting cruel, inhuman, or degrading treatment) not only to prohibit such treatment but to ensure that there was some "machinery of control" and adequate investigation of complaints and punishment of wrongdoing – even, crucially, when carried out by "persons acting outside our without any official authority."[78]

The IACtHR had been careful in both of these cases to situate its decisions in the context of a political or security environment in which disappearances and politically motivated killings could be perpetrated "impunely [*sic*]," but the CEDAW Committee has vastly expanded that position in its own interpretive practice. This was evident even in General Recommendation No. 19, which among other things recommended that State parties to the Convention take measures to ensure that the media respect and promote respect for women, to protect women from sexual harassment in the workplace, to provide appropriate services in regard to fertility control, to provide training and employment opportunities for women, to monitor employment conditions of domestic workers, to provide support services for families where sexual abuse has occurred, to carry out public information and education programmes to change attitudes about the roles and status of men and women, and so on.[79] Where the "due diligence" obligation as it was envisaged in *Velasquez Rodriguez* concerned the obligation to investigate or prosecute specific crimes and to prevent a culture of impunity from arising, and while that conceptualisation has found expression in some of the CEDAW Committee's jurisprudence,[80] the interpretation found in General Recommendation No. 19 was much broader in scope and nature, involving an extensive range of positive duties. While not put explicitly, the interpretive approach is clear: the Committee has identified an object and purpose for the CEDAW ("[enjoying] rights and freedoms on the basis of equality with men"),[81] and it reads the treaty text through its own understanding of what the underlying principles mean in their fullest expression. In its view, this means there is not merely a duty for States to refrain from violating the rights of women, but a duty to eliminate violence against women wherever it might take place, including through diffuse and indirect methods such as eliminating media stereotypes and pornography;[82] helping women overcome poverty and employment so that they do not engage in prostitution;[83] ensuring that women do not experience "sexually coloured remarks [*sic*]" in the workplace because it would create a hostile working environment;[84] and so on.

The argument of this section is not to suggest that teleological interpretation of the character outlined is illegitimate or unwarranted in general or in reference to any particular instance. Rather, it is to demonstrate that this stance towards treaty interpretation readily facilitates the turn towards solipsism and imperialism which Koskenniemi identified, because it removes textual, institutional, or even legal constraint (it ignores, for instance, traditional rules concerning State responsibility which may also have something to say with respect to due diligence obligations),[85] and because of the ease with which it can be turned through "ingenuity" towards any subject or concern.[86] Housing is linked to the protection of the fundamental dignity of the human person, and hence the right to housing must be read to include obligations to provide rent controls and locations allowing access to childcare; a clean water supply is indispensable to leading a life of dignity, and hence a right to water must exist; the object of the CEDAW is to achieve equality between men and women, and hence obligations must exist to eliminate stereotypes in the media and "sexually coloured remarks" in the workplace. To reiterate, none of those interpretations is in itself undesirable. But they indicate the extent to which a purposive interpretation of the treaty text – whether offered explicitly in that spirit or otherwise – results in expansion of human rights law's overall purview.

Human rights in the positive dimension

Obligations to respect, protect, and fulfil

As we have already seen in this chapter, in modern human rights practice, very wide-ranging positive obligations are frequently said to be imposed on States – from the duty to promote the Irish language to the obligation to eliminate gender stereotypes in the media. This tendency, of course, has some roots in the Universal Declaration of Human Rights (UDHR), which contains such obligations, but it primarily originates in the sphere of economic, social, and cultural rights. It is nowadays unfashionable to suggest that there is any inherent distinction between "positive" economic, social, and cultural rights, on the one hand, and "negative" civil and political rights, on the other. But it is nonetheless the case that we must look to the ICESCR in particular and social and economic rights in general to locate the initial impetus for the expansion of positive human rights obligations.

This is because the history of economic, social, and cultural rights must be understood in part as a purposive attempt by the CESCR itself, the UN Commission on Human Rights and its Sub-Commission on the Promotion and Protection of Human Rights, and sympathetic academic commentators and non-governmental organisations (NGOs) to give better definition to the obligations contained in the Covenant than their original, somewhat amorphous, formulations, and rebut accusations that the ICESCR was unenforceable or merely aspirational and hence in some sense inferior in importance to its civil and political cousin.[87] This has resulted in the development of a number of principles or institutional tactics, by far the most important of which is the evolution of the doctrine of "respect, protect, and fulfil." First introduced in 1987, this formulation is now often described as "classic,"[88] and has come, in effect, to be the orthodox understanding of States parties' obligations under not just the ICESCR but all the international human rights treaties, as we shall see.

The essence of this tripartite framework is set out in the first document in which it appeared, Asbjorn Eide's 1987 report as SR on the right to adequate food.[89] Here, Eide first expressed concern that the "indivisibility and interdependence" of human rights might be undermined by questioning of the status of economic and social rights; that the content of economic and social rights was "extremely vague"; and that there were arguments that such rights (and in particular the right to food) were not legally enforceable, but merely "broadly formulated programme[s] for governmental policies." He then went on to set out a new framework for understanding social and economic rights in order to rebut these criticisms.[90] He prefaced his comments by arguing that while human rights constitute "in the first instance" a relationship between the individual and the State, "all members of society share a responsibility for the realization human rights" and the State can hence "call on and oblige all individuals to participate in the realization of human rights."[91] He concluded that this meant that State responsibility for human rights operated at three levels. First, there was an obligation to respect human rights, which meant abstaining from doing anything that would infringe the freedom of an individual, including the freedom to use material resources necessary to satisfy their needs. Second, there was an obligation to protect human rights, which meant the duty on the part of the State and its agents to prevent other individuals or groups from violating the rights of an individual. And third, there was an obligation to fulfil human rights, which constitutes a requirement for the State to take measures necessary to "ensure for each person within its jurisdiction opportunities to obtain satisfaction of those needs...which cannot be secured by personal efforts."[92] His conclusion was that the role of the State was "double-faced, like Janus" – it must respect human rights limitations and constraints on its scope of action, but also had an active role as "protector and provider."[93]

While Eide was careful to add the caveat that economic, social, and cultural rights might be achieved merely through non-interference with the freedom of individuals,[94] his tripartite framework – enthusiastically adopted across the field – has generally been used since to advocate for a robust role for the State in society and the economy. The Maastricht Guidelines of 1997, widely understood to be the authoritative statement on the classification of economic, social, and cultural rights violations, illustrate this pithily:

> The obligation to respect requires States to refrain from interfering with the enjoyment of economic, social and cultural rights. Thus, the right to housing is violated if the State engages in arbitrary forced evictions. The obligation to protect requires States to prevent violations of such rights by third parties. Thus, the failure to ensure that private employers comply with basic labour standards may amount to a violation of the right to work or the right to just and favourable conditions of work. The obligation to fulfil requires States to take appropriate legislative, administrative, budgetary, judicial and other measures towards the full realization of such rights. Thus, the failure of States to provide essential primary health care to those in need may amount to a violation.[95]

The implications of this paragraph are clear. The State's duties with respect to economic, social, and cultural rights cannot realistically be fulfilled except through intervention – whether by ensuring that third parties do not act in such a way that would prevent an individual's human rights from being realised, or taking appropriate measures to "fully realise" those rights (whatever those measures might be). While in some sense the obligation to respect might be fulfilled through non-interference, or "*laissez-faire*" as the

CESCR had put it in its General Comment No. 3,[96] that simply cannot be the legal position for economic, social, and cultural rights *in toto* if the tripartite framework is adopted. In case there was any doubt about this, the Office of the United Nations High Commissioner for Human Rights' (OHCHR's) *Handbook for National Human Rights Institutions* dispels it: the obligation to protect, as elucidated in that handbook, "requires the State and its agents to prevent the violation of any individual's rights by any other individual or non-State actor";[97] the obligation to fulfil requires "positive measures by the State" to "guarantee each person within its jurisdiction opportunities to have full access to all entitlements ... that cannot be secured through exclusively personal efforts";[98] and even the obligation to respect requires States to "abstain ... from tolerating any practice, policy or legal measure"[99] violating economic, social, or cultural rights – something which is obviously worded in such a way as to go beyond mere "*laissez-faire.*"

This approach, initially developed in order to render the rights contained in the ICESCR more concrete and clear, has now come in one form or another to permeate the corpus of international human rights law, appearing in the practice of all of the UN treaty bodies and Charter-based mechanisms, as well as, to a certain extent, the various regional human rights systems and domestic theatres. This includes the Children's Rights Committee (CRC Committee),[100] the CEDAW Committee,[101] the CRPD Committee,[102] and the OHCHR itself, as we have seen.[103] Even where the framework is not explicitly referred to, most notably in the work of the HRC, it is implicitly substituted with a similar legal concept which operationalises positive actions on the part of the State in order to bring about an indirect horizontal effect for the relevant rights: the HRC, for instance, as we have seen, holds that the ICCPR imposes positive obligations on States parties to exercise due diligence in preventing harm caused to individuals by private persons or entities, and to take "positive measures" to protect individuals from discrimination on the part of other individuals, amongst other things.[104]

Expanding positive obligations and the duty-bearer perspective

The result is what is sometimes referred to as a "duty-bearer perspective" on human rights obligations,[105] which emphasises the responsibilities of those which have duties under the relevant legal instruments – namely, in the first instance, States (although, as we shall see next, the duty-bearer perspective is also increasingly argued to extend to other actors, such as international organisations and other non-State actors). The primary interest, in other words, is in what actions are taken by the State in order to improve human rights outcomes – that is, to protect, respect, and fulfil human rights – rather than on inhibiting the capacity of the State to violate the human rights of its citizens. This vision permeates the system, but three examples will serve to illustrate. These examples are chosen without particular design other than to demonstrate the widespread nature of the phenomenon being observed; others are abundant and will be evident to any cursory examination of the functioning of the UN treaty- and charter-based mechanisms.

The first is the CRC Committee's fifth General Comment, on "General measures of implementation of the Convention on the Rights of the Child,"[106] which illustrates the way in which UN treaty bodies tend to approach State party obligations in general. The CRC's fifth General Comment is an outline document serving to provide greater detail on the nature of States parties' obligations under Article 4 of the Convention: the nebulous requirement to "undertake all appropriate legislative, administrative, and other measures for the implementation of the rights recognized" in the CRC.

The Committee begins with the observation that while the State takes on obligations under the Convention, "its task of implementation ... needs to engage all sectors of society,"[107] and cites with approval General Comment No. 14 of the CESCR:

> While only States are parties to the Covenant and thus ultimately account-able for compliance with it, all members of society – individuals, including health professionals, families, local communities, intergovernmental and non-governmental organizations, civil society organizations, as well as the private business sector – have responsibilities regarding the realization of the right to health. States parties should therefore provide an environment which facili-tates the discharge of these responsibilities.[108]

The CRC Committee then goes on to detail how this is to be achieved in the field of children's rights, "through legislation, the establishment of coordi-nating and monitoring bodies – governmental and independent – compre-hensive data collection, awareness-raising and training and the development and implementation of appropriate policies, services and programmes."[109] States parties are encouraged to develop "comprehensive national strate-gies rooted in the Convention"[110] – nothing less than "national plans of action for children" which are to be endorsed at the highest level of govern-ment, linked to national development planning and included in national budgets, adequately resourced, and given real and achievable targets. These are not to be "one-off tasks" but continuously monitored, reviewed, and updated, the overall aim being to describe a "sustainable process for real-izing the rights of children throughout the State."[111] But the Committee's recommendations do not end there. They also include, for example, ensur-ing coordination across government departments to ensure effective imple-mentation,[112] the creation of a "specific department or unit close to the heart of Government,"[113] the carrying out of systematic and ongoing training and capacity-building for government officials, parliamentarians, and members of the judiciary, and for "all those working with and for children,"[114] as well as the creation of independent national human rights institutions to develop projects to enhance the promotion and protection of children's rights and to monitor the compliance and progress of the State concerned.[115]

The second example is the Concluding Observations of the CEDAW Committee on the combined second and third periodic reports of Timor-Leste,[116] which illustrates more specifically how State parties are encouraged to proactively enact policies to realise human rights which go far beyond mere legislative change. The government's efforts to institutionalise gender-responsive budgeting and the creation of an interministerial working group on gender mainstreaming and national and district gender working groups are noted, but the Committee recommends they be given more resources, that more data is gathered to improve impact assessment, and that monitoring mechanisms be put in place to measure progress towards strategic plans on gender equality.[117] The State party is called upon to adopt a comprehensive strategy with clear goals and timetables for the elimination of "discriminatory stereotypes and harmful practices" and to reinforce awareness programmes targeting the judiciary, law enforcement personnel, teachers, parents, and community leaders, "as well as women and men and girls and boys [sic]."[118] It is asked to strengthen the assistance to and rehabilitation of women who are victims of violence, through establishing a "comprehensive care system" and ensuring access to legal aid, medical and psychological support, shelters, counselling, and rehabilitation services.[119] It is recommended to carry out a study on the prevalence of trafficking in women and girls and prostitution and continually update data, and to provide victims of trafficking with access to shelters and other forms of assistance as well as alternative income-generating opportunities.[120] And it is told to adopt measures to increase the percentage of female village chiefs and to develop targeted training and mentoring programmes for potential women candidates;[121] to provide safe transportation to and from schools; to strengthen incentives for parents to send daughters to school; to eliminate child marriage; to raise awareness of the importance of education for girls and women; to conduct literacy programmes in local languages and Portuguese; to adopt an official re-entry policy for girls dropping out of school due to pregnancy; to take measures to encourage girls to report sexual violence in educational institutions to the police[122] – and, at the risk of producing a litany, much more besides.

The third example is the report of the SR on the Right to Food given to the Human Rights Council after her visit to Poland in 2016.[123] As with all the UN special procedures, the SR on the Right to Food occasionally conducts country visits in order to gather information and propose recommendations. The visit to Poland is a typical example.

The report begins with an overview of the legal framework on the right to adequate food in Poland, recommending that explicit recognition of the right to food be enacted in national legislation: an overarching legal framework on the right to food would help ensure the integration of a "plethora [*sic*]" of policies, strategies, and programmes, harmonise coordination mechanisms between relevant ministries and stakeholders, and ensure greater efficiency of policies and programmes designed to respect, protect, and fulfil the right to food.[124] It would also, in the SR's view, institutionalise a coherent and integrated approach through the creation of an "independent council" to advise the government on food and nutritional security, ground policy in a "society-wide consensus," allow the ring-fencing of resources, and strengthen accountability and institutional oversight of food programmes.[125] The notion that such programmes exist and will continue to exist goes without saying; the interest is in how policy can be centralised and a "master plan" developed,[126] and then, subsequently, in the goals of that plan. While these are not explicitly stated as such, those goals can be easily gleaned from the SR's various recommendations, which include, among other things, mainstreaming of the right to food in national social assistance programmes; support for women farmers with additional incentives and access to credit; control of advertising of unhealthy foods, particularly with respect to children; implementation of environmental regulations to protect against soil degradation and water pollution; enhanced control and monitoring of the use of pesticides; and the promotion of organic agriculture and agroecology through financial mechanisms and training programmes.[127] Other recommendations can be gleaned from various comments in the SR's report, for instance in her concern expressed that there is no specific government programme for monitoring food waste;[128] her exhortation that the government include access to food for the Roma population as a focus area in national programmes;[129] her interest in statistics on breastfeeding;[130] and her welcoming of government efforts to combat obesity.[131]

Belabouring the point with further examples could hardly make it clearer. The sole question of interest for the CRC, HRC, and SR in the aforementioned examples is what is being done by the holders of obligations to improve conditions in a particular regard (the rights of children in general; women's rights in Timor-Leste; the right to food in Poland). It is not so much that the obligations of the duty-bearer to act (or refrain from acting) are emphasised in these documents; it is that they are the exclusive focus. Individual rights-holders are barely mentioned, if at all. Where individuals do appear, it is either as members of society who themselves have responsibilities vis-à-vis realising the right in question – and whose efforts in this respect are to be facilitated and encouraged by the State – or as the passive beneficiaries of its positive action. Human rights, then, appear in essence as the justifications for imposing positive duties to act on the duty-bearer, and what the rights-holders might wish to do to exercise them disappears from consideration almost entirely. In some formulations, the situation is put even more starkly: in the words of the author of perhaps the most widely used textbook on international human rights law, "the State can never simply 'abstain' from interfering with a right, since the right *cannot exist* without State action."[132]

The overall impression given by this picture is one in which human rights obligations are all-pervasive and the interest of human rights bodies all-encompassing. Not even breastfeeding is an event which escapes consideration as a topic of interest to the overarching legal regime. This single example in itself perhaps serves to prove the general point that, to a solipsistic and imperialistic international legal regime such as human rights law, there is truly nothing that cannot be viewed through the lens of its overriding purpose, and there is nothing that its purpose – protecting human rights – cannot be conceived to mean; provided, of course, there is no external or self-imposed restraint on its self-centredness and ambition.

The relationship between the expansion in the scope of positive obligations that has taken place since the late 1980s and the teleological interpretive stance described in the previous subsection is a direct one, although it is not often explicitly spelled out by the bodies performing the interpretation in question.[133] Evidently, the UN treaty bodies and charter-based mechanisms operate on the generally implicit understanding that what they are called to do with respect to the text of the relevant treaty is give effect to its "moral truth," as they see it, rather than the intentions of the drafters or its ordinary meaning, whatever that might be. The expansion of positive obligations, in other words, must be seen as being entwined with the teleological approach to interpretation, because of what the latter does to facilitate the former. If one considers one's role to be to bring about the object and purpose of a treaty or treaty provision, and one is not otherwise constrained, whether by internal or external forces, then one can, with the correct "ingenuity," construe essentially any event as relevant, and hence read an additional positive duty into the text accordingly.

As we shall now see, it is also only a short step from expanding the scope and number of positive obligations in this fashion to expanding the range of duty-bearers themselves. That the concept of the "duty-bearer" extends beyond the State has, of course, been foreshadowed by much of what followed. The CESCR was quite clear about this in its General Comment No. 14,[134] when it described effectively any and all conceivable actors as having responsibilities regarding the realisation of the right to health. But it is also implicit in the mere existence of the obligations to protect and fulfil, and the requirement to exercise due diligence, which at the very least suggest that the State must take an interest in the actions of private actors. This cannot help but result, in many cases, in duties being imposed on such actors. In many such scenarios, the State remains the locus in the sense that it must carry out its own obligations through creating duties for others. Yet, as we shall see, there are specific areas where it is increasingly common to also speak of, if not out-and-out binding human rights obligations, then at least "responsibilities" for private actors arising independently of the duties of States – the most notable of these areas being transnational commerce and international organisation.

Duty-bearers beyond the State

Expanding the range of duty-bearers

We have already noted that the doctrine of due diligence quickly extended beyond the specific circumstances of the *Velasquez Rodriguez* and *Godinez Cruz* cases, and of the general international legal principles of State responsibility, in order to provide the justification for detailed and elaborate positive obligations to be imposed on States parties to the CEDAW. This approach has become evident in many other areas since the early 1980s. The results can be very fine-grained. The Committee on the Elimination of Racial Discrimination (CERD Committee), for example, in 1995 interpreted Article 3 of the CERD Convention – which requires States parties to prevent, prohibit, and eradicate all practices of racial segregation and apartheid in their jurisdictions – as including a positive obligation to work to eradicate "partial segregation" arising as an "unintended by-product of the actions of private persons" in the form of residential patterns resulting in group differences in income.[135] The CRC Committee, meanwhile, speaking to adolescent health and development in 2003, called upon States parties to adopt programmes to improve road safety and designate pedestrian areas because of a concern about disproportionate numbers of adolescents affected by road traffic accidents.[136] At the same time, the expression of this obligation can be much more general, as in the Convention on the Rights of Persons with Disabilities' (CRPD's) inclusion of an explicit requirement to "take all appropriate measures to eliminate discrimination on the basis of disability by any person, organization or private enterprise,"[137] or the HRC's broad reading of the rights contained within the ICCPR as containing positive obligations which "will only be fully discharged if individuals are protected by the State, not just against violations of Covenant rights by its agents, but also against acts committed by private persons or entities."[138]

Clearly, in many of these cases no significant legal duty extends to the private actor in question – at least where none was already in existence.

There is no particular additional obligation imposed on drivers by road safety and pedestrianisation programmes except the existing prohibitions of the criminal law widened slightly in scope. But, equally, in many such cases there will be an additional legal duty imposed. The most obvious examples for this are found in the arena of employment law. In order to satisfy the obligation to protect individuals from violation of their right to freedom from discrimination on whatever grounds, States may, for example, impose requirements through legislation on employers not to discriminate – the UK's Equality Act 2010 being an obvious example of this. In such circumstances, private actors are given what is, in effect, the duty to carry out the State's own obligation to eliminate discrimination arising from the various treaties in which this is found. Employment law may indeed be thought of as the paradigm case in which the duty of the State to "protect" human rights finds expression in the imposition of duties on private actors, and the list of jurisprudence concerning this issue, domestic and international, is long indeed.[139]

Increasingly, however, the duties that are imposed are becoming more pervasive even while they are ostensibly softer and more diffuse, being described in many circumstances only as "responsibilities" rather than obligations. Perhaps more significantly in terms of general international law, many of these duties and responsibilities are said to be "inherent" for certain private actors – that is, distinct from the State's delegated obligation to protect – despite the justification remaining largely undertheorised.[140] In the examples which follow, I describe how businesses and international organisations are becoming subject to ever more such duties, whether in the "hard" form of obligation or "soft" form of responsibility – with the important caveat that the following chapters will elaborate much further on the nature of such duties and the relationships they create between the powerful actor and its beneficiaries.

The human rights responsibilities and duties of businesses

Human rights may have been "universal" since 1948, but of course at that time it was hardly envisaged that private firms had human rights obligations towards employees, much less "stakeholders" (had that concept then existed). Nonetheless, it is now widely believed that businesses have human rights responsibilities of various kinds, and that businesses are capable indeed of violating the human rights of their employees and stakeholders. The change in the way rights are conceptualised – essentially from an instrument of public law exercised by the individual against the State to hold it to its international obligations, to a much broader category of obligations which can be held by private actors towards individuals – has happened rapidly. An example from the British context will serve to illustrate. In 2009,

Parliament's Joint Committee on Human Rights (JCHR) issued a report on *Human Rights and the UK Private Sector*.[141] In it, the Committee set out what was, in effect, a regulatory understanding of the relationship between businesses and human rights. While private sector entities "cannot be considered directly subject to the state's obligations,"[142] as the report put it, the activities of UK businesses could affect the ability of the UK Government to meet its human rights obligations, and hence "certain obligations may require the regulation of business."[143] This was, in effect, a mere extension of the logic of the "obligation to protect": the activities of businesses can be understood in that context as being underneath the umbrella of private actors from whom individual rights-holders must be protected by the State. In 2017, by contrast, the same Committee, in its report on *Human Rights in Business*,[144] took the stance in the first paragraph of its opening summary that "Human rights violations ... all occur with the realm of business activity [and] examples of multinational companies violating the human rights of their workers or of local communities are extensive."[145] That is, business activities were now understood not merely as part of the penumbra of factors to be taken into account in assessing whether a State was doing enough to fulfil its due diligence obligations and its obligations to protect, respect, and fulfil human rights; rather, they were of direct interest to human rights law itself. The transformation in the understanding of businesses as actors whose activities might impact on the ability of the State to meet its own obligations, to actors with direct human rights obligations of their own, seems to have taken less than a decade.

The immediate reasons for this transformation are well known and the background is well rehearsed. In 2005, John Ruggie, the Special Representative of the Secretary-General of the UN on human rights and transnational corporations, began a project to develop a series of international standards or norms governing the relationship between human rights and businesses, which culminated in the so-called Ruggie Principles of 2013.[146] These principles, the UN Guiding Principles on Business and Human Rights, place responsibilities on businesses to respect human rights that are distinct from the duties of the State. While these responsibilities are not binding inasmuch as the "Ruggie Principles" are not contained in a binding instrument, they have found widespread acceptance among G20 countries in particular.[147] There will be much more to say about the content of the Principles in due course. For the moment, it suffices to note that their existence provides what might be thought of as the proximate cause for the sea change in the way the human rights responsibilities of businesses are conceptualised: as actual duties, albeit non-binding on their face, which businesses inherently possess irrespective of any relationship to the State.

While the "Ruggie Principles," the Organisation for Economic Cooperation and Development (OECD) Guidelines, and other international standards and instruments concerning business and human rights are typically non-binding, however, the general shift in emphasis identified in the preceding paragraphs has resulted in many domestic and regional legislative changes which have led to binding statutory duties for duties specifically concerning human rights. Businesses, for instance, are now in many jurisdictions required to report on the potential impact of their operations on human rights, typically in their annual reports. In the case of the UK, this comes in the form of the "strategic report" now appended to annual reports, which is required to be prepared by the directors of all medium and large quoted companies.[148] This must, among many other things, include information about "human rights issues" in the context of the "principal risks and uncertainties facing the company."[149] Similar requirements in, for example, the EU and Canada, whether hard or soft, result in similar reporting practices.[150] More concretely, in some jurisdictions businesses are being given obligations with respect to the behaviour of their overseas suppliers, often under the rubric of preventing human rights violations, and frequently coming in the form of a requirement to conduct "due diligence" in preventing the risk of such violations taking place in their supply chains. Examples of this include enacted legislation in France requiring due diligence (or "duty of vigilance") plans with respect to human rights risks in their operations to be drawn up and implemented by large limited liability companies,[151] a similar draft piece of legislation currently being considered at the time of writing by the German Federal Ministry for Economic Cooperation and Development,[152] and s. 1502 of the US Dodd Frank Act 2010, which requires publicly listed US companies to report to the Securities and Exchange Commission on their efforts to identify conflict minerals in their supply chains.

In all of these circumstances, while a legal duty *per se* has come into existence, it consists primarily of an obligation either to report or to plan. Yet the imposition of much more direct duties on businesses has also lately taken place in certain jurisdictions, most notably South Africa. Here, courts have developed a principle that even the most quintessential area of private law, the law of contract, is subject to the requirements of the Constitution, particularly as they concern human rights. In *Bondev Midrand (Pty) Ltd v. Mulatedzi Alton Madzhie, et al.*,[153] for instance, a term in a deed of sale of land to the effect that the land must be returned if the buyer did not build a house on it within 18 months was held to be unenforceable. This was because, in the view of the High Court, that clause put the developer, which had sold the land, in breach of not only a negative duty under section 26(1) of the Constitution ("Everyone has the right to adequate housing") – which is to say, a duty not to infringe on the rights of others to access adequate housing – but also a positive one to facilitate the provision of it.[154] Here, the duty of the private actor extends far beyond mere reporting or exercising due diligence in the making of contracts, but into the undertaking and performance of contracts themselves.

International organisations

As is the case with businesses, none of the main international human rights treaties contains direct obligations for international organisations, for the simple reason that only States can be parties to them.[155] International organisations are mentioned in the major texts of the UN treaty system, but only in advisory or supervisory roles.[156] Yet it is regularly claimed that international organisations do have human rights obligations. Doctrinally, it is argued that the UN itself has human rights obligations by virtue of the protection of human rights being part of the UN Charter, with the content of those obligations being those of the ICCPR and ICESCR because they "partake of the creative force" of the UDHR.[157] This, it is further argued, extends into other UN specialised agencies such as the International Monetary Fund (IMF), World Health Organization (WHO), Food and Agriculture Organization (FAO), and United Nations International Children's Fund (UNICEF) through their relationship agreements with the UN, which are said to require them to respect the principles of the UN Charter, including, therefore, protection of human rights (although it is not abundantly clear which rights are included).[158] Alternatively, because some human rights standards are part of customary international law – though there is no widespread agreement on what that corpus contains[159] – and international organizations are thought to be bound by "general international law" (which would presumably include customary international law),[160] this would indicate that customary norms concerning human rights would be part of the obligations of international organisations.[161]

Irrespective of whether these arguments are convincing, it is undoubtedly the case that they have proved influential in practice, at least insofar as they have informed the work of the UN treaty- and charter-based mechanisms and NGOs. The Commission on Human Rights had already tasked the CESCR to consider how measures to promote economic, social, and cultural rights could be integrated into the activities of UN agencies working in the field of development in 1989,[162] and the topic has only broadened and deepened since then. Where in 1990, for example, the CESCR stuck fairly strictly to the text of Article 22 of the Covenant in defining its role vis-à-vis the specialised agencies as merely being to advise or make recommendations concerning measures taken,[163] by the early 2000s it was describing the UN, the FAO, UNICEF, the World Bank, the IMF, and so on, as having "obligations" concerning human rights with some regularity,[164] with those obligations typically being framed as cooperating with States parties to the Covenant to help them implement the relevant rights and taking into account the goal of promoting those rights in their activities.[165]

But it is in the charter-based mechanisms that the issue has been most prominently addressed, primarily through the creation of special procedures with thematic mandates. The most obvious example of this is the establishment of the Independent Expert on the effects of foreign debt and other related financial obligations of States,[166] whose extended mandate expressly concerns structural adjustment reform programmes and policy conditionalities (clearly in respect of the IMF) and their "inadequate attention to the provision of social service." It also groups "the United Nations system [and] the Bretton Woods institutions" under the rubric of "the international community" in general with respect *inter alia* to the implementation of the outcomes of the World Conference on Human Rights.[167] The Guiding Principles on Foreign Debt and Human Rights, developed by Cephas Lumina, a previous holder of the office, state that international organisations, along with private corporations, have an obligation to respect international human rights – "[implying] a duty to refrain from formulating, adopting, funding and implementing policies and programmes which directly or indirectly contravene the enjoyment of human rights."[168] And the current office holder at the time of writing, Juan Bohoslavsky, has shown a particular interest in labour rights in the context of austerity, calling for international and regional financial institutions to include explicit commitments to respecting human rights in their lending policies and to exercise human rights due diligence in lending,[169] and arguing that the EU institutions themselves have obligations respect human rights obligations that are binding on Member States, particularly in the context of austerity and economic adjustment programmes.[170]

But many of the other office holders of other special procedures have also spoken to the purported human rights obligations of international organisations, and the topic has a long pedigree in the charter-based mechanisms. An early and perhaps unexpected example is the Commission on Human Rights' Sub-Commission on Prevention of Discrimination and Protection of Minorities and its working paper on "Human Rights as the Primary Objective of International Trade, Investment and Finance Policy and Practice," which argued that by dint of the UDHR's preamble (calling on "every individual and every organ of society"), international organisations had obligations to promote and strive to secure the recognition and observance of human rights.[171] Among the mandate holders who have spoken to the issue include the SR on adequate housing,[172] the SR on the right to food,[173] the Independent Expert on the promotion of a democratic and equitable world order,[174] and the SR on extreme poverty and human rights.[175] Illustrative of the general position is the letter sent by a group of mandate holders, among them the Independent Expert on foreign debt, in late 2017, to the Executive Directors of the IMF on the subject of social protections.[176] While refraining from addressing the topic of whether the IMF itself has binding human rights obligations directly, the letter calls upon the organisation, among other things, to provide its own staff with guidance so as to "avoid interfering in an impermissible way with the right to social security when providing technical support to Member States" – as close as it is possible to come to suggesting that the Fund's conduct might breach a human rights obligation without actually doing so.[177] It also requests the Fund to conduct human rights impact assessments when recommending reform and fiscal consolidation, and monitor the impact of its policies, as well to support countries in achieving universal social protection "according to the right to social security"[178] – all of which coming very close, of course, to drawing a direct link between the activities of the Fund and human rights protection.

Summary

To various extents, then, human rights duties (whether couched as "responsibilities" or actual binding legal obligations) have proliferated for non-State actors, and they increasingly do so outside the rubric of the State's obligation to protect. Rather, they exist in many cases as free-standing duties which are said to be inherent in the status of the new duty-bearers, much as rights and obligations under international law, in the traditional view, are said to inhere in an entity's status as a State.[179]

As with the expanding scope of positive obligations, it is appropriate to describe the position of international human rights law in this respect as solipsistic, for the way that it continually conceptualises new species of relationship – employer and employee, purchaser and supplier, international organisation and population – through its own lens, and in such a way that the bounds of its purview extend ever further across the field of human activity. For many of those existing relationships, there already exist applicable non-international civil and criminal duties, or the potential for such duties to exist, but, unrestrained, the international legal regime incorporates them within its purview regardless.

We also see in the account offered here the clear relationship between the three different phenomena I have described and the solipsism and imperialism which underlie them. The teleological approach to interpretation which is generally adopted by any given "interpreter" of human rights treaty provisions results, in the first instance, in a tendency to widen the scope of applicability in an effort to realise the "moral truth" underpinning them. What typically follows is a broadened range of obligations, particularly across the positive dimension, and a concomitant requirement for the duty-bearer (in the first instance the State) to take on obligations with respect to the conduct of private actors. From there, it is only a short conceptual step to hold that the "moral truth" which is the object and purpose of the relevant treaty requires duties to be imposed on other powerful actors beyond the State. This will include any actor which has the capacity to affect any aspect of what can be understood as relevant to the purposes of human rights law (which is to say, almost anything) – and even, indeed, to view any distinction between State and non-State actor in this regard to be mythical or perverse.[180]

The reason why this is so is that, if one considers human rights law to have a purpose, with that purpose being the universal protection of human rights, then one will view it as quite natural that any entity which has the potential to influence human rights outcomes ought to come within the purview of human rights protection – especially since, as we have noted, any event (such as one concerning purely private actors) is capable of being conceptualised as of concern to human rights law and hence as affecting such outcomes. As De Schutter puts it, perfectly channelling this view, there is now "general agreement" that since "private compulsion may exercise an equally powerful constraint on the free will of the individual right-holder ... [particularly] in situations where the right holder is in need and where he/she faces few alternatives ... the possibility for the private actor with whom the rights-holder interacts to withhold certain goods or services ... may in fact lead to a form of coercion equivalent to that at the disposal of the State."[181] That is, the purpose of human rights law – the universal protection of human rights – trumps the legal fiction of the distinction between State and non-State actor, and makes the imposition of the duties on the latter perfectly reasonable, even inevitable. The private actor (by which De Schutter quite clearly means businesses) ought to be bound by human rights obligations simply by dint of its power or purported capacity to influence human rights outcomes – and for that reason alone.

And, indeed, in much of the literature on businesses and human rights, this is the reasoning we encounter. Corporations, the argument frequently goes, may be implicated in all manner of activities capable of being conceptualised as abuses of human rights, such as employing child labourers, discriminating against groups of employees, failing to provide safe and healthy working conditions, discouraging collective bargaining, and dumping toxic waste.[182] They may, in more general terms, contribute to rising poverty, environmental degradation, poor labour standards, and ill health – all of which are also just as capable of being thought of as of concern to the project of human rights.[183] And they may, like States, have the "resources and power to escape responsibility."[184] Given that all of this is the case, it should, of course, appear entirely natural in the solipsistic and imperialistic style of international human rights law's legal reasoning that they must have responsibilities in human rights law accordingly.[185] It should also be entirely natural for the same reasons that other potential mechanisms for ameliorating such concerns – such as criminal law, tort law, or labour law – should be downplayed or ignored, or operationalised for human rights law's purposes. This goes to explain why even contract law is increasingly argued to have implications for human rights. Since any relationship in which one party is stronger than another can be conceptualised as a potential threat to human rights outcomes, and since contracts are always "per definition" between parties with unequal bargaining power, why should courts not interpret and execute them so as to contribute to the fulfilment of human rights?[186]

For international organisations, similar reasoning is typically applied, though the justifications usually concern the "public" nature of the roles and powers of such organisations. Since, the argument usually goes, the international legal order is, or should be, invested with constitutional ideals (among them the protection of human rights), international public authority in whatever form should be bound by those ideals.[187] And since international public authority, like domestic public authority, has the "legal capacity to determine others and to reduce their freedom," it must be bound as domestic public authority is by principles concerning democracy, transparency, the rule of law, human rights, and so on. By dint of their being "fiduciaries of humanity,"[188] as it has been put, international organisations cannot but be subject to human rights obligations – just as is true for the State. Other, more functional perspectives would hold simply that, since in certain circumstances international organisations have State-like functions, it must be the case that they are bound by human rights obligations. In the words of Mégret and Hoffman, "the wedging criterion for ultimate human rights responsibility" is the exercising of sovereign control, and, therefore, where in particular the UN exercises what is in effect sovereign control (for instance when administering refugee camps or even entire territories such as Kosovo), it must have human rights obligations "*tout court.*"[189]

To bring us back to a case discussed earlier in this chapter, it is instructive in closing to consider the decision of the ECHR in *Young, James and Webster* to illustrate how the relationship between teleological interpretation, the expansion of positive duties for the State, and the expansion in the number of actors given human rights obligations plays out in the rather mundane circumstances of UK labour law. It will be recalled that in that case, workers at British Rail were required to join one of three trade unions, and the existence of the law which enabled such "closed shop" arrangements to exist, namely the Trade Union and Labour Relations Act 1974, was held to have placed the UK in breach of a negative aspect of the right to freedom of association under Article 11 of the Convention. This was done in spite of the fact that the intentions of the parties to the Convention at the time of drafting had clearly been to exclude "closed shop" arrangements from the scope of Article 11. This interpretation of the text of Article 11 – which was given in order to realise the freedom that text had been "designed to guarantee"[190] – then had the effect, quite naturally, of requiring the respondent State to take steps to make "closed shop" arrangements unlawful (a positive duty), which could only have full effect by imposing additional duties on private actors – that is, trade unions and employers. And this is indeed the sequence that followed the decision: shortly afterwards, the Employment Act 1982 made closed shop arrangements in effect so impractical as to be impossible, with the Employment Act 1990 making them unlawful outright.[191] This, of course, imposed a series of obligations on employers, including not to refuse employment to a person on the grounds of not having membership of a particular trade union or unwillingness to become a member of one.[192] It is not, to reiterate a point emphasised earlier, that this chain of events is illegitimate or undesirable. Rather, it is that it demonstrates how attempts to read human rights treaty provisions in light of their purpose typically result in an expansion of human rights law's purview and scope of application, in such a way as to appear in new contexts (the employment relationship) and new forms (duties being imposed on private actors who are employers). The system's solipsism – its willingness to view any event as being of relevance to human rights – and imperialism cannot be separated from each other.

Conclusion

In the account provided in this chapter I have, borrowing from Koskenniemi and Kelsen, described the international human rights regime as solipsistic, for the tendency it shows to interpret any and all events (from suicide to breastfeeding) as of relevance to its purpose, and imperialistic, for its tendency, for the most part, to avoid imposing self-restraint in declaring such events to be the subject of that purpose.

The next task is much more complex, and concerns the "purpose" of the regime itself. As was alluded to earlier in this chapter, it is one thing to suggest that international legal regimes have their purposes or projects, but quite another to account for why and how one such purpose or project comes to dominate or become mainstream (if indeed one does at all). Put in a different way in light of the preceding description of the development of international human rights law, what is it that gives those engaged in the system a sense of its "moral truth," what is it that defines what that "moral truth" might be, and how is it that a particular method of implementation for realising that "moral truth" comes to prominence? Above all, and perhaps this is the most fundamental question, why do those engaged in the interpretation of human rights obligations see their task (implicitly or explicitly) as the realisation of a "moral truth" to begin with? That task will be dealt with in Chapters 2 and 3.

Notes

1 Stephen Holmes and Cass Sunstein, *The Cost of Rights: Why Liberty Depends on Taxes* (WW Norton, 1999), p. 48.
2 See, for instance, W. Enteman, *Managerialism: The Emergence of a New Ideology* (University of Wisconsin Press, 1993).
3 M. Koskenniemi, "International Law: Constitutionalism, Managerialism and the Ethos of Legal Education," 1, *European Journal of Legal Studies* (2007) 1, p. 6.
4 *Ibid.*, p. 2.
5 Case C-459/03, *Commission v. Ireland* [2006] ECR I-04635.
6 Koskenniemi, "International Law," pp. 2–5.
7 *Ibid.*, p. 7.
8 *Ibid.*
9 *Ibid.*, p. 12.
10 M. Koskenniemi, "The Politics of International Law – 20 Years Later," 20 (1), *European Journal of International Law* (2009) 7, p. 13.
11 *Ibid.*, p. 12.
12 *Ibid.*, p. 13.
13 *Ibid.*, p. 11.
14 *Ibid.*, p. 13.
15 Koskenniemi, "International Law," p. 11.
16 See especially M. Koskenniemi, "Constitutionalism as Mindset: Reflections on Kantian Themes About International Law and Globalization," 8 (1), *Theoretical Inquiries in Law* (2007) 9; M. Koskenniemi, "The Fate of Public International Law: Between Technique and Politics," 70 (1), *Modern Law Review* (2007) 1.
17 Koskenniemi, "International Law," pp. 10–12.
18 *Ibid.*, p. 10.
19 In H. Kelsen, *Pure Theory of Law* [2nd edition, 1960] (University of California Press, 1967; trans. M. Knight), pp. 340–345.
20 A. Somek, "Kelsen Lives," 18 (3), *European Journal of International Law* (2007) 409, p. 432.
21 Vienna Convention on the Law of Treaties 1969, Article 31 (1) and (2).
22 *Golder v. United Kingdom* (1975), Series A No. 18.
23 *Ibid.*, para. 34.
24 *Ibid.*, para. 36.
25 *Tyrer v. United Kingdom* (1978), Series A No. 26.
26 *Ibid.*, para. 31.

27 *Ibid.*, para. 38.

28 *Goodwin v. United Kingdom*, App no. 28957/95 (ECtHR, 2002), para. 74.

29 See, in the general context, G. Nolte, Report of the International Law Commission, 60th Session (2008), UN Doc. A/63/10; GAOR, 63rd Session, Supplement No. 10 (2008), Annex A, para. 1; and, in the human rights context, K. Dzehtsiarou, "European Consensus and the Evolutive Interpretation of the European Convention on Human Rights," 12, *German Law Journal* (2011) 1730.

30 In *Matthews v. United Kingdom*, App no. 24833/94 (ECtHR, 1999).

31 *Tyrer v. United Kingdom*, dissenting opinion of Judge Sir Gerald Fitzmaurice, para. 11.

32 *Ibid.*, Judgment, paras 30–33.

33 *Ibid.*, para. 30.

34 *Ibid.*, para. 33.

35 G. Letsas, *A Theory of Interpretation of the European Convention on Human Rights* (Oxford University Press, 2007), pp. 78–80.

36 *Young, James and Webster v. United Kingdom* (1981), Series A No 44.

37 *Ibid.*

38 *Ibid.*, para. 52.

39 Letsas, *Theory of Interpretation*, p. 70.

40 *Ibid.*, p. 79.

41 *Young, James and Webster v. United Kingdom*, para. 52.

42 F. de Londras and K. Dzehtsariou, "Managing Judicial Innovation in the European Court of Human Rights," 15 (3), *Human Rights Law Review* (2015) 523, p. 524; C. Rozakis, "The European Judge as Comparatist," 80, *Tulane Law Review* (2005) 257, p. 276.

43 L. Hoffmann, "The Universality of Human Rights," 125, *Law Quarterly Review* (2009) 416, p. 428.

44 Letsas, *Theory of Interpretation*, p. 79.

45 Judgment (Preliminary Objections) *Velasquez Rodriguez v. Honduras*, Inter-American Court of Human Rights, Series C no. 4, 26th June 1987, para. 30.

46 Advisory Opinion OC-16/99, Inter-American Court of Human Rights, Series A no. 16 (1999), paras 114–115.

47 *Austria v. Italy*, App no. 788/60 (1961), para. 140.

48 *Caesar Case*, Inter-American Court of Human Rights, Series C no. 123 (2005), separate opinion of Judge Trindade, para. 7.

49 *Kindler v Canada*, Comm. 470/1991, Views under Article 5, para. 4 of the Optional Protocol, CCPR/C/48/D/470/1991, 30th July 1993.

50 *Ibid.*, para. 10.1.

51 HRC, General Comment No. 6, UN Doc. CCPR/GEC/6630/E (1982).

52 *Kindler v. Canada*, para. 14.3.

53 *Ibid.*, Individual opinion submitted by Mr Bertil Wennergren (dissenting).

54 *Ibid.*

55 *Ng v. Canada*, Comm. 469/1991, Views under Article 5, para. 4 of the Optional Protocol, CCPR/C/49/D/469/1991, 5th November 1993.

56 *Cox v. Canada*, Comm. 539/1993, Views under Article 5, para. 4 of the Optional Protocol, CCPR/C/52/D/539/1993, 31st October 1994.
57 *Judge v. Canada*, Comm. 829/1998, Views under Article 5, para. 4 of the Optional Protocol, CCPR/C/78/D/829/1998, 5th August 2002.
58 *Ibid.*, para. 10.3.
59 *Ibid.*, paras 10.5–10.6.
60 *Kindler v. Canada*, Dissenting opinion by Mr Francisco Jose Aguilar Urbina.
61 *Golder v. United Kingdom*, Separate Opinion of Judge Sir Gerald Fitzmaurice, para. 2.
62 M. Sepulveda, *The Nature of the Obligations Under the International Covenant on Economic, Social and Cultural Rights* (Intersentia, 2003), p. 83.
63 The European Court of Human Rights is, from time to time, criticised for showing either too much self-restraint (see e.g., De Londras and Dzehtsariou, "Managing Judicial Innovation") or too little (see e.g., D. Popovic, "Prevailing of Judicial Activism Over Self-Restraint in the Jurisprudence of the European Court of Human Rights," 42, *Creighton Law Review* (2008–2009) 361.
64 *Hatton and Others v. United Kingdom*, App no. 36022/97 (ECtHR, 2003).
65 CESCR, General Comment No. 4, UN Doc. E/1992/23 (1991).
66 *Ibid.*, para. 7.
67 *Ibid.*, para. 8.
68 CESCR, General Comment No. 12, UN Doc. E/C.12/1999/5 (1999). The right to water had also been mentioned in the earlier General Comment No. 6, UN Doc. E/1996/22 (1995).
69 *Ibid.*, paras 1, 2, and 3, respectively.
70 *Ibid.*, paras 12 and 13.
71 CEDAW, General Recommendation No. 12, UN Doc. A/44/38 (1989).
72 CEDAW, General Recommendation No. 19, UN Doc. A/47/38 (1992).
73 *Ibid.*, para. 6.
74 *Ibid.*, para. 9.
75 *Ibid.*
76 *Godinez Cruz v. Honduras*, Series C no. 5 (1989).
77 Judgment, *Velasquez Rodriguez v. Honduras*, Series C no. 4 (1988), para. 172.
78 HRC, General Comment No. 7, UN Doc. CCPR/GEC/6629/E (1982), paras 1–2.
79 CEDAW, General Recommendation No 19, para. 24.
80 See e.g. *AT v. Hungary*, Comm. 2/2003, Views under Article 7, para. 3 of the Optional Protocol, CEDAW/C/32/D/2/2003, 26th January 2005.
81 CEDAW, General Recommendation No 19, para. 1.
82 *Ibid.*, para. 12.
83 *Ibid.*, para. 14.
84 *Ibid.*, para. 18.
85 See, for instance, J. Klabbers, *International Law* (2nd edition, Cambridge University Press, 2018), pp. 137–153.
86 I make this observation in full awareness that an argument can be made that the "return to the text" is just as much an interpretive tactic as any other – see

S. Fish, "What Makes an Interpretation Acceptable?" in S. Fish, *Is There a Text in This Class: The Authority of Interpretive Communities* (Harvard University Press, 1980), 338, pp. 353–355.

87 J. Welling, "International Indicators and Economic, Social and Cultural Rights," 30 (4), *Human Rights Quarterly* (2008) 933, p. 937.

88 See e.g., D. Desierto, *Public Policy in International Economic Law* (Oxford University Press, 2015), p. 75.

89 UN Commission on Human Rights, *The New International Order and the Promotion of Human Rights: Report on the Right to Adequate Food as a Human Rights*, UN Doc. E/CN.4/Sub.2/1987/23 (1987).

90 *Ibid.*, paras 40–43.

91 *Ibid.*, para. 65.

92 *Ibid.*, paras 66–69.

93 *Ibid.*, para. 70.

94 *Ibid.*, para. 72.

95 CESCR, Maastricht Guidelines on Violations of Economic, Social and Cultural Rights (1997), Guideline 6. The Guidelines were initially produced as an academic project but were formally adopted by the CESCR in UN Doc. E/C.12/2000/13.

96 CESCR, General Comment No. 3, UN Doc. E/1991/23 (1990), para. 8.

97 OHCHR, *Handbook for National Human Rights Institutions* (2005), p. 17.

98 *Ibid.*, pp. 18–19.

99 *Ibid.*, p. 15.

100 The tripartite framework was first adopted by the CRC Committee in its General Comment No. 4, UN Doc. CRC/GC/2003/4 (2003).

101 See e.g., General Recommendation No. 28, UN Doc. CEDAW/C/GC/28 (2010).

102 See e.g., General Comment No. 3, UN Doc. CRPD/C/GC/3 (2016), para. 24.

103 OHCHR, *Handbook for National Human Rights Institutions* (2005), pp. 15–19.

104 See e.g., HRC, General Comment No. 31, UN Doc. CCPR/C/21/Rev.1/Add 13 (2004).

105 See e.g., S. Fukuda-Parr, T. Lawson-Remer, and S. Randolph, "An Index of Economic and Social Rights Fulfilment: Concept and Methodology," 8 (3), *Journal of Human Rights* (2009) 195, p. 197.

106 CRC, General Comment No. 5, UN Doc. CRC/GC/2003/5 (2003).

107 *Ibid.*, para. 1.

108 CESCR, General Comment No. 14, UN Doc. E/C.12/2000/4 (2000).

109 CRC, General Comment No. 5, para. 9.

110 *Ibid.*, paras 28–36.

111 *Ibid.*, para. 32.

112 *Ibid.*, para. 37.

113 *Ibid.*, para. 39.

114 *Ibid.*, para. 53.

115 *Ibid.*, para. 65.

116 CEDAW, Concluding Observations on the combined second and third periodic reports of Timor-Leste, UN Doc. CEDAW/C/TLS/CO/2–3 (2015).

117 *Ibid.*, para. 13.
118 *Ibid.*, para. 15.
119 *Ibid.*, para. 17 (g).
120 *Ibid.*, para. 21 (c).
121 *Ibid.*, para. 23 (b).
122 *Ibid.*, para. 27.
123 Human Rights Council, Report of the Special Rapporteur on the Right to Food on Her Mission to Poland, UN Doc. A/HRC/34/48/Add.1 (2016).
124 *Ibid.*, para. 14.
125 *Ibid.*, para. 15.
126 *Ibid.*, para. 22–23.
127 *Ibid.*, para. 73.
128 *Ibid.*, para. 58.
129 *Ibid.*, paras 54–55.
130 *Ibid.*, paras 46–51.
131 *Ibid.*, paras 37–38.
132 O. de Schutter, *International Human Rights Law: Cases, Materials and Commentary* (3rd edition, Cambridge University Press, 2019), p. 303 (emphasis added).
133 This lack of a rigorous doctrine of interpretation within the UN human rights system in general is occasionally criticised, most notably in K. Mechlem, "Treaty Bodies and the Interpretation of Human Rights," 42, *Vanderbilt Journal of Transnational Law* (2009) 905.
134 See above, at fn. 108.
135 CERD, General Recommendation No. 19, UN Doc. A/50/18 (1995), para. 3.
136 CRC, General Comment No. 4, UN Doc. CRC/GC/2003/4 (2003), para. 21.
137 International Convention on the Rights of Persons with Disabilities 2006, Article 4.1 (e).
138 HRC, General Comment No. 31, para. 8.
139 See, for example, *Griggs v. Duke Power Co.*, 401 US 424 (1971).
140 See e.g., E. de Brabandere, "Non-State Actors, State-Centrism and Human Rights Obligations," 22, *Leiden Journal of International Law* (2009) 191, p. 192.
141 JCHR, *Any of Our Business? Human Rights and the UK Private Sector, First Report of Session 2009–2010* (The Stationery Office Limited, 2009).
142 *Ibid.*, p. 12, para. 18.
143 *Ibid.*, p. 12, para. 20.
144 JCHR, *Human Rights and Business 2017: Promoting Responsibility and Ensuring Accountability, Sixth Report of Session 2016–2017* (2017).
145 *Ibid.*, p. 5.
146 For a general history, see e.g., S. Aaronson and I. Higham, "'Re-Righting Business': John Ruggie and the Struggle to Develop International Human Rights Standards for Transnational Firms," 35 (2), *Human Rights Quarterly* (2013) 333.

147 See the G20 Leaders' Declaration, July 8, 2017, available at www.g20.utoro nto.ca/2017/2017-G20-leaders-declaration.html (accessed 18th November 2020).

148 This duty is imposed by Chapter 4A of the Companies Act 2006 as amended by the Companies Act 2006 (Strategic Report and Directors' Report) Regulations 2013, which applies to all UK quoted companies except for those entitled to the small companies exemption.

149 *Ibid.*, s. 414C (7).

150 See EU Directive 2014/95/EU and Canada's Strategy to Advance CSR in Canada's Extractive Sector Abroad, available at www.international.gc.ca/ trade-agreements-accords-commerciaux/topics-domaines/other-autre/csr-strat-rse.aspx?lang=eng (accessed 18th November 2020).

151 Loi no. 2017–399 du 27 Mars 2017 relative au devoir de vigilane des sociétés mères et des enterprises donneuses d'ordre.

152 Legislative Proposal: Corporate Responsibility and Human Rights, 15th June 2017, available at www.business-humanrights.org/sites/default/files/ documents/17-06_QuA_mHRDD%20German%20Law%20%20Proposal. pdf (accessed 28th November 2019) [English].

153 *Bondev Midrand (Pty) Ltd v. Mulatedzi Alton Madzhie, et al.*, High Court of South Africa (Gauteng Div., Pretoria) 19th December 2016.

154 *Ibid.*, para. 37.

155 They are, for example, open to signature by State members of the UN, State members of its specialised agencies, State parties to the International Court of Justice (ICJ) Statute, or State invitees, in the case of the ICCPR and ICESCR (under Articles 48 and 26, respectively); the CRC is open for signature "by all States" (under Article 46).

156 Article 22 of the ICESCR, for instance, allows ECOSOC to bring matters arising in State party reports to the attention of other UN organs or specialised agencies to assist them on "the advisability of international measures likely to contribute to the effective progressive implementation" of the Covenant; the CRC provides for the CRC Committee to request expert advice from UNICEF and other UN organs and specialised agencies under its Article 45.

157 See e.g., L. Sohn, "The Human Rights Law of the Charter," 12, *Texas Journal of International Law* (1977) 129. It must be said that this argument has little basis in existing principles of law.

158 See e.g., P. Alston, "The International Monetary Fund and the Right to Food," 30, *Howard Law Journal* (1987) 473, p. 479.

159 Some would argue that human rights standards achieving customary status include the entire UDHR (see e.g., T. Franck, "The Emerging Right to Democratic Governance," 86, *American Journal of International Law* (1992) 46, while others would limit them to a very restricted "core" (see e.g., T. Merson, *Human Rights and Humanitarian Norms as Customary Law* (1989)).

160 The Advisory Opinion of the ICJ which is often cited in support of this argument is actually ambivalent on this point: see *Interpretation of the Agreement*

of 25 March 1951 Between the WHO and Egypt ICJ Reports, Advisory Opinion of 20th December 1980, paras 40–42.

161 See e.g., A. Reinisch, "The Changing International Legal Framework for Dealing with Non-State Actors," in P. Alston (ed.), *Non-State Actors and Human Rights* (Oxford University Press, 2005), 37.

162 In UN Commission on Human Rights, Resolution 1989/13 (1989).

163 See e.g., CESCR, General Comment No. 2, UN Doc. E/1990/23 (1990).

164 The notion of international organisations having human rights obligations first appears in the CESCR's activities in General Comment No. 8, UN Doc. E/C.12/1997/8 (1997); it is then used again throughout most of the General Comments which follow through to General Comment No. 18, UN Doc. E/C.12/GC/18 (2006) – although, as has been observed, the Committee's practice in this regard has not been particularly coherent (see Mechlem, "Treaty Bodies").

165 See e.g., CESCR, General Comment No. 19, UN Doc. E/C.12/GC/19 (2008), paras. 82–84.

166 Established in 2000 under resolution E/CN.4/RES/2000/10; the full title is the "Independent Expert on the effects of foreign debt and other related financial obligations of States on the fully enjoyment of human rights, particularly economic, social and cultural rights."

167 Human Rights Council, "Mandate of the Independent Expert on the effects of foreign debt and other related international financial obligations of States on the full enjoyment of all human rights, particularly economic, social and cultural rights," UN Doc. A/HRC/RES/25/16 (2014), at paras 2 and 5, respectively.

168 Human Rights Council, "Report of the Independent Expert on the effects of foreign debt and other related international financial obligations of States on the full enjoyment of all human rights, particularly economic, social and cultural rights, Cephas Lumina: Guiding principles on foreign debt and human rights," UN Doc. A/HRC/20/23 (2011), para. 9.

169 Human Rights Council, "Report of the Independent Expert on the effects of foreign debt and other related international financial obligations of States on the full enjoyment of all human rights, particularly economic, social and cultural rights," UN Doc. A/HRC/34/57 (2016), para. 64.

170 Human Rights Council, "Report of the Independent Expert on the effects of foreign debt and other related international financial obligations of States on the full enjoyment of all human rights, particularly economic, social and cultural rights, on his mission to institutions of the European Union," UN Doc. A/HRC/34/57/Add.1 (2016).

171 Commission on Human Rights, Sub-Commission on Prevention of Discrimination and Protection of Minorities, "Human Rights as the Primary Objective of International Trade, Investment and Finance Policy and Practice," UN Doc. E/CN.4/Sub.2/1999/11 (1999), para. 13.

172 OHCHR, Addendum – Mission to the World Bank, UN Doc. A/HRC/22/46/Add.3 (2012).

173 Interim Report to the General Assembly of the Special Rapporteur on the right to food, UN Doc. A/60/350 (2005).

174 OHCHR, Mandate of the Independent Expert on the promotion of a democratic and equitable world order, Consultation on the role of the international financial institutions in promoting an equitable and democratic international order, especially in the field of taxation, 14th October 2016, available at www.ohchr.org/_layouts/15/WopiFrame.aspx?sourcedoc=/Documents/Issues/IntOrder/AgendaEMOctober2016.doc&action=default&DefaultItemOpen=1 (accessed 28th November 2019).

175 OHCHR, Report to the Human Rights Council of the Special Rapporteur on extreme poverty and human rights, UN Doc. A/HRC/38/33 (2018).

176 See OHCHR, Mandate of the Independent Expert on the effects of foreign debt and other related international financial obligations of States on the full enjoyment of all human rights, particularly economic, social and cultural rights, et al., Letter to Ms Lagarde and Executive Directors, 21st December 2017, available at www.ohchr.org/Documents/Issues/Development/IEDebt/Open_Letter_IMF_21Dec2017.pdf (accessed 28th November 2019).

177 *Ibid.*, p. 5.

178 *Ibid.*

179 The classical statement here is, of course, that of Vattel, who defined international law itself as "the science which teaches the rights subsisting between nations or States, and the obligations corresponding to those rights" (in *The Law of Nations: Or, Principles of the Law of Nature Applied to the Conduct and Affairs of Nations and Sovereigns* [1758/1797] (Liberty Fund, 2008; ed. R. Whatmore, trans. Anon.), s. 3).

180 See, for example, C. Lafont, "Accountability and Global Governance: Challenging the State-Centric Conception of Human Rights," 3, *Ethics & Global Politics* (2010) 193; or C. Harding, "Statist Assumptions, Normative Individualism, and New Forms of Personality: Evolving a Philosophy of International Law for the Twenty First Century," 1, *Non-State Actors and International Law* (2001) 107.

181 O. De Scutter, *International Human Rights Law*, p. 498.

182 D. Weissbrodt and M. Kruger, "Human Rights Responsibilities of Businesses as Non-State Actors," in Alston, *Non-State Actors and Human Rights*, 315, p. 317.

183 L. McConnell, *Extracting Accountability from Non-State Actors in International Law: Assessing the Scope for Direct Regulation* (Routledge, 2017), p. 1.

184 C. Wells and J. Elias, "Catching the Conscience of the King: Corporate Players on the International Stage," in Alston, *Non-State Actors and Human Rights*, p. 142.

185 This is indeed the basic justification for assigning them "responsibilities" under the United Nations Guiding Principles on Business and Human Rights (UNGPs). See J. Ruggie, Commentary on the Guiding Principles on Business and Human Rights, 29 (2), *Netherlands Quarterly on Human Rights* (2011) 224, p. 237.

186 S. Liebenberg, *Socio-Economic Rights: Adjudication Under a Transformative Constitution* (Oxford University Press, 2010), p. 360.

187 This is as true of those interested in global constitutionalism (for instance, M. Kumm, "The Legitimacy of International Law: A Constitutionalist Framework Analysis," 15, *European Journal of International Law* (2006) 907) as it is for those writing from a perspective of global administrative law (for instance, D. Esty, "Good Governance at the Supranational Scale: Globalizing Administrative Law," 116, *Yale Law Journal* (2006) 1490), or a "public law approach" (such as A. von Bogdandy, P. Dann, and M. Goldmann, "Developing the Publicness of Public International Law: Towards a Legal Framework for Global Governance Activities," in A. von Bogdandy et al. (eds), *The Exercise of Public Authority by International Institutions: Advancing International Institutional Law* (2010).

188 E. Criddle and E. Fox-Decent, *Fiduciaries of Humanity* (Oxford University Press, 2016), pp. 287–289.

189 F. Mégret and F. Hoffman, "The UN as a Human Rights Violator? Some Reflections on the United Nations' Changing Human Rights Responsibilities," 25, *Human Rights Quarterly* (2003) 314, p. 341.

190 *Young, James and Webster v. United Kingdom*, para. 52.

191 Though it is, of course, impossible to disentangle the influence of the ECtHR's decision in *Young* on the legislative agenda from the broader domestic political context; trade union reform was clearly an inevitability once Margaret Thatcher's Conservative Party had won the UK general election of 1979.

192 s. 137 (1).

2

Between *nomos* and *telos*

[T]he era of declaration is now giving way, as it should, to an era of implementation.

(Kofi Annan, Address to the UN Commission
on Human Rights, 7th April 2005)

Introduction

We have established that the international human rights regime has a solipsistic and imperialistic character, given to continually expanding the nature and scale of legal obligations, and the range of actors bearing them. For Koskenniemi, this ultimately derives from a sense that the purposes of the law are known, and hence that what matters is how to achieve them. In such circumstances law *per se* becomes seen at best as declaratory: "a pointer to good purposes, but pointless if those purposes [are] known, and harmful if poised against them."[1] There follows an overall shift in tenor within the regime in question – from law to regulation or "governance." As a result, the regime itself is transformed into a technical enterprise which is preoccupied with how to give effect to declared purposes, and which rarely, if ever, subjects them to critique.

This observation is undoubtedly correct, and indeed much of it can of course be gleaned from the materials examined in Chapter 1, but it is also impressionistic. It is here given flesh by the work of Michael Oakeshott, one of whose chief concerns was the relationship between law and purposiveness or what he called "enterprise association."[2] For Oakeshott, law in the modern State is caught between two apparently conflicting ideal types. In the first, it is merely a set of prescriptive conditions within which decisions can be freely made. In the second, it is a "set of prudential managerial conclusions specifying a common purpose and the manner in which this purpose shall be contingently pursued."[3] Law, in other words, exists in a tension between *nomos* and *telos*. And clearly, Koskenniemi's account suggests to us that law has a similar ambivalence in the international sphere, capable of embodying either *nomos* or *telos* or, as Oakeshott put it, comprising an "equivocal mixture" of the two.[4] Koskenniemi's managerialism, then, does not represent the replacement of law *per se* with purposive regulation or governance, but rather an unbalancing of the mixture between *nomos* and *telos* within law itself, such that it becomes primarily conceived as being declaratory of purposes – with an expanding apparatus of regulatory mechanisms the inevitable result.

What Oakeshott's work suggests, therefore, is that law can be tugged one way or another in the ambiguous position which it occupies, particularly in the direction of *telos*. It is readily enlisted in order to declare purposes and prescribe the methods for achieving them. And when this takes place, its character itself shifts. This means that managerialism is not to be understood as law's replacement, but rather the consequence of law taking on a largely *teleocratic* orientation.

As I shall argue in the closing section of this chapter, international human rights law is a particularly clear illustration of Oakeshott's depiction of law in general. Looking through the lens of his work allows us to see international human rights law's programmatic nature in a fresh light: as the consequence of it being "beckoned," to use his word, in the direction of *telos*. It also, however, gives us an even more significant insight in that it shows us something about the developing role of human rights within the international sphere. That is, for Oakeshott, law creeps towards *telos* as a result of the State itself becoming conceptualised as purposive or "*teleocratic.*" Law's ambivalence resolves in a purposive mode when it becomes associated with a programmatic understanding of the State. Hence, I will argue, international human rights law, which is itself as ambivalent as any other body of legal rules, tends to become oriented towards *telos* as a result of the coming into focus of a certain conceptualisation of global constitutionalism or indeed global governance – with that being the subject of the following chapters.

Koskenniemi on law and governance

As we saw in the previous chapter, for Koskenniemi, the description of international legal regimes as solipsistic and imperialistic was ultimately a way of providing a proximate causal explanation for their dominance by notions such as "governance" and "regulation." Such regimes have projects or purposes to realise. But realisation is fraught with difficulty – circumstances constantly change, future events are unpredictable, and if rules are too strict they may prove inflexible. This means that standards are best left open-ended, which in turn means that a class of experts must come into existence "with sufficient latitude to adjust and optimise, to balance and calculate."[5] Implementation of the purpose, in other words, is too nuanced and complex for as blunt an instrument as law, and must be replaced with the "contextual *ad hocism*" of technical expertise.[6]

The result is a turn to policy making: a shift from "international law's archaic *mores* [to] a political science-inspired language of 'governance,' 'regulation,' or 'legitimacy.'"[7] The preference is not for hard rules but softer standards which refer to, and are often fixed by, experts in the "box" – that is, within the regime.[8] And political concerns consequently diminish. Technical expertise does not concern itself with normative analysis but compliance; "the vocabularies of constraint [become] cognitive rather than normative."[9] If the objectives are known, in other words, then what is left is simply how they are to be realised. Since "[matters of] distribution and preference have already been decided elsewhere [...] all that remains are ... questions about how to smooth the prince's path."[10] The final outcome is a "takeover" by the managerial mindset – "a jargon of 'legitimate govern-ance' set[ting] up an ersatz normativity that replaces the conservatism of law [with] empirical political science, thoroughly instrumental and committed, as a world tribunal assisting whoever is in charge."[11] The "legal" regime of international law ceases to be indeed "legal"[12] – and becomes instead regulatory or governance-based. Law as such becomes vestigial in this picture, useful when necessary to provide a justification for one course of action rather than another, but otherwise irrelevant – or even counter-productive if it would appear to stand in the way of a desired interpretation or activity.

Koskenniemi's somewhat schematic account, as bleak as it might appear, is a compelling one. Impressionistically, at least, it would seem to provide a rather apt description of much of the subject matter of Chapter 1. There, international human rights law was shown to be a field characterised by technical questions – particularly of a statistical nature – and an aware-ness of law not as constraining action or being used to settle disputes, but rather declaratory of "moral truth," open to whatever interpretation would appear most favourable to the desired ends of those in a position to deter-mine what that moral truth might be.

A fitting illustration of Koskenniemi's concern is found in the case of the death penalty, which we have already examined in Chapter 1. It will be recalled that Article 6 (2) of the International Covenant on Civil and Political Rights (ICCPR) reads as follows:

> In countries which have not abolished the death penalty, sentence of death may be imposed only for the most serious crimes in accordance with the law in force at the time of the commission of the crime and not contrary to the provision of the present Covenant [...]. This penalty can only be carried out pursuant to a final judgement rendered by a competent court.

It will also be recalled that over the course of 10 years, the Human Rights Committee (HRC) developed a reading of this provision in its jurisprudence to the effect that a State which had abolished the death penalty could not lawfully expose any person within its jurisdiction to a "real risk" of the application of that penalty. This, among other things, would prevent a State which did not practice the death penalty, such as Canada, from deporting or extraditing an escaped criminal to a death penalty State, such as the United States, without the assurance from said State that the death penalty would not be carried out. This was not based on the ordinary meaning of the text – which does not of course mention deportation or extradition – but chiefly on the fact that "the spirit of [Article 6] is to eliminate the death penalty as a punishment."[13] This was ultimately rooted in the Committee's own General Comment No. 6, in which it had expressed the view that "[Article 6] ... refers generally to abolition in terms which strongly suggest (paras. 2 (2) and (6)) that abolition is desirable."[14] That is, by framing the death penalty in the terms in which it does, Article 6 (2) of the ICCPR is said to suggest that, by default, its expectation is for States not to carry out the death penalty. Exceptions are permitted for States which at the time of the Covenant coming into force had not abolished the practice, but those exceptions existed within strict limits (i.e., sentence of death may only be imposed for the most serious crimes, and so on). This meant, as Francisco Urbina later put it, that the Article's "spirit" must be viewed as leaning against the death penalty *per se*. It hence could not be re-introduced once abolished, even "indirectly" through deportation or extradition to a death-penalty State.

Whether or not this is persuasive is immaterial. It suffices to note that the Article is viewed by the Committee as essentially being declaratory of principle: abolition of the death penalty is "desirable." It follows that "all measures of abolition should be considered as progress in the enjoyment of the right to life"[15] and that "the expression 'most serious crimes' must be read restrictively to mean that the death penalty should be a quite exceptional measure."[16] In other words, the law as such is not merely a rule which could either prohibit or permit the application of the death penalty in some circumstances or others. Rather, it is considered to stake out a distinct purpose.

The result is that the law, viewed as declaratory of principle, becomes merely the justification for an essentially programmatic interest in achieving an end-state – in this case, the universal abolition of the death penalty. That this is the case was already implicit in the Committee's General Comment No. 6, wherein the Committee expressed concern that "progress made towards abolishing or limiting the application of the death penalty is quite inadequate."[17] But over time, this has become pronounced. Considering the question of the legality of the death penalty to be concluded as a matter of law (permitted as an exception for States which have not yet abolished it, but to be eliminated over time and certainly not reintroduced, even indirectly through deportation or extradition) the interest of the United Nations (UN) treaty- and charter-based mechanisms has entirely transferred to how to achieve abolition. And the answer to this has primarily taken on a technical bent. The question of the correct interpretation of Article 6 (2), either generally or on the specific points concerning re-introduction or deportation or extradition, has never been revisited. Instead, the matter of the death penalty now only generally appears in the context of attempts to eliminate it altogether, largely as a technical question of implementation and compliance. Hence, it is the subject of high-level panel discussions in the Human Rights Council,[18] expert seminars and strategic development sessions under the auspices of the Office of the High Commissioner for Human Rights (OHCHR),[19] advocacy materials,[20] and country-specific "expert meetings" designed to find "ways forward."[21] States which do practice the death penalty are encouraged to collect and report statistics on its use, and to create statistical indicators to measure progress towards abolition.[22] While such States are still subject to what might be called persuasion in the UN's political fora, the overwhelming trend is to view the elimination of the death penalty as a matter to be resolved through technical expertise in global fora.

What this brief illustration demonstrates to us is the impressionistic plausibility of Koskenniemi's account. Law, conceived as declaratory of "good purposes" – in this case, the abolition of capital punishment – becomes in essence the justification for a managerial process for realising those purposes. The validity of the original interpretation of the legal text consequently becomes closed to further interpretive debate. With the answer to that question settled, the only ongoing relevance for the existing legal instrument is to provide the legitimacy from which the resulting technical process derives its authority – and to specify the necessary obligations for achieving it (such as the obligation not to extradite or deport anybody at risk of being executed in the home State).[23]

But it must be emphasised that this plausibility *is* impressionistic. It has a descriptive accuracy. Yet it raises many questions which require further elucidation. The first of these is why this takes place at all. How is it that law becomes conceived of as purposive in to begin with? (One might indeed ask how it could be otherwise.) The second of them is, what determines the purposes to which law is put? To begin answering those questions, which are of course linked, we turn to the work of Michael Oakeshott and his thoughts on law in particular.

Oakeshott on law in human association

The civil condition and enterprise association

Oakeshott begins his essay "On the Civil Condition" by postulating the existence of what he calls an "ideal character."[24] By this – and it is important to emphasise this from the very beginning – he is quite clear that he is referring neither to an actual "association of ascertainable persons in respect of a place or time," nor to a "wished-for perfect condition of things."[25] Rather, his aim is to describe an ideal in the sense of a set of postulates abstracted from the ambiguity and complexity of existing human association in the real world, which he is consistently at pains to insist cannot and should not be reduced to any one particular schema.

This ideal character he calls the "civil condition," which can be summarised as follows, using his definition of "civil freedom":

> [T]he condition of being associated solely in terms of the recognition of authority (not the choice or the desirability) of the adverbial conditions of conduct specified in *respublica*, distinguished from that of having chosen to be associated in terms of a common purpose and of choosing to acknowledge or not to acknowledge the performances in which this purpose is contingently pursued.[26]

This is opaque, but can be made clear by boiling it down to three essential characteristics. First, the civil condition is association based on the shared recognition of the authority of "conditions of conduct" – something which Oakeshott refers to as *lex* in order to distinguish it from law in general. Second, it is contingent upon the existence of institutions and administrative rules and procedures concerned with the application of *lex*, which Oakeshott refers to as *respublica*. Third, it is to be compared to another ideal type – one of association on the basis of a shared purpose, which Oakeshott calls "enterprise association." From this, a number of secondary characteristics then follow. The most significant of these are that people associated in the civil condition, *cives*, are united only by a "'watery' fidelity" through a shared moral practice – summarised as "being 'just' to one another";[27] and that "politics," strictly speaking, is an activity taking place in the civil condition and concerning the desirability of the conditions of *respublica*. This is distinct from "policy," which is purposive and hence alien to that condition.

Initially, then, we are presented with an ideal form of human conduct or association which is predicated above all on having no overarching purpose and of having nothing to do with the achievement of individual or collective purposes of any kind. Rather, it is association based purely on a shared commitment to a particular practice: that of abiding by a system of rules.

And central to this is a particular understanding of law, which is its most significant feature.[28]

Lex *in the civil condition*

Cives, Oakeshott tells us, are related in terms of a practice. But he is careful to begin by defining this as being a "moral practice" – that is, a "set of conditions to be subscribed to in all or any of an agent's actions or utterances, which has no extrinsic purpose and is not related to procuring any substantive satisfaction or to the pursuit or achievement of any substantive purpose."[29] It is moral in the sense that it is not instrumental. Rather, it is based in a shared recognition on the part of its participants that one another are *cives*, and only that. This makes it useful to think of it as being akin to a "language" which *cives* have in common. Those who are familiar with it are able to "think and to speak about themselves and their conduct, about the conduct of others, and about their relations with one another in a manner otherwise impossible."[30] This makes the civil condition a relationship between agents performed through a continuously used, and continuously evolving, language of understanding and intercourse. It is, in other words, association on the basis of shared fidelity to form rather than content; it is a relationship akin to that of French speakers "in respect of their language, not in respect of what they have to say."[31]

Like all languages, this practice has a grammar – it is "composed entirely of rules."[32] These rules concern any and every transaction between *cives*, while at the same time being indifferent to the outcome of those transactions. That is to say, they are not requirements to perform any particular course of action or another, but are simply the recognised framework within which *cives* participate in their interactions. They are prescriptions – they neither initiate particular activities nor forecast in advance what particular actions or utterances will be done or said.[33] And they are not contingent for their existence or validity on the actions of *cives* or their lack of approval. The only reason why an agent may legitimately refuse to obey is if he or she does not fall within the jurisdiction of the rules at all; that is, if he or she is not in fact a *cive* in the first place.[34]

These rules are what Oakeshott called "*lex*," in order to distinguish them from the more general term "law" (which as we shall see, he considered to be ambiguous). He defined *lex* as "rules which prescribe the common responsibilities (and the counterpart 'rights' to have these responsibilities fulfilled) of agents and in terms of which they put by all that differentiates themselves from one another and recognise themselves as formal equals – *cives*."[35] The shared commitment of those subject to such rules is the "practice of being 'just' to one another"[36] and following this practice in all or any of their actions.[37]

It follows that *lex* must, for Oakeshott, have the following characteristics. Most obviously, it must have the basic elements of any sensible system of rules, as commonly acknowledged: it must prescribe conditions that do not conflict with one another; it must not conceal itself from those with the obligation to follow it; and it should have no arbitrary exemptions. Much more importantly for definitional purposes, it must be a self-contained system. It is not merely a set of rules for a game, which relate to one another incidentally for the purposes of prescribing what can be done in terms of play. And nor is it the rules of an association set up for a particular purpose, such as a hospital or orchestra, which derive from an instrumental relationship to that common purpose. Rather, it is a set of rules governing the conduct of agents "who are joined in no common purpose or engagement, who may be strangers to one another [...] and who may lack any but this moral allegiance to one another."[38] In this sense, it is self-sufficient: it is the sole terms in which *cives* are related, and it therefore itself constitutes that relationship, constructing a "*persona civica*" which depends entirely upon it.[39]

From this, a number of further characteristics follow. First, *lex* is contingent or uncertain in a specific sense: it does not set out in advance how its norms relate to any given actual circumstance. It provides a set of obligations which are known by *cives*, and which are generally observed by them. But this is predicated on its own norms being subject to adjudication in order to determine, when there is a dispute about their application in a particular circumstance, "what has been said or done on a particular occasion, and where the responsibility for it lies, and to determine its relation to the conditions prescribed in *lex*."[40] This is an adversarial process in which the judge takes on the role of "the custodian of the norms of *lex*," and reaches a conclusion not based on the "relative bargaining strengths of the disputants but the relative strengths of their claims measured on the independent scale of these norms of conduct."[41]

This means that civil association, which is to say, association in terms of *lex*, presupposes a judicial procedure so that the "meaning of *lex* in a contingent situation may be authoritatively determined and the adequacy or inadequacy of the subscription of an action to if this declared."[42] This brings us to the second of its characteristics, which is that it must itself, as a self-sustaining system, contain rules and procedures to prevent its own abuse, harshness, error, or ossification.[43] The first three of these potential problems are, of course, straightforward. The third concerns the nature of adjudication itself. Since the role of the judge is to determine the meaning of the norms of *lex* in a given situation, his or her task is not strictly speaking to treat "like cases alike." There are no like cases, because no two cases are identical. This makes precedent a matter of elucidation or amplification of the meaning of *lex*. It is not to be treated as dispositive, but rather a further illustration of what the applicable norms mean. This makes the entire process of adjudication a delicate balancing act. A court decision must "amplify" or "illuminate" the meaning of *lex* in a contingent situation, such that other judges may in future draw upon that amplification. But it must not go so far that the amplification becomes a definitive reading which is applicable simply by rote in similar cases thereafter.[44]

And, third, *lex* must also be amendable as required by an internal procedure of legislating. There may have been a notable change or belief or sentiment among *cives* about the desirability of the conditions of their association, and in those circumstances enactment of new or altered norms must be possible. Here, an authoritative text is created containing conditions to be subscribed to by *cives* from a certain point onwards, and hence specifying a new general norm of conduct.[45] This is not to be done in order to specify conclusions about the particular meaning of *lex* in contingent circumstances, but rather to create a new condition whose own meaning itself may be subject in turn to amplification through adjudicative procedures in the future. Since this new condition will apply throughout the civil association among all *cives* to whom it becomes relevant, it must also be determined by a legislator or legislators who have the authority to make that determination and do so on the basis of certain rules and procedures which are also properly to be understood as part of the system of *lex*.[46]

In summary, then, *lex* is to be understood as a relationship based on rules which prescribe conditions to be subscribed to by all of the parties to that relationship in their self-chosen interactions with each other, which is to say, the *cives*. These rules also specify the jurisdiction of *lex* itself; procedures for ascertaining its meaning and adjudicating disputes in contingent situations; procedures for making or amending *lex*; and rules for specifying the powers and duties of legislators in making or amending *lex*, and the procedures which they must follow. This, Oakeshott finishes, constitutes the "practice of civil association."[47]

Law and enterprise association

All of the above, as the reader will no doubt have recognised, is both highly abstract and idealised. It is made much less so by contrasting *lex* with what it is not: a "rule-book," as Oakeshott calls it, for achieving purposes of any kind. Since civil association is characterised by having no extrinsic purpose, and having no relation to the procuring of substantive satisfaction of any kind, this must also be true of the rules or norms comprising *lex*. They are conditions which *cives* subscribe to in their actions and utterances, and only that.

But where human agents do join together to achieve a purpose of a particular kind, they may create systems of rules accordingly. These are the

circumstances which Oakeshott called "enterprise association" – relationships between agents who share the joint purpose of "some imagined and
wished-for common satisfaction … common purpose … [or] condition of
things to be jointly procured."[48] This might be a common faith which the
"enterprisers" seek to propagate, a literal "enterprise" in the sense of a
business concern, a political or charitable cause, an expedition, a criminal
conspiracy, a trade union, a guild, and so on. Their ties may be tight or
loose, long-lasting or soon dissolved; their purpose or interest might be simple or complex, clear or vague, near or distant. As long as it is a common
substantive purpose which is "recognisable as a substantive condition of
things imagined and wished-for as the outcome of human activity,"[49] then it
is an enterprise association. It is also (and this point will become significant
in the final chapter of this book) a relationship entered into by choice, albeit
choice very broadly defined. Enterprise association proper is the joint pursuit of a common purpose by agents who acknowledge themselves to have a
common purpose, and who, while they may not expressly have "enrolled"
in an organisation or participated in deciding what the purpose is, are at
least able to extricate themselves by choice.[50]

However, Oakeshott's enterprise association is also not to be understood
merely as a group of agents who happen to share a common goal or interest.
It is also, in his own word, "managerial."[51] Pursuing a purpose or promoting an interest is "nothing other than responding to continuously emergent
situations by deciding to *this* rather than *that*."[52] And such decisions cannot, except in very exceptional circumstances, be deduced and performed
automatically by reference to the common pursuit in question. One thinks,
for example, of a professional football club. While it might have a particular common purpose or interest (say, good sporting performance), this
cannot simply be unreflectingly applied in order to determine what to do
in response to actual real-world events. So agents in enterprise association
must be able to either jointly make decisions about how to proceed in their
enterprise, or at least have a way of acknowledging such decisions as being
their own. Whether this is done through majority voting, by a directorate,
by a single leader, and so on, is immaterial. There must be some form of
"management" taking place, defined as "the engagement to make substantive choices of actions or utterances which are not entailed in the common
purpose but which contingently constitute its pursuit."[53]

Enterprise association will not necessarily, but will usually, have some
form of rules having authority over the relevant agents concerned. A business, for example, will have its Articles of Incorporation or similar, and
employee rule-books and the like; a golf club might have rules for joining. However, these rules differ in important respects from *lex* as described
above. First, where *lex* is the very stuff of civil association – the system of

norms to which *cives* subscribe and which thus constitutes their relationship – the rules of an enterprise association "do not even identify, much less
define" it.[54] If the associates themselves are asked to give an account of their
relationship, they will do so in terms of the purpose, object, or interest they
have in common, not their rules. Second, where *lex* is defined most strongly
by lacking any purpose, the rules of an enterprise association will be decidedly instrumental. Any single such rule will be judged to be desirable or
not in terms of whether it promotes or hinders the pursuit of the overall
purpose. By the same token, the rules comprising *lex* are not amenable to
assessment in this way – since there is no "social policy" or common interest in the civil condition, and since *lex* cannot prescribe a desired outcome
in human conduct, no single such rule can be determined to be good or bad
through reference to its instrumental worth.[55] The same is true of adjudication. The decision of a court in the civil condition cannot be understood to
have the task of resolving an uncertainty in light of policy, because there
is no such policy.[56] For an enterprise association, however, uncertainties
must clearly resolve in favour of achieving the purpose of the association
(or at least in a manner not antagonistic to that purpose). Third, where civil
association concerns nothing else but the subscription to and observance
of the norms constituting *lex* (with the association dissolving where those
norms are no longer generally subscribed to), the purpose of an enterprise
association cannot be identified simply as the observance of particular rules.
To use Oakeshott's own example, the workers at a fire station (an enterprise
association with the joint purpose of preventing and putting out unwanted
fires) may have a set of rules of conduct. But no fire will ever be prevented
or put out if the workers only recognise themselves as being related in the
observance of their rules of conduct, or do nothing but observe them.[57]

Hence, where the civil condition is articulated through rules, enterprise
association is primarily a matter of decisions exercised managerially. The
attempt to realise some purpose, interest, or prevailing condition cannot be
brought about simply through proclaiming rules. This does not mean that
any given enterprise association will lack rules – it may have many of them.
But they do not identify or constitute its common purpose or interest, the
agents engaged in the enterprise are not associated primarily on the basis of
subscription to them, and they are capable of being assessed in the abstract
as being desirable or otherwise in terms of policy – which means that they
are not self-contained or self-sustaining as are the rules of *lex*.

Summary

Oakeshott thus provides us with two contrasting ideal modes of human
association and therefore of law or rules. On the one hand, there is the
civil condition, which is a moral practice of just conduct constituted by a

self-sustaining system of law (*lex*) whose rules are only conditions to be taken account of and subscribed to in otherwise freely choosing what to do. This condition is entered into by *cives*, who are associated only in a "language" of civil intercourse, which is to say the system of *lex* and the rules governing its adjudication, creation, alteration, enforcement, and so on. On the other, there is enterprise association, which, while in many cases entailing moral relationship, is primarily an instrumental practice concerned with the achievement of a purpose or pursuit of an interest, however broadly or vaguely defined, and whose rules are concerned primarily with furthering the enterprise in question in some sense. Agents freely choose to engage themselves in enterprise association, and to disassociate themselves if they no longer approve of the enterprise or wish to further it.

Law as "equivocal mixture"

At the beginning of this exposition, I emphasised that Oakeshott was keen to make clear that neither of these forms of association exists in reality in pure form. This ambivalence is important to emphasise, because Oakeshott is sometimes portrayed as suggesting that there could be anything in reality resembling his civil condition and its system of *lex*.[58] This is a mischaracterisation. In the first place, it is a brute fact that there are no entirely non-instrumental rules, at least to the extent that all rules exist for *some* reason or connection of reasons.[59] And Oakeshott was perfectly aware of this. All rules exist for purposes, whether "formal," as he elsewhere put it, or "substantive."[60] *Lex* is therefore an entirely unrealistic proposition, and deliberately so. Likewise, enterprise associations clearly often have something of the character of the civil condition in their agents' recognition of the authority of rules, and as they become more organised, their distinction from "civility" will surely blur and their rules will become more akin to the formal conditions of *lex*. Individual human beings may belong to any number of enterprise associations in coexistence with their role as a *cive* in the civil condition. And the civil condition itself in particular is merely "glimpsed here or there in the features of human goings-on," and nowhere does it constitute a "premeditated design."[61] Human "inadvertence," "folly," and "crookedness" are inescapable,[62] not to mention "eccentric adjudicators" and "corrupt or careless legislators."[63] But it would be a mistake to portray Oakeshott's view of the civil condition as being realisable if only there were better people. Human societies, as he consistently made clear in all of his work on the matter, he saw as being untidy – impossible to reduce to ideals, and indeed corrupted in any attempt to do so. Nothing would be worse, or more self-defeating, for Oakeshott than an attempt to bring about the civil condition through willed design.[64] This is indeed what separates him from thinkers on the libertarian right, particularly Hayek, with whom he is sometimes grouped.[65]

While these two ideals are useful, then, in considering how human societies are arranged and develop, and indeed, as we shall see, for critiquing those arrangements, reality is messy – and desirably so, if the alternative is enforced tidiness. This is nowhere more true than in the case of law. Law is "in abundance," Oakeshott notes, but it is "an exceedingly ambiguous" phenomenon.[66] This is the case both in its substance and its theory. It might, on the one hand, resemble the ideal of *lex* as merely the conditions which agents acknowledge and subscribe to as the norms of "just conduct" within which they interact. It might, on the other, resemble the rules of enterprise association – rules which are conceived of in instrumental terms in light of the purpose or interest which they are supposed to help secure, and which hence give rise to managerial efforts to realise that purpose. In reality, it will be what Oakeshott later calls an "equivocal mixture" of the two.

This is so even with individual rules themselves. Consider the example of the prohibition of murder. Such a rule could on its face be interpreted straightforwardly as a general condition prescribing just conduct and hence as *lex*: *cives* must not kill one another, subject to certain exceptions. But equally, such a prohibition could be seen as a purposive rule designed to make society more peaceful, and hence more prosperous, and so on. And in the latter circumstance, it may well give rise to attempts to regulate behaviour so as to reduce the rate of violence. It is hence impossible to categorise even such a seemingly simple prescription as the prohibition of murder fully as either an item of *lex* or a "rule-book rule." And this will, of course, be more true of more complicated laws.

It is not, then, that law in general or a specific law in particular can be categorised either as non-instrumental *lex* or an item in an instrumental rule-book: to attempt to do this would be to fall prey to the "craving for … certainty" which Oakeshott called "the relic of a belief in magic."[67] Rather, it is that the perception of a particular law can be oriented towards the ideal of *lex* or the ideal of rule-book. There will always be a way of reading it in the light of the civil condition – as simply part of the framework of just conduct within which *cives* freely act. And there will always be a way of reading it through the lens of enterprise association as a way of declaring broader ends and justifying programmatic attempts to achieve them. In reality, the law will be oriented in both directions, depending on its formulation and other contingent circumstances – although one such orientation may very well tend to be stronger, and even dominant. Clearly, Oakeshott's sympathies lay in general in orienting law in one direction rather than another, for reasons which we will come to, but this must not be seen as an absolutist position and certainly not as advocating the wholesale rejection of purposive or instrumental law-making.

International law as lex *and rule-book*

Reading Koskenniemi's schema of international law and managerialism in light of Oakeshott's account of the civil condition and enterprise association is, then, illuminating. It will be recalled that for Koskenniemi managerialism was in effect the replacement of what he called "law" with concepts such as regulation, legitimacy, and policy. To use his own words, the result of solipsism and imperialism in an international legal regime was that "law is finally drained out of international law, conceived as a professional technique for the management of values, purposes, ideals."[68] Once the purpose of the regime is known and accepted, it becomes, at best, the declaratory justification for the existence of an array of regulatory practices concerned with the implementation of that purpose. At worst, it is ignored or reconfigured. What Oakeshott's discussion of the civil condition suggests is that Koskenniemi's concern is in effect an expression of dissatisfaction with the possible composition of the "equivocal mixture" between law in the mode of *lex*, as the general conditions of just conduct, and law as the rule-book for enterprise association – understood in instrumental terms in view of the ends which are hoped to be achieved. It might be read in other words not as a concern that "law" as such will be marginalised or even corrupted, but that there is a tendency for the balance between two competing conceptualisations of law to tip too far in one direction, so that the mixture itself becomes too strongly oriented towards law in its guise as an instrumental rule-book providing the authority or justification for managerial decision making, and too weakly oriented towards providing a moral framework within which actions are freely chosen.

There is much more to be said about this, of course, not the least of which being that Oakeshott paid little attention in his writings (though not no attention whatsoever) to international relations or international law. It is not absolutely clear, then, whether he viewed what he called the civil condition as being limited to the domestic sphere. Here, however, the position must surely be that, because the civil condition and enterprise association are only ever abstracted ideals – just "glimpsed here or there" in real human societies – there is no reason why one should not view them as appearing in some form or other in both the domestic and international realms alike, given that the latter of these is, after all, just as much an association of intelligent human agents as the former. That is to say, in describing the existence of these two ideals, we are in the end simply observing that wherever human beings associate and create rules concerning their association, there will almost certainly be an untidy mixture of two ways of conceiving of the nature of those rules. The sphere of international association should be no different in this respect to what takes place within the confines of the State.

It would be a crude misreading of Oakeshott's essay to propose therefore that a given international association, whether in a formal organisation such as the UN or the Council of Europe, a long-standing treaty relationship, or simply the informal sphere of the "international community," can be categorised as either civil association or enterprise association. And nor can its rules therefore be described as either embodying *lex* or an instrumental rule-book accordingly. Rather, such international associations are an untidy mixture of both civil condition and enterprise association, and their rules occupy an ambivalent position between those two poles. International law in this context must be seen as a blend of two abstractions, perhaps more closely resembling *lex* in some contexts, and an instrumental set of rules for bringing about certain purposes in others. It will be oriented this way or that depending on who is looking at it. But in no circumstance will it be entirely one or the other.

A straightforward example of this is the customary norm of non-intervention. On the one hand, this might be thought of as a rule strongly resembling the ideal of *lex*: a law which specifies a norm of just conduct of general and abstract application (i.e., not addressing any specific States, who can be thought of in this context as something akin to *cives*) and without a substantive purpose. This is indeed how it has tended to be formulated, in, for example, the Declaration on the Inadmissibility of Intervention in the Domestic Affairs of State and the Protection of Their Independence and Sovereignty of 1965,[69] and by the International Court of Justice (ICJ) in its judgment in *Nicaragua v. USA*.[70] But the rule is equally as capable, as has been shown in recent decades, of being conceptualised as merely a facet of a wider movement towards what a policy-oriented jurist would call "an optimum public order."[71] Here, the purpose of international law is to usher in a "world public order of human dignity,"[72] and hence the principle of non-intervention must be understood with that purpose in mind. This means that in general it exists to prevent "harmful" effects such as "destabiliz[ing] the order of states" or "fanning ethnic or civil strife."[73] It "encourages states to solve their own internal problems" and prevent those problems "spilling over into a threat to international peace and security"[74] and hence threatening that emergent "public order." But this also means that where the principle of non-intervention no longer serves that purpose, but appears "poised against it" – such as when civil conflict and repression are severe and widespread – it ought to be read as *permitting* military intervention within certain bounds. This has, as a consequence, given rise to the doctrine of the Responsibility to Protect, which seeks in effect to regulate the principle of non-intervention in light of achieving the greater purpose of ensuring stability of the public order and ultimately of securing "human dignity."[75]

International human rights law between lex *and rule-book*

This brings us, then, to the main focus of this book, which is of course international human rights law. We shall now briefly consider the composition of the "equivocal mixture" between *lex* and rule-book in this context, before going on to consider why it is that the mixture might be said to have taken on a dominant orientation through reference to Oakeshott's thinking on the nature of the modern State and the role of law within it.

It is tempting, of course, to put civil and political rights in juxtaposition with economic, social, and cultural rights as a reflection of something akin to the distinction between *lex* and law as rule-book. Civil and political rights in such a schema would be construed as "negative" conditions of just conduct applying in general across States parties. Economic, social, and cultural rights would, on the other hand, present themselves as a kind of rule-book for declaring particular ends to be achieved, such as the elimination of poverty or the realisation of material well-being. The former would therefore simply be restrictions on conduct enforceable through courts; the latter would be construed as declaratory of purposes and hence the justifications for extensive arrays of programmatic regulatory or managerial apparatuses.

This would be naive and simplistic. It would not reflect either the theory or practice of modern human rights law, in which it is perfectly normal to see civil and political rights as imposing positive obligations on States, and indeed declaratory of purposes (such as the elimination of discrimination). Instead, it is more sensible to suggest that the two spheres of so-called "negative" and "positive" rights are both "equivocal mixtures," capable of resembling *lex* and rule-book in different guises, often at the same time. And, indeed, it would be undesirable to try to prevent this from being the case.

To use a basic example, the ICCPR contains the provision that "No one shall be held in slavery; slavery and the slave-trade in all their forms shall be prohibited."[76] This, on the one hand, appears to be oriented towards *lex* – a general norm of just conduct to which States are expected to conform (and indeed all persons within such States accordingly). But implicit in it is also a purposive role for the State in acting to eliminate slavery, particularly between private individuals. Few would disagree with the proposition that it is desirable for the State to undertake positive and indeed purposive action to eliminate the slave trade within its jurisdiction – in other words, that it is perfectly reasonable to view the law in this sense as declaratory of an "end" which ought to give rise to regulatory apparatuses and managerial decision making that go beyond mere criminal prohibition.[77] Another way of putting this is that it is unrealistic, to say the least, to conceive of human rights laws merely as specifying the conditions of just conduct among *cives* (i.e., States) absent of any programmatic element, because it is only natural for human beings to seek to diminish or eliminate practices which they consider to be harmful. The same is just as true of more contentious "hard cases" than the slave trade, such as the death penalty, discrimination, and so on. Perhaps facially resembling conditions of *lex*, such prohibitions will also inevitably give rise to programmatic attempts to eliminate harmful practices, simply because societies are comprised of human beings with goals other than maintaining a non-existent and pure "civil condition." Solely "negative" civil and political rights do not exist, and advocates for them are a non-existent extreme.

So even where human rights laws appear to resemble Oakeshott's ideal of *lex*, they always in practice contain a managerial or "rule-bookish" element. Naturally, this element will be stronger the more inherently purposive a right's formulation is (one might think, for example, of the International Covenant on Economic, Social and Cultural Rights (ICESCR's) rights to social security, or to "the continuous improvement of living conditions.")[78] In such circumstances, rights will readily take on the guise of providing the declaratory justifications for extensive managerial programmes. Yet, just as even the apparently purest negative rights will never entirely appear as conditions of *lex*, nor will positive obligations ever entirely dissolve into being the mere authorities for programmatic regulations. They will, in practice, also be hedged by a concern not to stray into authoritarianism or by a doctrine of proportionality which prevents untrammelled pursuit of a particular purpose entirely overriding individual freedoms. There are very few theorists of positive rights who would suggest, for instance, that the right to housing should be achieved universally through compulsory evictions of wealthy home-owners without judicial oversight, or that realising the right to social security would legitimate the compulsory confiscation of all privately held assets. And it is certainly at least possible to argue that even the most apparently "purposive" right, such as that to social security, could be achieved through the actions of civil society left untrammelled rather than through programmatic action on the part of the State.

It is not particularly accurate, then, to suggest that there is some opposition in this respect in the substance of rights themselves; they are capable of being viewed as oriented in either direction, to varying degrees. To a certain extent, the modern history of the philosophy of human rights can be read as being a dialectic between the disposition to prefer an orientation of rights towards *lex* and the disposition to prefer them as orientations towards purposive or instrumental "rule-book rules."[79] But this does not entirely derive from the nature of rights themselves, however they are formulated. It is just as much a function of the position from which they are seen.

The setting up of the two opposing ideals or antinomies of *lex* and rule-book, civil condition and enterprise association – a technique which anybody coming to Oakeshott's work cannot fail to notice is a repetitive theme or even a "tic"[80] within it – is therefore not to be understood as a zero-sum game. There is no law which appears solely as *lex*, nor as the item in a rule-book. And this is just as much the case with human rights laws. They exist rather on a spectrum in the tension between those poles. In some circumstances, they will be tugged closer to one pole than the other. But this is contingent on context. The appropriate questions, then, are not at this stage whether one is "better" than the other or what the right blend in the mixture would be in the abstract. They are, rather, to ask what it is that results in human rights laws being tugged in one particular direction, and the effects of this in a given set of circumstances.

The answers to those questions, somewhat obliquely, bring us to Oakeshott's thoughts on the nature of the State. Here, Oakeshott's work again offers us a much richer layer of detail to add to the picture we have already sketched out. In the third essay of *On Human Conduct*, he turned his attention to the "equivocal mixture" between the two different ways of conceiving of law which he had established as they appear in the modern State. His thoughts in this regard help to cast light on possible answers to those two crucial questions, and it is therefore necessary to investigate them in some depth.

Oakeshott on the State

Societas *and* universitas

Oakeshott begins his essay "On the Character of a Modern European State" by emphasising the historical ambiguity of the nature of those States.[81] They "began as mixed and miscellaneous collections of human beings precariously held together" within a territory and were already under rulers of various kinds when the concept of a "State" itself came into common usage. They were not, in other words, born, but emerged. And they did so as "ramshackle" constructions, made by designers who themselves were following no accepted pattern.[82] This meant that the character of a State cannot be a "model from which copies [can] be struck off" but is rather "what the effort to understand [the experience of its emergence] has made of it."[83] So the matter of how this new form of association was to be understood was, of course, of great significance during the period in question, the sixteenth century. And, indeed, it has been "puzzling" us ever since: the subject of "five centuries of speculative thought remarkable both for the variety of its arguments and for the inconclusiveness of its outcome."[84]

It will not be surprising to learn that Oakeshott grouped such bodies of speculative thought roughly into two categories, loosely corresponding to his abstract ideals of the civil condition and enterprise association. These were originally known as *societas* and *universitas*. Initially concepts existing in Roman law, neither of them proved in the long term to be able to provide on its own an adequate representation of the "equivocal character of a State," because their apparently exclusionary nature was unable to properly reflect the ambivalence of what a modern State is, or the ambiguity of its vocabulary (in terms such as "law," "politics," "ruling," and so on). In fact, as Oakeshott sees it, the State is best thought of as existing in, and produced by, the unresolved tension between these two concepts.[85] Yet for this reason, Oakeshott considers them still to be useful as expressing that unresolved tension.

The first, *societas*, is the notion of agents being tied together by bonds of loyalty so as to produce the outcome of *socii*: a collection of agents pursuing their own interests, individually or with others, but related by the continuous acknowledgement of the authority of rules of conduct indifferent to those interests. Intrinsic, then, to *societas* as a concept of the State is that is based not on the choice of relationship of the agents, but on their recognition of a common "predicament" and loyalty to one another on that basis. In a State conceived in such terms – clearly bearing a close relationship to what Oakeshott had earlier described as the civil condition – the ruler and government are effectively the custodians or perhaps repositories of the loyalties of the agents in question. Their role is to be the "master of ceremonies," with the task of "keeping the conversation going [rather than] to determine what is said." Government here is a *"nomocracy"* whose laws are to be understood as conditions of conduct, i.e., *lex*, and it does not manage or direct its subjects, but only administers those conditions.[86]

The second, *universitas*, is a corporate mode of association which is the origin of the notion of a corporation or other entity as a legal person. Here, the relationship between the agents is one of recognising each other as being engaged in a joint enterprise to satisfy some common substantive want or wants – a "many become one," not in the sense of a common will but simply in the sense of having a common engagement which they pursue together. When the State is imagined on these terms, government is a set of managerial offices making decisions about how that engagement is to be pursued. This means that law is a set of rules prescribing conduct considered instrumental to that pursuit, and the land, resources, and even talents of the State's members are considered to be property of the corporation, to be utilised for carrying out the decisions of the government in its managerial capacity. This makes government in this context a *"teleocracy,"* concerned above all with the implementation of a purposive concern or concerns.[87]

What we have, then, is two analogies, both of them pointed in two different directions, which have been present as aids to reflection on the nature of the State since its emergence. Tracing their heritage back to Roman times, in the early modern period both already existed in some form or other with respect to various disparate phenomena, which we will discuss in due course, and they became thereby inherited as conceptual frameworks by thinkers engaged in the tentative exploration of Statehood once that concept came into consideration. There is a great deal more to be said about this historical picture, which when read alongside Foucault's thought on the matter proves to be a highly productive way of describing the origins and characteristics of modern Statehood. For now, it suffices to note that these two analogies exist and have generally informed attempts to understand or define the State through to the present day, and that indeed the "political imagination" of modern Statehood is itself constituted by the tension between them. About this, Oakeshott is very firm: "my contention is that the modern European political consciousness is a polarised consciousness, that *these* are its poles and that all other tensions (such as those indicated in the words 'right' or 'left' or in the alignments of political parties) are insignificant compared with this."[88]

Tipping the balance

Oakeshott is clear that the tension between *universitas* and *societas* is unresolved. But he is also clear that history had shown a "teleocratic drift" – with "the notion of the State as an all-embracing, compulsory corporate association and of its government as the manager of an enterprise" slowly becoming the "most obtrusive of the strands which constitute the texture of modern European political reflection."[89]

This is due to two groups of reasons (although Oakeshott himself does not quite state it in this way). The first might be described as conditional or circumstantial, deriving effectively from historical accident. The second can be thought of as in some sense deliberate or rooted in what we now think of as political philosophy.

To begin with, then, there are a range of circumstantial factors that Oakeshott describes as "beckoning" civil understanding and imagination in a *teleocratic* direction.[90] The first of them is, most simply, that it became not only possible to conceive of the State as an enterprise association in a fanciful sense, but plausible to describe it as a somewhat feasible potential reality, thanks to the relentless expansion and elaboration of centralised administrative apparatuses of ruling.[91] Medieval rule was a matter of "indis-criminate" judicial and administrative engagement. Afterwards, forms of administrative engagement emerged which were entirely separate from judicial processes, and outside of the purview of judicial officers – in short, a bureaucracy. It would be impossible to sustain the State as *universitas* without such an extensive suite of centralised administrative functions, and their coming into being thereby made it possible to imagine the State in a managerial form.[92]

Second, there remained an "unpurged relic" of a notion of "lordship" in the emergence of the offices of modern monarchs and their successors, which conceptualised the ruler as being concerned with the beneficial ownership of an estate. This made the modern State recognisable as a domain: "eligible to be understood as an enterprise of a certain sort, its territory as an 'estate,' its laws as rules instrumental to the success of the enterprise, the office of its government as estate-management, and 'subjects' as role-performers in an undertaking."[93] This was not the result of "compelling belief." It was, rather, because of the obscurity of the distinction between monarchy and lordship which had emerged in the late medieval period, with kings often also being great landowners having extensive lordly rights over their subjects' property, control of foreign trade, power to license monopolies, and so on. While, of course, the office of the monarch disappeared entirely in most cases and sub-stantively in the rest, the sense that rulership concerned estate management had in any case become partially ingrained in the manner of rule.

This was furthered by two other circumstances which fostered a sense of the office of government as the exercise of seigneurial management. The early modern period was characterised by the birth of colonialism, in which States were engaged in precisely such projects.[94] Colonialism may have had many and varied origins, but it was always fundamentally an extension of the lordship of rulers, who granted commissions, concessions, and licenses to settlers and traders in order to exploit notionally uninhabited lands which the ruler had obtained by conquest or occupation, in return for supplying the ruler with monies, goods, or services. It was always and everywhere therefore an enterprise, and one in which those engaged physically in that enterprise – such as merchants, settlers, and corporations – were simply the arms of various States. While the character of colonies evolved over time, the concept of the colony as a private estate managed by agents of a *grand seigneur* remained a physical reality even until 1908 in the form of the Belgian Congo, ensuring that Europe was thoroughly familiarised over the course of 400 years with the concept of a State as an enterprise and the government as its manager.[95]

Similarly, while war was hardly alien to Europe during the medieval period, from the early modern period onwards it became incessant and more organised. This resulted in it becoming necessary for the incipient States of that period to continuously maintain the capacity to attack and to resist, to prepare for or make war, to counteract the consequences of war elsewhere, or to recover from conflict in its aftermath. In such circumstances, the latent element of managerial lordship "comes decisively to the surface and is magnified" in the name of mobilising resources towards specific ends: belligerence is enterprise association writ large, and is "alien" to the civil condition.[96] This tendency became more pronounced over time as bureaucracies grew, such that whereas in the fourteenth century war may have been experienced "only in the demands of tax collectors" outside regions which were physically ravaged by the conflict itself, by the twentieth wars were "occasions for the almost total mobilization, management and direction" of energies and resources in pursuit of a single purpose.[97]

Hence, an already latent tendency towards conceiving of the office of government as akin to that of a managerial lord over an estate was accentuated and concentrated over time by the historical experiences of colonialism and warfare, ensuring that modern European States never "lacked invitations" to recognise themselves as enterprise associations on the analogy of *universitas*.

A third and final circumstance drawing thinking on Statehood towards the analogy of *universitas* concerns what Oakeshott calls the "human postulate" of such a State – the character of its subjects. Here, he puts in place two obliquely opposed characters, which he calls the individual and the individual manqué.[98] There is no avoiding that this passage has a somewhat mean-spirited tenor. Indeed, it may have been one of the main sections of the book which Hannah Pitkin had in mind when she described the overall flavour of *On Human Conduct* (accurately) as "crotchety."[99] But it is nonetheless significant, for reasons which will become clear. In essence, Oakeshott observes that modernity brought with it the dissolution of the old certainties of belief, occupation, status, community, and so on, ushering the human being into a world of autonomous individuals – a point that is hardly novel.[100] The emancipation which was thrust upon all people alike was embraced by some, but it equally "depressed and discomforted" others – those who "by circumstances or temperament" were unwilling or unable to seize the benefits of their new-found freedom. This latter group, who had suffered both substantive loss and "moral defeat," were led to a position of "needs rather than wants" – for the alleviation both of poverty and the loss of the old "warmth of solidarity" in community life now disappearing. The individual manqué, Oakeshott tells us, "sought a patron rather than a ruler, a lord able to make for him the choices he was unable to make for himself," and hence "invoked [the] unpurged relic of lordship" in the office of government of the State. To this, he "found some response." Hence the

modern State may in part be recognised as an "[invention] for making circumstantially unavoidable choices for those unable to make them for themselves."[101] In short, although Oakeshott does not use this word, a certain
impulse towards a paternal form of government grew over time. This could
be nothing but *teleocratic*.

In the early modern period, then, European States already had features
which "beckoned" thinkers towards the analogy of *universitas*, and those
features gradually became more pronounced as the conditions of history
made the analogy increasingly appropriate. In short, these were a growth
in centralised non-judicial administrative apparatuses; a concept of the government as the "lord" of an estate with the goal of managing its resources,
fostered by the experiences of colonialism and war; and a conceptualisation
of the individual as incapable of exercising new-found freedom and hence
requiring the protection of a patron to exercise choice on his or her behalf.
This picture was of course mixed. Different States "have trodden [the] path
with varying degrees of consistency and commitment, some inadvertently or
merely in response to local and temporary exigencies," and there is nowhere
in which "allegiance" to the idea of *societas* has been abandoned.[102] But
there has been, to use Oakeshott's term again, a drift towards a conception
of the State as an enterprise association – a *teleocracy* defined by the pursuit of purposes or projects, and the management of society and resources
with those purposes or projects in mind. And in his view those purposes or
projects had tended to cohere around a notion of improving "well-being"
or similar.

On "well-being" and enlightened conduct in the State

While the circumstances of European history might have gestured towards
teleocracy as described above, and while therefore there is a certain uncon-
scious or even accidental quality to proceedings in Oakeshott's account,
he also makes clear that history was also, in a sense, deliberately driven.
As well as it becoming possible to imagine the State as an enterprise association, it was also possible for this to become the subject of "visions,"
oriented around notions such as "well-being," the "common good," *salus
populi*, and so on.

By far the most important of early such visions was, in Oakeshott's view,
that of Francis Bacon, which managed to produce a particular "idiom" of
teleocracy, concerned with the organisation of society along the lines of
enlightened conduct so as to improve human well-being, and operationalised
primarily through the economy, that has prevailed to the present day.[103] Here,
the State is seen as a territory whose inhabitants are incorporated in the shared
pursuit of well-being, under a government who in cooperation with a technical *illuminati* was custodian and manager of this enterprise. This paved the

way for what Oakeshott describes as an understanding of the State as *civitas cupiditatis*: "a corporate productive enterprise, centred upon the exploitation of the material and human resources of an estate and managed by a government whose office it was to direct research, to suppress distracting engagements and to make instrumental rules for the conduct of the enterprise."[104]

While Bacon's vision was rooted in theology, it became the progenitor in Oakeshott's account for more secular subsequent elaborations, such as those of Fourier, Owen, Louis Blanc, Bellamy, Webb, Lenin, St Simon, and Comte. Critical in this was the recognition of the State as an economy. Here, the State was conceived as having an income, with the manner in which it was shared among its members being as much a matter of concern as its production. There must therefore be a general rule of distribution or an administrative apparatus to assign shares to the members accordingly. As a result, the question of the economy became a subject of intense reflection. The political economy which was the result of this reflection on the part of the classical economists ultimately produced a dominant style of rule which is of course familiar. This is predicated on people being essentially free to buy what they desire, which is the root of productivity in any economy and hence of the growth which will provide the stuff of raised living standards. But, since the classical economists recognised that such a system would not be self-sustaining, the "freedom" of economic actors was itself made subject to civil institutions, and the State gradually began to engage, not in the distribution of benefits *per se*, but in the satisfaction of wants.[105] Ultimately, this is in effect, of course, a description of the modern welfare State: a mixture of free market principles, which are the roots of economic growth, with a range of policies designed to provide a "safety net," and both in combination achieving an overall purpose – the "well-being of the associates," or the "common good."[106] Within this picture, enlightened conduct is understood as being the arrangement of affairs within the State such that overall health, prosperity, and happiness is secured.

So for Oakeshott, the distinction between socialism and capitalism (or indeed any other modern political ideology) is in essence a false one, in that it is distinction *within* the concept of the State as enterprise association or *teleocracy*, and one without significant difference.[107] These two purported ideologies are "irrelevant designations"[108] inasmuch as they are both rooted in the same impulse to understand the State along the analogy of *universitas*, with the office of government being to manage affairs in view of the overriding (if amorphous) purpose of promoting well-being.[109] Naturally there is always a wide range of interpretation in what the promotion of "well-being" might mean, which of course is what allows one to speak of distinctions such as socialism and capitalism or others besides, but both are predicated on the same basic conceptualisation of the role of the State.

Thus, while no State has ever been conceived entirely along the lines of *universitas* alone, the analogy has "bitten deep" into the civil institutions of modern Europe, such that it now has the character of a received idea, no longer even the subject of reflection. All modern political doctrines are for Oakeshott "indelibly Baconian," with the differences between them long "worn smooth."[110] Each is concerned with the purposive pursuit of well-being, and each has a vision of itself as operationalising enlightened conduct – a vision of the "virtuous life,"[111] whether this be the "'righteousness' of the Calvinist," "the moral *vérité* of Bossuet," the "*homo felix* of the enlightenment," the cogs in the machine of the Cameralists or Fabians, or whatever else.[112] The result is that the "commonplace concerns" of modern European governments, whatever their local variations, have at the end of a long, gradual but inexorable process come to be essentially uniform. Oakeshott summarises this as

> substantial command over the resources of the estate, including the energy and the talents of its inhabitants; the directions of productive activity controlled by agreements, subsidies, exemptions, licenses, penalties, man-power budgets, or orders, etc.; full employment or a guaranteed income; taxation transformed into a means of acquiring direct control over a large part of the "national income" to be expended in favoured projects or distributed in the form of "truck" …; a so-called rising standard of life; a concern for compulsory generalised education and technological training,

and so on.[113]

Summary

What Oakeshott's historical survey provides, then, is a picture of Statehood as emerging "coevally" with both historical circumstances and philosophical visions that steered it in the direction of *teleocracy*. On the one hand, the practical potential inherent in a growing bureaucracy, the experiences of colonialism and incessant warfare, and the effects of secularisation and industrialisation gave the State an orientation towards *universitas* through force of circumstance. And that process was also propelled by particular conceptions of Statehood as having the purpose of improving the well-being of subjects. Over time, therefore, while there were competing understandings of what the State signified (i.e., along the analogy of *societas*), "actually existing States," so to speak, have been tugged strongly towards the analogy of *universitas* and hence have become to more strongly resemble *teleocracies* than *nomocracies*.

This is not, of course, a process that has been completed or which could ever become complete. *Nomocracy* and *teleocracy* are set up as non-existent abstracted ideals in exactly the same way as are the civil condition and enterprise association, and Oakeshott is clear that he did not think that any States – even the Soviet Union or Germany under Nazi rule – are constituted purely as purposive *teleocracies*.[114] All of them are mixtures, caught between both ideals and pulled toward one and the other by circumstance and the ideas which have currency at any given moment.[115] Their institutions and laws, and indeed everything about them, he stressed repeatedly, were ambivalent. The conclusion is not therefore that States are in the modern age all *teleocracies* conceived on the analogy of *universitas*. Rather, it is that conditions have tended to orient themselves in that direction, and political doctrines have tended to strengthen that orientation in the main.

The State's "manifold character quality"

That the picture Oakeshott paints is at best a schematic abridgement and at worst unhistorical have been frequent accusations.[116] It has also been argued that he was corrupting what he had declared elsewhere to be his views on the studying of history, namely that it was an exercise to be performed for its own sake.[117] However, these criticisms are less biting if we emphasise that Oakeshott's project in *On Human Conduct* was not primarily a historical but a philosophical one. It is true that his two ideals of *societas* and *universitas* were historically derived, but ultimately his aim was to theorise them as philosophical constructions – to uncover "what ... this activity called governing [really is]."[118] As Boucher puts it, they are "philosophical constructions philosophically conceived and 'on the analogy of human history.'"[119] They are best understood, in other words, as historically derived metaphors used to aid reflection on the predicament of governing a modern State. And in this sense they are hardly schematic or ahistorical. They are, as has been pointed out, corroborated entirely by thinkers ranging from Rosanvallon to Jellinek, from Mortati to Fraenkel, and from Hayek to Habermas.[120]

What Oakeshott stressed, then, was not the descriptive accuracy of *universitas* and *societas* as existing forms of government, but rather their aptness as descriptors of particular orientations towards the nature of governing. They are aids to reflection on a genuine "fissure" in the way in which the State is conceived.[121] Real governments have a "manifold character quality" and are never homogenous.[122] Thinking about the *nature* of government, on the other hand, is given to take "flight to extremes" whether through design or "negligence."[123] It is more helpful, then, to think of *universitas* and *societas*, or *teleocracy* and *nomocracy*, as being the poles between which dispositions towards governing are situated – with real-world goings-on being the product of those competing orientations. Thinking about the State is polarised, but the real mixture is anything but.

In the end, then, what Oakeshott provides us with is a method for thinking about the nature of government, combined with an understanding of what tends to influence the project of government, and the ideas of those who are governing or theorising the practice of governing, over time. In summary, these are external circumstances or contingencies, and the ideas and purposes of those theorising the practice of governing. At different times, and in different situations, that combination will result in different mixtures – although of course Oakeshott emphasised that overall the general tendency has been a *teleocratic* "drift."

Law in the modern State and beyond

Having noted this, it will be apparent that this also gives us a framework within which to think about the nature and role of law within the modern State. At the centre of the tension between the two poles of *societas* and *universitas* sits law. Is law, Oakeshott asks, "a system of prescriptive conditions, indifferent (and not merely impartial) to the satisfaction of wants, to be subscribed to in making choices about what to do or say, or is it a set of prudential managerial conclusions specifying a common purpose and the manner in which this purpose shall be contingently pursued?"[124] Clearly, this is a question that harks back to the distinction between *lex* and the rule-book of an enterprise association. It is easy, then, to see which direction Oakeshott's train of thought will go. When the State is understood in terms of *societas*, law will be understood to resemble something like Oakeshott's indifferent *lex*. Where the State is understood to be a *universitas*, law will be his "set of prudential managerial conclusions" specifying purposes and the manner of their pursuit.

Equally clearly, this provides us with the beginnings of an explanation as to what it is that causes law to be conceived of as *lex* or rule-book and *vice versa* within modern States. It depends on its prevailing position in the poles between *societas* and *universitas*, or *nomocracy* and *teleocracy*. The result will always be an "equivocal mixture" between *lex* and rule-book. But in different situations we will be able to describe it as a whole or in part as leaning towards one pole or other. This is not to suggest that the correspondences between visions of the law and the State in this respect are direct or monolithic. Those correspondences will be contingent, indirect, and fluctuating. Rather, it is to suggest that when law is reflected upon (whether as a single rule, a body of rules, a field of law, or simply law *per se*), it will be seen to resemble *lex* or rule-book depending on its composition and context. And this will tend to reflect a certain understanding of the State within that context.

This also, therefore, gives us an explanation for what it is that gives law its particular composition in respect of *lex* or rule-book at the international, transnational, or global levels.[125] As I noted above, while the civil condition and enterprise association were linked very strongly in *On Human Conduct* to different analogies for theorising the nature of the State, there is nothing to prevent us from using those two ideals as aids to reflection in respect of other forms of political organisation – such as at the international or global scale.[126] Here, too, such forms of organisation will tend to be considered as, and comprise, mixtures of *societas* and *universitas*, civil or enterprise association, in much the same way as are States. And, concomitantly, the rules of those organisations will likewise be considered as, and comprise, an "equivocal mixture" of *lex* and rule-book accordingly. That is, they will sometimes be understood to be indifferent prescriptive conditions, and sometimes managerial conclusions specifying and operationalising purposes. And, indeed, individual rules will take on different guises accordingly. When they do so, they will tend to suggest one particular analogy for reflecting on the nature of international organisation – that is, *societas* or *universitas*.

The final stage of this schema will now be clearly evident. If the State is a fluctuating mixture of *societas* and *universitas* and law derives its own composition from those analogies, then international law will likewise derive its composition from those analogies as they appear in reflection on the nature of international, transnational, or global organisation. And if the composition of the mixture of *societas* and *universitas* with respect to the modern State is influenced by external circumstances or contingencies, and the ideas and purposes of those theorising the practice of governing, then much the same will be true of political organisation at the international, transnational, or global scale. This means that international law, in other words, will also find its particular mixture of *lex* and rule-book fluctuating in accordance with external circumstance or contingencies, and the ideas and purposes of those theorising the practice of governing at that level.

Notes

1 M. Koskenniemi, "International Law: Constitutionalism, Managerialism and the Ethos of Legal Education," 1, *European Journal of Legal Studies* (2007) 1, p. 12.
2 M. Oakeshott, *On Human Conduct* (Clarendon Press, 1975/1991).
3 *Ibid.*, p. 231 and p. 326.
4 *Ibid.*
5 Koskenniemi, "International Law," p. 8.
6 M. Koskenniemi, "The Fate of Public International Law: Between Technique and Politics," 70 (1), *Modern Law Review* (2007) 1, p. 9.

7 M. Koskenniemi, "The Politics of International Law – 20 Years Later," 20 (1), *European Journal of International Law* (2009) 7, p. 15.

8 Koskenniemi, "International Law."

9 Koskenniemi, "Fate of Public International Law," p. 8.

10 Koskenniemi, "Politics of International Law," p. 16.

11 M. Koskenniemi, "Constitutionalism as Mindset: Reflections on Kantian Themes about International Law and Governance," 8 (1), *Theoretical Inquiries in Law* (2007) 9, pp. 13–15.

12 Law, as Koskenniemi puts it, is "drained away" from international law. See Koskenniemi, "International Law," p. 12.

13 *Kindler v. Canada*, Comm. 470/1991, Views under Article 5, para. 4 of the Optional Protocol, CCPR/C/48/D/470/1991, 30 July 1993, Dissenting opinion by Mr Francisco Jose Aguilar Urbina.

14 HRC, General Comment No. 6, UN Doc. CCPR/GEC/6630/E (1982), para. 6.

15 *Ibid.*

16 *Ibid.*, para. 7.

17 *Ibid.*, para. 6.

18 See, for instance, Human Rights Council, High-level panel discussion on the question of the death penalty – Report of the UN High Commissioner for Human Rights, UN Doc. A/HRC/30/21 (2015).

19 See for instance *Moving Away from the Death Penalty: Lessons from National Experiences* (OHCHR, 2013), available at https://www.ohchr.org/Lists/MeetingsNY/Attachments/27/moving_away_from_death_penalty_web.pdf (accessed 1st December 2020).

20 See, for instance, *Moving Away from the Death Penalty: Arguments, Trends and Perspectives* (OHCHR, 2015), available at www.ohchr.org/Lists/MeetingsNY/Attachments/52/Moving-Away-from-the-Death-Penalty.pdf (accessed 28th November 2019).

21 See, for instance, OHCHR, Expert Meeting on a Moratorium on the Death Penalty with a View to its Abolition in Malawi, 12th November 2015, available at www.ohchr.org/Documents/Issues/DeathPenalty/ConceptNote12Nov2015.doc (accessed 28th November 2019).

22 The use of the death penalty is one of the attributes of the Right to Life in the OHCHR's project to encourage the use of human rights indicators, with a number of relevant indicators being suggested. See OHCHR, Human Rights Indicator Tables, available at www.ohchr.org/Documents/Issues/HRIndicators/SDG_Indicators_Tables.pdf (accessed 28th November 2019).

23 This is not to say, of course, that this is a settled matter as far as all of the States parties to the ICCPR are concerned. Rather, it is no longer a subject for debate within the international human rights law regime.

24 Oakeshott, *On Human Conduct*, p. 108.

25 *Ibid.*, pp. 108–109.

26 *Ibid.*, p. 184.

27 *Ibid.*, pp. 124–128.

28 *Ibid.*, p. 111.

29 *Ibid.*, p. 122.
30 *Ibid.*, p. 123.
31 *Ibid.*, p. 121.
32 *Ibid.*
33 *Ibid.*, p. 126.
34 *Ibid.*
35 *Ibid.*, p. 128.
36 *Ibid.*
37 *Ibid.*, p. 122.
38 *Ibid.*, p. 129.
39 *Ibid.*
40 *Ibid.*, pp. 130–133.
41 *Ibid.*, pp. 132–133.
42 *Ibid.*, p. 137.
43 *Ibid.*, pp. 137–138.
44 *Ibid.*, p. 137.
45 *Ibid.*, pp. 138–139.
46 *Ibid.*, p. 139.
47 *Ibid.*, p. 141.
48 *Ibid.*, p. 114.
49 *Ibid.*, pp. 114–115.
50 *Ibid.*, p. 115.
51 *Ibid.*, pp. 115–116.
52 *Ibid.*, p. 115.
53 *Ibid.*
54 *Ibid.*, p. 116.
55 *Ibid.*, p. 134.
56 *Ibid.*
57 *Ibid.*, pp. 116–117.
58 William Galston, for instance, excoriates Oakeshott for the "outright implausibility" of his "radicalism" in this regard. See W. Galston, "Oakeshott's Political Theory: Recapitulation and Criticisms," in E. Podoksik (ed.), *The Cambridge Companion to Oakeshott* (Cambridge University Press, 2011), 222, p. 242.
59 One is reminded of Joseph Raz's argument that even an entirely morally neutral "rule of law" will have the purpose of "guiding behaviour efficiently." See J. Raz, *The Authority of Law: Essays on Law and Morality* (Oxford University Press, 1979), p. 223.
60 M. Oakeshott, *Lectures in the History of Political Thought* (Imprint Academic, 2006), p. 473.
61 Oakeshott, *On Human Conduct*, pp. 180–181.
62 *Ibid.*, p. 165.
63 *Ibid.*, p. 141.
64 It would indeed go against the entire tenor of his thought. See M. Oakeshott, *Rationalism in Politics* (Methuen, 1962), in particular the essays "Rationalism in Politics" (*ibid.*, 1) and "The Tower of Babel" (*ibid.*, 59).

65 Writing on *The Road to Serfdom*, Oakeshott concluded that Hayek still in the
    end had a doctrine – a "plan to resist all planning." See Oakeshott, "Rationalism
    in Politics," p. 21. This is, in essence, the same critique which has been levelled
    from the left against the thought of Hayek and other (purported) neoliberals.
    See, for instance, M. Vatter, "Foucault and Hayek: Republican Law and Civil
    Society," in V. Lemm and M. Vatter (eds), *The Government of Life: Foucault,
    Biopolitics, and Neoliberalism* (Fordham University Press, 2014).
66 Oakeshott, *On Human Conduct*, p. 181.
67 M. Oakeshott, "Rational Conduct," in Oakeshott, *Rationalism in Politics*, p.
    93.
68 Koskenniemi, "International Law," p. 12.
69 UN Doc. A/RES/2131(XX), 21st December 1965.
70 *Case Concerning Military and Paramilitary Activities in and Against Nicaragua
    (Nicaragua v. USA)*, ICJ Reports 1986, 14, Judgment, paras 202–209.
71 S. Wiessner and A. Willard, "Policy-Oriented Jurisprudence and Human Rights
    Abuses in Internal Conflict: Toward a World Public Order of Human Dignity,"
    93, *American Journal of International Law* (1999) 316, pp. 319–324.
72 *Ibid.*
73 International Commission on Intervention and State Sovereignty, *The
    Responsibility to Protect* (December 2001), available at http://responsibilit
    ytoprotect.org/ICISS%20Report.pdf (accessed 28th November 2019), paras
    4.11 and 4.12.
74 *Ibid.*, para. 4.12.
75 On the Responsibility to Protect, see e.g. W. Knight and F. Egerton (eds), *The
    Routledge Handbook of the Responsibility to Protect* (Routledge, 2014).
76 Article 8.
77 An prominent example of this is the UK's Modern Slavery Act 2015, which as
    well as introducing new criminal offences, also requires businesses to audit and
    report on the existence of slavery in their supply chains, and has resulted in the
    creation of a government "task force" and an open register of company state-
    ments on modern slavery, among other things.
78 Articles 9 and 11, respectively.
79 See, for example, D. Kelley, *A Life of One's Own: Individual Rights and the
    Welfare State* (Cato Institute, 1998) on the one side, and S. Moyn, *Not Enough:
    Human Rights in an Unequal World* (Belknap Press, 2018) on the other.
80 See e.g., N. McInnes, "A Sceptical Conservative," 61, *The National Interest*
    (2000) 82.
81 M. Oakeshott, "On the Character of a Modern European State," in *On
    Human Conduct*, 185. Oakeshott framed his discussion around "European"
    States, but he also suggested that States in other areas of the world largely have
    the same ambivalent natures – and a very strongly *teleocratic* bent – because
    they were in effect forced simulacra of European polities owing to their colonial
    legacies. See pp. 296–297, fn. 2.
82 *Ibid.*, p. 198.
83 *Ibid.*

84 *Ibid.*, p. 197 and p. 189.

85 *Ibid.*, pp. 200–201.

86 *Ibid.*, pp. 201–203.

87 *Ibid.*, pp. 203–206.

88 *Ibid.*, p. 320.

89 *Ibid.*, pp. 311–312.

90 *Ibid.*, p. 266.

91 *Ibid.*, p. 267.

92 *Ibid.*, p. 268.

93 *Ibid.*

94 *Ibid.*, p. 270.

95 *Ibid.*, pp. 270–272.

96 *Ibid.*, p. 273.

97 *Ibid.*

98 *Ibid.*, pp. 274–275.

99 H. Pitkin, "Inhuman Conduct and Unpolitical Theory," 4, *Political Theory* (1976) 301, p. 302.

100 Oakeshott, *On Human Conduct*, p. 275.

101 *Ibid.*, p. 276.

102 *Ibid.*, p. 279.

103 *Ibid.*, pp. 287–288.

104 *Ibid.*, p. 290.

105 *Ibid.*, pp. 293–295.

106 *Ibid.*, p. 298.

107 *Ibid.*, p. 321.

108 *Ibid.*, p. 318.

109 *Ibid.*, p. 308.

110 *Ibid.*, pp. 311–312.

111 *Ibid.*, p. 298.

112 *Ibid.*, p. 297 and pp. 299–300.

113 *Ibid.*, pp. 300–301.

114 Oakeshott did not explore either form of totalitarianism in any depth in *On Human Conduct*, but it is clear that he viewed both Soviet Communism and Nazism as the ultimate expressions of the amorphous drive to improve well-being taken to its furthest conclusions (in *On Human Conduct*, pp. 285–286). In respect of this, his reading was similar to that of Foucault's: see M. Foucault, *Society Must Be Defended: Lectures at the College de France 1975–1976* (Penguin, 2003; ed. M. Bertani and A. Fontana, trans. D. Macey), pp. 239–263 and M. Dean, *Governmentality* (2nd edition, Sage, 2010), pp. 163–174.

115 This is often misunderstood, and Oakeshott portrayed as advocating that the State should instantiate civil association. See e.g., O. Letwin, "Are Adverbial Rules Enough?" Michael Oakeshott Memorial Lecture, LSE, 19th October 2011, available at www.lse.ac.uk/lse-player?id=1199 (accessed 28th November 2019).

116 For an example of the former, see L. O'Sullivan, "Michael Oakeshott on European Political History," 21 (1), *History of Political Thought* (2000) 132; for an example of the latter, see P. Anderson, "The Intransigent Right at the End of the Century," 14 (18), *London Review of Books* (1992) 7, p. 11.

117 M. Oakeshott, *On History and Other Essays* (Liberty Fund, 1999), p. 3. On his inconsistencies of method, see S. Soininen, *From a 'Necessary Evil' to the Art of Contingency: Oakeshott's Conception of Political Activity* (Imprint Academic, 2005), p. 11.

118 M. Oakeshott, *Morality and Politics in Modern Europe: The Harvard Lectures* (Yale University Press, 1993), p. 14.

119 D. Boucher, "Politics in a Different Mode: An Appreciation of Michael Oakeshott 1901–1990," 22 (4), *History of Political Thought* (1991), 717, p. 723.

120 M. Loughlin, *Political Jurisprudence* (Oxford University Press, 2010), pp. 163–164.

121 *Ibid.*, p. 164.

122 M. Oakeshott, *The Politics of Faith and the Politics of Scepticism* (Yale University Press, 1996; ed. T. Fuller).

123 *Ibid.*, p. 127 and p. 12.

124 Oakeshott, *On Human Conduct*, p. 231.

125 I use these terms loosely to refer to inter-state relations, cross-border private law, and global governance, respectively.

126 This observation has occasionally been made elsewhere. See J. Klabbers, "Two Concepts of International Organization," 2, *International Organizations Law Review* (2005) 277, discussing Oakeshott at pp. 285–287.

3

Human rights' directing idea

I don't like to see other people suffering.
(Peter Tatchell, Interview with *Triggernometry*,
27th May 2018)

Introduction

In the first chapter of this book, we saw that international human rights law has a tendency to expand its purview in a manner which is largely unfettered. We observed that this results from a conception of human rights law as being purposive. In Chapter 2, we noted that law in general has a tendency to be conceived of as a *teleocratic* rule-book, declaratory of purposes and specifying the actions and duties necessary to achieve them programmatically. We saw that this often derives from a conception of the State itself as a *universitas* – an enterprise association with the amorphous goal of improving the well-being of its members. In such circumstances, law is frequently mobilised to achieve that goal. We concluded that international law will be similarly led to take on a *teleocratic* guise when international political organisation is thought of in terms of a *universitas*, and that this will therefore be true of international human rights law specifically. This suggests that international human rights law will become oriented towards *teleocracy* where international political organisation is considered to have the purpose of improving human well-being. In such circumstances, human rights law will become the rule-book for the programmatic achievement of that purpose.

In this chapter, I argue that this way of thinking about human rights and their role within the international order tends to be taken as a given, even if it is not generally put in these terms. At an abstract level, human rights are often described as having a constitutional character. Global law is constitutionalising, it is said, and human rights provide part of the fundamental underlying framework of principles or norms on which the process of constitutionalisation is based. Since that process is often described as having the goal of improving human well-being, human rights naturally take on a purposive or *teleocratic* bent in that context. More concretely, human rights are frequently deployed on a piece-meal basis as the legal justifications for expanding the administrative authority of the State or international organisations where a specific problem is identified as requiring a solution. Here, too, human rights laws appear in strongly *teleocratic* guises.

I then argue that this is hardly accidental. International human rights law, while never having been an entirely cohesive regime, has always been imbued with what the French constitutional theorist Maurice Hauriou called a "directing idea" – in this case, that it is the duty of the powerful to care for and look after the powerless, and that this should be operationalised through the imposition of legal obligations.[1] This derives ultimately not from reason but from a shared sense of emotion animating the adherents of the regime – namely, compassion. This gives international human rights its particular character, and is the source of its ready mobilisation for programmatic projects for the universal improvement of human well-being.

Human rights law and its purposes

Accounts of what human rights are "for" are, occasionally, put in descriptive or empirical terms.[2] But it is far more common to encounter them being thought of as having purposes of a much grander normative scale, as being the means "to ensure that people's life chances aren't held back by barriers in their way";[3] as being the promotion of "social progress and better standards of life in larger freedom";[4] as being nothing less than the means by which "human dignity" will be secured.[5] And, similarly, interpretations of rights in specific contexts are often also described as having purposes of vast and idealised scope: to provide "an agenda for the future for tackling inequality";[6] to "ensur[e] that societies recognize that all people must have the opportunity to reach their full potential";[7] to "help to pursue justice for minorities without a voice";[8] and so on. All law can be conceived as purposive in some sense, as we saw in the previous chapter. But human rights law takes on a *teleocratic* guise particularly readily.

In this section, I describe the dominant mode of engaging with human rights law as envisioning them as the means by which ends are to be realised. These ends are often presented in a fashion that is idealised and rhetorical, perhaps even utopian: to fully realise universal human well-being (although this can be put in various other ways). But, as I will argue, this finds much more concrete effect at two different levels. First, it results in human rights being described as constitutional in the sense of being fundamental or structural norms both for individual States and the "international community."

Second, it gives rise to an instrumentalist approach to human rights which sees them being deployed to achieve specific ends – the meeting of "felt needs."[9]

"All human rights are achieved for all"

The introduction to the Office of the High Commissioner for Human Rights' (OHCHR's) 2018–2021 "Management Plan" – in effect, a strategy document for human rights across the UN – strikes a note of cautious positivity.[10] The Universal Declaration of Human Rights (UDHR), with the help of "brave human rights defenders and visionary human rights leaders," has, it declares, "changed the world."[11] It has brought freedom, equality, and access to justice and opportunity; it has reduced poverty and exploitation; it has meant more young people going to school; it has meant the eradication of disease; it has brought an end to "oppressive dictatorships" and replaced them with participatory systems of governance.[12] While the authors observe that inequality is growing, that there remain problems such as corruption and the criminalisation of public dissent, and that "a more unequal world has encouraged a retreat to nativism and hostility,"[13] ultimately the conclusion is optimistic – one is even tempted to describe it as millenarian. "Human rights remain our most sure and universal point of reference," the document declares, "[and] can help set us on a course towards inclusion, sustainable prosperity, justice, dignity, freedom and sustained peace."[14] It closes,

> Each day, together, one person at a time if needs be, we can face down hatred, despair and selfishness, and build societies in which everyone has a chance to survive and flourish. In a world divided in so many ways, human rights can unite us. In a world so uncertain, human rights are our sure and steady guiding star.[15]

This rhetoric could be easily lampooned as "human rightism."[16] But one need only cast a glance at the literature (whether in practice or the academy) on international human rights law to find sentiments of its kind being expressed – albeit typically put in somewhat subtler tones and emphasising different aspects or interpretations of human rights. The basic conceptual framework, however, is plain: the ultimate goal is to "build societies in which everyone has a chance to survive and flourish," and the way to get there is through human rights (often expressed as through "realising" human rights). This is, in essence, more or less exactly as Franklin D. Roosevelt had put matters in his famous "four freedoms" speech in early 1941. Through freedom of expression, freedom of worship, freedom from want, and freedom from fear ("the supremacy of human rights everywhere"), a new "kind of world" would be attainable.[17] While the career of human rights has followed a convoluted path since then,[18] that basic vision has continued to dominate rhetorically. What, of course, the realisation of human rights actually consists of is a source of keen debate in the academic literature, as the reader will likely be aware. But that in some conception achieving it would usher in better societies and a better world is a commonplace.

This produces two particular effects. The first is a view of human rights as being progressive in the sense of moving towards "full realisation."[19] While it may be true that "the struggle for human dignity ... has no beginning or end,"[20] and remains an ongoing project, it is still one in which there must be momentum forward – as "expeditiously and effectively as possible," in the words of the Committee on Economic, Social and Cultural Rights (CESCR).[21] The language everywhere is one of travel, with the making of "strides"[22] and "advances."[23] It is said to be important to develop "roadmaps [towards] realising the full potential of human rights."[24] There must be no "retrogression."[25] Where the International Court of Justice (ICJ) lags behind human rights courts in its support for human rights claims it must "catch up."[26] Frequently, this also results in a rhetoric of *joint* endeavour; it is, of course, common to speak of there being a human rights "movement," but other metaphors are also used: the Chairperson of the Coordination Committee for United Nations (UN) Special Procedures, citing the Secretary-General's concerns that the "human rights agenda is losing ground," reminded his colleagues that "We are all climbing the same mountain tied with the same rope [and] have therefore no choice but to support each other and move together in the right direction."[27]

The second is a sense of human rights as being somehow structural or foundational in the formation of a particular kind of State or, much more significantly, a particular kind of world. The human rights movement, in the words of perhaps the most prominent current writer on the subject, must concern itself with the "designing [of] good states";[28] for the UK Equality and Human Rights Commission (EHRC), the aim is to have "strong foundations on which to build a more equal and rights-respecting society";[29] for the current UN High Commissioner for Human Rights, a major goal of human rights is "creating resilient and peaceful societies."[30] For Cancado Trindade, it is something altogether greater: the creation of an "international law for humankind" – a new *corpus juris* on which to found a world society "[fulfilling] of the needs and aspirations of human beings, of peoples and of humankind as a whole."[31] For Hersch Lauterpacht, it was simply a new kind of international community.[32]

These two perspectives are of course complementary, and the neatness with which they interlock is amply demonstrated by the OHCHR's 2019 appeal to donors, which contains an "Organizational Management Plan" or OMP, which functions as a strategic plan through to 2021.[33] This is underpinned by a "Theory of Change" which contains three steps towards a final goal. The first step, "What We Do," is a list of the OHCHR's activities, which includes facilitating learning, delivering human rights education, raising human rights awareness, monitoring and publicly reporting on human rights situations, facilitating dialogue between stakeholders, and so on. The second step, "Our Pillars," can be thought of as intermediate or bridging goals: strengthening the rule of law, enhancing equality, integrating human rights into sustainable development, preventing violence, and so forth. The third step, "The Results We Contribute To," contains desired outcomes: these include State laws and policies which protect and promote human rights; state institutions, non-State actors and the private sector promoting, protecting, and respecting human rights; a growth in public support for human rights; human rights being effectively integrated into UN programmes; and the international community responding effectively to critical human rights situations. Beyond these three steps is the ultimate goal: "All Human Rights Are Achieved For All."[34]

While this "Theory of Change" describes the OHCHR's vision of its own role very clearly, its conceptualisation of human rights in general could also not be put more simply. They are themselves both an end state to which progress must be directed, and also the mechanism and justification for achieving it. This is to take place through the restructuring of States, non-State actors, and private sector organisations; the integration of human rights into the activities and aspirations of the international community; and the invigoration of "the public" as participants in, and supporters of, the overall project. All that is left open is what exactly the end state of "All Human Rights Are Achieved For All" looks like, although the High Commissioner herself makes clear in her foreword that it will consist of "greater well-being for all" and "greater justice and equity."[35] The words are Michelle Bachelet's, but they could just as easily have been Roosevelt's. The essence of the project is identical but for the fact that the former is more detailed: ushering in a new kind of world through the supremacy of human rights everywhere.

Of course, such rhetorical commitments are just that. But it would be a mistake to view them as having no impact beyond rhetoric. For, as we shall see, these ideals imbue the worlds of human rights practice, activism, and academia alike.

Human rights and global constitutionalism

It is natural to think of the perspectives described in the previous subsection – an understanding of human rights as at once a progressive project and a restructuring of entire societies and indeed the world – against the backdrop of general international law, because, of course, public international law has also been thought of in such terms for centuries. One might root this in Grotius, with his vision of a legal morality structuring all human life,[36] Pufendorf and his image of States as bound by a universal and natural law guiding them towards peace and welfare,[37] Vattel's "delightful dream" of a universal republic,[38] Bentham's "universal international code" with its designs on the "common and equal unity of all nations,"[39] Kant's vision of a cosmopolitan world order,[40] or elsewhere. But few would dispute that thinking on international law has long held a tendency towards (one might say an obsession with) the purposive achievement of desired end states.

Likewise, few would disagree that this purposiveness characterises itself by visions of both *progress* and *structure* – the former often described as inevitable (at worst resembling a kind of naive Whiggish historicism), the latter as strongly desirable: international law as both ushering in a new world and providing the fundamental rules by which it will, or should, be governed. That this has often caused international legal scholars to tie themselves in knots over whether their work is descriptive or normative is beside the point;[41] the fact of the matter is that to "'do' international law" is to participate in a field which has a long and continuing impulse to describe itself as a *project*.[42] And human rights have, of course, become inextricably bound up in that project – no doubt because the kinds of things that they are said to enshrine are so closely associated with the purported aims – welfare, peace, equality, and so on – of the wider project as a whole.

The locus at which we can most clearly see that relationship finding traction in recent decades is in the notion of global constitutionalism. Analogies between international law and domestic public law have a very long pedigree, and there are some fairly old antecedents for the position that the international community does or should have a constitution. But in the last two decades a distinct preoccupation with constitutionalist thinking has emerged among international lawyers. The reasons for this have been the subject of some reflection,[43] but they need not detain us at this stage. It is sufficient merely to observe that the international legal system (and there is here a strong sense that there is such a *system* and it can be described with that word)[44] is very frequently presented in contemporary accounts of international law as undergoing a process of integration through globalisation, such that it no longer resembles a group of sovereign States on the Westphalian model negotiating reciprocal obligations on the basis of consent. Rather, in these accounts, the system must be thought of instead as becoming "verticalised" by the existence of certain overarching norms.[45] These norms, it is often said, reflect shared values of the international community, and it is proper therefore to describe them as constitutional, given that they provide the legal structure or foundation upon which law is made. Depending on one's perspective, these might be specified minimally as the maintenance of peace and security and the prohibition of the use of force, the peaceful settlement of disputes, the sovereign equality of States, the principle of cooperation, and, of course, self-determination and respect for human rights.[46] More maximally, they may be the dense network of laws, rules, norms, and procedures contained in the "global administrative space" in which States, international organisations, transnational governmental networks, and public-private hybrid regulators operate, and which is designed to protect individuals against the arbitrary deployment of official power within it.[47] Here, a "'small c' constitutionalism"[48] is said to exist in the form of a decentralised and bottom-up evolution of common administrative practices combined with certain fundamental principles – such as transparency, administrative review, and respect for human rights – underlying them.

There are some who view human rights in this context as being a kind of epiphenomenon of globalisation and modernity. Gunther Teubner, for instance, has observed the development of "subsystems of world society."[49] Here, the old nexus between State and law is described as a mere historical interlude in which certain concepts such as "jurisdiction," "territory," and "State" developed "in order to appreciate specific, historically grown or politically constituted, frameworks of legal evolution at a particular time and place – no more and no less."[50] In the world society which is said to be developing, transnational law is freed from that connection, and generates itself autonomously through many different and diverse legal orders – a society "without peak or centre," as Luhmann memorably put it[51] – just as domestic law self-generates through autopoiesis. Human rights in this literature tend to be described as one of the "distinguishing values/premises" which help determine the legitimacy of "constituted social objects" in the polycentric world society.[52] Alternatively, rights are interpreted as underpinning the global system of governance by offering "structural points of orientation" through, for instance, courts, which connect the national and international layers of governance (when, for example, a domestic court applies international human rights law), and the public and private dimensions of global order (by regulating private activities and giving private bodies governance functions if they are rights-compliant).[53]

Yet the vast bulk of the literature on human rights in global constitutionalism has a distinctively normative tenor. This is sometimes disguised by the fact that the development of global constitutionalism can have the tendency of being presented as a *fait accompli*,[54] and its proponents described as merely "exploring" or "mapping" developments.[55] But most theorists in the field tend to adopt the perspective, formulated by Scheingold in another context, that rights can be "constitutive of, rather than simply a reflection of, social practice."[56] In other words, if a global constitution is developing or has developed, human rights can and should give it a particular character – one which has the protection of human well-being at its core. In the words of Macklem, international law "*shape[s]* an international political reality into an international legal order," and does so by regulating the distribution of sovereignty such that it requires the sovereign to "represent the whole of its population within its territory consistent with principles of equality, non-discrimination, and self-determination" – that is, with the most elementary principles of international human rights law.[57]

Some argue that it is a global network of judges who ought to be at the centre of that "shaping" project, through their engagement in a "common enterprise of protecting human rights" in whatever court in which they sit.[58] This has certainly been the attitude of judges in the European Court of Human Rights (ECtHR) and Inter-American Court of Human Rights (IACtHR), the former of which described the European Convention on Human Rights (ECHR) as a constitutional charter for Europe in one of its earliest decisions,[59] the latter of which has spoken of itself, as we have seen, as part of an "international *ordre public* based upon the respect for human rights in all circumstances."[60] Others suggest that the UN Charter, which embodies "common values, goals and principles" of the international community, among which are of course respect for human rights, is part of "a larger process of building a world order of law and justice" and thereby *constitutive* of that world order.[61] Still others suggest that it is human rights obligations' nature as duties owed *erga omnes* that gives them their particular structuring nature, because it results in the "constitution of an international community, community being a term suitable to indicate a closer union than between members of a society."[62] What these different conceptualisations have in common is that they each propose not only that the protection of human rights is one of the fundamental values underpinning a global constitution, but that human rights should also have a specific structuring role in bringing that constitution about and a guiding one in ensuring that it fosters an international community as the guarantor of peace and human welfare.

It is not so much, therefore, that globalisation is integrating States into an international community which just happens to have respect for human rights as one of its fundamental constitutive norms. It is rather that the process of global integration is and must be shaped and guided by human rights principles – and that, indeed, human rights are essential to ensuring that the result of that integrative process is an international community founded on achieving universal human well-being.[63] In other words, scholars in this field are not, generally, only describing a process, but furthering the expansion of a "normative horizon" through upholding human rights as a set of constitutional principles and promoting their implementation.[64]

But as well as being thought of as having a structural purpose at the global level, human rights are also often described as being constitutive of a particular kind of State. Here, given the highly variable levels of effectiveness given to human rights laws in different States, few would suggest that this is merely a matter of mapping developments. Instead, it is presented as a project of, as we have seen, the "*designing* [of] good states.*"

An illustrative example of this view, chosen only because its author is so eminent, is that set forth by Jeremy Waldron. Beginning with the principle that States are not ends in themselves but only "exist for the sake of human individuals" or as "trustees for the people committed to their care,"[65] he goes on to suggest that this means they are "supposed to operate lawfully and in a way that is mindful that the peaceful and ordered world that is sought in international law [is] for the sake of the millions of men, women, communities, and businesses who are committed to their care."[66] And since international law is "oriented to the well-being of individuals" rather than States in this way, the role of international law is to "articulate a set of common standards for the protection of human rights" – which is "in the end" nothing less than the "*telos* of international law."[67] This produces an understanding of the State not as the subject of international law but as an "agency" whose task (acting alone or in coordination with others) is to improve the lives of all of the individuals on the earth.[68] In other words, since the State is an artificial construct to begin with, rather than something whose value is to be "assumed as a first principle" like the human individual, the nature of sovereignty can be "determined by the rules of the international order."[69] It follows that human rights, as part of the corpus of the most fundamental of those rules, can and indeed should therefore have a role in determining the nature of sovereignty itself – so as to achieve international law's humanitarian *telos*.

Other authors have provided elaborations on this theme, arguing that the time has come to "retire" the conception of State sovereignty as exclusive jurisdiction and replace it with a sense of sovereignty as "emanating from a fiduciary relationship between states and the people subject to their jurisdiction."[70] Here, a "compelling philosophical account of contemporary international law's focus on human security and human rights" is provided by considering a State's claim to exercise sovereign authority as being derived from "the satisfaction of its relational duties to the people subject to its legal powers."[71] International law thus endows States with a "fiduciary mission," reliant on them as it is in its aim (what Waldron would have called its *telos*) of bringing about "secure and equal freedom for humanity."[72] The result is that international law can be thought of as "constitut[ing] the State as an international juridical institution and defin[ing] its legal capacity ... to exercise rights, assume liabilities and assert immunities as a fiduciary representative of its beneficiaries."[73] And it does so in such a way that States are placed under "fiduciary obligations to exercise that power in a manner that is consistent with the other-regarding purposes of their entrusted authority (e.g. international human rights)."[74] Lest this be thought of only as a series of academic arguments, such conceptualisations of human rights as fundamentally restructuring the nature of Statehood have also entered the realm of international politics. "State sovereignty," as Kofi Annan put it to the General Assembly in 1999, "is being redefined, [with] States now widely understood to be instruments at the service of their peoples,"[75] and this he explicitly linked to the "renewed and spreading consciousness of individual rights." The relationship between those two phenomena is clear: if States are instruments at the service of their peoples, then human rights are the legal principles upon which that service is enshrined and realised.

Human rights, then, are frequently understood to have purposes, operant in the two different spheres of the global and the domestic, that can be described as constitutional. They are said to comprise part of the structuring of global legal order, or of the fundamental legal framework of "good States." And they are said to do so in terms which are not merely descriptive of a certain process of integration, nor merely aiming towards a legal framework for protecting human individuals from political power in a globalised world (as important though that may be). Rather, they are supposed to imbue the international community with indelible values concerning the universal achievement of human well-being.

Human rights and felt needs

As well as being purposive at the grand scale outlined above, however, human rights – individually or read alongside or in conjunction with each other – are often deployed in much more specific contexts in order to achieve aims that are narrower or more focused in scope, and more concrete in nature. Human rights are increasingly seized upon and instrumentalised for what might be described as more detailed goals of public policy – as the justifications for purposive social action of particular kinds.

The most frequent way in which this finds expression is through identification of a need and subsequent identification of a right which entitles the right-holders to a benefit to resolve it. This is sometimes stated quite starkly. In the training manual for social workers on human rights, produced by the forerunner to the OHCHR, for example, we find it expressed as follows: "A substantive need can be translated into an equivalent positive right, and entitlement to the benefits of that right is sought from the State and beyond. It follows that the search for the realization of positive rights and entitlements is an *inseparable twin to the meeting of needs* [emphasis added]."[76] But in most circumstances it is simply implied and taken as a given – so pervasive that it passes without remark.

The first chapter of this book was of course filled with examples to illustrate this mode of thinking. Whether the need identified is to end racist bullying in schools, to end harmful stereotypes of women present in pornography, or to halt the disappearance of the Irish language, human rights are provided both as the justification for why the need exists at all, and the legal mechanism by which a positive resolution is to be determined. To take, for example, the matter of racist bullying in schools, human rights were both the means by which the problem was conceptualised and identified in the first place (broadly, as a matter of freedom from discrimination) and also the legal mechanism whereby it was to be resolved (by placing a legal obligation on the State to take positive action to remedy it).

This identification of needs takes place at differing levels of abstraction. As we have seen, it can occur at an almost microscopic level of detail, as in the Committee on the Elimination of Discrimination Against Women (CEDAW Committee)'s interest in ending the making of "sexually coloured remarks" in the workplace. It can be much broader in scope, such as the Human Rights Committee's (HRC's) interest in reducing the suicide rate. Or it can be a large, society-wide objective, such as ending discrimination against women in Timor-Leste. And, of course, these different levels at which needs are identified flow into one another, producing concatenations of needs from the large-scale society-spanning objectives down to the small-scale steps to be taken to achieve them.

To illustrate this, we will take the 2019 annual report of the Special Rapporteur on the Right to Health, which took mental health as its main focus.[77] The report is framed at the highest level of abstraction. It posits that the State's obligation is to "create and sustain enabling environments that incorporated a rights-based approach to mental health," resulting in the "promotion of a life of dignity and well-being for all persons throughout their lifetimes." This is because good mental health derives from the "psychosocial, political, economic and physical environment that enables populations to life a life of dignity, with full enjoyment of their rights and in the equitable pursuit of their potential."[78] The State is conceptualised not merely, then, as being the means by which treatment is provided for mental health problems, but as the guarantor of a "healthy psychosocial environment" sustaining "well-being" and "respect, social connection, equal opportunities and dignity."[79] Here, the need is identified at the grandest possible scale: "to create and sustain specific conditions that promote a life of dignity and well-being for all," and the solution put firmly within a "rights-based" approach.[80]

From this flow further intermediate needs, and rights-based solutions for them. This includes, for example, the provision of "equitable health care" and "alternatives to the biomedical model," as well as "actions ... in homes, schools, workplaces and communities" so as to promote conditions for good mental well-being.[81] This will include, among other things, "evidence-based family support," parental leave, early childhood education, "supportive parenting interventions" and "rethinking" the processes of "social healing" – not to mention "eliminating the toxicity of the physical and psychosocial environment."[82] This of course means in the first place more resources, non-discriminatory provision of services, and benchmarks and indicators to measure progress.[83] But ultimately it leads to human rights presented as the solution for felt needs at an extremely granular scale: requiring the State to intervene in order, for instance, to provide support in cases of early childhood trauma (including where there has been a bereavement), to provide maternal education, to fully eliminate institutional care of children, to provide "skills-based interventions" to stop adolescents from joining gangs, to prevent bullying in schools, to provide inclusion programmes for older people, and so on.[84] Here we can see how clearly how the abstract felt need of improving well-being finds expression in a deep and broad identification of further felt needs being identified accordingly – with human rights being the justification for solving them, and the means by which obligations are said to accrue to the State in order to provide a solution.

The relationship between this instrumentalisation of human rights to identify and remedy perceived problems at the local scale, and the grand rhetorical and constitutionalist purposes of human rights identified in the previous subsections, is complicated. On the one hand, it is undoubtedly the case that the former is frequently motivated by the latter. This is certainly so with the Special Rapporteur on the Right to Health, for example, who explicitly ties his aims with respect to mental health to the broader aim of human rights in general ("protecting the well-being of people").[85] That is, there are many who would see the achievement of incremental improvements – reducing the suicide rate in Scotland, promoting the Irish language, eliminating racist bullying in UK schools, or whatever else it might be – as steps on the "path towards the full realization of the rights enshrined in international human rights law."[86] And this is, of course, implicit in the OHCHR's Theory of Change, which contemplates the gradual realisation of the ultimate goal of "all human rights achieved for all."

At the same time, however, there are many circumstances in which human rights are put to the resolution of felt needs in the absence of any particular relationship to, or awareness of, the wider rhetorical or constitutionalist aims at the grand scale. They are rather deployed in an attempt to achieve a particular social (or indeed individual) goal simply because they happen to be the "ideas lying around,"[87] as it were, that might be of use in doing so.

Two brief examples of this, chosen only because they are illustrative of this highly instrumental usage of human rights, follow. The first concerns the role human rights could play in preventing childhood obesity. Here, since "global childhood obesity has reached epidemic proportions," there is argued to be a requirement for "powerful global actors" to address its "drivers."[88] And this, it is postulated, could be solved by making human rights a source of obligations for States to prevent and treat obesity, and for food and drink companies to take responsibility for consumer health, particularly with regard to children.[89] The reasoning is simply stated. Since the Children's Rights Committee (CRC Committee) and International Covenant on Economic, Social and Cultural Rights (ICESCR) both enshrine the rights to health and adequate food, "which have a clear link to obesity,"[90] States must take steps to promote the healthy development of children, and to prevent, treat, and control diseases. And since companies have the responsibility to respect all rights contained in the ICESCR under the United Nations Guiding Principles on Business and Human Rights (UNGPs), they should act to prevent harm vis-à-vis the rights to food and health, and certainly should not act in such a way as to cause it through, for instance, directly advertising foods with high sugar content to children.[91] It follows that human rights could be a "force to demand accountability" for companies' negative impacts on childhood obesity if only human rights practice in the field of obesity prevention could be better developed.[92]

The second is the use of human rights to protect children from the health harms associated with tobacco smoking.[93] Here, a range of reasons are offered for why children are particularly vulnerable to tobacco-related harm: many long-term tobacco-related harms originate during the pre- and post-natal periods; most adult smokers start smoking before the age of 18; the tobacco industry specifically targets children; there is an increased risk of adolescents beginning to smoke if a family member does; and children are often exploited in tobacco farming.[94] It is then argued that children's rights could be a "valuable mechanism to protect children against tobacco-related harm."[95] This could be achieved, for example, by requiring States to create "enabling environments" in which children can achieve agency over, and participation in, their own health and well-being through promotion of their "health capability."[96] It could be through giving the State a protective function in "specific vulnerable settings."[97] Or it could be through "shaping what exactly governments must do" in order to take into account the best interests of children in policymaking, particularly of course with respect to tobacco control.[98]

It is irrelevant whether the basis for the arguments presented above as a matter of law is in either case weak or strong, or likely to have a material impact on policy. They simply serve to demonstrate a particularly instrumental approach to human rights law. In each case, the basic pattern is the same. A problem or series of problems (childhood obesity or tobacco-related health harms) is desired to be solved. The person desiring a solution then seeks a method for solving it in the legal mechanisms that are "lying around," and human rights is the method which is fixed upon. The problem is then conceptualised as a human rights concern – however tenuously – and an argument is then made that a positive duty deriving from a human rights obligation or obligations should be placed upon a powerful actor (typically the State or businesses) to find a resolution. In other words, there is no particular sense in which the purposive usage of human rights in these contexts is linked to the very broad and ambitious "human rightism" evident in, for instance, the rhetoric of the High Commissioner.

Nonetheless, it is my argument that there is an underlying connection between these highly instrumental deployments of human rights law to resolve felt needs and the wider constitutional aims identified earlier, which is that they ultimately resort to and buttress an understanding of the relationship between the powerful and the powerless as one of benevolent care. In other words, in all of the different ways in which human rights are conceived of as purposive or deployed for instrumental ends, we find an implicit or explicit understanding that those purposes are to be realised through making powerful actors not merely accountable to, but responsible for the well-being of, the individuals, groups, and populations under their care. That is to say, the purposive impulse driving those advocating for and deploying human rights is imbued with what I will call, borrowing from the French constitutional theorist Maurice Hauriou, a "directing idea." This directing idea has at its centre the improvement of human well-being through imposing obligations on the powerful. And it motivates both the grandest constitutionalist theorising and the most instrumentalist deployment of human rights law to resolve "felt needs" alike.

The directing ideas of human rights

Hauriou on law and directing ideas

In his "Theory of the Institution," Hauriou sought to given an account of how social institutions are given a distinctive life by what he called the "directing ideas" which animate them.[99] Far from being inert, institutions are filled with the notion of "work to be realised" that transcends mere function, or indeed even ends in the sense of results. The directing idea, rather, is more properly to be understood as the object of the institution – an ongoing and continuous project that encompasses plans of action and results, but which also necessarily includes "undetermined or unrealised" elements which drive its sense of purpose.[100] For a corporation, the directing idea is as simple as profit; for the State, it is in Hauriou's words "a protectorate of a national civil society by a public power having a territorial jurisdiction, but distinct from territorial property, and thus leaving a great scope of liberty for its subjects."[101] What makes these notions directing ideas is their encapsulation of both function and ends and their surpassing of both to suggest an ongoing (and potentially unending) realisation. Indeed, it is this latter indeterminate element which is critical, because it has far more influence in the minds of those engaged in the project than existing functions. To take the State, for example, it is not the administration of existing public services which is of vital interest to the citizens, but "political government, which works in the undetermined arena"[102] of potential future services.

While given a "subjective gloss" in the mind of each individual perceiving them, these directing ideas take on an objective existence, according to Hauriou, separable from the minds of individuals and "pass[ing] from one mind to another by their own force of attraction without losing their identity."[103] It is this which gives to institutions their distinctive life – a continuous existence independent from the individuals who might be engaged in that life at any given moment, and of course open for other individuals to become engaged in at any given time. Thus, for example, the corporation's directing idea of profit exists independently of the mind of any given person, and passes into the minds of those engaged in the corporation's enterprise until such time as they cease to be so engaged. This is not to suggest that these subjective glosses are not of any significance: over time, the directing idea may be come to be understood in different ways, just as for instance the plays of Racine are understood differently in the twentieth century from how they would have been in the seventeenth, or the ideal of "justice" is interpreted to mean different things in different contexts and over the course of time. "But we cannot say that there is nothing lasting, nothing real, nothing objective in the idea of justice."[104] This objective existence of the idea allows it to "pass from one mind to another and to be refracted differently in each mind without dissolving and disappearing."[105]

Hauriou's thoughts concerning the directing idea were underdeveloped. They do not give an account of how different such ideas might compete within the same institution-person with one coming to dominance, and nor do they provide any explanation for how such ideas come into being in the first place. At most, he gives us only a Jungian gloss: "men do not create ideas, they simply find them."[106] Yet he was clear that at the heart of such ideas was a sense of common emotion. There were moments, which he called "manifestations of communion," when a directing idea was able to pass into the subjective state of a social group – moving them by their contact with it and making them aware that they are bonded by a shared feeling. Here the idea is "refracted into similar concepts in thousands of minds ... [it] passes momentarily into the subjective state in the thousands of individual minds that are united in it; these individuals invoke its name and it descends among them, adapted by them to the subjective state."[107] This was not Durkheim's concept of collective conscience, of which Hauriou was dismissive, but rather an *individuated* experience. "It is individuals who are moved by their contact with a common idea and who, by a phenomenon of interpsychology, become aware of their common emotion."[108] It is this awareness that then compels these individuals to act: "it connotes not only intellectual assent but also the will to act and the initial step forward that ... engages the whole being in the common cause."[109] Thus it is through this sense of communion that individuals come to adopt a sense of ownership over a shared idea.

These manifestations of communion do not have to be as dramatic as the founding of the French Republic or the moment at which the Israelites ask for a king.[110] Hauriou's more mundane examples – the formation of labour unions in the nineteenth century or the founding of private institutions such as charities and companies – are more illustrative. Here, the foundation of such institutions is preceded by meetings in which the directing idea is enthusiastically acclaimed. It is these meetings that constitute the so-called communion of action at which the objective and subjective meet.[111] Here, the individuals present interiorise the idea, and it comes to "obsess" them.[112] As Hauriou noted, the objection immediately presents itself that such manifestations of communion are rare, sporadic, and discontinuous – "rapid flashes of light that fade away in the night."[113] But the directing idea, in his view, remains in the subjective state (that is, in the minds of its adherents) in a continuous manner thereafter. This is because it assumes a trajectory, entering into the voluntary acts and wills of the individuals who hold it, and hence becoming the subject of power. Directing ideas are thus given continuity by the fact that there are acts of conscious will involved in their perpetuation. Such acts of power thus "throw bridges between ... states of consciousness like the couplings thrown between rail-road cars to establish the trembling continuity of an express."[114]

Chief among these acts of power are laws and regulations. Such juridical rules, in his view, were "institution-things" which are propagated and live in the social milieu,[115] particularly within constituted bodies such as the State or a private entity. They regulate the present consequences of situations created in the past and anticipate the future by regulating situations which are to come.[116] This fact, that laws and regulations "rule the future," means that they prolong the subjective manifestation of directing ideas and thus provide a subjective continuity in the minds of the individual members of the relevant group, acting as "tentacles" of power which bind sporadic manifestations of communion together.[117]

In the constituted bodies which they inhabit, these institution-things (such as laws and regulations) thus can be thought of as "borrowing" the body's power of sanction in order to "realise [an] idea."[118] That is, such juridical rules are not dependent only on the will of particular individual subjects (as for instance in the case of contractual obligations) or simply self-sustaining (as for instance in the case of customary rules).[119] Rather, they exist within Hauriou's "institution-persons" in order to give effect to the directing ideas which sustain them and to, in turn, provide those ideas with a continuous existence in the minds of their adherents. Such laws can even themselves be thought of as instantiating such ideas, although Hauriou was careful to be clear that, in his view, they could not themselves "incarnate" or create an enterprise or give life to an organisation.[120] "Institutions," by which he meant institution-persons or constituted bodies, "make juridical rules; juridical rules do not make institutions."[121]

This means that Hauriou had a keen sense that juridical rules, as he called them, were of secondary importance to the realm of ideas or, as one might put it, politics. The power of creation or incarnation was not in rules, but in the actors – the individuals and institutions – who make them. Or, rather, it is was in the directing ideas which inhabit or "obsess" those individuals and institutions:

> Directing ideas, which are of a comprehensive objectivity since they pass from one mind to another by their own force of attraction without losing their identity, are the vital principle of social institutions. They communicate to institutions a distinctive life, as separable from that of individuals as ideas themselves are separable from our minds and capable of reacting upon them.[122]

Laws and regulations in turn, then, can be seen in this context as the mechanism by which this "vital principle" of the directing idea is perpetuated and given effect – ready to pass from one mind to another across time. This is because they both give the directing idea force, and also allow it to find expression across time, having been enacted in the past and continuing to "rule" present and future action.

Hauriou gave this account in order to elucidate what he meant by institution-persons. He was not interested here in developing his notion of the institution-thing, and indeed never did so subsequently. Nonetheless, his article, as he put it, had as its entire aim the study of "social vitalism," and it is in this wider context that we find its usefulness for understanding what I have previously called the "purposes" of human rights as a legal regime.

First, Hauriou's account helps us to locate the origins of legal and regulatory rules in the realm of ideas, particularly the kind of ideas which he thought of as directing. That is, such rules can embody a sense of both function and end while transcending both to suggest an ongoing, indefinite, and indeterminate "project." Second, those ideas in turn are created (or, more properly in Hauriou's terminology, "found") not in abstract discussion but in *feeling* – a communal sense of shared emotion which gives the impetus to individuals to engage in acts of will in order to further that project. Third, they tend to manifest themselves in the form of rules because such rules give effect to power, in the sense that they manifest the conscious will of those engaged in the project in such a way that governs the past, present, and future and hence provides the directing idea with its necessary "trajectory" and sense of continuity. As well as having their own particular effects, that is, they guarantee the ongoing existence of the directing idea in a way far superior to the mere sporadic acts of communion of its adherents.

The reader will already have identified certain points of convergence between Hauriou's account presented here and those provided by Koskenniemi and Oakeshott as described in previous chapters. Chiefly, this is the sense that law is readily enlisted in ongoing and limitless projects which instil within it a continuous purpose. But Hauriou takes us a step further by showing us how this purpose is driven by a sense of communal emotion which both gives individuals the desire to act and unites different individuals across time, providing the purpose with an objective continuity or "trajectory." He also shows us why it is that law in particular comes to be not only put to a purpose but to act as a repository for it: this is because law ties the past, present, and future together through its governance of all three – like, to repeat Hauriou's memorable phrasing, "the couplings thrown between rail-road cars to establish the trembling continuity of an express."

Human rights and compassion

Our inquiry turns, then, to the directing idea of human rights law. We have already established that the regime is characterised by the desire to put human rights to particular purposes, whether at what I earlier called the grand constitutional scale or the purely instrumental level. Certainly, in the case of the former, the sense of human rights as an indeterminate project transcending both end and function is writ large in the practitioner and academic literature alike. But as I also sought to demonstrate, human rights are additionally put to much more localised or narrow uses to attempt to achieve particular outcomes or resolve felt needs in specific contexts, and there is not necessarily any clear relationship between this instrumental outcomes-based deployment of human rights and the grander vision which dominates the rhetoric of the High Commissioner, for example. Yet, as I will now argue, there is such a relationship, and indeed the two are very closely tied. This is because, as Hauriou reminds us, the directing idea of an institution – and here we will consider human rights law or the human rights movement in general as an "institution-thing" – is rooted in emotion. And one emotion in particular is held in common across those using human rights for purposive ends at whatever "scale" those purposes are to find effect. This emotion is what I will call "compassion." What this means requires brief explanation, because of course the word "compassion" has a variety of uses both within the English language, and between languages.

Milan Kundera sheds light on this in a short passage in *The Unbearable Lightness of Being*. Here, he distinguishes between two different approaches to words for "compassion." In languages deriving from Latin, he observes, the word derives from combining the prefix for "with" (*com-*), with that for "suffering" (*passio*). Hence, "compassion" means "we cannot look on coolly as others suffer; or, we sympathise with those who suffer."[123] This is distinct from other languages in which the word is translated by a noun formed from the prefix for "with" and the word for "feeling" (hence the German *mitgeful*). In such languages, the word has a broader tenor, he argues: "to have compassion" (that is, in the sense of "with-feeling") "means not only to be able to live with another's misfortune but also to feel with him any emotion – joy, anxiety, happiness, pain."[124]

English does not, of course, derive from Latin, but the word "compassion," like much of its vocabulary, does. And the sense in which I use the word is quite deliberate in signifying what Kundera identifies as being the feeling that one "cannot look on coolly as others suffer." It is this emotion – this sense of sympathy with suffering, or indeed the sense that suffering ought not to be tolerated – which is held in common by human rights advocates, whether in practice or academia, and it is this shared feeling in which we find the roots of the regime's "directing idea."

This calls us, of course, to human rights' roots in the Enlightenment – that era in which, as Arendt put it, the "age-old indifference [to human misery] was about to disappear."[125] For Arendt, compassion was at the centre of the French Revolution and all of the revolutions which followed. It was what "haunted and [drove]" them.[126] Rousseau and his contemporaries, who felt an "innate repugnance of seeing a fellow creature suffer,"[127] were led inexorably to conclude that the welfare of the people was the "most sacred of all laws."[128] And the result was Robespierre's attempt to unify the French nation through "the compassion of those who did not suffer with those who were *malheureux*."[129] This makes compassion, for Arendt, the "most powerful and perhaps the most devastating passion motivating revolutionaries."[130] The rights of man, in other words, sprang from a movement which was guided more than anything else by an intolerance with, or even a disgust for, suffering. For Lynn Hunt, the role played by compassion or empathy is much wider and more pervasive: growing notions of "bodily integrity and empathetic selfhood" during the eighteenth century making it possible for new social and political concepts – such as human rights – to come into being.[131] Human rights here were integrally related to broader changes in human psychology which made it possible for compassion to be felt universally (i.e., not merely for one's family or tribe).

And few would dispute the argument when put to them that human rights advocates in the modern day tend to be motivated by compassion, least of all human rights advocates themselves. Geoffrey Robertson, for instance, describes how the millions of ordinary people making up global society feel unable to "avert their eyes from repression in foreign countries."[132] Ken Booth calls human rights "the politics of the-I-that-is-another," which is "badged with common humanity."[133] Upendra Baxi writes that it is "axiomatic" that human rights' "historic mission ... is to give voice to human suffering."[134] Wheatley identifies the Sharpeville Massacre of 1960 as a critical event in which "moral shock" brought about a radical shift in how the UN viewed the relationship between human rights and sovereignty.[135] And Gunther puts it more starkly still: if you wish to know what human rights "means," then "you can think of the German Gestapo torturing a political opponent."[136] But it is important to emphasise how pervasive this motivation is through the field of practice. Perhaps the best illustration can be found in the form in which most future advocates will encounter formal human rights doctrine – academic textbooks. Take, for example, the introduction to Goodhart's *Human Rights: Politics and Practice*.[137] Here, in a common pattern, we find a series of events described, all of which "would be difficult," we are told, "to talk about [...] without invoking human rights."[138]

> [An] authoritarian government silences a critical independent media; rural villagers and the urban poor endure sickness caused by the lack of clean water; criminal networks traffic women and girls for sex; transnational corporations shift manufacturing jobs to low-wage countries with lax labour standards; gay men and women organise to win the right to marry and found families; refugees fleeing tribal or religious violence are denied asylum in nearby wealthy countries; suspected terrorists are captured and detained without trial or review; reformers organise resistance to a repressive military regime; an international air campaign helps to topple a regime that has threatened to massacre its own people; a campaign eliminates school fees and makes education available for all.[139]

While this list of events is presented ostensibly to illustrate the point that human rights have become an all-pervasive concern within the political world, it is also hard to escape the rhetorical imperative to sympathise. These events call upon the reader to identify with the suffering of the subject, be they the women and girls trafficked for sex, the gay men and women struggling to be allowed to marry and form families, or the refugees fleeing violence and denied asylum – or, for that matter, the workers in low-wage countries with lax labour standards and those who lose their manufacturing jobs as a result of the corporation's actions. Our sense of compassion – compassionate outrage, even – is aroused, and we are enjoined to engage in a shared sense that in such circumstances of suffering something must be done.

Similarly, in Alston and Goodman's *International Human Rights*, the text begins with a long introductory sequence of media stories raising human rights issues, which concern, in order, the summary execution of a child in Sri Lanka; voter disenfranchisement in the United States; women's global lack of representation in politics; the "public health disaster" of unhealthy food; the problems confronting women in the aftermath of the Arab Spring; the involvement of a former Guatemalan head of state in acts of torture and displacement; civilian deaths in the North Atlantic Treaty Organization's (NATO's) military campaign in Libya; poverty; the mass rape of women during the Liberian civil war; persecution of homosexual people in Africa; Britain's thorny relationship with the ECtHR; organ transplants carried out after executions in China; Hungary's laws constraining the independence of the judiciary and media; a recent coup d'état in Mali; and a decision by the US Supreme Court to the effect that strip searches were permitted in principle for any arrest.[140] Two of these examples, concerning poverty and Britain's relationship to the ECtHR, respectively, are presented as exhibits of at least partial scepticism about rights. But in all of the other circumstances, the examples invite nothing if not a feeling of compassionate concern with the plight of the subjects involved and, equally, a sense that their suffering ought to be ameliorated through human rights – indeed, that this is what human rights are *for*.

What these relatively simple examples show is that often our typical first encounters with the notion of human rights in an educational or doctrinal context are framed in a particular way: we are enjoined to engage with the subject in a spirit of compassion. It is compassion, this sense of sympathy with suffering – of being unable to "look on coolly" – which is central to the emotional experience of engagement with human rights. And it is here, of course, that Hauriou's work comes into particular relevance, because he saw with such sharp focus how it was that the directing ideas of an institutional project are rooted in these moments of shared feeling, and because he understood that this gave them not only their willed impetus, but also their continuity and "trajectory" across time through the creation of laws. The import of this will already be clear: compassion is not only the locus for "manifestations of communion" between adherents of human rights. It is also the driving force behind the creation, interpretation, and implementation of human rights laws, which unite adherents across time by communicating the project's directing idea from the past to the present and into the future – like "the couplings thrown between rail-road cars to establish the trembling continuity of an express."

One does not, of course, need to look far to find that sense of emotional commonality in the literature on human rights, nor to discover it as the source of the impetus of the making of laws. One thinks, for example, of the Chairperson of the Coordination Committee of Special Procedures' reminders that "Human rights ... bind humanity together with shared principles and a better future" and that "We are all climbing the same mountain tied with the same rope."[141] One also thinks of Fassbender's sense of human rights as embodying the "common values, goals and principles" of the international community and the consequent importance of enshrining them as constitutional norms, or Waldron's vision of a "peaceful and ordered world" hoped for by "millions of people" that is the very *telos* of international law in general and human rights law in particular. Equally, one thinks of Moyn's claim that "human rights norms and organisations remain the chief source of idealistic passion in the world" and that the "power of their current ethic" must be "put to good use" – through law's role in his "designing [of] good States."[142] But one also thinks of more concrete developments: the incipient human rights *jus commune* or *jus gentium* (or *ordre public*) brought about by judicial dialogue between human rights courts around the world, which is often said to be creating a "common law of human rights"[143] and which, of course, embodies Slaughter's vision of a global network of judges engaged in the "common enterprise of protecting human rights."[144] Most plainly and obviously, though, one thinks above all of Roosevelt: in the name of a common desire to make a more humane world order, a new legal framework must be created and put into effect.

In making this observation, it is also useful to return to Kundera. For as Kundera reminds us, movements of any kind – religious, political, national, and so on – are rooted in understandings of shared sentiment which he called "kitsch." For Kundera, kitsch is a feeling which in its very nature also contains an awareness that it is a feeling held in common with a multitude of others. Seeing a group of children running on a large expanse of grass in the sunlight, a character is moved to observe, "Now, that's what I call happiness." This image, that of children running on grass, is kitsch not because it is a feeling merely that it is "nice" to see children running on grass, but because even in communicating that sense of "niceness" the character also understands that the image is one which the rest of mankind is also moved to feel is nice. "Kitsch," Kundera tells us, "causes two tears to flow in quick succession. The first tear says: How nice to see children running on the grass! The second tear says: How nice to be moved, together with all mankind, by children running on the grass!" He concludes that "It is the second tear that makes kitsch kitsch."[145] Kitsch inheres in the understanding that even as one feels an emotion, one partakes in it with others.

Kitsch is at the heart of political movements for Kundera because such movements "rest not so much on rational attitudes as on the fantasies, images, words and archetypes that come together to make up this or that political kitsch."[146] In other words, these movements derive from feeling. But it is not feeling that an individual has alone. Rather, it is feeling that is shared: an emotion that is first felt, and then understood as being felt in communion with others. It is this commonality of emotion and, moreover, the very sense that there *is* such a commonality that gives such movements their power. This is what "intoxicates" their adherents and sets them on the path to action.

It is also what gives them their trajectory, because ultimately kitsch is an aesthetic ideal: that there can and should be an absolute "agreement with being."[147] It rests on the notion that, while there may be obstacles, there are in the end no complications or contradictions – there will be a final point of union between the world as it is, and the world as it is should be. ("All human rights are achieved for all," as the OHCHR would perhaps put it.) It is this which produces the desire for continuity and a feeling of forward momentum, and this which gives a movement its sense of purpose.

The work of Hauriou and these observations of Kundera's allow us to perceive the contemporary field of human rights in a particular light. First, they show us how a shared emotion, and an understanding in those who share it that it is indeed shared with others, can be the origin of, and driving force behind, movements of any kind, political or religious or otherwise. Second, they show us how this instils in such movements a sense of trajectory or continuity across time. And third, they show us that this trajectory or continuity is often given effect through law, intrinsic to which is the capacity to transmit feelings and ideas between past, present, and future so as to govern and control the latter. In combination, this allows us to see human rights as a purposive project which is rooted in emotion and given continued life through law. But it also allows us to define that project's directing idea as being to end human suffering through the placing of a responsibility on powerful agents – be they the State, businesses, international organisations, or otherwise – to act to improve the well-being of those under their care. At the root of human rights' purpose, in other words, lies the feeling of compassion: that something must be done.

Human rights and its directing idea

We have seen how modern human rights practice has resulted in an expanding range of positive legal duties (whether binding obligations or softer responsibilities) being placed on an increasing array of actors. The regime's "solipsism and imperialism," in this respect, has here been explained partly by its rooting in a shared sense of compassion for suffering which gives its adherents the will to act and particularly to do so through the creation and application of laws. This leads us to a summation of its directing idea – its purpose – as being to construct legal relationships of benevolent care in which the powerful are conceptualised as having the duty of improving the well-being of the powerless.

This, of course, is also what unites what I earlier described as being the constitutional and instrumental senses in which human rights are purposive. While the deployment of human rights language and the imposition of human rights obligations to ameliorate childhood obesity or the harmful effects of tobacco smoke on children may have no explicit and obvious connection to the constitutionalist vision of the role of human rights in a global society, when boiled down to their essence such usages of human rights clearly share a broader impulse. It is the imagining of human rights as the means by which well-being can be secured. That is, human rights become thereby conceived not merely as limitations on the capacity of the State, or indeed other powerful actors, to interfere with the freedom of subjects. Rather, they become conceived as the justifications for the State and such powerful actors to take on benevolent roles towards the powerless. Such actors become, in effect, made responsible for improving human well-being, not merely for securing freedom from interference. This may take place at the grandest scale of an incipient global constitution based on the universal promotion of human welfare, or at the most relatively minor, such as the prevention of childhood obesity.

It is, of course, this which Koskenniemi would describe as being the transformation of human rights into a purposive or managerial regime, and which Oakeshott would see as a drift within the field of human rights towards a *teleocratic* mode. Human rights advocates, driven by compassion, the unwillingness to watch others suffer, read human rights as declaratory of the principles of a directing idea: human well-being secured through the benevolent actions of the powerful. This provides a lens through which all human rights law is conceived, such that it is consistently read as being the legal mechanism for securing that particular "moral truth."

This directing idea is, of course, extremely amorphous and broad. Indeed, it is almost a floating signifier, capable in any context of being interpreted to mean more or less anything – with, it will be remembered, "the right amount of ingenuity." This is, as we saw so clearly in Chapter 1, the cause of its imperialism – its rapid and boundless sense of expansion, and its unwillingness to accept limitations. Why, indeed, accept the traditional limitations placed on the purview of human rights by sovereignty, when there are values (such as universal human well-being) which "deeply [cut] across" those precepts?[148] Why talk about such outmoded legalistic concepts as Article 2 (7) of the UN Charter when the "simple language of the Universal Declaration" provides the justification to act?[149] Why let what Koskenniemi sarcastically referred to as law's "archaic *mores*" hold back the "politics of cosmopolitan dreams"?[150] As Arendt put it, once the "magic of compassion" has "opened the heart,"[151] the "processes of persuasion, negotiation and compromise" (which might be said to be at the heart of traditional international law-making) seem only "wearisome."[152]

The result, as we have already observed, is dissatisfaction with formal law-making and enforcement and an attraction towards the "contextual *ad hoc*-ism" of concepts such as governance or regulation. If the purpose is to improve human well-being, then the strictures of legal rules should be rendered more flexible. One should not focus mainly on doctrinal matters but balance legal requirements against the broader concept of legitimacy.[153] Roberts, speaking about humanitarian intervention but in terms which could apply much more broadly across the system of international human rights law in general, expresses no concern that the concept is "shrouded in "legal ambiguity," because that allows a more flexible principles-based approach that can "reflect the perspectives and interests" of various parties in any particular circumstance.[154] That stands, indeed, for the general approach taken by the UN treaty bodies and charter mechanisms to human rights law; their recommendations and statements are generally described ambivalently as "authoritative" without being binding, or perhaps as statements of soft law, which allows them to issue interpretations with a degree of looseness which would not generally be considered appropriate in a domestic court.[155] But it even applies to the jurisprudence of the ECtHR, which as we have seen retains the flexibility to interpret the Convention teleologically so as to realise "moral truths" from case to case.

This provides us with a particular viewpoint on the turn to managerialism in international human rights law. Compassion gives rise to a particular directing idea, which sees the promotion of human well-being as an aim to be realised through the (voluntary or forced) benevolence of powerful actors. This gives rise to a sense of the law as, at worst, a body of "archaic mores" to be ignored, but at best as a set of declared purposes, and obligations specifying how they are to be achieved. The next stage naturally then becomes how to implement those purposes and give effect to those obligations through managerial techniques. We see in this schema, in other words, precisely how it is that international human rights law might begin to orient itself away from *nomocracy* and towards *teleocracy*, or away from formal limitations and towards purposive and programmatic regulation. And what we see in turn is human rights becoming a matter of governance. That is the subject of the next chapter.

Notes

1 M. Hauriou, "The Theory of the Institution and the Foundation: A Study in Social Vitalism," in A. Broderick (ed.), *The French Institutionalists: Maurice Hauriou, Georges Renard, Joseph T Delos* (Harvard University Press, 1970), 93.
2 This is at least partly the project, for instance, of C. Beitz, *The Idea of Human Rights* (Oxford University Press, 2009).
3 EHRC, *Strategic Plan 2019–22*, available at www.equalityhumanrights.com/en/publication-download/strategic-plan-2019-2022 (accessed 29th November 2019), p. 18.
4 Charter of the United Nations, Preamble.
5 There are myriad formulations of this notion. See e.g., W. Moka-Mubelo, "Human Rights and Human Dignity," in *Reconciling Law and Morality in Human Rights Discourse: Beyond the Habermasian Account of Human Rights* (Springer, 2017), pp. 89–125.
6 Human Rights Council, Report of the Special Rapporteur on extreme poverty and human rights, UN Doc. A/HRC/29/31 (2015), Summary.
7 OHCHR, *From Exclusion to Equality: Realizing the Rights of Persons with Disabilities* (OHCHR, 2007), available at www.ohchr.org/Documents/Publications/training14en.pdf (accessed 18th November 2020), p. iv.
8 *Ibid.*, p. 19.
9 M. Oakeshott, "Rationalism in Politics," in *Rationalism in Politics and Other Essays* (Methuen, 1962), 1.
10 OHCHR, *United Nations Human Rights Management Plan 2018–2021*, available at www.ohchr.org/Documents/Publications/OMP_II.pdf (accessed 29th November 2019), p. 5.
11 *Ibid.*, p. 6.
12 *Ibid.*
13 *Ibid.*
14 *Ibid.*, p. 7.
15 *Ibid.*
16 A. Pellet, "Human Rightism and International Law," Gilberto Amado Memorial Lecture, 10, *Italian Yearbook of International Law* (Brill, 2000), 1, pp. 1–3.

17 State of the Union Address of 6th January 1941, Franklin D. Roosevelt Presidential Library and Museum, available at https://www.fdrlibrary.org/documents/356632/390886/readingcopy.pdf/42234a77-8127-4015-95af-bcf8 31db311d (accessed 29th November 2019), pp. 21–22.

18 The history and historiography of human rights is, at the time of writing, undergoing something of a boom, but an especially useful account is provided in M. Mazower, *Governing the World: The History of an Idea* (Penguin, 2012), pp. 317–331. See, also, J. Eckel and S. Moyn (eds), *The Breakthrough: Human Rights in the 1970s* (University of Pennsylvania Press, 2014).

19 This is effectively the OHCHR's mission statement. See OHCHR, "Our Priorities," available at https://www.ohchr.org/EN/newyork/Pages/Ourprioriti es.aspx (accessed 29th November 2019).

20 J. Mendez and C. Cone, "Human Rights Make A Difference: Lessons from Latin America," in D. Shelton (ed.), *The Oxford Handbook of International Human Rights Law* (Oxford University Press, 2015), 955, p. 955.

21 CESCR, General Comment No. 3, UN Doc. E/1991/23 (1990), para. 9.

22 See e.g., K. Cope, C. Crabtree, and Y. Lupu, "Beyond Physical Integrity," 81, *Law & Contemporary Problems* (2018) 185, p. 185.

23 S. Fukuda-Parr, T. Rawson-Lemer and S. Randolph, *Fulfilling Social and Economic Rights* (Oxford University Press, 2015), p. 1.

24 J. Ferrie, R. Wallace, and E. Webster, "Realising International Human Rights: Scotland on the World Stage," 22 (1), *The International Journal of Human Rights* (2017) 1, p. 1.

25 A. Nolan, N. Lusiani, and C. Courtis, "Two Steps Forward, No Steps Back? Evolving Criteria on the Prohibition of Retrogression in Economic and Social Rights," in A. Nolan (ed.), *Economic and Social Rights After the Global Financial Crisis* (Cambridge University Press, 2014), 121.

26 B. Simma, "Mainstreaming Human Rights: The Contribution of the International Court of Justice," 3 (1), *Journal of International Dispute Settlement* (2012) 7, p. 25.

27 Human Rights Council, 40th Session, General debate under item 5, Statement by Dainius Puras, Chairperson of the Coordination Committee of Special Procedures, 13th March 2019, available at https://www.ohchr.org/Document s/HRBodies/SP/HRC40_ChairItem5_13_March2019.docx (accessed 29th November 2019), p. 2.

28 S. Moyn, "Epilogue," in S. Moyn, *Human Rights and the Uses of History* (Verso, 2014), p. 146.

29 EHRC, *Strategic Plan 2019–22*, p. 19.

30 OHCHR, *UN Human Rights Report 2018*, available at www.ohchr.org/Documents/Publications/OHCHRreport2018.pdf (accessed 29th November 2019), Foreword, p. 5.

31 C. Trindade, *International Law for Humankind* (Brill, 2010), p. 4.

32 H. Lauterpacht, *International Law and Human Rights* (Stevens & Sons, 1950).

33 OHCHR, *United Nations Human Rights Appeal 2019*, available at www.ohchr.org/Documents/Publications/AnnualAppeal2019.pdf.

34 *Ibid.*, p. 11.

35 *Ibid.*, p. 4.

36 H. Grotius, *De iure belli ac pacis* [1625] (Cambridge University Press, 2012; trans. S. Neff).

37 S. von Pufendorf, *De iure naturae et gentium* [1672] (Oceana, 1964; trans. W. Oldfather and C. Oldfather).

38 E. de Vattel, *The Law of Nations: Or, Principles of the Law of Nature Applied to the Conduct and Affairs of Nations and Sovereigns* [1758/1797] (Liberty Fund, 2008; ed. R. Whatmore, trans. Anon.).

39 J. Bentham, *An Introduction to the Principles and Morals of Legislation* [1789] (Oxford University Press, 1970; ed. J. Burns and H. L. A. Hart) and "Plan for An Universal and Perpetual Peace," in *The Principles of International Law* [1786–1789] (Sweet & Maxwell, 1927).

40 I. Kant, *Perpetual Peace: A Philosophical Sketch* [1795] (Hacket Classics, 2003; trans. T. Humphrey).

41 See e.g., J. D'Aspremont, "The Foundations of the International Legal Order," 18, *Finnish Yearbook of International Law* (2007) 219.

42 See M. Koskenniemi, "Law, Teleology and International Relations: An Essay in Counterdisciplinarity," 26 (1), *International Relations* (2011) 3, esp. pp. 3–9.

43 See e.g., J. Klabbers, "Constitutionalism Lite," 1, *International Organizations Law Review* (2004) 31; C. Schwoebel, "The Appeal of the Project of Global Constitutionalism to Public International Lawyers," 13, *German Law Journal* (2012) 22.

44 M. Koskenniemi, "Between Coordination and Constitution: International Law as a German Discipline," 15, *Rediscriptions* (2011) 45, p. 63. See also S. Kadelbach, T. Kleinlein and D. Roth-Isigkeit (eds), *System, Order and International Law* (Oxford University Press, 2017).

45 E. de Wet, "International Constitutional Order," 55, *International & Comparative Law Quarterly* (2006) 51.

46 C. Schwoebel, "Situation the Debate on Global Constitutionalism," 8, *International Journal of Constitutional Law* (2010) 611.

47 See B. Kingsbury, N. Krisch, R. Stewart and J. Wiener, "Foreword: Global Governance as Administration – National and Transnational Approaches to Global Administrative Law," 68, *Law & Contemporary Problems* (2005) 68, p. 4.

48 M-S. Kuo, "Taming Governance with Legality?" 44, *NYU Journal of International Law & Politics* (2011–2012) 55, p. 103.

49 G. Teubner, *Constitutional Fragments: Societal Constitutionalism and Globalization* (Oxford University Press, 2012).

50 P. Zumbansen, "Defining the Space of Transnational Law: Legal Theory, Global Governance, and Legal Pluralism," 21, *Transnational Law & Contemporary Problems* (2012–2013) 305, p. 309.

51 N. Luhmann, *Political Theory in the Welfare State* [1981] (Walter de Gruyter, 1991; trans. J. Bednarz Jr), p. 22.

52 L. Cata Backer, "Transnational Corporations' Outward Expression of Inward Self-Constitution: The Enforcement of Human Rights by Apple, Inc.," 20 (2), *Indiana Journal of Global Legal Studies* (2013) 805, p. 810.

53 C. Thornhill, "A Sociology of Constituent Power: The Political Code of Transnational Societal Constitutions," 20 (2), *Indiana Journal of Global Legal Studies* (2013) 551, esp. pp. 576–577.

54 See e.g., D. Kennedy, "The Mystery of Global Governance," 34, *Ohio Northern University Law Review* (2008) 827.

55 N. Krisch, "Global Administrative Law and the Constitutional Ambition," in P. Dubner and M. Loughlin (eds), *The Twilight of Constitutionalism* (Oxford University Press, 2010), p. 252.

56 S. Scheingold, *The Politics of Rights: Lawyers, Public Policy and Political Change* (2nd edition, University of Michigan Press, 2011), p. xxi.

57 P. Macklem, "What is International Human Rights Law? Three Applications of a Distributive Account," 52, *McGill Law Journal* (2007) 575, pp. 586–588 (emphasis added).

58 See A. M. Slaughter, *A New World Order* (Princeton University Press, 2005), p. 81.

59 *Ireland v. UK*, App no. 5310/71 (ECtHR, 1978).

60 *Caesar Case*, Inter-American Court of Human Rights, Series C no. 123 (2005), separate opinion of Judge Trindade, para. 7.

61 B. Fassbender, "The United Nations Charter as Constitution of the International Community," 36, *Columbia Journal of Transnational Law* (1998) 529, esp. at pp. 616–619.

62 C. Tomuschat, "Obligations Arising for States Without or Against Their Will," 241, *Recueil des Cours* (1993) 195, p. 211.

63 J. Waldron, "The Rule of International Law," 30, *Harvard Journal of Law & Public Policy* (2006) 15, p. 17.

64 A. Peters, "Global Constitutionalism," in M. Gibbons (ed.), *The Encyclopedia of Political Thought* (Wiley, 2015), 1484, pp. 1485–1486.

65 J. Waldron, "Are Sovereigns Entitled to the Benefit of the International Rule of Law?" 22 (2), *European Journal of International Law* (2011) 315, p. 325.

66 *Ibid.*

67 *Ibid.*, pp. 325–326.

68 *Ibid.*, pp. 327–337.

69 *Ibid.*

70 E. Criddle and E. Fox-Decent, *Fiduciaries of Humanity* (Oxford University Press, 2016), p. 3.

71 *Ibid.*

72 *Ibid.*, p. 46.

73 *Ibid.*

74 *Ibid.*

75 K. Annan, Annual Address to the General Assembly, UN Doc. SG/SM/7136, 20th September 1999.

76	Centre for Human Rights, *Human Rights and Social Work: A Manual for Schools of Social Work and the Social Work Profession* (UN Publications, 1994), para. 19–20.

77	Human Rights Council, Report of the Special Rapporteur on the right of everyone to the enjoyment of the highest attainable standard of physical and mental health, UN Doc. HRC/41/34 (2019).

78	*Ibid.*, Summary.

79	*Ibid.*, para. 5.

80	*Ibid.*, para. 1.

81	*Ibid.*, para. 20.

82	*Ibid.*

83	*Ibid.*, paras 21–23.

84	*Ibid.*, paras 59, 58, 61, 64, 68, and 79, respectively.

85	*Ibid.*, para. 8.

86	*Ibid.*, para. 12.

87	M. Friedman, *Capitalism and Freedom* (University of Chicago Press, 1982), Preface.

88	K. O Cathaoir, "Children's Right to Freedom from Obesity: Responsibilities of the Food Industry," 36 (2), *Nordic Journal of Human Rights* (2018) 109, p. 109.

89	See e.g., A. Garde, "Advertising Regulation and the Protection of Children-Consumers in the European Union: In the Best Interests of … Commercial Operators?" 19, *International Journal of Children's Rights* (2011) 523; E. Handsley, C. Nehmy, K. Mehta, and J. Coveney, "A Children's Rights Perspective on Food Advertising to Children," 22 *International Journal of Children's Rights* (2014) 93.

90	O Cathaoir, "Children's Right to Freedom from Obesity."

91	*Ibid.*, pp. 117–120.

92	*Ibid.*, p. 130.

93	M. Gispen and B. Toebes, "The Human Rights of Children in Tobacco Control," 41 (2), *Human Rights Quarterly* (2019) 340.

94	*Ibid.*, pp. 340–341.

95	*Ibid.*, p. 341.

96	*Ibid.*, pp. 344–345.

97	*Ibid.*, p. 345.

98	*Ibid.*

99	Hauriou, "Theory of the Institution and the Foundation," p. 123.

100	*Ibid.*, pp. 101–102.

101	*Ibid.*, p. 101.

102	*Ibid.*, p. 102.

103	*Ibid.*, p. 123.

104	*Ibid.*, p. 103.

105	*Ibid.*

106	*Ibid.*

107	*Ibid.*, p. 108.

108 *Ibid.*
109 *Ibid.*
110 *Ibid.*, p. 107.
111 *Ibid.*, p. 108.
112 *Ibid.*
113 *Ibid.*, pp. 112–113.
114 *Ibid.*, p. 113.
115 *Ibid.*, p. 100.
116 *Ibid.*, p. 113.
117 *Ibid.*, pp. 113–114.
118 *Ibid.*, p. 99.
119 *Ibid.*, pp. 93–99.
120 *Ibid.*, p. 123.
121 *Ibid.*
122 *Ibid.*
123 M. Kundera, *The Unbearable Lightness of Being* (Faber & Faber, 1999; trans. M. Heim), p. 19.
124 *Ibid.*, p. 20.
125 H. Arendt, *On Revolution* (Viking Press, 1965), p. 65.
126 *Ibid.*
127 *Ibid.*, citing Rousseau.
128 *Ibid.*, p. 54.
129 *Ibid.*, p. 74.
130 *Ibid.*, p. 66.
131 Hunt, *Inventing Human Rights: A History* (WW Norton, 2007), pp. 30–34.
132 G. Robertson, *Crimes Against Humanity: The Struggle for Global Justice* (Penguin, 1999), p. 82.
133 K. Booth, "Three Tyrannies," in T. Dunne and N. Wheeler (eds), *Human Rights in Global Politics* (Cambridge University Press, 1999), 31, p. 66.
134 U. Baxi, "Voices of Suffering and the Future of Human Rights," 8, *Transnational Law and Contemporary Problems* (1998) 125, p. 127.
135 S. Wheatley, *The Idea of International Human Rights Law* (Oxford University Press, 2019), pp. 82–83.
136 K. Gunther, "The Legacies of Injustice and Fear: A European Approach to Human Rights and Their Effects on Political Culture," in P. Alston, M. Bustelo and J. Heenan (eds), *The EU and Human Rights* (Oxford University Press, 1999), 117, p. 126.
137 M. Goodhart (ed.), *Human Rights: Politics and Practice* (2nd edition, Oxford University Press, 2012).
138 *Ibid.*
139 *Ibid.*, p. 2.
140 P. Alston and R. Goodman (eds), *International Human Rights: Text and Materials* (Oxford University Press, 2013).
141 Statement by D. Puras.
142 S. Moyn, "Epilogue."

143 See e.g., C. McCrudden, "A Common Law of Human Rights?: Transnational Judicial Conversations on Constitutional Rights," 20, *Oxford Journal of Legal Studies* (2000) 499, or the useful overview provided by De Schutter in *International Human Rights Law: Text, Cases and Materials* (3rd edition, Oxford University Press 2019), pp. 36–57.

144 Slaughter, *A New World Order.*

145 M. Kundera, *The Unbearable Lightness of Being*, p. 248.

146 *Ibid.*, p. 254.

147 *Ibid.*, p. 246.

148 A. Bianchi, "Immunity versus Human Rights: The Pinochet Case," 10, *European Journal of International Law* (1999) 237, p. 260.

149 Robertson, *Crimes Against Humanity.*

150 D. Archibulgi, "Demos and Cosmopolis," 13, *New Left Review* (2002) 24.

151 Arendt, *On Revolution*, p. 76.

152 *Ibid.*, p. 82.

153 A. Roberts, "The So-Called 'Right' of Humanitarian Intervention," 3, *Yearbook of International Humanitarian Law* (2000) 3.

154 *Ibid.*, p. 51.

155 See e.g., M. O'Flaherty, "The Concluding Observations of the United Nations Human Rights Treaty Bodies," 6, *Human Rights Law Review* (2006) 27, M. Scheinin, "International Mechanisms and Procedures for Implementation," in R. Hanski and M. Suksi (eds), *An Introduction to the International Protection of Human Rights* (Institute for Human Rights, 1997), 369.

4

The governmentalisation of global human rights governance

You know, ultimately we should judge any system, shouldn't we, by whether or not in the end it maximizes human welfare?
(Matthew Taylor, "The Fall of the Berlin Wall,"
The Moral Maze, BBC Radio 4 6th November 2019)

Introduction

We have seen in previous chapters, then, why it is that law will take on a *teleocratic* orientation, driven by the directing idea of making the powerful responsible for the well-being of the powerless, and hence being construed as declaratory of purposes and specifying the methods by which they are to be achieved. We turn, now, to the consequences of this. These are described by both Koskenniemi and Oakeshott with the word "managerial," and it is clear that they both mean something broadly similar with the use of that term. In short, this can be taken to be an interest in achieving the outcomes which law declares or mandates through programmatic action.

This is a useful and important observation, but it only takes us to the threshold of understanding what managerialism, in this sense, entails. Having established that it constitutes the technical implementation of outcomes, we must then investigate what this means in practice, so as to properly understand its effects. Here, we are drawn inevitably to the work of Michel Foucault, particularly with respect to the influential concept of governmentality which he developed later in his life. As we shall see, Foucault trod over much of the same ground as Oakeshott in theorising the history of this particular form of political rationality. And he did so in such a way that, when he is read alongside Oakeshott, it gives a very rich perspective on the way in which international human rights law is developing. This is because it gives us an understanding of how the mixture of historical conditions and ideas about the role of rulership in a particular context can produce a certain governing style, which is on clear display in the structure which international human rights law has taken. This governing style, highly technical and abstract, and primarily functioning through indirect "tactics" rather than binding law, closely mirrors and indeed springs from the same phenomena which Foucault identified in the history of the State. Observing this allows us then to consider the nature and effects of that governing style in detail. That is the project of the last two chapters of this book.

This chapter begins by describing Foucault's thinking on the nature of law within the modern State, and then widening the discussion to his history of the development of Statehood. In doing this, I draw on the work of Oakeshott to further elucidate that narrative. Ultimately, as we shall see, in combination the accounts of these thinkers produce a rich understanding of the origins and effects of the conception of the State as having the purpose of improving human well-being. In particular, they furnish us with an understanding of the role that law occupies in such notions of Statehood, and the way in which it gives rise to highly complex and pervasive regulatory techniques or tactics in order to achieve wide-ranging effects across societies and populations. In the third section, I discuss how an analogous process, based on analogous reasons, is taking place in the field of something which I will call – following in Foucault's tradition of "ugly" terminology[1] – the "governmentalisation of global human rights governance."

Foucault on law and government

The juridico-legal, disciplinary, and security modalities

Foucault's thoughts as they concern law have been subject to a certain amount of discussion.[2] This is not the place to enter that debate. This is because much of the writing on the subject has been dominated, naturally enough, in reference to the penal system and the criminal law, which is only a very small part of a modern legal system and not the specific area of interest for this book. In this section, I am chiefly concerned with the picture which Foucault paints of law within the framework of the development of the modern State. Put somewhat crudely, this is how law functions with respect to rulership in that context.

He begins his discussion here by setting out three different mechanisms or modalities by which rule is constituted.[3] In doing so, he uses the "simple, childish" example of a ruler's concern with theft. How, one might ask, does a ruler respond to that phenomenon? In the first place, there is the legal or juridical response: "laying down a law and fixing a punishment for the person who breaks it."[4] Hence, there is a law prohibiting theft, and a punishment stipulated. Second, there is the disciplinary mechanism (which of course Foucault elaborated on in much more detail elsewhere),[5] that is contingent on the existence of a prohibitive law, but which aims to prevent the breaking of the rule in advance and correct such breaches, if they do take place, retrospectively. Hence, surveillance takes place to attempt to discourage theft before it is committed, and punishment takes on a corrective or transformational aspect.[6]

Third and finally, however, there is an additional modulation layered upon those mechanisms, called the "apparatus of security"[7] – namely, those efforts to "keep a type of criminality, theft for instance, within socially and economically acceptable limits and around an average that will be considered as optimal for a given social functioning."[8] What are relevant to security are questions such as, what is the average rate of theft in the population and what will increase or reduce it? What is the generalised economic cost of theft on society? What is the cost of policing and preventing it? And does the cost of prevention outweigh the cost of non-prevention?[9] Put another way, it is an interest in theft as a naturalised phenomenon: as probabilistic, as calculable (and therefore subject to cost-benefit analysis), and as non-binary (i.e., not absolutely prohibited or permitted, but permitted within accepted bounds).[10] Notably, it is an interest in theft that is amoral. It understands the phenomenon as natural and hence neither good nor evil: "it is what it is."[11] It is not to be eliminated, but rather to be regulated – to be kept at a level which is socially optimal in terms of cost-benefit vis-à-vis the expense of policing and deterring it.

What naturally follows, then, is for the analysis to "move back a notch"[12] – to abstract itself from the underlying phenomenon (of, for example, individual instances of theft) to factors which ultimately might seem remote but which are known (or thought to be known) to affect its overall prevalence. The main aim ceases be to get subjects to obey the law or the sovereign's will – i.e., to get them not to steal – but rather "having a hold on things that seem far removed from the population, but which, through calculation, analysis and reflection, one knows can really have an effect on it."[13] The aim, in other words, becomes the indirect manipulation of factors remote from the underlying phenomenon in an attempt to control it and keep it within optimal bounds.

Governmentality

Foucault was at pains to emphasise that what he was calling security did not replace or "bracket off" the disciplinary or juridico-legal modalities. Nor was the relationship between those three different modalities to be understood as a shift from one particular era to another. All three have always been present to some degree or other, and in some form, in the way in which rule is constituted. What changes are the *type* of techniques which each modality deploys and the level of their complexity, and also the relationships or "correlations" between the three of them.[14] What he argued in his forthcoming lectures was that a way of thinking about power from the perspective of security – a striking development in both its own complexity and its correlations with the disciplinary and juridico-legal modalities – emerged, distinct and new, in the sixteenth and seventeenth centuries, and it was this which could be understood by the word "governmentality."

This concept has proved highly influential, and has given rise to a very extensive range of academic literature.[15] This should not lead one into the error of being doctrinaire. Governmentality is a fungible notion, and Foucault never gave, nor apparently intended there to be, a fixed definition. It is rather presented as a new formulation of the relationship between the juridico-legal, disciplinary, and security modalities, with the emphasis on how the connections between them strengthen the latter. Nonetheless, it is possible to tease out some of the main characteristics of governmentality, and of these there are five.

The first is that governmentality takes as its primary object the population, rather than the territory or the individual. Whereas, before the notion of government had "broken out," the concern of the sovereign was essentially that of Machiavelli – how the Prince could hold on to his territory[16] – it became, afterwards, something altogether more pervasive: improving the health, welfare, prosperity, and happiness of the population as a distinct object in its own right. And while individuals are hardly immaterial in this, they are not the ends, as it were, but only the means:

> The final objective is the population. The population is pertinent as the objective, and individuals, the series of individuals, are no longer pertinent as the objective, but simply as the instrument, relay, or condition for obtaining something at the level of the population.[17]

Governmentality operates, that is, at the level of generality. It leaves details – what is taking place at the individual level – alone, to be "what they are"; to be simply part of what is taking place "situated at the level of the population."[18] Put very crudely, governmentality's purview is not the individual theft, the individual suicide, or the individual illiterate. It is the rate of theft within the population, the suicide rate, and the literacy rate; what can be done to improve them; what the cost of such improvements might be and whether the cost would be worth the potential result; and so on.

Second, governmentality is concerned with what Foucault called the "intrication" or "complex" between "men and things."[19] In acting at the level of the population and what can be known to affect phenomena occurring within it, one must not interest oneself particularly in the people themselves. They cannot be simply forced or commanded to become healthier, wealthier, and so on. Rather, one must interest oneself in the world of objects and how those objects affect the ways in which the people conduct (and improve) themselves. Two of Foucault's own examples will serve to illustrate. The first of these is the proposed design of the town of Nantes in the eighteenth century. Here, the aim was not to reconstruct the town in detail. Rather, it was to achieve particular ends through working with "givens" – maximising existing positive elements in the town, and minimising negative ones.[20] This meant, in essence, simply cutting new routes through the town and widening streets. This would have the effect of improving hygiene by opening up densely crowded areas, improving the internal circulation of trade in the town, connecting this trade with the outside world through better links to roads leading elsewhere, and improving surveillance.[21] In other words, through manipulating things – roads – one would indirectly be able to increase the health, wealth, and security of the town's population (or, more properly, one would ensure that the population would increase *its own* health, wealth, and security). The second example is grain. Whereas scarcity of grain would, in the past, have been remedied with juridical methods such as the prohibiting of hoarding, prohibits on exports, and price controls, in the era of governmentality the new concept of economy does the opposite. It encourages the free circulation of grain through the removal of such restrictions. This allows prices to rise at times of scarcity, which will result in greater cultivation by peasants and hence abundance of production, followed by a proportionate decrease in prices. The problem of scarcity of grain, or what might be thought of more broadly as the health of the population, is remedied or improved not through close supervision at the level of detail but through allowing things to circulate.[22] The population is not made healthier through decree or command, but through acting on factors which are remote from questions of health at all – in order to create the conditions in which the population acts so as to become healthier. The result of this intervention at the nexus between "men and things" is that the aim of government can come to be described as "the right disposition of things arranged so as to lead to a suitable end," as La Perrière had put it.[23] More pithily, governmentality acts on humanity's "milieu."[24]

The third characteristic of governmentality is that it is predicated upon, and indeed must be realised through, freedom – in the sense of free circulation and movement. It "thinks before all else of men's freedom, of what they want to do, of what they have an interest in doing, and what they think about doing."[25] The regulation of the population can only be carried out "through and by reliance on the freedom of each" – freedom of movement, both of people and of things.[26] Indeed, failing to respect freedom is not merely an abuse of rights but a failure to govern properly.[27] This is because governing is fundamentally an exercise in framing conditions so that natural processes occurring within the population reach their full effect. It is about managing natural phenomena so that the ordinary impulses of the population result in its self-improvement. The basic principle of the State's role is to "get [natural processes] to work, or to work with them," and while this is a task which requires much intervention, this takes place at the level of facilitation and encouragement rather than prohibition or interdiction.[28] This should not be misunderstood as freedom untrammelled. Governmentality exists in the correlations between the juridico-legal, disciplinary, and security modalities even if it appears predicated on the latter. Rather, it should be understood as a structuring of the possibilities and limitations in which free action can take place. All of this is, of course, evident from Foucault's two examples of the design of Nantes and the free trade in grain, both of which concerned the removal of particular restrictions (physical and legal) to not only allow but to *stimulate* free circulation to take place for particular ends.

Fourth, governmentality must present itself primarily as an overweening interest in statistics, particularly statistical norms, for reasons which will be obvious. Statistical knowledge of the population provides both the raw material by which to understand exactly what natural phenomena are taking place within it, and also the justification for improvement or intervention. Statistics "[reveal] that the population possesses its own regularities: its death rate, its incidence of disease, its regularities of accidents"[29] – and, therefore, in their very production suggest and frame how the "governor" ought to act. Is the rate of disease straying beyond acceptable norms? And, if so, what if anything is to be done? "Wisdom," as Foucault puts it, discussing La Perriere, is "the knowledge of things, of the objectives that can and must be attained," and, naturally therefore, "the 'disposition' one must employ in order to attain them."[30] Statistics are the very stuff of this.

Fifth and finally, governmentality is composed largely of what Foucault refers to as techniques or "tactics" of government. Since its interest is in stimulation or facilitation of particular kinds of freedom within particular bounds, and since it takes as its point of intervention the nexus between "men and things," laws – at least laws in the prohibitive sense – are not the primary mode of operation for government. Rather, governmentality consists of, indeed is comprised by, tactics rather than laws – "the perfection, maximisation, or intensification of the processes [government] directs."[31] This does not mean that the juridico-legal modality is non-existent. Indeed, as we shall see, it has a significant role. It is rather that the way in which governmentality operates at its most pervasive extent is as a regulatory rather than a legal phenomenon: a matter of management rather than the imposition of duty. Ideally, as the bumblebee rules the beehive, in La Perrière's text, without need of a sting, it should be possible for government to take place without using the "sword" of the law but simply through the correct disposition of things.[32] It should be possible, for instance, to achieve greater wealth and improved health for the population of Nantes chiefly through the cutting of new roads – an activity which has its legal ramifications but is hardly to be achieved simply through the making of laws. From this observation, ultimately, we derive the description of governmentality as the "conducting of conduct" – the attempt to arrange the field in which the free conduct of the individuals comprising the population takes place, such that it results in desired ends.

Governmentality, then, can be understood as a way of thinking about rule which attempts to achieve its ends at the level of the population rather than the individual or the territory, and which functions through a relationship of abstraction or remoteness from it. This means its interest is in the general rather than the specific; in the nexus between "men and things"; in the recognition of and respect for freedom or at least free circulation; in statistical forms of knowledge; and in the deployment of regulatory or management-based techniques or tactics rather than laws to "conduct the conduct" of all of the multiplicity of individuals who comprise the population.

Governmentality and managerial law

Immediately, for the purposes of this monograph, I must first address Foucault's remark that governmentality concerns tactics rather than laws. As mentioned above, this does not mean that law ever disappears or becomes irrelevant. It means, rather, that the complex between what Foucault had originally called the juridico-legal, disciplinary, and security-based modalities changes its composition and form, such that the character of what we call "law" itself also changes. This is made clear by his comments in *The History of Sexuality* to the effect that law as a "juridical system" is in large part repurposed in modernity so as to take on a regulatory function.[33] The point is neither that law in its juridical form becomes outmoded (clearly, in the case of the criminal law this is hardly so), and nor that it is entirely replaced by policy or regulatory apparatus. Rather, it is that law begins in large part to take on the function of setting and maintaining the rules or principles within which the conducting of conduct will take place, such that it clusters around a particular "norm." Governmentality will hence necessarily involve the full range of juridico-legal, disciplinary, and security-based responses. This is because activities in the juridico-legal mode make those in the others possible.

A brief example to illustrate this comes in the form of minimum alcohol pricing in Scotland. Concerned about the effect of high levels of alcohol consumption on public health and public order, the Scottish Parliament passed a piece of legislation in 2012, the Alcohol (Minimum Pricing) (Scotland) Act. This stipulates that it is a condition of any licence granted to sell alcohol that it must be sold at or above a minimum price – currently 50p per unit.[34] Failing to comply with this condition will result in the revocation of the relevant license to sell alcohol, with any unlicensed sale being a criminal offence under the Licensing (Scotland) Act 2005. Here, we see a combination of all three of Foucault's modes of rule acting in consort to achieve a particular effect. First, in the juridico-legal sphere, we see the prohibition on the sale of alcohol below the minimum price, with according criminal sanction if this prohibition is breached. Second, in the disciplinary sphere, we see the requirement to evidence compliance with the terms of a license, under the oversight of Licensing Boards with the authority and power to grant, review, and revoke licenses. And third, in the sphere of security, we see the attempt to manipulate natural processes within the population (the drinking of alcohol) by permitting its unrestricted purchasing and consumption, while at the same time attempting to make it undesirable to sell alcohol (and, by implication, drink it) "irresponsibly" through the mechanism of increased cost.[35] Hence, law takes on a regulatory function by creating a framework within which free actions (the buying and selling of alcohol) can take place, in order that a particular social norm of responsible drinking is produced and behaviour becomes clustered around it. But this does not mean that law entirely loses its prohibitive or "hard" character. On the contrary, its prohibitive, punitive aspect is an important part of the "complex" which upholds that framework. And juridical institutions are far from absent in all of this. The decisions of Licensing Boards will of course be subject to judicial review, but the entire regime of minimum alcohol pricing was itself given the imprimatur of the UK Supreme Court in 2017 when that Court found in judicial review that the Alcohol (Minimum Pricing) Scotland Act 2012 was not in breach of the Treaty on the Functioning of the European Union (TFEU) as a measure having the effect of a quantitative restriction on imports.[36]

Another way of putting this will likely already have suggested itself to the reader: what we call "law" has an ambivalence for Foucault, just as much as for Oakeshott. It is capable of taking on different guises. It can be prohibitive but also permissive, restrictive or expansionary. And it can give rise to a very wide range of regulatory measures as equally as it can provide decisive and instant resolution. It, as Golder and Fitzpatrick put it, "vacillate[s]."[37] And this ambivalence means that law is always available to be put to the use of "interests" of various kinds.[38] "Rules are empty in themselves" and hence can be "bent to any purpose."[39] Law has no external existence, in other words, from which it acts to limit the application of government power – far from it. It is always available, acting in the correlation between the juridico-legal, disciplinary, and security modalities, to set out whatever framework is necessary to bring about desired ends.

Clearly, then, for Foucault, law can and does readily take on a managerial function in the modern State, but it does not do so simply through the expurgation or supervention of it in its juridical form. Rather, it does so through continually being repurposed to take on regulatory functions in a variety of different guises. And, indeed, this can even involve apparently restricting or limiting, through juridical prohibition, the capacity of the State to act. This allows the preservation of freedom, within particular bounds, so as to allow given natural processes within the population to flourish, and thereby produce desired effects. Hence, for example, EU law prohibits Member States from acting so as to restrict trade in goods between Members, and courts, enforce the relevant provisions of the TFEU accordingly, but it would be a mistake to conceptualise this as being a break or limitation on the application of rule. It is quite the opposite: it is the achievement of desired outcomes (European integration, economic growth, greater tax revenues, etc.) through indirect rule, operationalised by the limits imposed in law. Governmentality, in other words, frequently works *through* legal restriction of the application of direct State power.

There is a striking adjacency, then, between Foucault's thoughts in this respect and those of Oakeshott. If the former were to recognise the concept of the civil condition, he would almost certainly suggest that the trappings, as it were, of *lex* within that condition can just as well be repurposed – that is to say, deployed *for* purposes. This is not altogether different from the way in which Oakeshott presented his own understanding of law. It will be recalled that, for Oakeshott, *lex* was simply an abstract ideal, and that actual law as we find it in the world frequently bears little resemblance to it – like the civil condition as a whole, it is only "glimpsed here or there." There is no single rule which resembles *lex*, let alone a legal system as a whole. Any given rule will be at most a mixture of moral condition and purposive conclusion, of *nomos* and *telos*, and it is frequently the case that court proceedings, statutes, rights, and the like will appear in highly instrumental guises, in which indeed the ideal of *lex* is barely visible. Put very crudely, in actual human societies, all laws are *teleocratic* to some degree, because they are always capable of being used in such a way that they give rise to regulatory and bureaucratic apparatus which ultimately amount to the "conducting of conduct." Put in terms more recognisable within the framework of Foucault's analysis, law – even when appearing as a restriction on State power – can be "bent to any purpose." It is always ready to be utilised to give birth to a range of techniques for the conducting of conduct, precisely as in the example of minimum alcohol pricing which we examined above.

This casts Oakeshott's comments on law (that it is an "equivocal mixture" between conditions prescribing just conduct, and conclusions specifying purposes or the actions to be taken to achieve them), in a different light. It reveals them to be yet more complex than seen at first glance, and shows that even where law appears only to prescribe just conduct, it is always capable, in doing so, of specifying purposes, or of providing the framework within which purposes can be specified – and hence of giving rise to bodies of managerial regulation with those purposes in mind. And this, in turn, allows us to understand managerialism as an inherent potential within law itself – not in opposition to it, as Koskenniemi suggests, but an ever-present tendency. As Oakeshott puts it, speaking about the human dispositions which he thought of as the roots of *societas* and *universitas* but in terms which could just as well be applied to *lex* and law-as-rulebook, "they are not exactly foes; ... their relationship is that of 'sweet enemies'."[40] Neither concept of law can fully exclude the other.

But this also means that, however much it might take on its *teleocratic* guise, law also always retains its tendency to resemble *lex*. It retains its status as *nomos*, if faintly. No matter how far the path of *universitas* is trodden, for Oakeshott, it remains "restrained by an allegiance to the idea of *societas*." The "relics of the civil condition," *lex* among them, are always available to be "resuscitated."[41] In other words, one might say that while law is always capable of being bent to any purpose, it is never forced completely perpendicular. To return to a previous metaphor, law may be thought of as existing in the tension between the two poles of *nomos* and *telos*. It may be strongly pulled towards the former, and become increasingly "managerial" as a result. But it still remains suspended in tension between them.

This is partly because of simple reluctance, stemming from an "allegiance," to use Oakeshott's word, to *nomocracy*. No State is homogenous or monolithic, and there is a resistance to *teleocratic* law-making from citizens and civil society alike[42] – a "*libertin*" spirit which is "irrepressible."[43] This is not to be confused with *laissez-faire* or free-market capitalism but rather the traditions of civility.[44] Put bluntly, human beings tend to resist when they are commanded to do something by the State. And there is a long-standing commitment to a concept of law as *lex* that Oakeshott identified in thinkers from Kant to Bodin, to Spinoza and Hegel, and which will always find its own expression in politics.[45] This means that even in the most highly centrally-planned societies there will always be a "bow in the opposite direction."[46]

But it is also because of pure practicality. Laws can never simply be deployed, as it were, in a purely *teleocratic* sense in order to achieve desired purposes by decree. Here, it is helpful to return to Oakeshott's example of the rules of conduct in a fire station. An organisation such as a fire station may specify rules of conduct for its members to follow, but as Oakeshott was keen to emphasise, no unwanted fire will be put out merely because of the existence of such rules, even if the fire fighters always follow them. At its heart, this example simply points out the obvious fact that purposive human action cannot be successfully guided only by rules, even on an algorithmic or heuristic basis. No set of rules will ever be remotely complicated or detailed enough in its own right to provide a comprehensive series of commands for an agent to slavishly follow and unfailingly achieve the outcome desired in the absence of prior knowledge, resources, and other external factors. This is true enough for a fire station, where the rule, "You must always put out unwanted fires," for instance, has to rely among other things on the existing abilities of fire fighters to put out fires, to know what counts as an unwanted fire, to have the tools to do so, and so on. But it is, of course, much more true at the social scale or at the level of the population and natural phenomena occurring within it – the literacy rate, the suicide rate, or the prevalence of cholera, for example. Put very simply and crassly, if one wished to reduce the suicide rate within a population, for instance, one simply could not do so through creating rules alone, however "*teleocratic*" they might be. It is difficult, indeed, even to imagine what rules one could enact, given the inherent complexity of the underlying phenomenon, but that of course is only one problem. Others are that whether a person commits suicide or not is contingent on a wide range of factors which have little or nothing to do with law at all; that the existence of rules does not guarantee the resources necessary to comply with them; and that compliance with any given rule is hardly guaranteed in the first place. Foucault was well aware of this point, of course: "the variables on which population depends are such that ... it escapes ... voluntarist and direct action in the form of the law. If one says to a population 'do this', there is not only no guarantee that it *will* do it, but also there is quite simply no guarantee that it *can* do it."[47] As well as there being what might be called a philosophical reluctance to achieve purposes through *teleocratic* law, then, it is also frankly impossible to do so.

This point leads us to a crucial observation about the nature of governmentality, which is that it is produced within that very tension. Post-Foucauldian accounts of governmentality have tended to take contemporary neoliberalism as their subject.[48] But this unnecessarily fetters a true conception of the origin and extent of what governmentality is. It is entirely natural to fall into this mistake, given Foucault's own focus in the series of lectures which immediately followed those on governmentality – those collected under the title *The Birth of Biopolitics* – in which his almost exclusive concern was the history of liberalism and its development into neoliberalism.[49]

But while it is important, of course, to subject liberal governmentality to analysis and critique, to do so exclusively is to miss what it is that produces the need for modern rule to function in this way. That is, governmentality arises precisely from the tension at the heart of law between *nomos* and *telos*. On the one hand is law's capacity to declare and specify purposes, and the means of achieving them – which it does in its highly ambivalent fashion, through a mixture of both positive obligation and prohibition depending on the context and the particular mixture of the juridico-legal, disciplinary, and security modalities within it. On the other is the undesirability and impossibility of its obtaining desired results on its own by decree. Put in this way, one sees governmentality not as characteristic of any given form of political organisation, but rather the consequence of ineluctable conditions stemming from the law's irresolvable tension between *telos* and *nomos*.

Governmentality beyond liberal rights

What this means, in effect, is that wherever there are laws which declare purposes or specify the means of achieving them, or are conceptualised or read as doing so, there will be a requirement to "govern" accordingly – to act indirectly so as to bring about the desired end. This is why, indeed, it is increasingly common to describe forms of governmentality appearing in decidedly non-liberal contexts, such as in modern China,[50] Bangladesh,[51] or South-East Asia.[52] This puts the way human rights are typically thought of in relation to liberalism in a different light.

Roughly, the schema which is often sketched out in this regard is as follows. As the early modern period progressed, rule became increasingly concerned with what Foucault called "biopolitics" – "the attempt ... to rationalise problems posed to governmental practice by phenomena characteristic of a set of living beings forming a population: health, hygiene, birthrate, life expectancy, race."[53] (Much of this will of course be evident from our previous discussion.) In other words, for reasons which we will come to, the matter of government became increasingly focused on topics such as life and death, physical and mental health, procreation, and so on, and its aim to optimise those factors in the population as a whole. But this coincided, more or less, with two other factors – the discovery of the economy and the theory and practices of sovereignty – which provided methods for restraining or critiquing bio-politics. For the first of these, of course, this is because the recognition of the existence of an economy led inexorably towards the understanding that economic growth must in large part derive from free commerce. This imperative meant that the biopolitical impulse, if it can be called that, was naturally restrained by the need for "frugal" government at least within the economy.[54] For the second, sovereignty as it was understood in the eighteenth century was contingent upon a framework of *right*, both of the ruler and subjects, and the emergent rights of subjects were a clear buttress against any attempt to directly achieve biopolitical goals.

This makes liberalism, in the words of Dean, an "ethos of review" – an ever-present "[suspicion] that one is governing too much."[55] It is not so much that liberalism is contingent on the doctrine of a minimal State, but rather that the biopolitical impulse, which drives towards the coordinated and centralised administration of life, "will need to be weighed against the norms of economic processes and the norms derived from the democratization of the sovereign subject of right."[56]

So far so good, and it will of course be evident that this provides us with an understanding of the role played within liberalism by law as perhaps the most important element of that "ethos of review." Law will be deployed for purposes which can be described as biopolitical in precisely the fashion which I outlined earlier in the chapter when discussing the example of minimum pricing for alcohol – a policy which, it will have been observed, is practically the quintessence of that concept. But it will also act as a brake on such purposes, so as to prevent the biopolitical drive to optimise the health and well-being of the population from interfering very far into the field of commerce, or into the rights of subjects. And it will not have escaped the reader's attention that it will do that chiefly through the mechanism of judicial review, which allows judges to carefully monitor the extent of such interference through doctrines such as reasonableness and proportionality.

Which is to say, of course, that it is law's capacity to act both as *telos* and *nomos* which makes it so crucial within what we understand as liberalism. It can both instigate and shape actions so as to achieve biopolitical purposes (through licensing requirements and punishment of transgression), and it will also act as a brake on the attempted achievement of those purposes from going too far and hence undermining the "freedom" upon which liberalism is predicated.

But the story does not end there. We should not conclude from all of this that biopolitics sits in antagonistic opposition to the economy or sovereignty within the liberal schema. Quite the opposite. The tension between the three, and hence between *nomos* and *telos* in law, is a highly productive one. For in restraining direct intervention in the economy or the overriding of the autonomy of individual subjects, a range of different desirable outcomes will result. A free economy provides the stuff of material human well-being which itself maximises biological processes within the population; a system of democratised right provides a stable and enduring framework of power relations in which material human well-being can flourish in an acceptable fashion through the indirect manipulation of remote variables;

and so on. (Oakeshott of course made precisely this observation in noting that for the classical economists, the aim of government was to "provide satisfactions for wants" by refraining from "suspend[ing] or qualify[ing] [...] ordinary transactions [or] the civil conditions imposed upon them," except in emergency).[57] That is to say, even in acting to restrain the biopolitical urge, law's role is hardly one of stark refusal. In fact, it is often part of the complex array of different factors which bolster that urge – albeit indirectly.

This account of the role that law plays in liberalism is neat and plausible. It portrays law as flexible and labile, able in whatever form to foster the interests of power. And it provides us with an understanding of governmentality as in large part deriving from the attempt to reconcile the drive towards *universitas* with loyalty towards the trappings of *societas*. That is, one can readily conceptualise liberal modern rule as being fundamentally a matter of achieving biopolitical ends, whatever those might be, in light of the "ethos of review" provided by enduring conceptions of civil society, individual autonomy, and nomocratic law. One can then readily recognise governmentality as the means by which the former can be achieved not only in spite of, but *through*, the latter. And if one accepts this sketch, then it is a simple enough step to draw the conclusion that law, in providing both the declaratory purposes from which regulatory or managerial implementation derives, and the restrictive *nomos* through which purposive action is limited, is absolutely central to how governmentality operates within liberal rule. This puts the emergence of rights in a particular context, because of course if law, in all of its ambivalence, lies at the heart of governmentality, then rights lie at the heart of the role played by law. It is rights which provide the buffering or restraining conditions which liberal rule imposes on itself as an "ethos of review," because it is in the form of rights that individual autonomy – the freedom to act – which is the stuff of governmentality is maintained. Other such limitations may be imposed in other legal forms, but it is individual civil liberties which are at the core of liberalism's self-restraint. This point is obvious, and has been made many times. It could, indeed, be said to be the standard understanding of rights in critical scholarship deriving from the work of Foucault.

However, in the light of what has preceded this section, we are able to recognise this schema as being only one facet of a much bigger and more complicated shape. It may be true that rights can appear in this guise within the liberal context. But this does not limit the capacity for rights, like all legal concepts, to "vacillate" depending on that context. In certain places and times, and in certain correlations between the juridico-legal, disciplinary, and security modalities, rights will serve the function of "review" or self-restraint precisely along the lines drawn above. But in other such correlations, they will be used in altogether more *teleocratic* forms – as part of a much more straightforwardly regulatory function. The reader only needs, of course, to cast his or her mind back to the contents of the first chapter of this book to see this phenomenon in action. What else, after all, is the concept of a duty to "fulfil" human rights, other than a volte-face in the standard conception of rights as liberalism's "self-critique"?

Summary

Law, then, is at the crux of governmentality. Capable of being "bent to any purpose" because of its potential as *telos*, it is always imminently at work within the complex between Foucault's juridico-legal, disciplinary, and security modalities in the attempt to achieve ends. Yet its nature is also fundamentally inhibitory because of its inherent and ineluctable nature as *nomos*. It can declare purposes and specify actions to be carried out accordingly. But on its own, it cannot secure them. It is the contradiction between these two competing impulses, the "sweet enemies" of *nomos* and *telos*, which therefore produces governmentality. It is instigated by purposive impulses, and necessitated by the need to regulate or "govern" in spite of law's *nomocratic* vestiges and imperatives. To go back to our example of minimum alcohol pricing in Scotland, law cannot reduce levels of drinking to "responsible levels" through mandate or decree, because law on its own, being merely *nomocratic* rules despite the *teleocratic* impulse behind them, will not be able to achieve that result. But law can act so as to give rise to regulatory apparatuses or "tactics" in order to achieve the stated goal indirectly. Law will in other words inescapably give rise to governmentality in some form or other wherever it is enacted for purposive ends. And given that all human laws will be enacted with a purpose in mind to some extent, as Oakeshott was keen to emphasise, governmentality will always be a consequence to some degree of the creation of laws.

That governmentality is a much broader and more fundamental phenomenon than any given category of political organisation, be it liberalism or any other, and indeed more so than the State itself, should therefore be obvious. Governmentality is not a phenomenon that is present only in liberalism, but is, rather, a necessary consequence of the purposive deployment of law. Foucault did not make this explicit. But he did make it absolutely plain that governmentality was a concept of much wider and more extensive scope than liberal Statehood. Indeed, it was a concept which extended far beyond the limits of Statehood *per se*: "the State is [only] an episode in governmentality."[58] Not *vice versa*.

This means, obviously, that governmentality will also be a productive concept for understanding the results of the purposive deployment of law (its *teleocratic* orientation) in the international sphere, as well. But in order to establish that more fully, it is necessary first to chart the history of the concept in greater depth.

Foucault and Oakeshott on the governmentalisation of the State

Foucault and Oakeshott cover much of the same ground in the *Security, Territory, Population* lectures and the final essay of *On Human Conduct*, respectively.[59] If that ground can be given a name, it would be the history, not exactly of the State, but of what Foucault calls "reflected practice" concerning it.[60] We have already examined a portion of Oakeshott's thoughts in that regard. As we shall now see, there are more examples of what I have previously described as the "striking adjacency" between their accounts on this subject. Put at its simplest, this is because both men ultimately arrive at the conclusion that the State, as we understand it, has come to us at the end of a long history of conscious and concerted reflection on what it means to govern in that particular form, and that underlying that history is a sense that the State is and should be driven by a purpose of a particular kind: the well-being of the population.

Foucault on the shepherd-flock and city-citizen games

Foucault frames his thoughts concerning "reflected practice" on the State by presenting an opposition between Greek and Hebraic/Christian concepts of government. In the former, the object of government is a thing: the city-state itself. The king governs as a helmsman or captain guides a ship, steering for it a safe course and avoiding danger, his "target" being "the city-state in its substantial reality, its unity, and its possible survival or disappearance."[61] And Greek religion illustrates this. The Greek god is a territorial god, one who founds a city and protects it, who "appears on the walls to defend his town."[62] The ruler is not concerned with directly governing the individuals living in the city-state and has no particular interest in them as individuals. They simply happen to live within the city and are themselves almost incidentally kept safe by virtue of that fact. The ruler does not interfere in their day-to-day lives; his object is rather to ensure that the city-state continues to exist – "what he leaves behind him is a strong city with laws enabling it to endure without him."[63]

By contrast, according to Foucault, in the ancient Near Eastern conception of power, particularly in that of the Hebrews (and ultimately therefore of Christians), the object of government is not things, but people themselves:

power is exercised over a flock.[64] Where the Greek god is a territorial one, the Hebrew God is a shepherd, whose interest is not territorial integrity or the ongoing existence of the polity but rather the well-being – spiritual as well as physical – of his people. His is a power which is exercised directly on people, who are its "target" just as the city-state is the target for the Greek ruler, and this gives it a markedly different character from that understood by the Greeks. Power in this context is characterised by *guidance*: a shepherd does not govern territory but leads a flock as it moves from place to place.[65] This makes it a power with a particular kind of purpose for those who are governed: to gather them together and lead them to fresh pastures, as distinct from power exercised merely for the purpose of the endurance of some superior unit such as the city-state or sovereign.[66] This also means that power in this mode is fundamentally *benevolent*. It is an exercise in "kindness."[67] Where power for the Greeks was characterised by its wealth and splendour, and defined as much by its ability to triumph over enemies and reduce them to slaves as to keep the polity safe, the aim of the Hebrew shepherd-God is only to do good: to ensure the salvation of the flock, to provide it with subsistence, to keep watch over it, to reduce its suffering, to treat those who are injured, and so on. It is a form of power which is "always a good in itself."[68] And this benevolent power of the shepherd is also *individualising*. The shepherd may direct the whole flock, but he also looks after each member individually: he counts them in the morning and the evening, and takes care of each one if they become lost or sick. "Not a single sheep escapes him."[69] The power of the shepherd is, Foucault declares, a pastoral power: a "power of care" – one which guides the flock to particular, benevolent ends, and which looks after all of those within it. It is a "constant, individualised, and final kindness."[70]

Foucault was at pains to emphasise that he was in all of this simply opposing two recurrent "themes" of government (which he called the "city-citizen" and "shepherd-flock" games). He was not attempting to provide an accurate depiction of how political power was actually used in either Greek or Hebraic societies.[71] He did not describe either as being monolithic. And nor did he consider them to be definitive: Western European States had invented "a great many different political forms" and "profoundly altered their legal structures several times."[72] Rather, his argument was that reconciling them was a problem spanning Western history from its ancient roots, and remaining of ongoing importance: what was the appropriate way to conceive of the relationship between "political power at work within the State as a legal framework of unity" and "a power we can call 'pastoral' whose role is to constantly ensure, sustain and improve the lives of each and every one"?[73] Western government, in other words, was an ongoing series of "tricky adjustments," as he put it, between political power as wielded over legal subjects and pastoral power as wielded over live individuals.[74] In the former conception, the State is a self-governing political community comprised of citizens with rights and obligations and founded on the basis of their equality; in the latter, it is a shepherd over a flock or mass of individuals who are "obedient and needful," each subsumed within the society or the population.[75]

To the reader familiar with Oakeshott's description of the modern European State, as described in Chapter 2, the similarities with Foucault's account are obvious. As will be recalled, for Oakeshott, the State is founded upon two competing "analogies." In the first, *societas*, the State is understood to be a unity of autonomous subjects sharing an acknowledgement of the authority of certain rules and conditions which they are all bound to follow, with the role of government being to preserve and improve upon those rules and conditions and maintain the unity of the association. In the second, *universitas*, the State is a purposive association in which the object of government is to arrange matters in an enlightened fashion such that the well-being of the population is improved. There, of course, is very little difference between this outline, which frames the State as existing in the tension between these two "analogies," and that of Foucault, in which the State is produced by the "tricky adjustment" between the city-citizen and shepherd-flock games. And there is also, as we shall see, a common understanding which both Foucault and Oakeshott share that the reconciliation of these two analogies or themes, whether one wishes to describe them as being in tension or "tricky adjustment," is highly productive of a particular mode of rule – which is, of course, governmentality, though Oakeshott obviously did not use the term. The reason for this is because, in both cases, that reconciliation is not merely coincidental, but driven. As we shall see, while there are important distinctions to be made between Foucault's account in this regard and that of Oakeshott, the thinking of the two men in this respect is ultimately complementary.

Political rationality and the "demonic" state

Having set up his opposition between the two themes of the city-citizen and shepherd-flock at the root of the modern European State, Foucault presents that opposition as being highly productive. This is for two distinct reasons.

The first of these reasons lies in the relationship between the two conceptions of *raison d'État* and *police*, which were developed sequentially in Europe from the sixteenth through to the eighteenth centuries. The former of these concerns the strengthening of the State versus the outside world – its ongoing rivalrous expansion against others, deriving from the necessity of perpetuating itself in a competitive order of sovereigns. The notions having been abandoned that all kingdoms would someday be unified in one final empire ushering in the Second Coming, or that the Roman Empire would be reconstituted, the early modern State came to be recognised as merely one among many – a competitive plurality of entities, each with its own history and also therefore historically limited by the possibility of absorption or dissolution through conquest.[76] The result was an interest in maintaining the State's security as an ongoing concern in itself.[77] For Foucault, while he does not make this absolutely explicit, it is clear that ultimately this represents a particular iteration of what he had elsewhere called the city-citizen game. While that theme of power was predicated on a particular *internal* conception of the human subject, as we have seen, it was also of course founded on a conception of rulership as existing primarily for the protection of the city against external threats and keeping the ship, so to speak, afloat. *Raison d'État*, in other words, is effectively a reappearance of that ancient motif – the understanding of the ruler as protector and ultimately glorifier of the polity.

The latter concept, *police*, concerns the happiness, health, well-being, and wealth of the population living within the State as itself an object of government. As States became modelled along the lines of *raison d'État*, it became necessary for regulations to be issued with respect to such matters, in order to maintain the capacity of the State to preserve its strength and security in the light of perpetual conflict and the threat of religious war and revolution.[78] Put simply, *raison d'État* required the object of the State to become the improvement of that from which it derived its strength: its natural resources, of course, but chiefly its population. "The main aim of modern government," as Foucault puts it, "is to develop those elements constitutive of individuals' lives in such a way that their development also fosters the strength of the State."[79] A healthy, wealthy, virtuous, and hard-working population is the basis of a strong and rigorous State. Hence, the aim of *police* becomes aligned with that of *raison d'État* in buttressing the State. And, of course, these two phenomena are mutually reinforcing, because a strong State is notionally better at improving the health and well-being of its population.

The second reason for understanding the relationship between the city-citizen and shepherd-flock games as being a productive one lies in the tension between conceiving of the individual as a legal subject or citizen, versus the "obedient and needful" member of the flock. A citizenry of autonomous legal subjects cannot be successfully enjoined to do anything by command: as we described in the previous section of this chapter, it might simply say "no" or disobey in other ways.[80] This provides a limit on what a sovereign can achieve. But there is no such limit in the context of the flock – the population of living individuals under the State's care. While the flock is a "thick natural phenomenon" which cannot be altered by decree, precisely as described earlier, it is hardly inaccessible or impenetrable.[81] Rather, it is open to calculation, analysis, manipulation, and management – to what Foucault called "tactics."[82] Indeed, that might be said to be the very essence of the shepherd's relationship to the flock – its knowledge of the individuals comprising it, and its guidance and management of them for their own benefit.

Hence, a political rationality is produced which, in attempting to achieve its purposes – improving the well-being of the population in order to strengthen the State – takes on a particular form and adopts a particular field of action. It may not successfully improve the citizenry by sovereign command, for reasons which we have discussed. However, it may successfully improve the *population* by conceiving of it as the "field of action" in the form, as it were, of a flock – and hence in knowledge, analysis, and manipulation of it. The result is governmentality – the form of power which works through a particular political or governing rationality predicated on the indirect management of a mass of individuals in order to achieve effects at the level of the population.

The combination of the productive relationship between these two themes makes the modern State truly "demonic,"[83] as Foucault puts it, because in their fusion the "fundamental experiences" of the living individual – birth, death, health, suffering, needs and desires, identity, labour, and so on – all become matters of concern for sophisticated forms of expertise and ultimately manipulation to fulfil the ends of the State.[84] That is, in short, the State's objectives become biopolitical. In turn, the population becomes conceived of as a "reality *sui generis*" to be acted upon and improved, rather than simply "the sum of the inhabitants within a territory."[85] All of which is to say, far from cancelling each other out, the city-citizen and shepherd-flock games combine in the union between *raison d'État* and *police* to produce a particularly vigorous and pervasive mode of political rationality in modernity – which is to say, governmentality.

For the purposes of comparison, it is worth briefly rehearsing Oakeshott's description of the rough historical timescale which is the subject of Foucault's account outlined here. For Oakeshott, those reflecting on the nature of the State during this period were "beckoned" towards doing so on the basis of the analogy of *universitas* by three particular historical conditions which faced them. Roughly, these were the appearance of bureaucracies and of increasingly advanced technical methods available to them; the concept of rulership as concerning the management of an estate, bolstered by the experiences of colonisation and warfare; and the "human postulate" of a newly alienated class of individual manqués requiring the provision of care and subsistence. At the risk of belabouring a point which will already be obvious, while these do not precisely map themselves onto Foucault's description of the fusion between *raison d'État* and *police* as outlined in this chapter, the parallels are plain: the appearance and then development of regulatory "tactics" equipping elaborate bureaucracies to achieve ends within the population; the threats of warfare (international and civil) and the ongoing necessity for the State to strengthen itself through its population; and finally a conceptualisation of the population as a thing in itself – a mass or "flock" of "obedient and needful" subjects requiring manipulation and management in order to improve along the dimensions required by the ruler.

What we find in both the Oakeshottian and Foucauldian understanding of the history of reflection on the nature of the State, then, is that such reflection has been invited towards conceiving of the State as having the function of improving the well-being of the population, not through command or edict, but through the elaboration of complicated systems of regulatory "tactics." But it is important also to make clear that for both thinkers, the story does not end at the observation that, as it were, improving the well-being of the population is always and everywhere simply a matter of *raison d'État*. Rather, in modernity the concern with biopolitics has frequently become unmoored entirely from that goal, such that the general purpose of improving the population has taken on a multiplicity of other ends. It is as though, indeed, having taken the step of recognising the population as a field of action in its own right, and having recognised that processes within it can be manipulated indirectly, those engaged in "reflected practice" on the nature of the State itself may now freely imagine it acting upon the population for a wide variety of purposes ranging far beyond the strengthening of its own internal forces. As Foucault puts it, once the State becomes envisioned as the "regulator of interests," questions then begin to open up: "What should the State's game be, what role should it play, what function should it perform in relation to that fundamental and natural game of private interests?"[86] Such questions are, indeed, an "essential element" of thinking on the State to this day.[87] And the scope of the answers to them will far exceed *raison d'État*. Oakeshott, of course, was keenly aware that this was the case – that once the improvement of well-being had become its interest, a wide and miscellaneous array of different fields would come under the purview of the State, and for an equally broad range of reasons – because "well-being" is open to so many interpretations.[88] This would allow that overriding purpose to be pursued in a "sordidly indiscriminate" manner, permitting extension of the State's interest into every corner of human life.[89] For Foucault, this would mean nothing less than "the governmentalisation of the State."[90] For Oakeshott, it would mean the State becoming synonymous with the "managerial apparatus" constituting it.[91] There is not a marked distinction between their understanding of the origins of these processes, which arise from the productive tension between *societas* and *universitas*, the city-citizen and shepherd-flock games, which existed during the period in which "the State" came into the consideration of those engaged in thinking about its character.

The governmentalisation of the State

For Foucault, as we have already seen, the State is to be conceptualised only as an "episode in governmentality." The previous section casts some light on what is meant by this. In the medieval period, the trappings of Statehood – armies, taxation, laws, administrative offices, and so on – were already in existence. But the notion of Statehood itself had not yet begun to crystallise. Those trappings were simply the tools of sovereigns ruling over realms. It was only thanks to the drive to govern that emerged in the early modern period that something called "the State" came into the "reflected practice" of "those who governed … those who advised the governors [and] those who reflected on governments."[92] That drive to govern, of course, arose from the confluence of certain forces already examined (new statistical methods and bureaucratic apparatus; the imperatives of rivalry, warfare, and civil unrest stemming from the emergent secularisation of rule; and the conception of the population *sui generis*) which "beckoned" thinking in that direction. Suddenly, the interest had shifted away from what had been Machiavelli's problem – how the Prince remains in possession of his polity – to what was Francis Bacon's: how the people living in a polity should be governed.[93] The efforts of those who governed became redirected towards managing and manipulating the population, its well-being, the flows of wealth within it, and the statistical "truths" about its composition. They became, in short, redirected towards "conducting its conduct."

This means that the State did not spontaneously develop so as to impose itself upon individuals, but was rather a practice – a *way of governing* – which emerged in thinking about the nature of rule within the context in which early moderns found themselves. This context led them to the analogies of *societas* and *universitas*, as we saw in Chapter 2, but it also provided the conditions which we have already sketched out. These were the competing conceptions of the city-citizen and shepherd-flock, brought into "tricky adjustment" against one another through the concepts of *raison d'État* and *police*; a bureaucratic apparatus restricted by law and the inherent immunity of the population from direct command or decree; and the recognition of the population as a thing in itself. This inexorably led to a form of political rationality which understood the State to be a purposive association along the lines of *universitas*, whose overriding purpose was to promote the well-being of the population in the name of a wide range of objectives, and who would achieve this through a correlation between juridico-legal, disciplinary, and security modalities that could be understood as being governmental. This resulted in what was, in effect, the birth of the State, with the State understood to mean the "regulatory idea of governmental reason"[94] – which is to say, the set of practices by which a way of governing came into existence that we now understand to be the State, and which had as its aim improving the well-being of its population.

Foucault describes this as the "governmentalisation of the State" because the modern State was almost literally constituted by this exercise of what we might call applied governmentality. This gets us part of the way to understanding what is meant by the State being merely an "episode in governmentality." To grasp it more fully, we have to turn to the thoughts of Foucault in respect of the Christian Church, which he identified as being in effect the intellectual crucible in which the methods or "tactics" which are the stuff of governmentality were created.

While the notion of God as a shepherd had only been one theme among many in Mosaic literature, according to Foucault, for Christianity it became the "keystone" for how the Church was organised.[95] For the Hebrews, the role of pastor was quite clearly taken on by God and God alone, but within Christianity the understanding of that role gave birth to an "immense institutional network" of pastoral relationships claiming to be coextensive with the entire Christian community, with the result that

> [I]n Christianity the pastorate gave rise to an art of conducting, directing, leading, guiding, taking in hand, and manipulating men, an art of monitoring them and urging them on step by step, an art with the function of taking charge of men collectively and individually throughout their life and at every moment of their existence.[96]

In the Church, that is, there developed an entire system of techniques designed for nothing less than the "government of men" – "the art by which some people were taught the government of others, and others were taught to let themselves be governed by certain people."[97] From Christ at the top of the Church, the ultimate shepherd who sacrifices his own life to save every individual in his flock, down to the lowly parish priest who even took on the title of "Pastor" in some Protestant denominations, "relationships of authority [within the Christian Church] are based upon the privileges, and at the same time of the tasks, of the shepherd in relation to his flock."[98] And these tasks are to guide the flock and all individuals within it to their salvation, to look after their physical well-being and protect them, and to therefore permanently intervene in everyday conduct – "the management of lives, as well as in goods, wealth and things."[99] The pastor must watch over every individual in his flock for the good of the whole, and is hence drawn into "manag[ing] the trajectories, circuits and reversals of fault and merit" amongst them.[100] And this is not simply a matter of telling the members of the community what they must know and do, at least not by laying out general principles of conduct for them to follow and letting that be the end of it. Since the flock is comprised of unique individuals in relationship to one another, the pastor must undertake a continual, daily modulation, requiring constant observation and supervision. "The pastor must really take charge of and observe daily life in order to form a never-ending knowledge of the behaviour and conduct of the flock."[101] And in return, of course, the individual "sheep" must put himself into his pastor's hands – subordinating himself not because of reason or principle but simply because the pastor is the pastor and must be obeyed.[102] He must "[know] that any will of one's own is a bad will."[103] This is an exercise in abnegating the self (the word Foucault uses is "destruction").[104]

The Christian pastorate is, then, to be thought of as a form of power which, first, creates an "entire economy and technique of the circulation, transfer and reversal of merits [and faults]"; second, establishes "a kind of exhaustive, total and permanent relationship of individual obedience"; and third, implements "a technique of … investigation, self-examination, and the examination by others."[105] This is what is essential to the organisation of the Christian Church, for Foucault, and it is here that we see the birth of an "absolutely new form of power" – namely, pastoral power.

But after having gone through a somewhat lengthy exposition of early Christian thought, Foucault stresses that the development of pastoral power which he describes stood in contrast to, and completely distinct from, political power until the seventeenth and eighteenth centuries. The pastor exercised power over souls, so to speak, and the king exercised power over the material world.[106] It was only in the early modern period that the art of government made its entry into politics, thereby ushering in the modern State. The Christian pastorate was hence only the background in which the practices and techniques of government began to develop – ready, as it were, to thrust themselves into the realm of political power and, in effect, help to governmentalise the State at the beginning of the modern era. This means that the modern State is, from the very beginning of its existence and through to the present day, governmentalised by a multitude of techniques for the government of men's conduct that were originally developed to deploy pastoral power within a religious context.

How the transposition of these techniques from the religious to the political spheres took place is one of the great lacunae in Foucault's late work:

in his own words, he did "not even try to sketch the series of transforma-
tions" that brought it about.[107] At most, he suggests that there was not,
strictly speaking, a transition of pastoral functions from Church to State
during this period. Rather, during the course of the sixteenth century, there
was a proliferation of the question of how to conduct, or direct, "men" –
that is, there was an "increased pursuit of being conducted."[108] This arose
because, in his view, in the period 1580–1650, the rise of reason and the
concomitant rejection of the anthropocentric view of the universe brought
about an understanding of the world as mathematical, intelligible, and literal – a world "purged of its prodigies, marvels and signs."[109] The world
had become knowable, and, more importantly, it had become a world to be
inhabited rather than merely passed through on the way to salvation. It was
a world of "open historicity" rather than a temporary staging post before
the ushering in of Christ's reign.[110] The result, we can infer, was that it began
to become possible to imagine its manipulation, and this meant that the role
of the sovereign was transformed. Where previously his duty may have been
conceptualised metaphorically as that of God in relation to nature, or the
father to children, it now became something for which there was no existing
metaphor or model – nothing less than being to *govern*.

   And thereby (though Foucault never spells this out clearly), the methodologies of government developed by the pastorate through the history of
the Christian Church, precisely for the purposes of "conducting conduct,"
made their *entrée* into the world of political power, ultimately shorn of their
religious ramifications, and evolving into something entirely secular. This
was the point at which the State emerged, as a more-or-less coherent set of
practices deployed for governing the population. It became possible, in that
moment, to imagine and envisage its existence for the first time. And this,
of course, is where we find the emergence of the notions of *raison d'État*
and *police*, described above: the understanding that there is such a thing as
State, competitive with others and requiring constant strengthening, with a
population from which it derives that strength and which, as a consequence,
it is to improve and "govern."

   Perhaps unsurprisingly, the missing link in this story – how it was that
the methods developed for the care of souls in the Christian pastorate made
their entrance into the political sphere for the government of men – is filled
in at least in part by Oakeshott. He attributes the initial reason for this
transition as being the result of early modern rulers engaging in projects of
nation-building – endowing their realms with "some semblance of substantive unity by imposing upon them a cultural and religious homogeneity."[111]
This meant the creation of national churches, and schools and universities
freed from ecclesiastical control, required to bring about religious and cultural integration and equipped with apparatus of control.[112] Rulers became

thereby the guardians of education and religious belief, and they were free to "plunder" Papal prerogatives accordingly.[113]

Where Catholicism remained the established religion, this was a matter of expropriating institutions, their property, and their offices in order to prevent the intrusion of protestantism, and resultant regimes of inspection, oversight and censorship.[114] Where protestantism was adopted, more decisive steps were taken. In such polities the ruler, in the very act of adopting his faith, was directly "displaying [himself] as the guardian of his subjects' moral and spiritual welfare."[115] Confiscations were made and had to be protected; populations had to be converted; institutions had to be reformed; and in the process, the ruler came to adopt extensive managerial control over his subjects.[116] This reached its apogee in the Calvinist States such as Geneva, in which the notion of salvation through predestination obviated any need for the ruler to act in order to improve those prospects for his subjects; rather, his office was to ensure that "the conduct of each of [his] subjects conformed at all times to the purpose of the enterprise: the glorification of God whose wrath would be visited upon a delinquent community."[117]

Irrespective of the established religion, in other words, at the dawn of the modern era the ruler, for Oakeshott, came to occupy – quite directly – a position which had previously, in a different form, been that of the Church. This resulted in the eventual secularisation of the concept of the ruler as guardian of welfare or well-being. And there is a definite echo in this, of course, of Foucault's account, which brings us neatly back full circle to *raison d'État* and the "demonic" character of Statehood. The ruler, intent on bringing about homogeneity in order to establish a secure domain, is led to an interest in the well-being of the living individuals within it. Governmentality, developed within the pastoral institutions and intellectual apparatus of the Church, thus makes its entrance into the secular sphere through the reconceptualisation of rulership arising from the birth of truly secular power. Governmentality, therefore, does not arise with or after the birth of modern Statehood: almost the opposite is true. The State is simply another iteration or "episode" of governmental reason, repackaged for parallel purposes.

Summary

What we have, then, in this reading of Foucault and Oakeshott on the history of reflected practice on the nature of Statehood, is in effect a history of the governmentalisation of the State. Here, the tension between two different poles – whether one prefers the description of *societas* and *universitas* or the city-citizen and shepherd-flock games – produces through "tricky adjustment" a method of rule which is concerned with the indirect "tactical" achievement of an overarching purpose: the pursuit of the well-being of the population as a thing in its own right. This adjustment, achieved through different correlations between what Foucault referred to as the juridico-legal, disciplinary, and security mechanisms, draws upon a form of governmental reason which originated long before the modern conception of the State, and which indeed can be thought of as constituting the State itself by turning its trappings (chief among which being law) to managerial or "*teleocratic*" regulation with the improvement of "well-being" in mind.

This lengthy exposition has been necessary in order to make absolutely clear why we must think of governmentality as a phenomenon that has a distinct existence from Statehood *per se*. It is rather to be thought of as a corpus of techniques for the indirect "government of men" in contexts including, but by no means limited to, the relationship between the State and its population. Understanding this permits us to understand how governmentalisation functions internationally or globally, and what it might thereby governmentalise in that sphere.

The governmentalisation of global human rights governance

The State, then, is only an episode in governmentality – an array of practices, emerging in the correlation between the juridico-legal, disciplinary, and security modalities, and deriving ultimately from particular ways of arranging relationships of power that were developed in the lifespan of the Christian Church. Matters have of course evolved in this respect since the early modern period to a quite bewildering and complex extent. But there is a rough essence that has remained basically the same: "conducting, directing, leading, guiding, taking in hand and manipulating men ... monitoring them and urging them on step by step" in the name of improving their well-being. Thinking of governmentality in this way allows us to see it in the terms in which Foucault referred to it: a type of political reason or rationality which is capable of being turned to wide and various ends in equally wide and various circumstances. There is no necessary connection between it and the State.

It is perfectly possible, then, to see this form of political rationality emerging in the global sphere, and indeed this has given rise to a sizeable body of literature. There is no particular requirement to survey this literature in detail, but it is worth investigating one of the crucial concepts developed in this field, which is Philip Cerny's *raison du monde*. This section begins by describing that concept, arguing that it captures an important aspect of what tends to be referred to as "global governance"[118] – namely, that just as the imperatives of *raison d'État* (security, strength, and hence the well-being of the population) came to be expressed through governmental techniques, *raison du monde* itself also has a set of similar imperatives that are expressed in similar ways. It then suggests that this results from an incipient understanding that there is developing such a thing as global governance, though it is referred to in different ways, and that thinking on the subject has led in a similar direction to that in which early thinkers on the State were "beckoned" in the early modern period. It closes in arguing that this can be thought of as a growing "governmentalisation of global governance," but that this process is necessarily much more fractured and pluralistic than the analogous governmentalisation of the State. This in turn means that we might more accurately and productively conceptualise it as a series of linked but separate global governances, of which human rights is a particular one.

From *raison d'État* to *raison du monde*

Cerny begins by presenting us with what might be called the orthodox Foucauldian reading of the relationship between governmentality and *raison d'État*.[119] Here, the neoliberal project is founded on the State "self-limiting" in order to foster the "one true and fundamental social policy" of economic growth.[120] Governmentality is thus depicted as the means by which the State encourages free competition through regulatory apparatuses in order ultimately to maintain the stability and security of the State and the structures of power within it. Cerny then suggests that through globalisation, a new hegemonic paradigm of *raison du monde* has emerged which effectively replicates this formulation in the international sphere.[121] In this understanding, governmentality is deployed globally across a complex array of agents, institutions, and fields in order ultimately to develop a stable world order. *Raison du monde*, therefore, conceives of all problems and issues as being transnational or global, and prioritises "groping towards" a world political superstructure for managing them.[122]

This is not to be understood as the emergence of a global State or even an integrated global marketplace, but something much more diffuse – "a complex, multi-layered, fungible ... set of simultaneously globalizing and governmentalizing political practices."[123] Yet – although Cerny does not himself make this point – there is a sense in which the transposition of governmentality from the Christian pastorate of souls to the State's government of men that occurred in the early modern period is replicated in his account, with a new iteration of governmentality occurring with the transference of techniques developed in the context of the State into the international sphere. What he calls the "governmentalisation of world politics" consists of the process by which a certain set of practices, "analogous in principle at least to that which has enabled liberal states to be so successful domestically" find themselves being repurposed or repositioned in the global arena.[124] This, in effect, allows us to think of the opening up of a new episode in governmentality occurring in this process, with the line of development running from the pastorate of souls in the Church, to the government of men in the State, to the government of States, non-State actors, populations, and individuals alike in the emerging arena of global governance. The important point to emphasise is that this is not so much a matter of the construction or strengthening of international institutions, though this might be part of the picture; rather, it involves the widening and deepening of particular *practices* that can be labelled as being "governmental" in the sense in which Foucault uses the term.

As facially plausible as it is, it misses out two important elements that I previously emphasised in the account of governmentality which I gave earlier in this chapter. The first of these is the relationship between governmentality and well-being. The pastorate of souls concerned the deployment of a "power of care," and the "government of men" arising from the imperatives of *raison d'État* likewise emphasised general welfare – initially at least due to the need to strengthen the population as the basis of the State's own strength, but developing into something much broader since then. This, of course, led govermentality in the latter context in a biopolitical direction. Clearly, then, one would expect governmentality to take on such a character in being deployed for the purposes of *raison du monde* – even if this is only to the extent that comfortable and happy populations will foster global stability. The second missing element is that of law. Cerny makes the point that, in his view, governmentality is a matter of balancing between or reconciling the "central contradiction of the modern era," which he describes as being that between top-down bureaucratic organisation and individual or civil society-based behaviour and values.[125] Undoubtedly that simply replicates the contradictions between the city-citizen and shepherd-flock games, or between *societas* and *universitas*, which we have of course examined and described as existing in productive tension. But, as we also saw earlier, it would be more accurate to suggest that in fact that central contradiction arises in large part due to the nature of law, which for all it can be turned to *teleocratic* or purposive ends cannot be relied upon to instrumentalise such ends on its own, and may indeed take a form contradictory to those ends. Rather, *teleocratic* law must work in tandem with other apparatuses within the modalities of discipline and security – through, that is, "tactics." Governmentality's usefulness is ultimately the result of the way that it both makes use of and circumvents the nature of law as such.

What this tells us is that in seeking to understand what I will call the "governmentalisation of global governance," we must emphasise these two things. The techniques in question will be performed upon populations broadly with the purpose of improving their well-being, whatever the ultimate objective might be (stability of the international order being the candidate put forward by Cerny). This will give that form of governmentality, and the global governance regimes which it constitutes, a particular tenor. And the process of governmentalisation will be, as always, taking place within the correlation between the juridico-legal, disciplinary, and security modalities – with the important point for our purposes being that this will both deploy legal rules and circumvent ineluctable characteristics which the law possesses.

Both of these matters, then, lead us back to certain observations made in the previous chapter concerning international law and global constitutionalism in general, and human rights' role in that context in particular. Clearly, the notion that international law is "for" human well-being is so widespread among those engaged in writing and thinking about the subject that the point hardly needs belabouring. And, just as clearly, human rights law as a subspecies of international law is at the heart of international law's nature in that regard. If international law is "for" human well-being, then international human rights law is one of the, if not the, primary means by which that is supposed to be achieved. At the same time, however, the mere existence of international human rights laws, despite their increased elaboration, cannot hope to bring about human well-being in their own right, partly because laws on their own cannot modify the underlying natural processes within populations, as we have seen, and partly because the law's predicates refute direct intervention (whether through the principle of non-intervention, on which the Westphalian system is founded, or through human rights laws' character as checks on the power of the State to directly command individuals).

These two considerations will be discussed in more depth in due course, but for the time being it suffices to raise their existence and then to point out that all of this arises not as a mere epiphenomenon of global interdependence and integration, but contingently on the fact that human beings have recognised and begun to think about global governance as a thing in its own right. In other words, just as in the early modern period the State became an object of "reflected practice" in the work of those such as Bacon or Von Justi and hence came into focus as a real phenomenon, so we are currently witnessing a similar process taking place with respect to global governance.[126] It is coming into focus as an object of knowledge and analysis. And, just as Foucault understood that in order to grasp the nature of the State one had to examine the thoughts and preferences of those who were performing knowledge and analysis of it during its emergence – "those who governed ... those who advised the governors [and] those who reflected on governments," so it is entirely appropriate therefore to say that understanding global governance will require performing the same examination of those who are engaged in thinking about its nature. This will quite naturally lead us to the question of which of Oakeshott's analogies of *societas* and *universitas* those people are beckoned towards. The answer to that question will already be clear to the reader. But it will be useful for what follows to make elements of that process clear.

Global governance as *teleocracy*

For Oakeshott, as we saw earlier, thinkers concerned with the nature of the State were drawn in the early modern period towards the analogy of *universitas* because of a mixture of both historical circumstance and visions of human progress. This mixture is, I will now argue, broadly similar to that which can be seen to prevail within the developing arena of global governance.

Dealing with the historical circumstances first, Oakeshott was keen to emphasise that part of the reason why *universitas* became a compelling analogy in early modern Europe was that it simply became practically possible to imagine an administrative State engaged in governing the lives of those living within its territory. This was partly because new administrative institutions and techniques of knowledge – such as statistics and the means of gathering and analysing them, and the concept of the average or "norm"[127] – came into being, and this made it possible to conceive of the population as amenable to bureaucratic organisation. But it was also because rulers were already engaged in something like purposive enterprise in their pursuit of colonies and engagement in war – two activities which allowed them to draw on the notion that the ruler was, in effect, a manorial lord administering an estate for its own improvement. And it was due also to the growing alienation of swathes of the population arising from the gradual secularisation of society and the slow collapse of communal ties which had hitherto served to ameliorate poverty. This created a rationale for understanding the State as having an obligation to care for this mass of individual manqués.

The parallels between these conditions and those which shape thinking about global governance are obvious. It goes without saying that a wide range of international organisations have come into existence, and continue to grow in number, scale, and complexity. And it has of course become possible, thanks to the further development and elaboration not just of statistics, but of statistical modelling and indices and rankings, for these bodies to

154 Critical theory and human rights

"know" about all manner of phenomena – concerning populations, natural resources, disease, climatic variations, and the like. It has, in short, become possible to imagine that something like global governance – centralised administrative management of global affairs – could conceivably take place.

Moreover, while of course States no longer engage in colonial projects, nor widespread warfare, with the exercise of some imagination it is plausible to suggest that at a certain level of abstraction there is a similarity between those conditions as they faced early modern rulers and certain conditions which face projects of global governance. The reason why Oakeshott insisted on the importance of colonialism in steering matters in the direction of *universitas* was because he believed it showed that even before States *per se* were in existence, rulers were already beginning to engage in activities resembling centrally directed estate management or improvement. They were, in that sense, "primed" to move in a particular direction. One can see something of the same process of priming taking place at the scale of global governance throughout the nineteenth and twentieth centuries, not through colonialism but through the gradual emergence of purposive international institutions and organisations such as the Rhine Navigation Commission, the International Telecommunications Union, and the International Labour Organisation (ILO). Such bodies, created for particular purposes and engaging in the administrative management of some specific transnational matter or other, had already begun to set the patterns of what we now describe as global governance before its widespread development in the second half of the twentieth century. There was already a predisposition, in other words, towards conceiving of there being a role for transnational institutions along the analogy of *universitas*, much as there was such a predisposition within the early modern State thanks to their incipient colonial projects. And the same can be said of warfare; if one thinks of warfare as simply an example of a transnational phenomenon requiring an energetic, organised response through the centralised administration and organisation of the resources of a polity, then one can just as well recognise other such transnational phenomena – disease, poverty, environmental problems, terrorism, and so on – as requiring similar such responses from existing institutions. That is, where for the early modern ruler the threat posed by warfare was an instigation to imagine that the State could have purposes and that it should be organised so as to pursue them, for the developing institutions of global governance a range of other perceived threats or problems also naturally "beckon" towards conceiving their role along the analogy of *universitas*.

Finally, it scarcely requires saying that globalisation and economic interdependence have resulted in both a discovery of hitherto-ignored poverty and an increased alienation of individuals that is analogous to – and probably more pronounced than – the processes which Oakeshott identified in the creation of what he called the individual manqué. Social and economic forces have conspired to produce a view of populations as masses of demoralised and impoverished individuals requiring the guidance of global governance regimes, just as they conspired in the period of the State's emergence to encourage the view that the State must manage such a mass of individuals manqués for their own good. One need only, for instance, direct oneself to the mission statements of the institutions of global governance, such as the World Health Organization (WHO) (which is "inspired by [a] vision of a world in which all peoples attain the highest possible standard of health [and a] mission to promote health, keep the world safe and serve the vulnerable")[128] or the United Nations International Children's Fund (UNICEF) (which is determined to "mobilize political will and material resources to help countries ... build their capacity to form appropriate policies and deliver services to children and their families")[129] to see this way of conceiving of the role of global governance in effect.

So the similarities between the historical circumstances which prevailed during the development of the early modern State and those which have done so at the emergence of global governance are, impressionistically at least, striking. And so indeed are the intellectual forces (or "speculative projects")[130] to which they give rise. For Oakeshott, these were the visions of Francis Bacon and his intellectual descendants: Von Justi and the other Cameralists, St Simon, the French *philosophes*, the classical economists, among others, all of whom created a kind of inheritance both of methods for thinking of the State along the lines of *universitas* and rationales for doing so. In much the same way, an intellectual inheritance of conceiving of global governance along such lines has been created for current thinkers in the mode of Waldron. This inheritance doubtless extends as far back as Grotius and beyond, but its more proximate interlocutors are that class of early twentieth-century "international civil servants" in organisations such as the ILO or League of Nations,[131] who described themselves as having "international minds,"[132] "trained to look upon social and economic phenomena without any national bias or predilection,"[133] and cooperating in the promotion of the "progress of civilization."[134] To observe how dominant the view contained within this intellectual inheritance has become, one need only examine the definition of "global governance" offered in a recent textbook on governance by Michael Zurn, chosen only for its representative quality: "Global governance refers to the entirety of regulations put forward with reference to *solving denationalised and deregionalised problems or providing transnational common goods.*" As if in anticipation of Oakeshott, he then adds that this is "more than just simple coordination between states to achieve a *modus vivendi* of interaction – [rather] it often aims actively at achieving normatively laden political goals."[135]

What we might describe as the framing conditions for thinking about the State during the course of its emergence, and those for thinking about global governance in its own development, are noticeably similar. It should hardly be surprising, then, that just as those framing conditions gave a *teleocratic* drift to how the State came to be conceived, global governance regimes have likewise tended to be conceptualised with a bent towards *teleocracy*. Put very bluntly, they are thought of as being projects, with purposes. And, like the State, those purposes tend to have the tenor of being designed to improve human welfare or well-being – along some dimension or other, or indeed all such dimensions.

This allows us to look upon the "governmentalisation of global governance" in a particular light. In Foucault's account, the State was "governmentalised" through instrumentalising and elaborating upon existing institutions and apparatuses, combined with taking on the intellectual technologies required for the care of souls within the Christian Church and deploying them to achieve the government of men. And this all took place because it was necessary to achieve that certain purpose, both very broad and very deep, of improving human well-being, and because it was impossible to achieve that purpose directly and straightforwardly through lawmaking or decree. What Oakeshott suggests to us is that this entire process was instigated in the first place by certain historical conditions and intellectual visions that drove thinking about the State towards the analogy of *universitas*.

What follows from our understanding of global governance as being framed by similar historical conditions and intellectual visions, and hence by the analogy of *universitas*, is that global governance will be "governmentalised" in a broadly similar fashion. It will consist of the instrumentalisation and elaborations of existing institutions and apparatuses – developed, as pointed out by Cerny, in the domestic sphere, and transposed to the transnational or global. And it will do so through the deployment of the very same intellectual technologies that derive ultimately from the context of the care of souls in the Christian Church, and which can be understood as governmentality broadly understood. And all of this will take place because of the need to achieve that very same purpose of improving human well-being, except at a different, bigger, and more abstract scale.

The governmentalisation of global human rights governance

A governmentalisation of global governance is taking place, then, analogous in large part to the governmentalisation of the State. But there are some important distinctions to be made. The most important of these is that, as is very frequently observed, global governance is highly fragmented and pluralised.[136] This is observable across several dimensions. Global governance encompasses a wide range of actors – State institutions, individuals, regional organisations, international organisations, non-governmental organisations, businesses, supranational bodies, and many other non-State actors of other kinds. It is practiced by all of these actors upon each other and between each other in different arrangements. It is practiced in different forms – negotiation, monitoring and verification, rule-making, standard-setting, evaluation, and enforcement. And it is split into different fields or sub-fields: trade, the environment, health, development, and so on, many of which appear almost hermetically sealed from one another and show radically different historical trajectories. We do not, in other words, see anything like the coherent, hierarchical structure which the governmentalisation of the State produced.

There is of course a good reason for this, which is that, as both Oakeshott and Foucault emphasised, the State was built upon the pre-existing territories, rulers, and institutions which were already well entrenched by the medieval period. The governmentalisation of the State was essentially a repurposing and elaboration on what went before – Oakeshott describes the State as being built from "second-hand materials."[137] The same is plainly not true in the arena of global governance, where there is no pre-existing structure whatsoever: there is no world ruler and there are no deep-seated and long-standing international institutions. And, indeed, the formal conditions of international relations themselves block the formation of such structures. There is no justification, then, in foreseeing the governmentalisation of global governance as resulting in a unified, hierarchical order along the lines of the State. Rather, has been pointed out many times, governance is better understood as a process than a set of institutions *per se*.[138] It arises as a "bricolage," as Cerny puts it,[139] through the experimentation and diversity of approach that is required in order to attempt to achieve ends in the absence of authoritative governmental institutions. This is why it is so fragmented and diffuse.

It makes sense, then, to think of the governmentalisation of global governance as really a governmentalisation of a series of many global *governances* – a multi-faceted and subdivided process which is made up of many linked but separate sub-processes. This is of course, in a sense, just another framing for what many others have said in slightly different ways, whether it be Gunther Teubner,[140] Peer Zumbansen,[141] or indeed Martti Koskenniemi himself.[142] But it emphasises that governmentality, while never monolithic, is in the global sphere especially pluralistic.

For this reason, for the remainder of this book – wherein our focus returns to human rights specifically – I will refer to the "governmentalisation of global human rights governance" as a specific item among these separate sub-processes of the wider series of processes comprising the whole. This is, in other words, the plethora of actors, the arrangements between those actors, and the laws and the regulatory "tactics" and managerial processes put in place to achieve the purpose which those laws are understood to declare. It is the entire structure which operationalises the "conducting, directing, leading, guiding, taking in hand, and manipulating men, [of] monitoring them and urging them on step by step, [with] the function of taking charge of men collectively and individually throughout their life and at every moment of their existence," and which has as its ultimate purpose the realisation of the directing idea of improving well-being through the benevolent exercise of authority.

In the following chapter, I describe how that finds expression in further detail.

Notes

1 M. Foucault, *Security, Territory, Population: Lectures at the Collège de France, 1977–1978* (Palgrave Macmillan, 2008; ed. M. Senellart, trans. G. Burchell), p. 115.
2 This is surveyed in B. Golder and P. Fitzpatrick, *Foucault's Law* (Routledge, 2009), pp. 12–39.
3 Foucault, *Security, Territory, Population*, p. 4.
4 *Ibid.*, p. 5.
5 In *Discipline & Punish: The Birth of the Prison* (Penguin, 1991; trans. A. Sheridan).
6 Foucault, *Security, Territory, Population*, p. 4.
7 *Ibid.*, p. 6.
8 *Ibid.*, p. 5.
9 *Ibid.*
10 *Ibid.*, p. 6.
11 *Ibid.*, p. 36.
12 *Ibid.*
13 *Ibid.*, p. 72.
14 *Ibid.*, pp. 6–8.
15 This is indeed too vast to catalogue in detail, but a useful overview is found in J. Donzelot and C. Gordon, "Governing Liberal Societies: The Foucault Effect in the English-Speaking World," in M. Peters et al. (eds), *Governmentality Studies in Education* (Sense, 2009), 3.
16 Foucault, *Security, Territory, Population*, pp. 91–92.
17 *Ibid.*, p. 42.
18 *Ibid.*, p. 45.
19 *Ibid.*, pp. 96–97.
20 *Ibid.*, p. 19.

21 *Ibid.*, p. 18.
22 *Ibid.*, pp. 32–38.
23 *Ibid.*, p. 96.
24 *Ibid.*, p. 23.
25 *Ibid.*, p. 49.
26 *Ibid.*
27 *Ibid.*, p. 353.
28 *Ibid.*, pp. 352–353.
29 *Ibid.*, p. 104.
30 *Ibid.*, p. 100.
31 *Ibid.*, p. 99.
32 *Ibid.*, pp. 99–100. As Foucault points out, La Perrière's understanding of government was not mirrored by any understanding of insect biology!
33 M. Foucault, *The History of Sexuality, vol. I* [1979] (Vintage, 1990), p. 144.
34 Alcohol (Minimum Pricing) (Scotland) Act 2012, s. 1 (2).
35 House of Commons Library, Briefing Paper 5021 (2019), available at http://researchbriefings.files.parliament.uk/documents/SN05021/SN05021.pdf (accessed 29th November 2019), p. 3.
36 *Scotch Whisky Association and Others v. The Lord Advocate and Another (Scotland)* [2017] UKSC 76.
37 Golder and Fitzpatrick, *Foucault's Law*, p. 39.
38 M. Foucault, "Lemon and Milk," in J. Faubion (ed.), *Power: The Essential Works of Foucault 1954–1984, Vol III* (Allen Lane, 2001; trans. R. Hurley et al.), p. 436.
39 M. Foucault, "Nietzsche, Genealogy, History," in Faubion, J. (ed.), *Aesthetics, Method and Epistemology: The Essential Works of Foucault 1954–1984, Vol II* (The New Press, 1999; trans. R. Hurley et al.), p. 378.
40 M. Oakeshott, *On Human Conduct* [1975] (Clarendon Press, 1991), p. 326.
41 *Ibid.*, p. 267 and 286.
42 *Ibid.*, pp. 301–302.
43 *Ibid.*, p. 286.
44 *Ibid.*, p. 301.
45 *Ibid.*, p. 252.
46 *Ibid.*, p. 321, fn. 1.
47 Foucault, *Security, Territory, Population*, p. 71.
48 A library search for articles, books, chapters, and reviews for "'neoliberalism' AND 'governmentality'" that I conducted on 29th November 2019 returned 10,599 results.
49 M. Foucault, *The Birth of Biopolitics: Lectures at the Collège de France 1978–1979* (Palgrave Macmillan, 2008; ed. A. Davidson, trans. G. Burchell).
50 The journal *Economy & Society* had a special issue devoted to this subject (35 (2006)).
51 S. M. Shamsul Alam, *Governmentality and Counter-Hegemony in Bangladesh* (Palgrave Macmillan, 2015).
52 S. Philpott, "East Timor's Double Life: Smells Like Westphalian Spirit," 27 (1), *Third World Quarterly* (2006) 135.

53 Foucault, *The Birth of Biopolitics*, p. 317.
54 *Ibid.*, p. 322.
55 M. Dean, *Governmentality* (2nd edition, Sage, 2010), p. 121.
56 *Ibid.*
57 Oakeshott, *On Human Conduct*, p. 295.
58 Foucault, *Security, Territory, Population*, p. 248.
59 It is also striking that they did so roughly contemporaneously, with *On Human Conduct* appearing in 1975 and the *Security, Territory, Population* lectures being given in 1977–1978.
60 Foucault, *Security, Territory, Population*, p. 247.
61 *Ibid.*, p. 123.
62 *Ibid.*, p. 125.
63 M. Foucault, "Politics and Reason," in L. Kritzman (ed.), *Michel Foucault: Philosophy, Politics, Culture – Interviews and Other Writings 1977–1984* (Routledge, 1988), 57, p. 62.
64 Foucault, *Security, Territory, Population*, p. 125.
65 *Ibid.*, pp. 125–126.
66 *Ibid.*, p. 129.
67 Foucault, "Politics and Reason."
68 Foucault, *Security, Territory, Population*, pp. 126–128.
69 *Ibid.*, p. 128.
70 Foucault, "Politics and Reason."
71 Foucault, "Politics and Reason," p. 63.
72 *Ibid.*
73 *Ibid.*, p. 67.
74 *Ibid.*
75 Dean, *Governmentality*, p. 93.
76 Foucault, *Security, Territory, Population*, p. 291.
77 *Ibid.*, pp. 291–292.
78 *Ibid.*, pp. 311–328.
79 Foucault, "Politics and Reason," p. 82.
80 Foucault, *Security, Territory, Population*, p. 71.
81 *Ibid.*
82 *Ibid.*, p. 99.
83 M. Foucault, "Lemon and Milk," p. 311.
84 Dean, *Governmentality*, p. 115.
85 *Ibid.*, p. 114.
86 Foucault, *Security, Territory, Population*, pp. 346–347.
87 *Ibid.*, p. 347.
88 Oakeshott, *On Human Conduct*, p. 308.
89 *Ibid.*
90 Foucault, *Security, Territory, Population*, p. 110.
91 Oakeshott, *On Human Conduct*, p. 301.
92 Foucault, *Security, Territory, Population*, p. 276.
93 *Ibid.*, pp. 271–272.

 94 *Ibid.*, p. 286
 95 *Ibid.*, p. 152.
 96 *Ibid.*, p. 165.
 97 *Ibid.*, pp. 150–151.
 98 *Ibid.*, pp. 152–153.
 99 *Ibid.*, p. 154.
100 *Ibid.*, p. 172–173.
101 *Ibid.*, p. 181.
102 *Ibid.*
103 *Ibid.*, p. 177.
104 *Ibid.*, p. 180.
105 *Ibid.*, p. 183.
106 *Ibid.*, p. 155.
107 *Ibid.*, p. 227.
108 *Ibid.*, p. 231 and at the footnote on that page.
109 *Ibid.*, p. 236.
110 See also *ibid.*, p. 260.
111 Oakeshott, *On Human Conduct*, p. 279.
112 *Ibid.*, p. 280.
113 *Ibid.*, p. 283.
114 *Ibid.*, pp. 280–281.
115 *Ibid.*, pp. 282–283.
116 *Ibid.*, p. 283.
117 *Ibid.*, p. 284.
118 See A. Kacowicz, "Global Governance, International Order, and World Order," in D. Levi-Faur (ed.), *The Oxford Handbook of Governance* (Oxford University Press, 2012), 686.
119 P. Cerny, *Rethinking World Politics: A Theory of Transnational Pluralism* (Oxford University Press, 2009), pp. 157–159.
120 Foucault, *The Birth of Biopolitics*, p. 144.
121 Cerny, *Rethinking World Politics*, p. 159.
122 *Ibid.*, p. 175.
123 *Ibid.*, p. 176.
124 *Ibid.*, p. 178.
125 *Ibid.*, p. 159.
126 N. Bhuta, "State Failure: The US Fund for Peace Failed States Index," in K. Davis, A. Fisher, B. Kingsbury, and S. Engle Merry (eds), *Governance by Indicators: Global Power through Quantification and Rankings* (Oxford University Press, 2012), 132.
127 F. Ewald, "Norms, Discipline and the Law," 30, *Representations* (1990), 138.
128 WHO, "Our Values," available at www.who.int/about/who-we-are/our-values (accessed 29th November 2019).
129 UNICEF, "UNICEF's Mission Statement," available at www.unicef.org/about/who/index_mission.html (accessed 29th November 2019).
130 M. Oakeshott, *On Human Conduct*, p. 279.

131 E. Phelan, "The New International Civil Service," 11, *Foreign Affairs* (1932–1933) 307.
132 N. Butler, "Development of the International Mind," 9, *American Bar Association Journal* (1923) 520.
133 N. Butler, cited in G. Fiti Sinclair, *To Reform the World: International Organisations and the Making of Modern States* (Oxford University Press, 2017), p. 73.
134 Butler, "Development of the International Mind," p. 522.
135 M. Zurn, in Levi-Faur (ed.), *The Oxford Handbook of Governance*, pp. 730–731 [emphasis added].
136 See e.g., E. Yip, "Globalization and the Future of the Law of the Sovereign State," 8 (3), *International Journal of Constitutional Law* (2010) 636.
137 Oakeshott, *On Human Conduct*, p. 198.
138 R. Rhodes, *Understanding Governance: Policy Networks, Governance, Reflexivity and Accountability* (Open University Press, 1997).
139 Cerny, *Rethinking World Politics*, p. 175.
140 See e.g., G. Teubner, "Fragmented Foundations: Social Constitutionalism Beyond the Nation State," in P. Dobner and M. Loughlin (eds), *The Twilight of Constitutionalism?* (Oxford University Press, 2010), 327.
141 P. Zumbansen, "Defining the Space of Transnational Law: Legal Theory, Global Governance and Legal Pluralism," 21 (2), *Transnational Law & Contemporary Problems* (2012) 305.
142 M. Koskenniemi, "Law, Teleology and International Relations: An Essay in Counterdisciplinarity," 26 (1), *International Relations* (2011) 3.

5

Tactics rather than laws

If you don't count it, it won't count … It is thanks to the indicators that we know where we stand and what we still need to do.
(Flavia Pansieri, then UN Deputy High Commissioner for Human Rights, Speech to the Human Rights Council, 28th July 2014)

Introduction

In previous chapters, we saw how the purpose of the international human rights regime can be discerned in a particular directing idea, which is to improve well-being through placing obligations on the powerful to conduct benevolent activities for the good of the powerless. This, combined with certain other circumstantial conditions, gives international human rights law a strongly *teleocratic* drift, and this results in a phenomenon which I described as the governmentalisation of global human rights governance. This refers to the deployment of regulatory or managerial tactics for the conducting of conduct in the manner which Foucault called governmental, and which derive from the correlations between the juridico-legal, disciplinary, and security modalities of rule. It is necessary for such governmental tactics to be used in order to realise the regime's directing idea, because ultimately, however *teleocratic* international human rights law might become, its provisions on their own will always partially retain their character as *nomos*. Another way of putting this is that the domain of the juridico-legal cannot on its own achieve the purpose which animates the regime. There must be recourse to other methods.

This chapter begins by elucidating the conditions which result in international human rights law retaining an "allegiance" to *nomocracy* despite its prevailing purposive orientation. As Oakeshott suggested was the case with law in general, these conditions partially exist in the realm of ideas and are partially simply pragmatic. In the first place, the international human rights system, like all international law, remains predicated on the principles of Westphalian sovereignty – irrespective of sustained and widespread scepticism, dissatisfaction, and rebuke – and the result of that brute fact is that direct rule-making and enforcement is conceptually impossible. In the second, the inability of law to achieve desired ends in its own right – its incapacity to, for instance, reduce the suicide rate through prohibition or decree – is even more acute in the international sphere than it is in the domestic. And the reasons for this are obvious. There are therefore readily discernible reasons why even a strongly purposive orientation to international human rights law, which is undoubtedly present, will not result in an outright *teleocracy*.

This will naturally therefore necessitate the deployment of governmental "tactics" in order to realise the regime's directing idea, and the bulk of this chapter describes some such tactics in order to show how a sphere of global human rights governance is becoming governmentalised. As we shall see, there is a widespread interest in contemporary human rights practice in quantitative performance measurement, and this is entirely in keeping with the governing style of late modernity in almost any politico-legal context – a point that hardly needs belabouring with examples. Contemporary thought has come to view statistics as in themselves both revelatory and explanatory of social phenomena,[1] and a host of different regulatory or managerial techniques have been developed in the domestic political sphere across the world as a result, designed to "improve" what those statistics reveal. This has given rise to a particular form of indirect rule which Miller and Rose called "governing at a distance."[2] And I shall argue that many of the techniques which comprise that phenomenon have been transposed into the international realm in order to realise the regime's directing idea. That is, as we saw in the last chapter, just as governmental reason evolved in the Christian pastorate before its repurposing in the modern State, so a similar process is taking place, in a much more diffuse manner, in the global sphere. Global human rights governance, seeking as it does to govern human rights "at a distance," is nothing more than an episode in governmentality. And ultimately, this is the explanation for its managerialisation – that preoccupation with process which Koskenniemi astutely observed.

The allegiance to *nomos*

We have seen how international human rights law has come to be strongly oriented towards *teleocracy*. The directing idea is to be realised. This means, for obvious reasons, that the concern of human rights practice turns very frequently to questions of how to achieve what are generally referred to, amorphously, as "compliance" and "effectiveness," but what in more general terms might simply be put as "[making] a difference to the lives of people throughout the world."[3] If achieving compliance is the traditional obsession of international law in general,[4] in the field of human rights it is an overwhelming one. And in turn it, of course, gives rise to other concerns: how compliance can be measured, what compliance actually means, how to remedy non-compliance, and so on.

This focus on compliance derives from problems which, while they confront any project of purposive social action, are particularly acute with respect to international human rights law. These are obvious, and as a result tend to be taken as givens. But they are worth briefly detailing in order to demonstrate how they map onto the broad sets of circumstances which Oakeshott identified as resulting in there remaining "relics" of *nomos* at the heart of law even in its most powerfully *teleocratic* guises.

First, it is impossible purely in practical terms to achieve the realisation of goals throughout all States parties to any given human rights treaty merely by decree. States may consent to be bound by the provisions of a given treaty. They may even consent to be bound by relevant judicial decisions where those exist, to incorporate treaty provisions into domestic law, and to regulate the actions of non-State actors in accordance with the rubric of "respect, protect, and fulfil." But the detailed and direct control required to operationalise a given human right to achieve a desired end – for example, to reduce racial discrimination, reduce the suicide rate in Scotland, increase female political participation, or whatever it may be – cannot be achieved simply through a chain of commands running from treaty body to State party to domestic public authorities and private actors and, finally, to individuals. Achieving any societal goal is, it should go without saying, hardly that simple. A fire station cannot operate simply on the basis of a set of operational rules, no matter how complicated and detailed they might be, and the "putting out of unwanted fires" is a straightforward matter in comparison to changing human behaviour within a population.[5]

And second, irrespective of the widespread rejection of "statism" by academic commentators, whether on normative or empirical grounds,[6] the system of international human rights law was founded upon and remains predicated on the principles of sovereign equality and non-intervention, however undesirable that might be thought to be by the relevant actors. Whether or not we are witnessing the withering of the State or will do so in coming decades, as a matter of law it is simply indisputable that States cannot be bound without their consent, and that they have exclusive territorial jurisdiction. They cannot – and this again goes without saying – be directly commanded to do anything with the expectation that it will be carried out. As well as it being circumstantially impossible to change matters "on the ground" through enacting law or issuing decrees or edicts, then, it is also impossible to achieve compliance through international law-making alone because of foundational principles which cannot be wished away and which the overwhelming majority of States insist on.[7]

Thus, both as a matter of both legal principle and ineluctable practical circumstance, there can be no possibility of direct realisation of outcomes purely by the creation or application of law in the sphere of human rights. It is worth re-emphasising that this point will be obvious and would not ordinarily require spelling out even in this cursory level of detail. But it is important to set it in the context of what has already been established. International human rights law is oriented towards *telos*. But it cannot entirely move beyond *nomocratic* constraint. Ultimately, the best it can do is to specify conditions which are to be complied with. But it retains its status as rules, and rules cannot in themselves achieve any desired purpose whatsoever.

Governing human rights at a distance

Governing at a distance

It is also important to make the observation that the two sets of conditions mentioned are very similar to those which, when combined with the desire to rule, will tend to produce what Miller and Rose described as "governing at a distance."[8]

Miller and Rose's project, described as an attempt to analyse political power in advanced liberal democracies, provided an important point of critique of changes that were taking place during the 1980s "New Public Management" era in the United Kingdom.[9] What Miller and Rose and others noticed during this period was that modern government had become characterised by *indirectness* – achieving desired outcomes through aligning the behaviour of ostensibly autonomous actors with the social and economic goals of the relevant public authorities and the State.

On the one hand, in Miller and Rose's view, the turn to indirectness had come about purely because of pragmatism. It was still the case that those in positions to govern and rule were concerned with directing the population towards desired end-states of whatever kind. But the vision of a "totally administered society … inspired by the utopian dream that all regions of the social body could be penetrated, known and directed by political authorities"[10] had long ago been abandoned because of its sheer practical impossibility. The history of the development of liberalism thus appears, in their account, partly just as the result of complexity, as those who desire to achieve their ends within the population learn repeatedly and with growing certainty that "'government' is a congenitally failing operation" – confronted at every turn with the fact that "'reality' always escapes the theories that inform programmes and the ambitions that underpin them."[11] In this context, the will to govern must be understood as being formed mostly by the difficulty of actually achieving anything in the complex environment of a human society. (One is perhaps reminded of Hayek's aphorism that "The curious task of economics is to demonstrate to men how little they really know about what they imagine they can design.")[12] The "murky plain of overwhelming detail" which presents itself to anyone expressing that will is impenetrable to his or her direct knowledge and intervention.[13] He or she must therefore develop indirect methods for doing so.

At the same time, however, the indirectness of advanced liberal rule is also predicated on the autonomy of its subjects. However one wishes to understand liberalism it is certainly the case that it self-describes as "a critique of excessive disciplinary power in the name of the rights and liberty of the individual."[14] Since this is the case, people cannot simply be commanded to act in certain ways in liberal societies except in very narrow circumstances; if the reverse were true, the society in question would quite obviously no longer be liberal. Rulers are in other words "confronted ... with subjects equipped with rights and interests that *should not* be interdicted by politics."[15] This means that liberal government is, in essence, an exercise in achieving desired ends without overriding the rights and liberties of individuals – hence, doing so indirectly.

These two different brute facts – that advanced human societies are extremely complex and largely impenetrable to direct political action, and that liberal societies must enshrine the rights and liberties of individual subjects – combine to produce a particular style of governing, which takes place "at a distance" rather than directly. Techniques of government are created so as to reflect and maintain the "distance" between the governing public authorities and the governed social actors, and this produces, in Miller and Rose's conception, three particular shifts.[16] First, there takes place the transference of powers from what they call "positive knowledges of human conduct" (medicine, engineering, science, education, etc.) to "calculative regimes of accounting and financial management" which subject expertise to constant critical scrutiny in the light of the goals of the governing body, chiefly through techniques of budget discipline, accountancy, and audit. These consist of enumeration, calculation, monitoring, evaluation, and so on, applied in settings as diverse as hospitals, schools, universities, and police forces. Second, there takes place a reconfiguration of political power which sees widespread "pluralisation and autonomisation" of accountability and responsibility, so that activities which were previously part of political apparatuses become (purportedly) apoliticised by outsourcing to quangos and other regulatory groupings. These new regulatory entities are given autonomy of decision making and are held accountable not through electoral mechanisms but through targets, indicators, and other performance measurement techniques, and through representation on their boards of "partners" from "communities" such as local residents, businesses, and charities. And third, individuals take on new subjectivities, called upon to "enterprise themselves" as "actively responsible," aligning their goals with those of their governors. This encourages them to voluntarily make choices that are healthier, better for their communities, and more productive, without being directly required to do so by law.

Caught between the Scylla of the sheer practical impossibility of direct political intervention and the Charybdis of the fact that such intervention should not take place, rule or government therefore takes on a particular mode or style simply as a necessary consequence of the desire to achieve things wished for within that context. The result of this is the attempt to "govern at a distance" through indirect means.

Miller and Rose's analysis is constrained by a focus on liberalism, which unnecessarily limits the scope of application of their concept. "Governing at a distance" on the terms which they describe is not merely a phenomenon confined to liberal government.[17] As I have sought to demonstrate, it is rather a combination of circumstances which are much more general. So we should not be restricted in discerning it elsewhere, and indeed the developing global governance of human rights replicates the model of "governing at a distance" closely.

In the remainder of this section, I utilise Miller and Rose's three "shifts" to analyse three characteristics of global human rights governance. These characteristics will be described here in shorthand as the shift to accounting and audit; pluralisation and autonomisation; and the specification of new subjectivities. How these characteristics reveal themselves in the context of human rights are set out next.

The shift to accounting and audit

Human rights governance as an "audit culture"

In recent years, it has become increasingly common for the international human rights system to be described as an "audit culture," or words to that effect.[18] Indeed, "implementation" in the modern international human rights context is often almost synonymous with supervision or monitoring.[19] This is largely because of a discernible trend since the mid-2000s within the United Nations (UN) treaty- and charter-based mechanisms and among non-governmental organisations (NGOs) and academics towards developing and deploying certain management techniques in order to more accurately monitor States' human rights performance. Among them are indicators and statistical measurement in general, budget analysis tools, the auditing of internal control and compliance, and on-site inspections. As the use (or at least development) of these different techniques has proliferated in order to monitor States' behaviour, they have also spread into other contexts, so that there is now a very wide-ranging, rich, and complex bricolage of different relationships of audit in the system of global human rights governance.[20] The UN treaty bodies and the National Human Rights Institutions (NHRIs) monitor States' human rights performance across statistically measured outcomes through the use of ever more detailed and extensive suites of indicators; NGOs examine the budgets of public authorities to assess whether reductions in given areas impact on human rights performance; large multinational firms employ teams of external or internal auditors to perform on-site inspections of firms in their supply chains; States are encouraged to audit each other's performance through the system of Universal Periodic Review; and so on.

Despite the myriad nature of all of these new developments, however, the essence of the entire phenomenon is relatively simple. The aim is to hold the relevant actor to account (to use an oft-repeated phrase)[21] through taking an interest in quantitatively measurable phenomena, which then has the effect of causing that actor to itself take an interest in those phenomena and attempt to improve against the relevant metrics. In other words, the fundamental principle is that which underpins almost all modern systems of performance review, whether in the field of education, product safety, academic research, health services, or otherwise.[22] In this respect, the recent history of the global governance of human rights mirrors quite closely what has taken place in most other governance contexts in the last several decades. Where once human rights was an "enclosure of expertise"[23] under the purview of a repository of positive knowledge – law – it has become penetrated by a different type of expertise altogether: calculation, monitoring, evaluation, and enumeration. That is, it has been permeated by the methods of management accounting.

The reasons for this are straightforward. Auditing *per se* has taken place since at least the Middle Ages in the context of church monies, but modern financial auditing was essentially born in the early modern era when joint stock companies first came to prominence. The strict separation of ownership (by shareholders) and management created a requirement for there to be a method by which the owners could control the direction of management without the capacity to command it directly. Hence the audit was developed, which provides the shareholders with the ability to align the operations of the company with their own goals by holding its performance to account on certain metrics (chiefly, of course, financial).[24] This has the virtue of both enshrining the autonomy of the company's management to make its own decisions, while also ensuring that it always does so in light of the shareholders' goals (e.g., maximising profit). This makes audit the quintessential technology for governing at a distance, and is why, of course, it has proliferated through both the public and private spheres in all advanced societies. It both recognises and protects the freedom of the actor who is being governed, while aligning that actor's goals with those of the governor so as to produce the desired conduct and outcomes. The management of a company are largely free to make their own decisions, as long as they achieve the goals of the shareholders as evidenced through the audit process. Similarly, the head of a school is largely free to make his or her own decisions, as long as they achieve certain outcomes measured through the relevant educational outcomes evidenced through exam results and inspections. An academic working at a university may make his or her own decisions, as long as the research produced is of a satisfactory quality and has "impact" as evidenced through research assessment exercises. The process of audit permits control to take place despite (or indeed, through) the autonomy of the subject.[25]

Precisely the same kinds of consideration underpin the shift towards regimes of audit in the system of the global governance of human rights: audit is a technology which allows indirect control to take place so as to achieve certain changes in conduct, in order to achieve certain goals or things wished for in a context in which direct control cannot. This can and does take place in many different forms; in the following section we examine some of them.

Technologies of human rights audit

Human rights indicators   The most prominent recent developments in the UN treaty-based sphere have undoubtedly been those centring around the creation and deployment of human rights indicators: numerical measures that purportedly provide an objective method for establishing whether human rights performance is declining or improving.[26] Seen as a way to open the human rights performance of States up to proper scrutiny by tracking how they perform against transparent and neutral metrics over time, human rights indicators began to be developed on an *ad hoc* basis by different treaty bodies and academics in the 1990s.[27] But they rapidly grew to prominence when the UN Office of the High Commissioner for Human Rights (OHCHR) undertook a project to systematise their use in 2005. This culminated in the OHCHR's 2012 *Human Rights Indicators: A Guide to Measurement and Implementation*, its stated goal being to act as a reference point for practitioners both within and outside the UN treaty-body system to enable them to bridge the gap between human rights standard-setting and implementation.[28]

What this meant in practice was a comprehensive and universal "framework" for developing and using suites of indicators that could be utilised among the UN treaty bodies, policymakers within States, public agencies, statistical agencies, development practitioners, NGOs, and international agencies alike – all deploying the same core methodology and rationale.[29] This involves, first, breaking down a given human right into four or five of its "attributes." For example, the right to health is subdivided into the attributes "Sexual and Reproductive Health," "Child Mortality and Health Care," "Natural and Occupational Environment," "Prevention, Treatment and Control of Diseases," and "Accessibility to Health Facilities and Essential Medicines."[30] Each of these attributes is then assigned a list of indicators, in three categories. These are structural indicators (which reflect the ratification and adoption of legal instruments and the existence of "basic institutional mechanisms necessary for the promotion and protection of human rights"), process indicators (which "measure duty bearers' ongoing efforts to transform their human rights commitments into the desired results" through, for example, statistics concerning policy measures, budget allocations, and public programmes), and outcome indicators (meaning "individual and collective attainments" such as literacy rates, life expectancy, percentage of the population experiencing crime, and so on).[31]

So, for instance, under the attribute "Sexual and Reproductive Health" for the right to health, we find structural indicators such as "time frame and coverage of national policy on sexual and reproductive health" and "time frame and coverage of national policy on abortion and foetal sex determination"; process indicators such as "proportion of births attended by skilled health personnel" and "medical terminations of pregnancy as a proportion of live births"; and outcome indicators such as "proportion of live births with low birthweight" and "perinatal mortality rate." (There are also some cross-cutting indicators across all attributes, such as the suggested structural indicator, "number of registered and/or active NGOs (per 100,000 persons) involved in the promotion and protection of the right to health").[32] The essential aim is to link commitments – in the form of structural indicators – to the efforts ("process") taken to achieve them, and then to measure the outcomes or results.[33]

This is by no means the only such project in contemporary human rights discourse – efforts are widespread and diverse[34] – but it serves as a paradigm case. The audited subject (the State) is opened up to review and rendered "knowable" through the deployment of statistical measurement, not to the tacit or intuitive expertise of the lawyer, civil servant, or politician, but to the apparently transparent, neutral, and objective expertise of the accountant. Performance review through indicators does not entirely replace the lawyer, civil servant, or politician, of course, but it subordinates their knowledge to the audit process.[35] What becomes relevant when evaluating whether a State is a good human rights performer becomes not the view of the independent expert but the abstracted measurement that, in effect, anybody can use to perform the evaluation. Whether the perinatal mortality rate is declining is transparent to observation, as is the status of ratification of the relevant treaty or the existence of a public health programme and expenditure on it.[36] Crucially, the abstracted measure also communicates in a highly efficient way to the audited subject how good performance is to be assessed, resulting in an alignment of goals between the "governor" (in this case, for example, the treaty body) and audited subject: good performance means increasing the proportion of births attended by skilled health personnel, decreasing the proportion of live births with a low birthweight, and so on. The audited subject is simply then to achieve the relevant statistical improvements.

Country visits   The shift to an accounting and audit culture is not limited to the deployment of indicators, however. More direct monitoring also takes place, in a wide variety of situations, in the form of actual on-site inspection. One prominent example of this is the country visit, widely used by the UN charter-based mechanisms such as the Working Groups, Special Rapporteurs, and Independent Experts (the so-called special procedures). Here, the mandate-holder visits a particular State to assess the human rights situation, whether at the request of the mandate-holder or at the standing invitation of the State concerned. While there, he or she typically meets with a range of actors – national and local public authorities, members of the judiciary, politicians, civil society organisations, and so on, as well as the press – and will often undertake a statistical audit of a kind alongside this, as well as making various recommendations.

To take one example, the Special Rapporteur on the Right to Education makes around one country visit each year. On her visit to Côte d'Ivoire in 2017, she met senior politicians, representatives of civil society organisations and teachers' unions, university presidents, and employees of the World Bank and various UN development programmes, and visited schools and universities. Her subsequent report is typical.[37] Beginning with an overview of Côte d'Ivoire's international legal obligations concerning the right to education, it then details the domestic legal framework before launching into a largely statistical overview of the current status of education in the country and recommendations for its improvement. Hence, for instance, we are told that 82% of pupils in the final year of primary school had not reached an adequate level in reading and mathematics and that the Government should take steps to improve this; that there were 4,471 pregnancies in general secondary schools in the country in 2016/2017 and that this was rising, but the Government should be commended for adopting a strategic plan to tackle the problem; and so forth.[38] The report ends with a list of "key issues" – such as inclusivity, child and adult literacy, academic performance, and vocational training – followed by various recommendations.

On the one hand, the country visit is another method by which the State becomes "known" and opened up to external scrutiny in much the same way that more purely statistical indicator-based techniques do, and it likewise has the effect of aligning the goals of the audited subject with those of the governing system – the improvement of educational outcomes for primary school pupils in reading and mathematics, a reduction in the number of pregnancies in secondary schools, and so on. However, the country visit also has a much more obvious auditory function: second-order observation. The modern financial audit is very much an assessment of internal control systems, for reasons of efficiency. If one can be certain that internal control is taking place adequately, one does not need to concern oneself particularly with detailed knowledge about the underlying activities (which would require a much more costly exercise).[39] Audit thereby becomes a process of external examination of the first-order control systems within the organisation itself, rather than an extensive inquiry into the nature of financial transactions taking place. Similarly, the country visit should not be understood as an attempt to generate detailed and wide-ranging knowledge about the actual underlying phenomenon – for instance, the status of the education system in Côte D'Ivoire, its effects and results, and the problems with it. Rather, it is more appropriately conceptualised as an assessment of the extent to which internal control is taking place within the State itself. It is an inquiry into the existence of relevant legal frameworks, policies, and strategies; the level of commitment of the relevant domestic actors such as politicians and civil servants; and the government's future intentions. This means that the actual phenomena underlying the statistics are almost irrelevant, and statistics themselves, where they appear, are frequently a veneer, important in large part merely because they signify that measurement is taking place. What matters is whether there is a strategy to reduce the number of pregnancies in secondary schools, for example, not necessarily its effects (and it appears in fact that there had actually been an *increase* in that number since the implementation of the strategy).[40] The government is congratulated for setting up monitoring committees regarding the number of girls who enrol and remain in school; there is no inquiry into the results of this.[41]

In a very different context, transnational firms increasingly adopt a similar approach to their suppliers, employing either their own auditors or external consultants to perform regular inspections at facilities to determine whether compliance with environmental or human rights standards is taking place. A prominent example is Levi Strauss, which regularly inspects firms in its supply chain to establish whether they are in compliance with its Business Partner Terms of Engagement – a detailed list of requirements, many of which concern human rights. These inspections can have concrete disciplinary effects (for instance, if on inspection a supplier is found to use forced or trafficked labour, it must immediately cease doing so).[42] But in large part, the purpose of such exercises is to reassure the purchaser that its suppliers have adequate internal control systems to ensure violations do not take place: verifying that factories have policies on termination of employment; that they publish lists of recruitment agencies they work with; and that they practice fire drills annually and document the results, among other things.[43] This means that Levi Strauss can satisfy itself that its suppliers have the necessary internal control systems in place to abide by the Terms of Engagement, without having to closely monitor actual performance continuously and in detail.

Budget analysis The most obvious arena in which parallels between human rights monitoring and financial accounting take place is that of budget analysis: "monitoring and analysing the public budget to assess the government's compliance with its human rights obligations" by reviewing expenditure and revenue, and auditing and evaluating the impact of the budget on human rights outcomes.[44] This is predicated on the notion that examining a State's budget can identify whether it allocates expenditure specifically towards attempting to improve human rights outcomes at all, whether its budget allocations are non-discriminatory and do not in themselves otherwise violate various human rights, and whether budget allocations in general do actually improve (or harm) human rights outcomes in a given context such as health or education.[45] (This is also often coupled with human rights budgeting, a technique which is discussed in more detail below.)

This approach is itself, of course, an exercise in statistical performance measurement of a particular type, and hence much of what was written in the previous section concerning indicators and quantitative human rights performance measurement and their effects and uses could be duplicated here. Through budget analysis, the State becomes "known" and its goals aligned with the monitor through the application of a technology which subordinates expertise in other fields such as law and politics to that of accounting in a particularly direct and obvious way. Again, it also bears emphasising that this is frequently observed and recommended as a virtue.[46] Shifting from law and adjudication to more "collaborative policy spaces" means translating the language of rights into "something meaningful and measurable,"[47] resulting in a much more effective way to hold governments to account. It also means that where previously the human rights movement has been "severely constrained [from addressing] broader issues of public policy" because of its focus on immediate obligations and their violations, it can now take the much wider perspective necessary to actually allow people to effectively enjoy their rights.[48]

Reporting But accounting and audit are, in their essence, exercises in reporting – this is indeed how the financial audit originated; as a public statement of accounts[49] – and modern human rights practice is strongly characterised by the making of public reports in a wide variety of fora. The most obvious of these is of course the actual State reporting procedures under each of the UN treaty regimes, whereby States are required to issue a public statement concerning their own human rights performance in the form of the State Report proper, the Common Core Document, and so on.

Yet this is far from being the only instance in which human rights obligations operationalise a system of reporting – be it formal or informal. The Universal Periodic Review (UPR), the Human Rights Council's equivalent to the state reporting procedure before the treaty bodies, likewise consists of a public report (referred to as a "national report") that is examined (alongside submissions by stakeholders, Special Procedures, and so on), by the Council's UPR Working Group as well as other States. The review itself takes place in an interactive discussion in an open forum, during which representatives from any UN Member State may pose questions, comments, or recommendations. This has itself been described as a "public audit ritual" because of the way in which it enrols the relevant actors into giving public accounts of themselves.[50]

And businesses in developed countries have recently begun to face increasing pressure to give reports concerning the impact of their activities on human rights, whether from shareholders or – much more prominently – as a statutory requirement. Within the EU, this comes in the form of the requirement under Directive 2014/95/EU for companies of certain types to issue "non-financial reports" containing, among other things, information concerning the impact of their activities on human rights.[51] In the UK, it appears in the Companies, Partnerships and Groups (Accounts and Non-Financial Reporting) Regulations 2016 (which gives effect in UK law to Directive 2014/95/EU), and the Companies Act 2006 (Strategic Report and Directors' Report) Regulations 2013. The latter of these requires any company which is not classified as small to issue a strategic report giving a holistic picture of the company's strategy, risks, future prospects, and the like; among these are any relevant "human rights issues" and policies concerning them.[52] In Canada, meanwhile, businesses in the mining and extractive sector are encouraged to engage in so-called CSR [Corporate Social Responsibility] Reporting alongside various other commitments under the government's Enhanced Corporate Social Responsibility Strategy to Strengthen Canada's Extractive Sector Abroad.[53] There now even exists a Reporting Framework, developed by Shift – an American non-profit organisation supported by the British, Norwegian, and Finnish governments, among others, which largely acts as a consultant concerning the UN General Principles on Business and Human Rights (UNGPs) – and the accounting firm Mazars, which is designed to allow businesses to directly evidence their compliance with the UNGPs in a format easily accessible to investors.[54]

What this means in practice is that businesses now routinely issue information concerning the human rights impact of their activities alongside various other matters in their annual reports, which would once traditionally have contained statements on financial performance alone. These can be extremely detailed or cursory, and hence it is difficult to make generalisable observations, but an example from a well-known firm operating in the UK's clothing industry is Next plc, which now issues a CSR Report based on the UNGP Reporting Framework described above. This document explains the salient human rights issues confronting the firm – for example, forced labour and modern slavery, fair living wages, discrimination, freedom of association, and child labour – and details how Next attempts to resolve those issues (in the case of child labour, this includes training for suppliers, educating "families, communities and business owners," working with NGOs to provide training, and supporting children back into education until reaching a legal working age).[55]

The matter of reporting, of course, brings us back full circle to auditing and accounting, and it is here we see the benefits of those technologies for those expressing the will to govern functioning most acutely. In the first place, through the requirement to report, the audited subject is required to display commitment to, and align its own goals with, those of the auditor – be it the treaty body, the Human Rights Council, investors and other stakeholders, and so on. (Notwithstanding the fact that this may of course be mere "buffering" or "game playing," displaying ritualistic compliance which masks the underlying reality, which is an ever-present problem.)[56] Thus, for instance, whenever a State makes its report to a treaty body and engages in the subsequent process – the exchange of the List of Issues, the constructive dialogue, and the Concluding Observations – it receives what is in essence feedback from the treaty body, which then informs both how it is supposed to act and also what it is supposed to *measure* in the following period. The process, then, is not solely or even very much concerned with the production of knowledge or the holding of the State to account for its performance in the previous period. It is rather an opportunity for the treaty body to communicate to the State what its goals are to be for the next. These could be substantive (improve the participation rate of children from a given minority group in the education system, reduce infant mortality, etc.) or they could be procedural (provide better data about the use of corporate punishment in schools, develop an indicator to statistically capture the extent to which people feel safe, and so on). In either respect, a signal is sent about what good performance constitutes, and the State is to respond accordingly.

Secondly, however, the reporting process also provides an opportunity for the audited subject to demonstrate that its own internal compliance structures are adequate. For example, when Next plc issues its CSR Report, what is being revealed and subjected to external scrutiny is not so much "facts on the ground" but what the firm is doing to monitor and control its own performance and relationships with its suppliers: it has a Human Rights and Modern Slavery Policy publicly available;[57] it trains 93% of its UK employees and 96% of its overseas employees concerning human rights;[58] it has "robust due diligence processes";[59] it has a Modern Slavery Steering Group;[60] and so on. And all of this information is assured by an external auditor, PricewaterhouseCoopers, which adds further reassurance that the firm properly self-scrutinises and self-regulates. The process of making the report must be understood, then, as being a display of self-assessment – a public demonstration that the firm audits *itself* – rather than an airing of relevant facts for the outside world to investigate in detail. Power refers to this as "structured self-observation" – the behaviour by which the audited subject comes to regard itself from the perspective of the auditor, and hence to align its goals with it.[61]

The characteristics of audit permeate the international human rights system, then, and the reasons for this are obvious. On the one hand, it is an attempt to resolve the practical difficulties of achieving things wished for in the "murky plain of overwhelming detail," and on the other it is an attempt to circumvent the legal and philosophical impossibility of simply ruling by decree. This is achieved through technologies of monitoring, reporting, measurement, and self-assessment, which render the subject knowable and accountable, and therefore – ideally – cause it to align its own goals with those of the governing body despite its formal autonomy. And this also has the effect, as will have been noticed, that the audited subject also begins to monitor and audit others, so that, for example, businesses begin inspecting their suppliers and States begin to monitor and report on goings-on in the private sphere. The result is a pluralisation of the actors carrying out the tasks of governance, and this is what we turn to next.

Devolving the task of governance: pluralisation and autonomisation

As we have already seen, the international human rights system touches a wide array of actors, and brings many of them into relationships of governance. And this takes place irrespective of whether those actors might formally exist in the public or private sphere. The State, which once engaged monolithically with international human rights law on the basis of entering into treaty commitments by which it agreed to be bound, and likewise was understood monolithically to violate rights or otherwise, has now been fractured. This has happened partly as a result of the turn to audit as already described, and partly because of the broader reconceptualisation of rights as requiring protection, respect, and fulfilment. As a consequence, there has been a vast and rapid proliferation of entities deemed to bear responsibility both for respecting human rights and also for controlling the conduct of others in that regard. In this respect what Miller and Rose described as pluralisation – the depoliticisation and dispersal of governance – is obvious and is, in many ways, the story of Chapter 1 of this book. It is also important to add, of course, that as well as pluralising human rights obligations and governance across a range of actors other than the State, this process has also autonomised such actors by separating their obligations from those attributed to the State. There is no better example of this than the transformation of the business into not merely the subject of human rights obligations but also a "responsible" actor with the requirement to carry out governance of suppliers and various stakeholder groups – and even, in some cases, States themselves – on the basis of its own free-standing obligations.

We have already seen much of this, in the manner in which businesses are increasingly required to report on the human rights impacts of their operations, and to carry out human rights due diligence with respect to their supply chains.[62] Here, the firm undertakes "a comprehensive, proactive attempt to uncover human rights risks, actual and potential, over the entire life cycle of a project or business activity, with the aim of avoiding and mitigating those risks."[63] This may include, for example, human rights impact assessments, which seek to measure the risk of human rights violations occurring in potential future operations. Or it might consist of ongoing human rights risk management, including ongoing monitoring and reporting, and integration of policies and protocols into corporate governance systems.[64] We earlier examined Levi Strauss's extensive efforts to externally audit its suppliers, and Next plc's CSR strategy, for example, both of which can readily be conceptualised in this way. However, due diligence may be much wider than this, both in the range of its subjects and the scope of its activities. For example, it is not unusual to find firms carrying out risk assessments and audits not only of suppliers but also of States themselves as locations to do business (often

through or with an external "partner" such as Transparency International).
Johnson & Johnson is typical in this regard, having a list of "High Risk
Countries" in which it invests, generated through assessments carried out by
Transparency International, and in which "outreach" is performed to ensure
conformance with human rights policies.[65] And "due diligence" can take on
a much more extensive and wide-ranging character than mere impact assessment and risk management to include capacity-building approaches – for
instance, by carrying out training for suppliers or capacity building.[66]

But even State apparatuses have gone through such a transformation.
The best example of this is the creation of the NHRI, a type of independent
ombudsman or commission formally accredited to be incorporated into the
UN human rights system by the Sub-Committee on Accreditation for the
International Coordinating Committee. These bodies, which are supposed
to act independently of the government in the State in which they operate
(and are given a status A-C to reflect whether they achieve this, among other
things) liaise with the UN treaty bodies by providing "shadow" reports,
contributing to the List of Issues when the State in question submits a
report, and so on. NHRIs are also expected to work to harmonise national
laws with international human rights law, encourage ratification of human
rights treaties, educate the populace, and so on. They also involve themselves in other activities more generally. The Equality and Human Rights
Commission (EHRC) in the UK, for instance, carries out investigations
into various issues concerning equality and discrimination, provides advice
and guidance to public authorities and employers, and also brings judicial
review proceedings where it considers it to be appropriate.[67]

The NHRI thus acts as a kind of outpost of the UN system within the
domestic apparatus of the State, working to bring about compliance "from
the inside." This might come in the form of encouraging governments to
comply with reporting obligations when they have failed to do so, urging
removal of reservations to treaty provisions, assisting in the preparation
of reports, and also providing supplementary information to treaty bodies
or encouraging NGOs to do so.[68] It also might include participating in the
official sessions of the treaty bodies, meeting informally with members of
the treaty bodies, and then later engaging in "follow-up" after Concluding
Observations have been issued.[69] Finally, it might also include disseminat-
ing information about individual complaint procedures where those exist,
assisting individuals to file complaints against the State, and initiating
inquiries where those procedures exist in the relevant treaty.[70]

In this way, the State becomes pluralised and its functions concerning
human rights separated out and autonomised from mainstream political
apparatuses. The EHRC, for instance, has a board of Commissioners formally appointed by the Minister for Women and Equalities but operating

under "as few constraints as reasonably possible in determining its activities, timetables and priorities."[71] It is directly accountable only to that Secretary of State and only to that extent. This means that democratic or political control is largely replaced by a stakeholder model with representation from different groups or "communities." Current board members, as of writing, include for instance the former Chair of Stonewall, the current Vice-President of Carers UK, the former Deputy Chair to the Business in the Community Gender Equality Campaign, and an expert on ethnicity and mental health. Thus the Commission operates largely (although not of course entirely)[72] autonomously from traditional political authority, and is constituted rather as a quango, carrying out an independent regulatory function with respect to other public bodies and private actors. The list of "current projects" on its website as of writing concern, for instance, anything from racial harassment in higher education, to disabled access at Premier League football stadiums, to equal pay for men and women in the BBC, to anti-semitism in the Labour Party – and everything in between.[73]

The phenomena of pluralisation and autonomisation are, of course, self-reinforcing and concatenating. Legislation requiring businesses to report on the impact on human rights of their operations, in turn, causes those businesses to require suppliers to perform similar rituals of audit, and so on down the supply chain. This transforms not just the largest firm into a human rights regulator in its own right, but also the suppliers vis-à-vis their own operations and stakeholders. The establishment of an NHRI such as the EHRC to perform a regulatory function likewise causes other public bodies and private actors to begin to put into effect their own human rights policies and procedures autonomously. Indeed, encouraging other regulators, ombudsmen, and the like to incorporate equality and human rights in their work is one of the goals in the EHRC's 2019–2022 strategic plan,[74] alongside priority aims such as "helping" employers provide fair opportunities, utilising public transport companies to promote social inclusion, and using the education system to "instil understanding of and respect for difference."[75] In this way, human rights regulation becomes further pluralised across an ever-widening range of actors (employers, public transport companies, schools, etc.), who are – at least, this is the intention – transformed into autonomous human rights regulators in their turn.

To take a brief illustration, the EHRC, as previously mentioned, lists disabled access at Premier League football stadiums as one of its current projects. This involves, among other things, producing annual reports on the "State of Play" concerning accessibility, which include a range of recommendations for individual clubs and the Premier League itself.[76] While the recommendations to the individual clubs chiefly concern best practices for improving accessibility for disabled fans, those addressed to the Premier League concern the "Premier League Pledge," an undertaking to abide by the Accessible Stadia Guide (ASG), to which clubs are required by the Premier League to commit. The ASG is itself produced by another quango, the Sports Ground Safety Authority (SGSA), and the EHRC likewise also issues that body with recommendations to work with the Premier League and other stakeholders to provide clearer and better guidance. And, finally, the EHRC also uses its report to urge other governing bodies such as the Football Association (FA), Sport England, Sport Scotland, and Sport Wales, and so on, to adopt similar "Pledges." In other words, if the EHRC's recommendations were to be carried out, human rights regulation – at least with respect to disabled rights – would be further pluralised and autonomised across sport's governing bodies, whether they are of a private or public character, including the Premier League, the SGSA, the FA, and so forth. These bodies would not, in other words, merely have human rights obligations in law, but the responsibility to perform governance of other relevant actors in their turn.[77]

Hence, the effort to govern human rights "at a distance" is both diffuse and capillary. On the one hand, it works not merely to enshrine autonomy but *through* it, devolving the task of "governance" to new actors irrespective of their public or private nature. And on the other, it causes that task to proliferate across an ever-widening range of actors in such a way that chains of governance, as it were, both spread and multiply. What is more, if the process of pluralisation and autonomisation has any effect on the behaviour of these actors at all, it cannot but be expected to also alter their subjectivity – indeed, that must be thought of as the ultimate end goal of that process: the production of a new subjectivity in which the actor is (at least partially) reconstituted as a "human rights governor" in its own right. Hence, of course, the process of pluralisation and autonomisation can be understood as simply another form or facet of the same underlying rationale or governing style. Just as technologies of accounting and audit produce the subject as an autonomous actor behaving in the manner that is desired by the auditor through the alignment of their goals, so those of pluralisation and autonomisation reconstitute an ever-increasing range of actors in a certain mould. And this leads us, quite naturally, to the third of Miller and Rose's groups of techniques: the creation of new subjectivities.

"A more proactive and systemic move": the construction of new subjectivities

At the time of the creation of the EHRC, the UK Parliament's Joint Committee on Human Rights was quite clear about the impetus behind the establishment of such a body:

> [A]n independent commission would be the most effective way of achieving the shared aim of bringing about a *culture of respect for human rights.*[78]

It is far from uncommon to find such desires expressed. The OHCHR, for example, describes its own task as "to inject a human rights perspective into all United Nations programmes."[79] The UNGPs are framed by their founder as having the goal of "embedding" businesses in transnational human rights norms.[80] And the task of the International Court of Justice (ICJ) regarding human rights is described by one of its most prominent judges as being to "integrate [human rights] into the fabric of general international law and its various other branches."[81] In other words, there is a frequent rhetorical commitment in modern human rights practice to not merely the advancement of legal protections *per se* but the systemic integration of a human rights "culture" into the functioning of States, businesses, international organisations, and courts.

This rhetorical commitment manifests itself in various techniques which are often framed as aspects of "mainstreaming."[82] The immediate goal of this is easily stated: ensuring that "due regard" is paid to human rights when planning or carrying out policy of any kind.[83] But that apparently simple formulation naturally gives rise to the perceived need for greater conceptual detail. It also conceals a vast array both of different species of mainstreaming and different techniques for achieving it. This section will focus in particular on three specific loci for human rights mainstreaming: the mainstreaming of human rights within UN institutions, national human rights action planning, and human rights budgeting (which is related to, but distinct from, the kind of human rights budget analysis described previously).

As we shall see, these techniques have the function of specifying the subjects of governance in a new way, that is, as active human rights protectors in their own right. This can be very explicit and directly stated, with the aim clearly intended to produce a particular kind of State, international organisation, business, and so on: one which acts to improve the enjoyment of human rights alongside or indeed through its activities. Through techniques of human rights mainstreaming, generally performed with the intention of achieving better and more widespread human rights protection, however formulated or understood ("cross[ing] over from the realm of rhetoric into the realm of reality," as Chalabi puts it),[84] the subject is itself produced as an actor which not only does not itself violate human rights, but takes an active role in spreading the global governance of rights. The existence of such subjects thereby becomes, indeed, the "ethical *a priori*"[85] for the way in which modern human rights governance functions.

Human rights mainstreaming

Fully integrating human rights The story of human rights mainstreaming effectively begins with Kofi Annan's proposal in 1997, as part of a much wider agenda for reform, to "fully integrate" the UN's human rights programme into the "broad range of the Organisation's activities."[86] At its most immediate and observable, this meant the reconceptualisation of human rights as a cross-cutting issue spanning the UN's four executive areas (peace and security, economic and social affairs, humanitarian affairs, and development cooperation) and the creation of a single Office of the High Commissioner for Human Rights (the OHCHR) to sit in all of the four corresponding executive committees of the UN. This Office was also then tasked with taking charge of the mainstreaming of human rights. But what it ultimately means, in fact, varies considerably depending on which part of the organisation's activities one examines, what definition of "full integration" one prefers, and which human rights are considered. This makes it difficult to make detailed observations which apply across the UN's activities *in toto*. This is not helped by a lack of recent academic surveys of the field – the most recent comprehensive attempt dates from 2008[87] – and a paucity of empirical studies on the actual implementation of human rights mainstreaming.[88] Yet some general characteristics can nonetheless be observed.

First, there is now a clear rhetorical commitment to human rights across the UN's specialised agencies. These commitments are often dismissed as being "half-hearted" or similar.[89] But there are essentially no UN agencies or bodies which do not at least purport to acknowledge a role for human rights to play in their activities. The United Nations International Children's Fund (UNICEF), for instance, puts a commitment to promoting the rights of children in the first sentence of its mission statement and says that it upholds the Convention on the Rights of the Child.[90] The Food and Agriculture Organization (FAO) has as one of its policy themes the promotion of a "cross-cutting human rights-based approach to food security and nutrition."[91] The Vision Statement of the World Bank Group's Environmental and Social Framework claims that the Bank's activities support the realisation of human rights and that it supports its member countries in achieving their human rights commitments.[92] And even the International Monetary Fund (IMF), often held up as the last bastion or holdout against ascribing human rights obligations to international organisations,[93] is careful to emphasise that its activities indirectly promote human rights through providing macro-economic stability, fostering respect for the rule of law, and so on.[94]

Second, human rights considerations now increasingly inform the policies and programmes of many UN organs, in two main ways. In the first place, policy is often formulated in such a way that it is said to further the protection of a given human right or human rights in general. Hence, for instance, the World Health Organization (WHO) has adopted the implementation of universal health coverage as one of its leadership priorities, specifically because it is viewed as an entitlement on the basis of its role in fulfilling the right to health – or simply, as the current Director-General puts it, because "universal health coverage *is* a human right."[95] Second, programmes are designed in such a way that they are informed by, or incorporate, human rights considerations. For example, UNICEF has a Gender Action Plan providing that the results of all UNICEF programmes are to be measured partly on the basis of gender equality – that is, so that all of its programmes will be designed with the elimination of gender inequalities, broadly understood, as specific goals.[96] In this way, gender equality is to become part of the "core of [UNICEF's] mission" – a theme integrated into all of UNICEF's "goal areas."[97]

Third, the staff of UN organs frequently undergo human rights-based training. This might occur internally (the United Nations Educational, Scientific and Cultural Organization (UNESCO), for instance, produces various learning modules for its staff, on the understanding that "building [their] capacities" is the basis of its efforts to mainstream human rights).[98] Or it might take place in a cross-cutting fashion across agencies (the General Assembly's Political Declaration on HIV/AIDS, for instance, calls on all UN agencies to provide training in HIV/AIDS awareness, including from a human rights perspective, to their staff).[99] The aim, however is frequently the same: to "promote organizational change and culture transformation"[100] through ensuring that staff have human rights values "in [their] DNA," to use the WHO's arresting phrase.[101] A related approach is the appointment of bespoke human rights officers and expert steering groups, which is the approach taken by, for example, the Global Fund to Fight AIDS, Tuberculosis and Malaria, a UN-affiliated financing mechanism. Its 2012–2016 strategy included an objective to "promote and protect human rights," and actions under this objective included the creation of a Community, Rights and Gender Department with a senior human rights advisor, and a Community, Rights and Gender Advisory Group and Human Rights Reference Group, both staffed by experts from NGOs. These various units carry out analyses and provide technical guidance and consultation within the Fund's activities in order to integrate human rights into its work.[102]

And fourth, human rights are very often becoming utilised as reference points or benchmarking criteria for establishing goals and targets, or for the assessment of the success or failure of policy outcomes. UNICEF's Gender Action Plan, briefly described already, is a typical example of the former. The plan includes, among other things, two "themes" – "Gender equality for girls and boys" and "Gender equality in care and support for all children" – and these are both to be assessed with four "demonstration results" each. These demonstration results are then broken down into a handful of different aspirations or broad goals. An example of a demonstration result for "Gender equality for girls and boys" is "Gender-equitable health care and nutrition for girls and boys." This is then broken down into the aspirations to collect sex-disaggregated data; to strengthen "community platforms" to address gender inequalities in care and counselling; and to develop indicators to improve data and measurement and test interventions so as to address the "gender dimensions" of adolescent mental health in low- and middle-income countries.[103] In other words, a particular conceptualisation of a given human right – in this case, the right to non-discrimination – is used as a broad-based framework within which to establish what the goals of programme making are to be. More directly, human rights may simply be the rationale or justification for the setting of performance targets. The UN Population Fund (UNFPA), for example, has at the core of its strategy the achievement of "three zeros" by 2030: zero unmet needs for contraception, zero preventable maternal deaths, and zero gender-based violence and harmful practices such as child marriage and female genital mutilation (FGM), all deliberately framed around empowering all women and girls to enjoy their rights.[104] Here, human rights provide the overarching targets by which the UNFPA's entire performance will be assessed. It will have succeeded or failed based on eliminating three phenomena which it deliberately conceptualises and describes as being barriers to the enjoyment of women's human rights.

The engines of implementation The purpose of mainstreaming human rights into the activities of UN organs is hardly hidden. It is to transform those organs into the "engines" of the implementation of human rights.[105] Given their role in providing States with technical assistance, policy guidance, capacity building, and so on,[106] the theory would have it, then the "indigenization" of human rights within UN agencies, funds, and programs would result in the entire corpus of the activities of such bodies being geared – to use another engineering metaphor – for the implementation of human rights.[107] Since this would mean that all of their work would be dedicated, at least in part, to achieving the enjoyment of human rights, this would then have the effect of finally bridging the gap between normative commitment and practical realisation which has obsessed the human rights movement from its very beginning.[108] Indeed, "the era of implementation," as Hunt puts it, "is also the era of mainstreaming."[109] The latter achieves the former through the integration of human rights considerations into the UN system's operations *in toto*.

That this should involve the reconceptualisation of the role of UN bodies goes without saying, but the intention, of course, is also to bring about a change in their self-perception. Their commitment to human rights is to be rendered "authentic."[110] This process is multi-faceted. On the one hand, it is described in terms that are best thought of as psychological. An institution must "question its very mandate." It must "take seriously" the call to mainstream human rights, and, if it "struggles" to do so, or displays "diffidence," then it must be categorised in an outer "circle of willingness."[111] The reformulation of its attitude must be total. UN bodies ought to "rediscover human rights in their respective mandates," and become aware that their work "has in fact always been linked to human rights."[112] To fail to base their activities on human rights should be "unimaginable".[113] (This personalisation of the abstract entity, of course, can disguise the ramifications for staff, whose potential "resistance [to] rights discourse" is to be "navigated strategically" by those carrying out the work of reconceptualisation).[114] Yet the aim is not only to bring about change in the way UN bodies self-perceive. It is also to result in their becoming active agents in the interpretation, development, and expansion of human rights norm making and standard setting.[115] Hence, for instance, UNICEF's interpretation of the content of the right of non-discrimination discussed previously so as to include, for instance, the issue of mental health in adolescence; the WHO's Gender, Equity and Rights Unit's elaboration of an entire set of principles and core attributes of the right to health;[116] UNESCO's efforts to render the right to science justiciable Action;[117] the UNFPA's interpretation of its mandate to include the elimination of child marriage on the basis of it being a violation of children's and women's rights; and so on. Through the creation of a devolved "human rights archipelago"[118] throughout the UN system, we see the production of UN bodies as a new type of actor – not merely international organisations who must respect human rights, but institutions who self-perceive and self-describe as having the implementation of human rights as their focus, and who work actively as norm-entrepreneurs to expand upon and detail the scope of human rights in their specific domains.

National human rights action planning

If the aim of human rights mainstreaming is to alter the subjectivity of UN bodies, then an equivalent process may be thought of as taking place for States through the technique of national human rights action planning (hereinafter "NHRA planning"), which often contains a mainstreaming component.

    NHRA planning has a comparatively ancient heritage, having been present conceptually in the system of international human rights law since its inception – Article 14 of the International Covenant on Economic, Social and Cultural Rights (ICESCR) explicitly requires States parties to "work out and adopt a detailed plan of action" for the implementation of universal compulsory free education. Though this is the only appearance of such a requirement in the international bill of rights, the Committee on Economic, Social and Cultural Rights (CESCR) has also consistently read the obligation to "take steps … by all appropriate means" to realise the rights contained in the Covenant, under Article 2, paragraph (1), to include an implied obligation to "work out and adopt a detailed national human rights action plan for the progressive implementation" of each such right. This was indeed one of the main subjects of its very first General Comment in 1981.[119] Since then, the CESCR has enthusiastically expanded upon and detailed this requirement in its General Comments and Concluding Observations on State reports. An illustrative list provided by Chalabi of areas which the Committee has urged States to adopt plans of action includes the reduction in disparities of living standards; improving housing and social inclusion; reforming the residential system of childcare; preventing suicide; reducing violence against women; eliminating gender inequalities; addressing school drop-outs and youth unemployment; eradicating slave labour and FGM; combating human trafficking and corruption; eliminating violence against children, child labour, and the sexual abuse, exploitation and prostitution of children; eliminating racism and discrimination, and eliminating domestic violence.[120] Such strictures have also spread across the different treaty bodies to a greater or lesser extent. They may simply be framed as requests for information on the existence and effect of such plans (which is the approach often taken by the Human Rights Committee (HRC));[121] they may be couched in the language of expectation (as, for example, the CRC Committee's expression of concern "at the lack of a comprehensive rights-based national plan of action for children covering all areas of the Convention" in Japan);[122] or they may be stated more directly (such as the Committee Against Torture (CAT)'s requirement put to Iceland to establish a national plan of action against trafficking in human beings).[123] In any event, the UN treaty bodies are generally unified in the view that, to some extent or other, NHRA planning arises as an obligation under their respective treaties – with failure to adopt and implement such a plan being *itself* a violation of the treaty text. This is typically on the basis of a requirement to take "all necessary measures" (or similar) to realise the rights recognised therein.[124] But requirements or recommendations for the creation of human rights national action plans are not limited to the UN treaty body system. Charter-based mechanisms, particularly Special Rapporteurs and Independent Experts, frequently also urge States to adopt such plans. The Security Council itself has repeatedly adopted resolutions on Women, Peace and Security which recommend the creation of National Action Plans on Women, Peace and Security.[125] And both the EU and UN Human Rights Council have requested that States develop national action plans on businesses and human rights and issued guidance accordingly.[126]

Naturally, there is a great deal of variation in what NHRA planning actually entails and is intended to entail, and the level of commitment given to it. The UN treaty bodies and charter-based mechanisms have typically refrained from offering detailed substantive recommendations, and limited themselves to addressing the structure and scope of such plans. The CRC's recommendation that Japan develop a national plan of action for children, discussed above, for example, specified that it ought to contain "medium and long-term targets" and monitoring mechanisms to control outcomes and make adjustments where necessary, with no particular substantive comment on what those targets or outcomes should be.[127] The recommendation of the Committee on the Elimination of Discrimination Against Women (CEDAW Committee) to Egypt regarding combatting violence against women and girls stipulated only that a national action plan in that regard ought to be "coherent and multi-sectoral."[128] The Special Rapporteur on torture, in urging Indonesia after a country visit to adopt an anti-torture action plan, specified only that it ought to contain "awareness raising programmes and training for all stakeholders ... in order to lead them to live up to their human rights obligations and fulfil their specific task in the fight against torture."[129]

Doubtless this lack of specificity on substance is for the most part due to the perennial issues concerning lack of time and resources about which anybody involved in the UN human rights system frequently complains. But it is not difficult to see another imperative at work in the general approach to NHRA planning. The aim not to oversee the minutiae of activities taking place within States, but rather their transformation into a particular kind of actor. An example is provided in the following set of Concluding Observations issued by the CRC Committee to Japan to those mentioned above.[130] Here, under the list of "Main Concerns and Recommendations," we find the State urged to fully harmonise its legislation with the principles and principles of the Convention, to develop a comprehensive child protection policy and a comprehensive implementation strategy for it, and to put in place a coordinating body with a clear mandate and authority to coordinate all activities in implementing the Convention at national, regional, and local levels. It is requested to improve data collection in all areas of the Convention, to establish independent monitoring mechanisms and ombudsmen for children's rights, and to carry out awareness-raising programmes and children's rights campaigns. It is urged to train teachers, judges, lawyers, investigating officers, social workers, law enforcement officials, media professionals, civil servants, and "government officials at all levels." It is tasked with producing a national action plan on business and human rights which integrates children's rights.[131] What is envisaged, in other words, is nothing less than a reconceptualisation of the Japanese State and its public, civic, and even private institutions as comprehensively and jointly engaged in the promotion of children's rights. The content of those rights is, of course, important to the CRC, and the Concluding Observations naturally go on to address them. But the planning component is distinct. It means a reconfiguration of the mechanisms of government so as to thoroughly encompass children's rights – to, borrowing again from Hunt, transform them into the "engines" of implementation.[132] The State, in other words, becomes re-conceived – if the process is successful – as an active coordinating entity. It is not merely called upon to refrain from violating the rights of children, but to become the active participant in a process of bringing about their enjoyment.

Human rights budgeting

The CRC's Concluding Observations on Japan's fourth and fifth periodic reports also contain a subsection of recommendations concerning the allocation of resources. In it, the Committee "strongly recommends" that Japan set up a budgeting process that includes a children's rights perspective, with amongst other things "detailed budget lines and codes for all planned, enacted, revised and actual expenditures that directly affect children," "budget classification systems that allow expenditures related to the rights of the child to be reported, tracked and analysed," and a means of ensuring "that the fluctuation or reduction of in budget allocations ... does not reduce the existing level of enjoyment of children's rights."[133] This brings us neatly, then, to our third example area in which we can discern the governing of human rights at a distance producing new subjectivities: human rights budgeting.

The deployment of human rights budget analysis has already been discussed earlier in this chapter. That technique can be understood most plainly as the attempt to use public expenditure in particular fields or in particular ways as a method of monitoring compliance with human rights obligations – particularly the obligations to use the maximum available resources to realise rights found in the ICESCR and CRC.[134] This is described as "hindsight" analysis: using the impact of expenditure as a way of establishing if it has resulted in failure to meet required standards.[135] In this sense, budget analysis can be thought of as one among many auditing tools, and indeed that was how it was conceptualised earlier in this chapter. The CRC Committee's comments on Japan's fourth and fifth periodic reports can also at least partially be understood in this way. If Japan were to provide budget lines and codes and budget classifications in such a fashion that it was clear how expenditures were intended to be used with respect to children's rights, then the process of audit from the Committee's perspective would be much simpler. It could identify failings more easily, and ideally shift closer towards the role of auditing internal control (i.e., the manner in which the budget was formulated) rather than actual outcomes.

But there is something more to the way in which budgets are described and conceptualised in modern human rights practice, such that it also makes sense to discuss "human rights budgeting" as a separate phenomenon. In our example, Japan is not simply being enjoined to systematise its budget in a particular fashion by the CRC Committee. It is also being asked to consider the very process of budgeting as an exercise in ensuring that "public budgets contribute to the realization of [children's] rights."[136] Japan must "specify clear allocations to children" and consider how to track and analyse "expenditures related to the rights of the child;" its budget must include a "child-rights perspective."[137] In other words, the State is being thought of as an institution whose role is not just to effectively administer resources in an abstract and general way – but that "mobilises" resources for particular ends (namely, the realisation of children's rights).[138]

The aim for the CRC Committee in respect of public budgeting, then, is not to create another technique simply for assessing compliance, but to advance implementation of the Convention through the way budgets are planned, enacted, executed, and followed up.[139] And this involves extensive structural change, such that the realisation of children's rights becomes integrated into the entire budget process – "all government branches ... that play a role in public budgets [must] exercise their functions in a way that is consistent with the general principles of the Convention," in an environment rendered "enabling" by the State.[140] This cannot simply be a matter of ensuring that budgets are non-discriminatory or that they do not divert funds from existing programmes concerning children's rights. The State must also "mobilise" sufficient financial resources by taking "all possible measures" in order to fulfil the economic, social, and cultural rights of all children.[141] It must "[equip] all levels and structures of the executive, legislature and judiciary with the resources and information required to advance the rights of children."[142] It must take "concrete [and] sustainable measures" to "mobilize domestic resources at the national and subnational levels, such as through taxes and non-tax revenues."[143] Put more bluntly, the "size" of the budget must be sufficient to realise children's rights.[144] Where it is insufficient – where the State lacks resources – it must seek international cooperation and technical and financial support from the UN, among others.[145] And all of this must take place in a context of stakeholder participation, legislative scrutiny, audit, and impact assessment, which ensures that the entire implementation process is "accountable, effective, efficient, equitable, participatory, transparent and sustainable."[146] It is no exaggeration to say that what is envisaged is for the State itself to be transformed into an active participant in realising children's rights – whatever that might mean, and whatever the cost – with the process of budgeting a programmatic tool in that very process.

The rationale here is obvious, and extends across the UN system. A budget "showcases the government's true priorities."[147] It, in an oft-quoted formulation of Wildavsky's, is "the lifeblood of the government ... the link between financial resources and human behaviour to accomplish policy objectives."[148] Hence, a budget does not simply evidence or plan expenditure. It also indicates and, more crucially, *formulates* aims and desires. A State which explicitly allocates fiscal resources towards achieving human rights-related ends is a State which actively attempts to promote the realisation of human rights. Its subjectivity, in other words, is changed through the process of budgeting in a particular fashion. Blyberg puts this quite starkly:

> Governments, if they have the political will, can shape their budgets and spend them in ways that help guarantee a more equitable distribution and use of the society's wealth [and thereby] enhance the access of each and every person in the country to those basic facilities and capacities that are essential for human dignity. *This is government at its best.*[149]

The reasoning could not be simpler. A State which budgets for human rights is a State which self-perceives and self-describes as being the means through which rights find expression and are realised. And this is indeed what we discover in the domestic context where arguments for human rights budgeting are being made. The Scottish Human Rights Commission (SHRC) has been at the forefront of such efforts in recent years, as part of its active role in the development of the Scottish government's national human rights action plan (Scotland's National Plan for Human Rights, or "SNAP"). The preamble to its background briefing paper on human rights budgeting, setting out the rationale for carrying such activities out, is worth quoting at length in respect of this:

> Governments' budgets, while comprising technical processes, are also political documents. They are shaped by the political debates within a country and embody the values of the decision-makers and, ideally, the people of the country. When a government is committed to values of social justice and equality, *as is the Scottish Government*, the public budget should mirror those values.[150]

The very process of public budgeting, that is, becomes part of a narrative in which a government self-describes as committed to realising the fulfilment of broad human rights-based goals ("social justice and equality") – to "systematically work to enhance the quality of life of all people."[151] The technology of public budgeting, if it could not be plainer, entails nothing less than the reconfiguration of the State so as to align itself with the purposes of the system of international human rights law.

Summary

We have come a long way from our beginning in this section, and it would be useful to briefly retrace our steps. I started with the initial observation that certain systemic conditions which confront a purposive orientation to international human rights law were different but analogous to those which tend to confront "governors" in advanced societies, and that we might therefore be able to identify the use of certain technologies of governing "at a distance" in the former that had been identified by other scholars in the latter. These, I suggested, could be grouped under the broad categories of a shift to techniques of accounting and audit; a growth in pluralisation and autonomisation; and the production of new subjectivities. The previous subsections evidence that this is indeed a persuasive way of thinking about recent developments in the field of what I have referred to as global human rights governance, because they show how those different technologies of government have proliferated in the human rights context, particularly in the last decade or so. In closing this section, it is worth emphasising some other aspects of these phenomena that have not already been discussed in great detail here.

The first is that – as the reader will undoubtedly have noticed – many of the technologies described in the foregoing sections are cross-cutting and there is considerable overlap between the three broad categories identified. The shift to accounting and audit, for instance, is of course in part a process both of autonomisation and the production of new subjectivities. While audit is primarily a matter of monitoring behaviour, as we have seen, it is also a method for producing *self-monitoring* behaviour, and also a way of aligning the goals and objectives of the subject with those of the governing entity which requires audit to take place. This could just as well be thought of as the autonomisation of the audited subject (its reconstitution as a self-auditor) and also a transformation in its very subjectivity (into an actor which actively audits itself and others in view of certain goals or purposes). Similarly, the growth in pluralisation might be conceived instead as the production of actors hitherto outside the purview of human rights – businesses, international organisations, etc. – as new subjects well within it. One should therefore not consider these technologies as deployed in isolation, but as part of a "bricolage," to use Cerny's phrase, for reconciling the goals of the system of global human rights governance with the ineluctable conditions confronting it.

The second is that one must be particularly careful to establish the appropriate level of abstraction at which to discern intent in the deployment of the technologies identified. The techniques used, and the manners in which they are used, are "pragmatically arrived-at for the most part."[152] While it is appropriate to understand them as being attempts to "govern at a distance," as in the domestic context, the actors concerned hardly, if ever, conceptualise them in that sense. Typically, if those advocating the use of such techniques describe themselves as attempting to achieve anything, it is couched in terms of bridging the gap between "rhetoric and reality" or "norms and implementation" or "ideals and practice." It so happens that the results of such efforts frequently amount to what could be described as governing human rights at a distance, but this is hardly – it ought to go without saying – the result of deliberate policy or even, often, awareness. It is simply the consequence of the project of attempting to effect the system's *teleocratic* project given the *nomocratic* constraints inherent within it.

Third, one must also be careful to avoid conflating the attempt to govern in advanced liberal societies, which Miller and Rose and others were attempting to describe, with the attempt to "govern human rights." My reasoning is strictly by way of analogy. It is important to be absolutely clear on this point, because of the associations, so frequently and naturally made, between liberalism and human rights, and because human rights are often said in the literature on governmentality to have a role, indeed, in the governmentalisation of liberal Statehood. It bears reiterating that governing at a distance is here advanced as a way of describing the deployment of a set of particular technologies of government which, in the context of human rights, bear a family resemblance to those deployed in the context of advanced liberalism, as they do to the drive to govern purposefully or *teleocratically* in any context.

Fourth, it is also crucial to emphasise that – as, again, will be obvious to the reader – the technologies grouped under the three categories in the previous subsection are only ever deployed partially, to some extent or other, and to varying degrees of success. It is perfectly possible for human rights auditing to be performed in an empty, game-playing, and perhaps even deliberately deceptive or fictitious form;[153] it is perfectly possible for human rights mainstreaming to be an entirely rhetorical exercise having no practical consequence in the behaviour of an organisation; and it is also perfectly possible for a business, notionally having human rights responsibilities, to simply comply with statutory reporting requirements in a fashion devoid of content. Another way of putting it is that there is always a gap, big or small, between even the stated goal of a policy or activity and its actual real-world effects, and unanticipated consequences are inescapable.

Conclusion

The reader will on reflection be struck by the descriptive accuracy of Koskenniemi's account, emphasising as it does the manner in which "law [becomes] drained out of international law"[154] to be replaced by the "global management" of optimisation, calculation, standard-setting, and the like.[155] A dissatisfaction – even a mistrust – with law is indeed evident in much of the literature on human rights implementation. Law is "necessary but not sufficient," and as time goes on the process will need to become "successively more executive rather than legislative";[156] human rights will need to "evolve" towards a new future of "governance."[157] Where law does appear it is frequently as the "enabling environment" for policy,[158] part of the framework of "institutional design"[159] or even simply the first "declaratory" stage before the work of implementation genuinely begins.[160] "A second best," that is – "a pointer to good purposes, but pointless if those purposes [are] known, and harmful if poised against them."[161]

Another way of formulating this is that law, while it might orient itself towards a particular purpose in the form of the directing idea which animates it, is insufficient because of its *nomocratic* residues. It will never take flight to a *teleocratic* extreme. The result is that it becomes, in effect, the declaratory justifications for the deployment of technologies of governing at a distance, analogous to, and deriving from, those which have developed over the course of hundreds of years in the domestic context. They result in other words in the dominance of a governmental reason which attempts to "conduct conduct" indirectly through "diverse tactics rather than laws." And this is closely associated with a turn away from the language and methodologies of law, strictly speaking, to those of governance, legitimacy, and policy. It is this which gives the system its managerial character. And it is this which in effect "governmentalises" a new sphere of global human rights governance, encompassing States, NGOs, businesses, and international organisations alike, cutting across whatever remains of the public/private divide, and predicated on the imperatives of a *raison du monde* for which the anachronisms of borders and jurisdiction and the other trappings of law are nothing but "wearisome."[162] And this, then, quite naturally, brings us to the final consideration, which is the consequence of all of this.

Notes

1 See e.g., I. Hacking, *The Taming of Chance* (Cambridge University Press, 1990); T. Porter, *Trust in Numbers* (Princeton University Press, 1995).
2 P. Miller and N. Rose, "Governing Economic Life," 19 (1), *Economy and Society* (1990) 1.
3 D. Shelton, "Introduction," in D. Shelton (ed.), *The Oxford Handbook of International Human Rights Law* (Oxford University Press, 2013), 1, p. 5.

4 H. H. Koh, "Why Do Nations Obey International Law?" 106, *Yale Law Journal* (1997) 2599.

5 The literature on this is legion, but the classic statement remains R. Merton, "The Unanticipated Consequences of Purposive Social Action," 1 (6), *American Sociological Review* (1936) 894.

6 See e.g., O. Schacter, "The Decline of the Nation-State and Its Implications for International Law," 36, *Columbia Journal of Transnational Law* 7 (1998); J. Cogan, "The Regulatory Turn in International Law," 52, *Harvard Journal of International Law* (2011) 321; M. Reisman, "Designing and Managing the Future of the State," 8 (3), *European Journal of International Law* (1997) 409; S. Marks, "State Centrism, International Law and the Anxieties of Influence," 19, *Leiden Journal of International Law* (2006) 339.

7 China and India being notable examples. See e.g., J. Gaskarth (ed.), *China, India and the Future of the International Society* (Rowman & Littlefield, 2015). See also UNGA Resolution 2625, Declaration on Principles of International Law concerning Friendly Relations and Co-Operation Among States in Accordance with the Charter of the United Nations (1970).

8 Miller and Rose, "Governing Economic Life."

9 See e.g., N. Rose, "The Death of the Social? Refiguring the Territory of Government," 25 (3), *Economy and Society* (1996) 327.

10 Miller and Rose, "Governing Economic Life," p. 33.

11 *Ibid.*, p. 35.

12 F. Hayek, *The Fatal Conceit: The Errors of Socialism* (Chicago University Press, 1988), p. 76.

13 G. Neave, "On the Cultivation of Quality, Efficiency and Enterprise: An Overview of Recent Trends in Higher Education in Western Europe 1986–1988," 23 (1), *European Journal of Education* 7 (1988), p. 12.

14 M. Dean, *Governmentality* (2nd edition, Sage, 2010), p. 133.

15 P. Miller and N. Rose, "Governing 'Advanced' Liberal Democracies," in A. Barry and T. Osborne (eds), *Foucault and Political Reason: Liberalism, Neo-Liberalism and Rationalities of Government* (University College London Press, 1996), p. 203.

16 *Ibid*, pp. 212–214.

17 A. Kipnis, "Audit Cultures: Neoliberal Governmentality, Socialist Legacy, or Technologies of Governing?" 35 (2), *American Ethnologist* (2008) 275.

18 See, for example, J. Cowan, "Before Audit Culture: A Genealogy of International Oversight of Rights," in B. Muller (ed.), *The Gloss of Harmony: The Politics of Policy Making in Multilateral Organisations* (2013), 103; and A. Rosga and M. Satterthwaite, "The Trust in Indicators: Measuring Human Rights," 27 (2), *Berkeley Journal of International Law* (2009) 253.

19 K. Arambulo, *Strengthening the Supervision of the International Covenant on Economic, Social and Cultural Rights: Theoretical and Procedural Aspects* (1999), p. 5.

20 See my own earlier article, D. McGrogan, "The Population and the Individual: The Human Rights Audit as the Governmentalization of Global Human Rights

Governance," 16 (4), *International Journal of Constitutional Law* (2018) 1073.

21 See e.g., N. Woods, "Held to Account: Governance in the World Economy," in A. Kuper (ed.), *Global Responsibilities: Who Must Deliver on Human Rights?* (Routledge, 2012), 251.

22 See M. Power, *The Audit Society: Rituals of Verification* (Oxford University Press, 1997).

23 Miller and Rose, "Governing 'Advanced' Liberal Democracies," p. 212.

24 See Power, *The Audit Society*, pp. 16–17.

25 *Ibid.*, pp. 41–69.

26 See e.g., J. Welling, "International Indicators and Economic, Social and Cultural Rights," 30, *Human Rights Quarterly* (2008) 933; M. Green, "What We Talk About When We Talk About Indicators: Current Approaches to Human Rights Measurement," 23 (4), *Human Rights Quarterly* (2001) 1062.

27 It may have begun with the Special Rapporteur on the Realization of Economic, Social and Cultural Rights in 1993. See UN GAOR World Conference on Human Rights, Report of the Secretariat: Report of the Seminar on Appropriate Indicators to Measure Achievement in the Progressive Realization of Economic, Social and Cultural Rights, UN Doc. A/CONF.157/PC/73 (1993).

28 OHCHR, *Human Rights Indicators: A Guide to Measurement and Implementation* (2012), Foreword by Navi Pillay, pp. III–IV.

29 *Ibid.*, p. 4.

30 *Ibid.*, p. 90.

31 *Ibid.*, pp. 34–38.

32 *Ibid.*, p. 90.

33 *Ibid.*, p. 33.

34 Other examples include the SERF Index, available at www.serfindex.org/about/ (accessed 29th November 2019); T. Landman's "principle, policy and practice" initiative, "Comparative Politics and Human Rights," 24 (4), *Human Rights Quarterly* (2002) 890; and the project to develop a specific suite of indicators for the right to health. See G. Backman et al., "Health Systems and the Right to Health: An Assessment of 194 Countries," 372 (9655), *The Lancet* (2008) 2047.

35 Subjective or qualitative assessments of performance are generally viewed as unreliable or lacking in transparency and hence not to be trusted. See e.g., R. Malhotra and N. Fasel, "Quantitative Human Rights Indicators: A Survey of Major Initiatives," Expert Meeting on Human Rights Indicators, Turku, Finland, March 2005, available at www.gaportal.org/sites/default/files/Quantitative%20Human%20Rights%20Indicators.pdf (accessed 29th November 2019).

36 There are, of course, huge methodological problems with this approach, but for the sake of argument these are not addressed here. See e.g., M. Strathern, "The Tyranny of Transparency," 26 (3), *British Educational Research Journal* (2000); H. Tsoukas, "The Tyranny of Light," 29 (9), *Futures* (1997) 827.

37 Human Rights Council, Report of the Special Rapporteur on the right to education on her mission to Côte D'Ivoire, UN Doc A/HRC/38/32/Add.1 (2018).

38 *Ibid.*, para. 61.
39 Power, *The Audit Society*, pp. 70–71.
40 Human Rights Council, "Report of the Special Rapporteur," para. 62.
41 *Ibid.*, para. 63.
42 Levi Strauss & Co., *Sustainability Guidebook* (November 2017), available at http://levistrauss.com/wp-content/uploads/2017/12/2017-Sustainability-Guidebook_December2017.pdf (accessed 29th November 2019), p. 17.
43 *Ibid.*, at p. 50, p. 50, and p. 57, respectively.
44 Scottish Human Rights Commission, *Human Rights Budgeting and Budget Analysis* (October 2015), available at www.scottishhumanrights.com/media/1706/human-rights-budgeting-and-budget-analysis-oct-2015-vfinal.doc (accessed 29th November 2019), p. 4.
45 See e.g., A. Nolan, R. O'Connell and C. Harvey (eds), *Human Rights and Public Finance: Budgets and the Promotion of Economic and Social Rights* (Hart, 2013).
46 In the OHCHR's *Guide*, using qualitative expert evaluations of governance, for example, is described as being of a "limited purpose." See OHCHR, *Human Rights Indicators*, p. 68.
47 M. Manion, R. Ralston, T. Matthews, and I. Allen, "Budget Analysis as a Tool to Monitor Economic and Social Rights: Where the Rubber of International Commitment Meets the Road of Government Policy," 9 (1), *Journal of Human Rights Practice* (2017) 146, p. 152.
48 E. Felner, "Closing the 'Escape Hatch': A Toolkit to Monitor the Progressive Realization of Economy, Social and Cultural Rights," 1 (3), *Journal of Human Rights Practice* (2009) 402, pp. 402–405.
49 Power, *The Audit Society*, at pp. 16–18.
50 J. Cowan, "The Universal Periodic Review as a Public Audit Ritual: An Anthropological Perspective on Emerging Practices in the Global Governance of Human Rights," in H. Charlesworth and E. Larking (eds), *Human Rights and the Universal Periodic Review: Rituals and Ritualism* (Cambridge University Press, 2015).
51 European Commission, Directive 2014/95/EU, amending Directive 2013/34/EU.
52 The Companies Act 2006 (Strategic Report and Directors' Report) Regulations 2013 s.7 (b) (iii).
53 See Global Affairs Canada, "Canada's Enhanced Corporate Social Responsibility Strategy to Strengthen Canada's Extractive Sector Abroad," available at www.international.gc.ca/trade-agreements-accords-commerciaux/topics-domaines/other-autre/csr-strat-rse.aspx?lang=eng (accessed 29th November 2019).
54 See "Human Rights Reporting and Assurance Frameworks Initiative," available at www.shiftproject.org/resources/collaborations/human-rights-reporting-assurance-frameworks-initiative/ (accessed 29th November 2019).
55 Next plc, Corporate Responsibility Report 2018 – Focus Updates, available at www.nextplc.co.uk/~/media/Files/N/Next-PLC-V2/documents/corporate-responsibility/focus-2018/focus-1-salient-human-rights-issues.pdf (accessed 29th November 2019).

56 J. Meyer and B. Rowan, "Institutionalised Organisations: Formal Structure as Myth and Ceremony," 83 (2), *American Journal of Sociology* (1977) 340.

57 Next plc, Corporate Responsibility Report 2018, available at www.nextplc.co.uk/~/media/Files/N/Next-PLC-V2/documents/cr-reports/cr-2018.pdf (accessed 29th November 2019), p. 5.

58 *Ibid.*

59 *Ibid.*, p. 8.

60 *Ibid.*

61 Power, *The Audit Society*, p. 83.

62 J. Ruggie and J. Sherman III, "The Concept of 'Due Diligence' in the UN Guiding Principles on Business and Human Rights: A Reply to Jonathan Bonnitcha and Robert McCorquodale," 28 (3), *European Journal of International Law* (2017) 921.

63 *Business and Human Rights: Towards Operationalising the 'Protect, Respect and Remedy' Framework*, Report to the UN Human Rights Council, UN Doc. A/HRC/11/13, 22nd April 2009, para. 25.

64 See e.g., G. Graetz and D. Franks, "Incorporating Human Rights Into the Corporate Domain: Due Diligence, Impact Assessment and Integrated Risk Management," 31 (2), *Impact Assessment and Project Appraisal* (2013) 97.

65 Johnson & Johnson, 2015 Citizenship and Sustainability Report, available at www.jnj.com/sites/default/files/pdf/cs/2015-jnj-citizenship-sustainability-report.pdf (accessed 29th November 2019), p. 68.

66 See R. Locke, *The Promise and Limits of Private Power: Promoting Labour Standards in a Global Economy* (Cambridge, 2013).

67 For a recent academic overview of the role of the EHRC, see D. Barrett, "The Regulatory Space of Equality and Human Rights in Britain: the Role of the Equality and Human Rights Commission," 39 (2), *Legal Studies* (2019) 247.

68 A. Muller and F. Seidensticker, *The Role of National Human Rights Institutions in the United Nations Treaty Body Process* (German Institute for Human Rights, 2007), pp. 36–42.

69 *Ibid.*, pp. 42–48.

70 *Ibid.*, pp. 51–60.

71 Equality Act 2006, s. 42, ss. (3).

72 See e.g., K. Tonkiss, "Contesting Human Rights Through Institutional Reform: the Case of the UK Equality and Human Rights Commission," 20 (4), *International Journal of Human Rights* (2016) 491.

73 See EHRC, "Our Projects," available at https://equalityhumanrights.com/en/our-work/our-projects (accessed 26th July 2019).

74 EHRC, Strategic Plan 2019–2022, June 2019, available at https://www.equalityhumanrights.com/en/publication-download/strategic-plan-2019-2022 (accessed 18th November 2020), p. 11.

75 *Ibid.*, pp. 21, 23, and 25, respectively.

76 The most recent of these reports at the time of writing is EHRC, "The State of Play: Progress on Premier League Clubs' Accessibility," May 2019, available at

www.equalityhumanrights.com/sites/default/files/the-state-of-play-progress-on -premier-league-clubs-accessibility_0.pdf (accessed 29th November 2019).

77 *Ibid.*, pp. 9–13.

78 JCHR, 6th Report, Session 2002–2003, *The Case for a Human Rights Commission*, HL Paper 67–I and II, HC 489–1 and II, para. 99 (emphasis added).

79 OHCHR, "What We Do," available at, www.ohchr.org/EN/AboutUs/Pages/ WhatWeDo.aspx (accessed 29th November 2019).

80 J. Ruggie, "The Social Construction of the UN Guiding Principles on Business and Human Rights" Corporate Responsibility Initiative Working Paper, June 2017.

81 B. Simma, "Mainstreaming Human Rights: The Contribution of the International Court of Justice," 3 (1), *Journal of International Dispute Settlement* (2012) 7, at p. 27.

82 An early survey of "mainstreaming" in general can be found in C. McCrudden, "Mainstreaming Equality in the Governance of Northern Ireland," 22, *Fordham International Law Journal* (1999) 1696.

83 See C. McCrudden, "Mainstreaming and Human Rights," in C. Harvey (ed.), *Human Rights in the Community: Rights as Agents for Change* (Hart, 2005), 9, p. 19, using the language of the Race Relations (Amendment) Act 2005.

84 A. Chalabi, *National Human Rights Action Planning* (Oxford University Press, 2018), p. 1.

85 Miller and Rose, "Governing 'Advanced' Liberal Democracies," p. 215.

86 UN, Report of the United Nations Secretary-General, Renewing the United Nations: A Programme for Reform, UN Doc. A/51/950 (1997), para. 79.

87 G. Oberleitner, "A Decade of Mainstreaming Human Rights in the UN: Achievements, Failures, Challenges," 26, *Netherlands Quarterly of Human Rights* (2008) 359.

88 Again, the most significant example, A. Frankovits, *The Human Rights Based Approach and the United Nations System* (UNESCO, 2006), is over a decade old.

89 See e.g., Oberleitner, "A Decade of Mainstreaming," p. 365.

90 UNICEF, Mission Statement, available at www.unicef.org/about/who/index_ mission.html (accessed 29th November 2019).

91 FAO, Policy Support and Guidance, available at www.fao.org/policy-support/ policy-themes/right-to-food/en/ (accessed 29th November 2019).

92 World Bank Group, Environmental and Social Framework, 2016, available at http://pubdocs.worldbank.org/en/837721522762050108/Environmental-and -Social-Framework.pdf, pp. 1 and 2, respectively.

93 See e.g., Human Rights Council, Report of the Special Rapporteur on extreme poverty and human rights, UN Doc. A/HRC/38/33 (2018), paras 1–8.

94 See e.g., Letter from Christopher Lane, Special Representative of the IMF to the United Nations, to Juan Pablo Bohoslavsky, Independent Expert on the effects of foreign debt, etc., 27th July 2017, available at www.ohchr.org/_layouts/15/

WopiFrame.aspx?sourcedoc=/Documents/Issues/IEDebt/impactassessments
/IMF.pdf&action=default&DefaultItemOpen=1 (accessed 29th November
2019).

95 WHO, *Together on the Road to Universal Health Coverage: A Call to Action*
(2017), available at apps.who.int/iris/bitstream/handle/10665/258962/WH
O-HIS-HGF-17.1-eng.pdf;jsessionid=DBB28DAFD0B64798C14D6B1D18
CE49B0?sequence=1 (accessed 29th November 2019), p. v.

96 See ECOSOC, UNICEF Gender Action Plan 2018–2021, 2017, UN Doc. E/
ICEF/2017/16 (2017), esp. pp. 6–16.

97 *Ibid.*, pp. 6 and 17, respectively.

98 See UNESCO, "Human Rights-Based Approach to Programming," available
at www.unesco.org/new/en/social-and-human-sciences/themes/human-rights-
based-approach/ (accessed 29th November 2019).

99 GA, Political Declaration on HIV/AIDS, A/RES/60/262, 15th June 2006.

100 WHO, *Integrating Equity, Gender, Human Rights and Social Determinants
into the Work of WHO: Roadmap for Action (2014–2019)*, p. 3.

101 WHO Assembly, *Gender, Equality and Human Rights at the Core of the Health
Response* (2012).

102 See e.g., S. Davis, "Human Rights and the Global Fund to Fight AIDS,
Tuberculosis and Malaria," 16, *Health and Human Rights Journal* (2014) 134.

103 ECOSOC, UNICEF Gender Action Plan, pp. 7 and 18.

104 UNFPA, *One Vision, Three Zeros: Annual Report 2018*, available at https://es
aro.unfpa.org/en/publications/one-vision-three-zeros (accessed 29th November
2019).

105 P. Hunt, "Configuring the UN Human Rights System in the 'Era of
Implementation': Mainland and Archipelago," 39, *Human Rights Quarterly*
(2017) 489, p. 498.

106 The description of such agencies as "operational" comes from P. Baehr and L.
Gordener, *The United Nations: Reality and Ideal* (2005), p. 33.

107 The word "indigenizing" is Hunt's: see Hunt, "Configuring the UN Human
Rights System," p. 529.

108 Mainstreaming will, as R. Thomas and V. Magar put it, "translate rights into
reality" – in "Mainstreaming Human Rights Across WHO," in B. Meier and L.
Gostin (eds), *Human Rights in Global Health* (Oxford University Press, 2018),
133, p. 134.

109 Hunt, "Configuring the UN Human Rights System," p. 501.

110 P. Alston, "Appraising the United Nations Human Rights Regime," in P. Alston
(ed.), *The United Nations and Human Rights: A Critical Appraisal* (Oxford
University Press, 1992), 1, p. 1.

111 Oberleitner, "A Decade of Mainstreaming," pp. 363, 369, 365, and pp. 364–
365, respectively.

112 *Ibid.*, pp. 360 and 370, respectively.

113 *Ibid.*, p. 369.

114 Thomas and Magar, "Mainstreaming Human Rights," p. 134.

115 See Oberleitner, "A Decade of Mainstreaming," p. 387.

116 WHO, *Report for the World Health Organization: Health and Human rights at the WHO* (cited in Thomas and Magar, "Mainstreaming Human Rights," p. 136).
117 See e.g., UNESCO, *Empowering the Poor Through Human Rights Litigation* (UNESCO, 2011), pp. 105–106.
118 Hunt, "Configuring the UN Human Rights System."
119 CESCR, General Comment No. 1, UN Doc. E/1989/22 (1981), para. 4.
120 A. Chalabi, *National Human Rights Action Planning* (Oxford University Press, 2018), p. 66.
121 HRC, Focused Reports Based on Replies to Lists of Issues Prior to Reporting (LOIPR): Implementation of the New Optional Reporting Procedure, 99th Session, UN Doc. CCPR/C/99/4 (2010), para. 11.
122 CRC, Concluding Observations: Japan, UN Doc. CRC/C/JPN/CO/3 (2010), para. 15.
123 CAT, Concluding Observations: Iceland, UN Doc. CAT/C/ISL/CO/3 (2008).
124 In the case of the CEDAW, for instance, this requirement is found in Article 24; in the case of CERD, Article 4 requires states to use "all appropriate means" to end racial discrimination; similar phrasing exists in all of the major international human rights treaties.
125 See A. Swaine, "Globalising Women, Peace and Security: Trends in National Action Plans," in S. Aroussi (ed.), *Rethinking National Action Plans on Women, Peace and Security* (IOS Publishing, 2017).
126 See European Parliament, Directorate-General for External Policies, *Implementation of the UN Guiding Principles on Business and Human Rights* (2017) EP/EXPO/B/COMMITTEE/FWC/2013–08/Lot8/09; UN Working Group on Business and Human Rights, *Guidance on National Action Plans and Human Rights* (2016).
127 CRC, Concluding Observations: Japan.
128 CEDAW, Concluding Observations: Egypt, CEDAW/C/EGY/CO/7 (2010), para. 24.
129 GA, Report of the Special Rapporteur on torture and other cruel, inhuman or degrading treatment or punishment, mission to Indonesia, UN Doc. A/HRC/7/3/Add.7 (2008), para. 76.
130 CRC, Concluding Observations on the Combined Fourth and Fifth Periodic Reports of Japan, UN Doc. CRC/C/JPN/CO/4–5 (2019).
131 *Ibid.*, at paras 7, 8, 9, 11, 12, and 13, 13 (b), and 15, respectively.
132 Hunt, "Configuring the UN Human Rights System."
133 CRC, Concluding Observations: Japan, para. 10 (a) through (c).
134 See e.g., D. Elson, R. Balakrishnan and J. Heintz, "Public Finance, Maximum Available Resources and Human Rights," in Nolan et al. (eds), *Human Rights and Public Finance*, 13.
135 A. Blyberg, "The Case of the Mislaid Allocation: Economic and Social Rights and Budget Work," 6 (11), *Sur: International Journal of Human Rights* (2009) 123, p. 128.
136 CRC Committee, General Comment No. 19, UN Doc. CRC/C/GC/19 (2016), para. 2.

137 CRC, Concluding Observations: Japan, para. 10.
138 The use of the word "mobilises" comes from Elson, Balakrishnan, and Heintz, "Public Finance," p. 14.
139 CRC Committee, General Comment No. 19, para. 14.
140 *Ibid.*, para. 19.
141 *Ibid.*, paras 28–30.
142 *Ibid.*, para. 27 (c) (i).
143 *Ibid.*, para. 74.
144 *Ibid.*, para. 12.
145 *Ibid.*, paras 35–39.
146 *Ibid.*, para. 11.
147 E. Ganguly Thukral, "Budget for Children," in Nolan et al. (eds), *Human Rights and Public Finance*, p. 139.
148 A. Wildavsky, cited in e.g., J. Kuosmanen, "Towards 'Human Rights Compatible' Public Budgets – An Account of Institutional Virtues," 64 (3), *Political Studies* (2016) 683, p. 683.
149 Blyberg, "The Case of the Mislaid Allocation," p. 137 (emphasis added).
150 SHRC, Background Briefing Paper, "Human Rights Budgeting and Budget Analysis," available at www.scottishhumanrights.com/media/1706/human-rights-budgeting-and-budget-analysis-oct-2015-vfinal.doc (accessed 29th November 2019), p. 3 (emphasis added).
151 *Ibid.*
152 P. Cerny, *Rethinking World Politics: A Theory of Transnational Neopluralism* (Oxford University Press, 2009), p. 178.
153 Meyer and Rowan, "Institutionalised Organisations."
154 M. Koskenniemi, "International Law: Constitutionalism, Managerialism and the Ethos of Legal Education," 1, *European Journal of Legal Studies* (2007) 1, p. 11.
155 *Ibid.*, p. 7.
156 Hunt, "Configuring the UN Human Rights System," pp. 496–497.
157 B. Meier and W. Onzivu, "The Evolution of Human Rights in World Health Organization Policy and the Future of Human Rights Through Global Health Governance," 128, *Public Health* (2014), 179.
158 Thomas and Magar, "Mainstreaming Human Rights," p. 142.
159 J. Kuosmanen, "Human Rights, Public Budgets and Epistemic Challenges," 17, *Human Rights Review* (2016) 247.
160 Kofi Annan, Address of the Secretary-General to the Commission on Human Rights, 7th April 2005, available at www.un.org/sg/en/content/sg/statement/2005-04-07/secretary-generals-address-commission-human-rights (accessed 1st December 2019).
161 Koskenniemi, "International Law," p. 11.
162 H. Arendt, *On Revolution* (Viking Press, 1965), p. 86.

6

Nothing but rejoicing

Development requires the removal of major sources of un-freedom: poverty as well as tyranny, poor economic opportunities as well as systematic social deprivation, neglect of public facilities as well as intolerance or over-activity of repressive states.

(Sen, *Development as Freedom*)[1]

Introduction

This book began by setting out Trilling's anxieties about how what he called "pity" would lead ultimately to coercion. The previous five chapters of this book have given us a framework within which we can understand how this takes place with respect to human rights. Compassion, the unwillingness to look on while others suffer, imbues the thinking of human rights advocates, whether in practice or the academy. This gives them a directing idea, realised through the capacity of law to span the present and future, which is that the powerful must be made responsible for improving the well-being of the powerless. The achievement of this purpose, however, cannot be done through law alone because of its inescapable "allegiance" to *nomos*. The result is the deployment of governmental reason, which manifests itself in managerial tactics for the indirect "conducting of conduct." This has the effect of creating or governmentalising a global sphere of human rights governance, based on the strictures of an overweening *raison du monde* which sees any and all problems as requiring global solutions, unbounded by the anachronism of prohibitory law. It is now our task to make clear the route from compassion to coercion taking place within that narrative.

In the first section, I lay out some of the potential criticisms of the managerialism which Koskenniemi identified as it appears in the arena of human rights. In the second, I suggest that these criticisms can ultimately be described as stemming from a particular view of the relationship between freedom and morality which can be found in the work of both Oakeshott and Foucault. That is, where freedom is conceived as a practice – a working out of individual selfhood – then anything which has the potential to impair agency will also necessarily have the potential to impair freedom. The consequence of this will be that the capacity to choose based on reason will be undermined. And the result of that will be to deprive the individual of the capacity to act ethically. He or she is reduced instead to a diminished sort of freedom, consisting only ultimately of the capacity to enjoy the "warm servility" of the obedient and needful member of the flock.

In the third section, I argue that orienting human rights law towards the ideal of *lex* is the only way of conceiving rights to be non-coercive. The alternative, which is to orient it towards being a managerial rule-book, results in the inevitable application of governmental techniques which reduce human choices to the results of mere "causes" rather than "reasons." The governmentalisation of global human rights governance, as a compulsory enterprise association, ultimately replicates a pastoral relationship between the powerful and the powerless, and the effect of this is Tocqueville's dystopia made real: an "immense and tutelary power" watching over a mass of "timid and industrious" animals: "absolute, minute, regular, provident and mild."[2]

In the fourth section, however, I argue that the picture which emerges as a result of all of this is mixed. On the one hand, it tends to produce in the minds of human rights advocates a view of the human individual as something akin to Oakeshott's individual manqué – demoralised, atomised, and able only to rely on the magnanimity and compassion of the powerful. The individual is ultimately, in other words, constructed as the passive beneficiary of Adam Smith's "man of system,"[3] the wise and knowledgeable "governors" who arrange the conditions of each individual's life so as to improve their own well-being and that of the people around them. Yet the reality is much more complicated. As Smith pointed out, the man of system is apt to forget that individuals have their own goals: the will to govern is always opposed by a corresponding will, in Foucault's words, "not to be governed quite so much."[4] The conducting of conduct has as its necessary corollary the performance of "counter-conduct" – ways in which individuals rebel against, refuse, or refute the governing apparatuses which seek to arrange their thoughts and actions. George Orwell, writing about socialism, considered one of the main reasons for its failure to be the vision of its adherents: "a set of reforms which 'we,' the clever ones, are going to impose upon 'them,' the Lower Orders."[5] This represented not a project of freedom but one deriving merely from a "hypertrophied sense of order,"[6] and it was no surprise therefore that the majority of working class people rejected it, often with outright hostility.[7] In other words, the conducting of conduct will often have the effect of encouraging thoughts and actions which directly oppose the ends which are determined by the conductors. That the entire human rights project is increasingly viewed not only with apathy but with open disdain around the world can be seen, therefore, as a direct consequence of its overreach.

The result of the governmentalisation of global human rights governance, then, may not in fact only be the construction of individuals as the obedient and needful components of "timid and industrious" masses,[8] but may also be the shrugging off of human rights as a tool of emancipation in the first place. The unpalatable conclusion for human rights advocates is that in order for the movement to gain widespread and popular appeal, it may be necessary to "govern a little less."

Critiques of managerialism

While "the governmentalisation of global human rights governance" is my own coining, I am far from being the only theorist to have identified a significant movement towards the managerialisation of human rights taking place, or to have developed a critique of it. And, of course, what is taking place in the field of human rights has much in common with developments in other fields of international law – not to mention across governance in general around the world. That is to say, the governance of human rights is of a piece with what might be called "new governance" more broadly. This consists of a move towards "reflexive governance" or "meta-regulation,"[9] and the destabilisation of traditional distinctions between private and public spheres, and of geographical limitations such as the local, regional, national, transnational, and global.[10] These developments have been subject to sustained critique, and as we shall see, much of this critique bears on human rights specifically.

Summarising some of these critiques is the task of this section. Here, it is useful to go back to Koskenniemi, who expresses a number of concerns about the managerialisation of international law. Many of them stem from his observation that for the managerial sensibility law was only a "second best" – "a pointer to good purposes, but pointless if those purposes were known, and harmful if poised against them."[11] This ultimately results in law being drained out from the international system, to be replaced by regulatory programmes. Clearly, as I have tried to argue, it is not so much that law *per se* becomes a second best in the managerial framework, but rather that its character increasingly resembles that of a programmatic rule-book of an enterprise association, being declaratory of ends or of the means of achieving them. But the ultimate consequences are the same, irrespective of how one chooses to define terms. These I will group as the consequences for the rule of law, the consequences for consent, and the consequences for ruling

– all of which are linked. As we shall see, existing critiques of the manage-rialisation of international law in general or international human rights law specifically have tended to group around these three sets of consequences (although they are not generally stated in these terms).

Consequences for the rule of law

The phrase "the rule of law" has had many interlocutors and almost as many definitions, some of which run against one another.[12] This is not the place to engage in a detailed exposition of the concept. Rather, I will reduce it to certain features which are most apposite in the case of managerialism and international law. These are two of the elements which Tom Bingham begins his exposition of the rule of law: that "laws [should be] publicly made [and] take effect (generally) in the future."[13] This can be expanded to the principles that law should be accessible, clear, and predictable, and that questions of legal right and liability should generally be resolved by the application of law rather than mere discretion.[14]

These two elements are, of course, related, in that they ultimately can be thought of as hedges against the law operating arbitrarily. If the law is read-ily knowable and understandable to those who must abide by it, and if those people can be relatively sure that they can predict how it will function in any given instance, then at least they will be able to conduct their affairs with some degree of consistency. They may still consider the law to be unjust or to have undesirable consequences. But it will perform one of the central functions which can reasonably be expected of a legal system and which is at the heart of most sociological thought regarding the object of law from Durkheim to Hart to Luhmann: stability of expectations.

Predictability, clarity, and consistency are clearly undermined where law is conceived as open-ended declarations of ends, for the simple reason that those engaged in interpreting the rules will always be encouraged to do so on the basis of their own conceptions about what those ends are and how best to achieve them. In short, it will grant them (or they will grant themselves) their own discretion in determining what laws mean. There is no clearer example of this than the jurisprudence of the European Court of Human Rights (ECtHR), examined in Chapter 1, in which a wide-ranging understanding of the object and purpose of the Court resulted in judges reaching interpretations which, it is fair to say, would not have been arrived at by a lay interpreter of the treaty text and the *travaux préparatoires*. But of course this interpretive expansiveness is hardly limited to judicial bodies, as was also evident from the discussion in that chapter. One thinks, for exam-ple, of the Committee on Economic, Social and Cultural Rights (CESCR)'s discovery of a right to water where none is contained in the International Covenant on Economic, Social and Cultural Rights (ICESCR), or indeed the development of the concept of the framework of "protect, respect and fulfil," which exists nowhere in the core international human rights treaties and has given to very far-ranging interpretations of the scope of international human rights law.

Judges and human rights scholars alike have tended to be "intensely relaxed" about the dangers posed by teleological interpretation to the predictability and consistency of the law.[15] If one is of the view, as for instance is Christian Tomuschat, that "States are no more than instruments whose inherent function is to serve the interests of their citizens as legally expressed in human rights,"[16] then insistence on the rule of law vis-à-vis consistency and predictability at the international level is unnecessary or even inappropriate. Law at the international level should simply be a matter of ensuring that the interests of citizens are served. There is no reason why States should be able to lay claim themselves to the predictable or consistent application of law, because they are simply agencies with the task of making things better for their citizens. This latter duty trumps the rule of law because it is what international law is "for." Individuals, living within States, are entitled to a predictable environment in which to organise their affairs, but there is no reason why this should apply to States with respect to each other or international organisations or courts. Letsas puts this rather bluntly: "[It] is hard to see why surprising [States] is morally wrong [...] What kind of harm does a State suffer when its expectations regarding its treaty obligations are defeated?"[17]

There is a fiction at the heart of this position, which is that there are obligations which can exist for States that will not ultimately result in consequences for, or duties being imposed upon, individuals. In fact, there are no such obligations. One does not need to be a Kelsenian to appreciate that individuals are always the final addressees of international law, because in the end States achieve nothing other than through the actions of their citizens, or through acting upon them. This will always mean that, at the very least, those citizens will have an interest in the effects which international law ultimately has, and it will very frequently mean they will be required to order their affairs in view of those effects. The decision in *Golder* may ultimately have had only indirect and minor consequences – chiefly the tax implications of a widened scope of interpretation of the right of access to courts. But the decision in *Young, James and Webster* clearly had an influence on industrial relations in the UK; and one of course will be struck by the very wide consequences resulting from the interpretations of treaty obligations by the United Nations (UN) treaty- and charter-based mechanisms if followed, touching as they do upon anything from road safety to breast-feeding to the gender composition of village chiefs. That is to say nothing of the duties which might be imposed upon individuals in international human rights law, particularly, for instance, employers with respect to the elimination of discrimination (but also, potentially, media companies to produce certain types of content, parents to refrain from smacking their children, employees to refrain from making "sexually coloured remarks" in the workplace, and so on).[18] Put perhaps crudely, unless it is completely ignored, international law always has consequences for individuals. And if it is unpredictable for States it will likewise be so for their citizens, whether because it imposes obligations or effects on them directly where it did not previously do so, or because it requires States to legislate in unforeseen ways. Put more bluntly still, if States should have no reason to expect that the rule of law will apply internationally, then individuals will likewise have no such expectation in the domestic context if international law is to have any force whatsoever.[19]

Consequences for consent

All of the foregoing is not to mention, of course, the basic democratic expectation that individuals are expected to have some ultimate say over the laws under which they are governed – however indirectly or diffusely. This leads us to the second set of consequences, which concern consent. Democratic accountability of courts and other institutions is a topic which tends to be treated in the literature on international human rights law in one of four ways. Occasionally, it is treated with blithe indifference. Since elected governments "privilege the interests of their own political quarter" and democratic choices might be "biased by self-interest,"[20] they are not to be trusted with the protection of human rights. Better, then, for global governance regimes to identify sympathetic "local advocates" in "islands of civility,"[21] so as to realise "democracy by articulation" rather than representation.[22]

Often, though, it is identified as an area of concern, or for improvement, but in a manner which does not suggest serious engagement. The Office of the High Commissioner for Human Rights (OHCHR), for example, while aware of the issue of accountability, appears to view it as fundamentally a matter of making its operations amenable to audit. It is a matter of providing "documentation and evidence"[23] so that UN Member States, right-holders, and funders can evaluate the "use of resources and the achievement of planned results."[24] It does not suggest that there ought to be any method by which the allocation of resources itself might be made amenable to democratic decision making, let alone what results are planned for (or indeed whether a given plan, if any, should be created or enacted in the first place).

In the academic literature, it is more typical (though by no means universal) to view democratic accountability somewhat unreflectingly as being the result or consequence of an expansion of human rights obligations. In this, while it is rarely made explicit, we tend to see the Tocquevillian "neutraliz[ation] of the vices inherent in popular government"[25] as being considered one of the chief virtues of human rights law. In this vision, human rights bolster a "thick" conception of democracy by ensuring that members of minorities have access to institutions, that such institutions take account of the interests of all citizens, or indeed that citizens have their needs met in such a way that they are able to participate in the goods which society provides.[26] Here, it is not unusual to describe human rights as *improving* accountability: even National Human Rights Institutions (NHRIs), with their acknowledged tendency to "take on a life of their own and produce unintended consequences" for governments,[27] are capable within this picture of being seen as "key to government accountability [and] democratic consolidation."[28]

But, finally, there is also a growing body of concern being expressed about the way in which human rights are framed within global governance so as to cloak political decision making or, perhaps worse, to obfuscate where accountability actually lies.[29] It places a technical or administrative facade in front of what is in fact an intensely political project, or set of projects: presenting sweeping and expansive interpretations of what "human rights" mean as being simply settled matters of law, which are then only to be implemented through following the advice of experts. Ordinary people – the very holders of the rights in question – are simply cut out from the subject entirely. This is, of course, a subset of a wider set of concerns about the "elitist tendencies" within new forms of governance, wherein democratically elected politicians find themselves in competition with, or made subservient to, technical "experts," judges, and other specialists.[30] It is hard not to see in what I have described in Chapters 1 and 5 of this book as simply a further development in what John Gray describes as the project of legal liberalism: "abolishing politics, or of so constraining it by legal and constitutional formulae that it no longer matters what are the outcomes of political deliberation."[31] We might only quibble that this is not merely the project of legal liberalism *per se*, but rather a characteristic of the State conceived along the analogy of enterprise association.

What this leads to is a variant on what Koskenniemi calls a "culture of bad faith" – the presentation of rights as being the sources of absolute normative claims with the capacity to trump the State, when in practice they are reduced to the mere bureaucratisation or "banalification" of politics.[32] Paradoxically, rights, which for Habermas were the very foundation of popular sovereignty and democratic politics, become instead a series of justifications for hedging politics entirely into matters of process and the balancing of interests so as to achieve pre-determined ends: the arrangement of society along benevolent, utilitarian lines.[33] The ultimate end-state is one in which no room is left for ordinary citizens to engage in the articulation or realisation of alternative conceptions of "the good" – or even to give or withhold their consent to whatever conception of "the good" which human rights are deemed by their governors (judges, experts, academics) to enshrine.

Consequences for ruling

Implicit in all of this is the matter of ruling or government in the traditional sense, and here we can identify a third set of potential concerns. One of these is that rights in this dimension simply serve to produce a "governable subject" – an individual who is "permanently observed"[34] but also, we might add, who permanently observes others and also himself. This is obviously a particular result of the turn to audit, which as we saw in the previous chapter has the primary effect of encouraging the audited subject to act in accordance with the wishes and ends of the auditor. The effect on the governed is that they come to order and arrange their behaviour within the bounds which are specified by the governors. As a consequence, they become pliant, obedient, and de-politicised. That is, as we also saw in the previous chapter, they take on new subjectivities which are highly regimenting and straightening for all that they are diffuse and invisible. Whether this new subjectivity resembles *homo juridicus*, a "predicate to neoliberal governmentality,"[35] or simply one of Tocqueville's "flock of timid and industrious animals," is rather beside the point. Whatever new subjectivities are produced, they hardly signify consent or genuine political engagement.

These arguments are anticipated and summarised by what Supiot refers to as "governance by numbers," a method of rule which has spread inexorably in the modern age, and continues to do so.[36] Here, the aim of governance is described as the "dream of an arithmetically attainable social harmony," a "new avatar" of Taylorism,[37] in which governing is understood as being the maximisation of numerically measurable outcomes through regulatory apparatus, rather than through respect for law.[38] Good governance relies on the programming of individuals so that they react flexibly and effectively so as to achieve the appropriate response to external stimuli.[39] As a result, to echo Koskenniemi, Oakeshott, and Foucault, "law loses its sovereign status and becomes simply an instrument for the realisation of programmes."[40] An autonomous realm of law is "obliterated" by the notion that science can ultimately specify desired outcomes and orientations, and as a result law simply becomes deployed to operationalise those specifications – a mere "technique of power."[41] It is no longer the condition on which the autonomy of individuals is based, but the tool of a form of governance which seeks quantitative results at every turn.

But the deficiencies of "scientism" – the tendency of governance by numbers to "replace the territory with the map" and hence take flights of fancy which "ensnare managers and workers alike" – will always lead to unsatisfactory, not to mention disastrous, results.[42] This is clearly evident in the history of Communism and other forms of central planning, of course. But is also for Supiot as much the cause of the present European predicament, with rampant unemployment, unhappy and over-worked employees, atomised and miserable citizens, and financial crisis an ever-present threat. The consequence for the human individual, therefore, is a turn in desperation to any group promising identity and physical and economic security – be they religious factions, ethnic groupings, or mafia networks (or, indeed, one might add brands, technology companies, or sports teams).[43] Most acutely, it results in "ties of allegiance" developing between employee and employer, such that the latter becomes ever more dependent on the former, no longer simply obeying orders for a certain period of time in exchange for money, but "totally mobilised" for its benefit in exchange for a kind of benign vassal status.[44]

That global human rights governance presents itself not as the means by which the turn to governance by numbers can be challenged, but rather a facet of the same phenomenon, is thus particularly poignant. As previous chapters of this book demonstrated, statistical performance measurement, often using the techniques of financial management and financial accounting, is fast becoming the weapon of choice of the human rights movement. This is presented as nothing less than a "science of human dignity"[45] – the creation of objective, trustworthy, and transparent methods of monitoring human rights performance that are far superior to qualitative methods, which are considered to be "too *ad hoc* [and] inadequate in establishing systematic patterns of violations, identifying clear failures by duty-bearers to fulfil their positive obligations, or motivating systemic reform."[46] The result is a plethora of initiatives to benchmark human rights performance through indicators, budget analysis, indices, and rankings. These are very often framed as being only a part of the solution, but they have a tendency to proliferate thanks to the allure of the measurable and the power of numbers to "create social worlds."[47] Far from providing any sort of legal barrier to the imposition of a "dream of an arithmetically attainable social harmony" and the negative consequences of that fantasy, the governmentalisation of global human rights governance is, bluntly, becoming part of the problem.

This range of concerns provide us with a powerful series of critiques of what I have called the governmentalisation of global human rights governance. And as we shall now see, they are in large part anticipated – and augmented – by the thought of both Oakeshott and Foucault, particularly as they concern the relationship between freedom and morality and how that relationship is formed in the nexus between law and politics. To expand on this, we first examine Oakeshott's rationale for preferring the State (and, by extension, international organisation) being oriented towards the ideal of the civil condition.

Freedom as the ontological condition of ethics

Oakeshott on free agency

Oakeshott defines free agency not on the basis of free will precisely, but rather on the basis of intelligence. This not meant in the sense that agency requires high intelligence, but rather in the sense that it requires the capacity to choose how to act in any given circumstance. This is because human conduct for him is the result of *reasons* (however adequate or inadequate they might be) but not *causes*. It is not, in other words, the impulsive or instinctive reaction to an external stimulus, but rather the agent "understanding (or misunderstanding) his situation and responding to it."[48] The response may be "wise or foolish," "adequate or inadequate," but in deriving from reason it is done with genuine agency.[49] It is nothing but the absence of causation.[50]

This results from human life's status as an "individual self-enactment." The self is a "substantive personality, the outcome of an education, whose resources are collected in a self-understanding [and] whose conduct is ... the adventure in which this cultivated self deploys its resources, discloses and enacts itself in response to contingent situations, and both acquires and confirms its autonomy."[51] Human association, therefore, is "dramatic and intelligent, not organic."[52] The joint pursuit of a common endeavour or cooperative undertaking of any kind is required to be in terms of continuous choices to be associated reflecting the self-understanding and autonomy of the individuals engaged in it.[53]

Oakeshott identifies a particular propensity or disposition to value this understanding of freedom as a strand within the European philosophical tradition.[54] This he describes as being the reading of the human condition as one in which individuals are "saddled with an unsought and inescapable 'freedom'" which they are not well-equipped to exercise, but which is nevertheless recognised to be the emblem of human dignity. It is a view of freedom as being "a condition for each individual to explore, to cultivate, to make the most of, and to enjoy as an opportunity rather than suffer as a burden."[55] And it acknowledges that "imagining, deliberating, wanting, choosing and acting" were not to be understood as "costs incurred in seeking enjoyments" but rather were enjoyments in themselves. They were "the exercise of a gratifying self-determination or personal autonomy."[56]

He identified this disposition in a long list of sources, ranging from Pico della Mirandola to Rabelais to Erasmus, but above all in the work of Montaigne, who understood the human condition as an adventure in personal self-enactment. There was in Montaigne's depiction of this adventure no promise of a discovery of the truth, nor of a technological breakthrough to satisfy all wants, but only "a prompting not to be dismayed at our own imperfections and a recognition that 'it is something almost divine for a man to know how to belong to himself' and to live by that understanding."[57]

Oakeshott is not to be misunderstood here as lionising a kind of Randian selfishness. While he recognised that this might be the consequence of such a disposition, he was keen to make clear that the "collected personality" of an autonomous self would we well aware of its own limits, and would on that basis be equally likely to show an interest in, and associate with, others.[58] That is, the free individual, far from being inclined to live and succeed by his own lights, is often in fact genuinely communally minded and given to social engagement – he or she is likely to take part in all manner of cooperative undertakings (or enterprise associations) provided they are freely entered into. He or she will be driven to relate to others, in other words, on the basis of equal terms; these relationships will be characterised by "humility," but will be "devoid of humiliation."[59] (Elsewhere, he put it that society is after all made up of individual selves who must find their place alongside and in cooperation with each other: "[o]nly through his particular station and the faithful performance of its particular duties, can [man] take hold of this thing called 'humanity'.")[60]

If a criticism is to be made, it is that the vision which Oakeshott paints is blithe about the effects which material conditions have on the ability to engage in self-determination, and romantic about its consequences. But Oakeshott was himself perfectly aware that he could be read in this way, and was careful to try to avoid any implication of suggesting that what he was depicting was anything other than a disposition – a way merely of conceiving of human nature and, he implies, not a realistic depiction of the lifestyle of anyone but "aristocrats," "angels," and "lunatics."[61] It is rather to be thought of as, if anything, a sentiment: a recognition of self-direction as "excellen[t] simply in respect of its authenticity."[62] And it was in this sense at least apolitical; he dismissed the description of it as "bourgeois market-society capitalism" as part of a "mountain of rubbish" burying it from view.[63] It was instead a "moral conviction."[64]

Free agency and civil association

It is this moral conviction that gives rise to an understanding of the State along the analogy of *societas*. This is because it gives that understanding its "chief theoretical postulate," which Oakeshott gives the name *civitas peregrina*.[65] This is an association not of pilgrims with a common destination, but one of "adventurers." These adventurers are not simply atomised individuals pursuing their whims and desires. They are instead "partners in a practice in civility" – in other words, the civil condition – which they have inherited from those who have gone before them, and which provides the framework of rules of just conduct within which they each undergo the process of self-enactment. This process, it bears re-emphasising, may and indeed would result in the creation and furtherance of purposive enterprise associations of various diverse kinds. And the existence of such purposive enterprise associations is envisaged by, and indeed made possible through, the prevailing practice of civility. But the overarching association itself is non-purposive.

Just as the disposition towards freedom is a moral conviction, the *civitas peregrina* is for Oakeshott a "faith" rather than an actual arrangement of government.[66] But it did imbue the thoughts of certain political theorists from the early modern period onwards. He identifies Machiavelli as one who "assumed a human being to be an intelligent agent seeking the satisfaction of his wants in self-chosen actions and utterances [and] guided by *la sua fantasia*."[67] But more pertinently he saw it also in the flourishing of thought concerning the nature of the State that took place during the enlightenment and thereafter. It was assumed, in his view, by the American founders and the authors of the Federalist papers and by those responsible for the French Declaration of the Rights of Man and the Citizen. And it was clearly evident in the work of a list of thinkers such as Montesquieu, Bodin, Hobbes, Spinoza, Kant, Fichte, and Hegel.[68]

It is in his reading of the last of these thinkers that we see something like a statement of the relationship between the moral conviction concerning freedom, law, and the civil condition – and ultimately of the position of rights implied by Oakeshott's thinking. For Hegel, Oakeshott tells us, human conduct is an engagement in which Subjects "continuously create and recreate themselves as the finite persons they wish to be." In doing so, each appears in his true character: an "independent exhibition of *der wirkende Geist*, active intelligence." And it is necessary in order for this to occur that the conditions governing the right and wrong of human conduct, *das Recht*, do not deprive Subjects of their "self-management in self-enactment." This is not because the authenticity of free conduct in itself ratifies *das Recht*. It is rather because the conditions of *das Recht* will compromise the integrity of the Subject unless they are understandable to him, unless he is free to subscribe to them or not, and unless that subscription is an intelligent, willed act. This does not require his approval of those conditions. It simply requires that they are the products of reflective intelligence, they are recognisable, and they do not necessitate substantive action but only acknowledgement *as* conditions.[69]

This means that whatever those conditions are, they can neither be commands to perform specified actions, nor immutable laws of nature. They must appear, at least in the context of the laws of a State, as "positive, self-authenticating, non-instrumental rules of law enacted by human beings according to a procedure authorised in the system of law [and] capable of being considered in terms of their desirability and deliberately altered."[70] They must not only allow free agency, but must postulate Subjects to be free agents.[71] And this means it is not necessary for all Subjects to approve of them; this does not deprive those Subjects of their self-enactment, because the rules make no substantive positive demands, nor enjoin or forbid other modes of association from being entered into. This is "law" of a particular kind, which Hegel called *Gesetze*.[72]

Taken together, then, this provides us with a sense of the relationship between disposition, theory, and legal form. It suggests that there is a certain conviction or sentiment concerning the human condition which prizes free agency; that this results in a theoretical postulate of human political association, namely the *civitas peregrina*; and that this finds expression in a particular formulation of law as *Gesetze*. These are the foundations, as it were, of the civil condition.

The civil condition as a moral association

It is this which makes the civil condition the only truly moral *compulsory* form of association for Oakeshott. This is because his understanding of morality was contingent on freedom. Moral practice must for him consist in activity which may be either good or bad. It is only possible to act morally when one is faced with alternatives – otherwise one is simply "disclosing" oneself as moral by abiding by the rules and other conventions. Response to command, obligation, or precept is simply the pursuit of morality "as the crow flies."[73] One is in responding simply reacting to circumstance – one's behaviour is only *caused*, rather than reasoned. Genuine moral action only exists where the agent is pursuing "self-enactment"; where she makes choices, and performs actions accordingly, in an attempt to actualise her self-understanding.[74] That is, when an agent exercises choice and reflects upon her motives for doing so, she reveals herself *to* herself – and in the

understanding of herself which is thereby revealed, she can elect to "cultivate some sentiments rather than others" in her own character.[75] This is the
true expression of virtue – the "requirement of thinking about [oneself] as
[one] should while doing what [one] ought."[76] Morality is thus a process
of self-realisation – freely choosing and cultivating sentiments or motives
within oneself as the basis of future action. And freedom is the necessary
postulate, therefore, of morality.

This means that morality cannot be judged on the basis of outcomes.
Evaluating the actions of agents on the basis of whether or not they procure
"the common good" has nothing to do with morality properly understood:
that would be to understand human beings simply as "role performers"
whose conduct is ultimately dictated by an overriding purpose.[77] They
are not freely electing to do this rather than that, but are *caused* to do
so. Moreover, acting to promote the good of others through compulsion is
thereby to destroy *their* freedom and hence "the [very] condition of moral
goodness."[78]

This puts Oakeshott's understanding of morality very close to Kant's.
For Kant, justice derived from the protection of freedom – not the natural
ends of man, achieving the common good or human happiness, or any other
such motive. And this meant that "a government [...] established on the
principle of benevolence towards the people" would be "the worst conceivable despotism."[79] Individuals are ends in themselves, not the means by
which the satisfactions of others are obtained, and the only form of genuine
morality therefore is one which enshrines their autonomy.[80] From this follows a very particular understanding of the relationship between freedom,
morality, and law.

The civil condition as the basis for the composition of the State, which
is to say, on the analogy of *societas*, is of course a compulsory association
in the sense that one is (usually) born into it and cannot simply dissociate
at will. But otherwise it consists only of a "watery fidelity" to a shared
practice – adherence to *lex*. And since *lex* is non-purposive, does not specify
purposes, and does not specify actions which particular *cives* must carry
out, it does not interfere (except to the extent necessary to have a functioning association at all)[81] with their free agency and their capacity therefore to
act morally. Its laws are of general application and simply specify what is
or is not "just conduct" within the practice in which the *cives* are engaged,
such that it is possible for them to obtain that "small amount of compulsory civilisation without which [people's] transactions would often be dis-
tressingly precarious and their lives more irksome and less enjoyable."[82]
This means that its rules do not affect underlying choices – they are simply
the "conditions to be taken into account and subscribed to in choosing
performances."[83]

What is so dangerous about compulsory enterprise association through the State-as-*universitas*, by contrast, is that it overrides the very possibility of individual self-enactment. Rather than being the result of reason, association on those terms is *caused*. And hence rather than allowing individuals to acquire and confirm their autonomy, it negates it. They are simply enlisted in a purported "common purpose" that is not their own. In effect, this means simply being "the property of the association, an item of its capital resources."[84] The only relevant consideration is whether they are hindering or undermining the purpose of the enterprise. If they are not, they have a certain license to act provided they stay within those bounds. But ultimately they are viewed only through the lens of the purpose which those who govern them have chosen. Oakeshott here cites Sydney Webb: "The perfect and fitting development of each individual is not necessarily the utmost and highest cultivation of his own personality, but the filling, in the best possible way, of his humble function in the great social machine."[85]

Oakeshott on law, politics, and morality

This means that Oakeshott had a particular view of the relationship between law, politics, and morality. *Cives* do have common concerns. They have an interest in what Oakeshott calls *"respublica,"* meaning both *lex* itself and the conditions which themselves determine the norms of *lex* – that is, adjudication, legislation, the conduct of office-holders, the procedures they are to follow, the delegation of authorities, the penalties for failing to abide by rules, and so on.[86]

This means that what is necessary for the civil condition to come into being is a general shared recognition, and acknowledgement of that recognition, that a certain system of law is indeed such a system and that it has authority. *Cives* are not, in that capacity, concerned with whether *respublica* is fit or unfit for achieving any substantive purpose, because of course there is no such purpose. They are not concerned with whether a rule is worthy of approval or disapproval, because this does not affect its character as a rule – "a rule is a prescription of conditions of conduct [and] since it cannot be denied its character as a rule on account of a disapproval of these conditions, it cannot be recognised in its character as a rule by approval of them."[87] *Cives* are, rather, concerned with whether *respublica* has authority. If it does so, then all of its rules will be recognised because they will be themselves derived from authoritative procedures.[88] Hence, the civil condition is predicated on the self-authenticating authority of *respublica* – the fact that it contains rules which themselves allow the authority of other rules to be recognised.

This point would appear almost banal – it is not significantly different from the thought of Kelsen or Hart. Here, Oakeshott is making the point only that the civil condition is entirely predicated on shared recognition of the authority of *respublica* on the part of the *cives*. If they cease for whatever reason to have that recognition, then there will be no civil condition.[89]

This causes Oakeshott to acknowledge that the recognition of the authority of *respublica* is conditional, but he quite deliberately dismisses the notion that it is conditional on anything other than recognition itself. The authority of *respublica* cannot derive from what can exist or be achieved in recognition of that authority. Civil association may bring value to human beings by "providing shelter from some of the uncertainties of a human life."[90] But this could not be the reason for recognition of the authority of *respublica*, for the simple reason that the benefits brought by civil association can only come into being on account of that recognition. If agents do not recognise the authority of *respublica*, there is no civil condition and hence no benefits arising from it. Those benefits can thus only be an epiphenomenon, as it were, of the civil condition, not its cause. To hold otherwise would be to make the circular argument that recognition derives from something which only comes about through recognition.[91]

Nor can recognition of authority derive from will, either in the sense of the will of a ruler, a majority, or indeed the "general will"; nor from a social purpose or approved moral ideas or distributive justice; nor from scientific knowledge about what is good for human beings; nor from laws of historical development. It is not a case of "deference to a trusted few who may be supposed to have such information or to be concerned with acquiring it" or a "schedule of inspired managerial decisions."[92] This is because, as Oakeshott never tired of emphasising, there was for him no "hovering *Volksgeist*" over human affairs, nor any such thing as "social forces," but only the individual decisions of individual human beings.[93] Hence the notion of universal approval or disapproval of some system, rule, or procedure or other could only ever be a figment of the imagination. A large number of human beings could never act to simply bestow authority on even one rule, let alone a system of rules, through their universal approval of its suitability, reasonableness, or worth. That would be an entirely unrealistic expectation of the muddle and messiness of the systems of rules which flawed human beings put into effect.[94] Put another way, the *only thing* capable of allowing a human society to generally recognise the authority of a system of rules is their shared recognition of its authority, irrespective of whether they approve of the individual rules comprising it, or whether individual rules appear reasonable to them, or not.[95]

This also means that Oakeshott accepts only a very limited definition of politics, which he contrasts with policy. Politics, in his understanding, is unique to the civil condition. It consists of the "engagement to consider the desirability or otherwise of the conditions prescribed [in *respublica*]"[96] – those being, of course, the conditions which themselves constitute the civil condition. This is deliberation on the desirability of those conditions, the imagining of them being different from what they are, and the undertaking to either change them or resist such change.[97] This means that political engagement consists of acting so as to bring about a change in the rules in a general sense – that is, to "prescribe [new] conditions to be subscribed to by all alike in unspecifiable future performances."[98] Such changes will not address particular specified groups or persons, or require them to perform specified actions, but will only be proposed and made to the general conditions of *lex* as they apply in the round. Politics is thus "at once acquiescent and critical." It requires assent to the ongoing authority of *respublica*, combined with a stance of criticism, questioning, or non-acceptance. To dissent from the authority of the system itself is to resolve to no longer be in a state of civil association.[99]

This means that politics is for Oakeshott a conservative practice in all senses. It is only the "holding up to inspection in terms of approval or disapproval some item ... of *respublica*, considering more desirable alternatives to it, and recommending and promoting the change from what is to the alleged more desirable condition." To engage in it is only to "focus attention on civility" – the practice of just conduct and the conditions which ought to be subscribed to within that framework.[100] This is to be contrasted of course with the wholesale rejection of the authority of civil association through civil war or revolution, but more importantly also with the "strategy and tactics" of policy – whether this be at the grand scale of "benevolent plans for the betterment of mankind, for diminishing the discrepancy between wants and satisfactions or for moral improvement," or the mere "proposals for awards of benefit or advantage to ascertainable individual or corporate interests."[101] Policy in this latter sense, Oakeshott is quite clear, has no place in civil association.[102]

Politics, which is a sphere exclusive to the civil condition, is not then a device for procuring substantive wants or achieving substantive purposes, but for making the prevailing conditions of *lex* more "just" in a piecemeal fashion. And this means that it is ultimately nothing to do with morality – except in the sense that it must not interfere with the underlying free agency of the *cives*.

Foucault and Oakeshott on freedom and ethics

The similarities between Oakeshott and Foucault with respect to the history of the State have already been identified. But both men also had two more foundational principles in common. The first of these is the sense of human activity as being the product of the internalisation of rules or norms.[103] The second is that it is possible for the self to "separate out from the contingency that has made us what we are, the possibility of no longer being, doing or thinking what we are, do or think."[104] That is, both were wedded to the possibility that the self could, through a process of care or self-enactment, transcend the contingent norms which mould it, while retaining its coherence – that one can achieve "self-transformation without self-destruction."[105] This results in a shared emphasis on freedom as a practice. For Foucault, freedom is something which is performed, a creative process, a project of "long practice and daily work."[106] Just as Oakeshott emphasised the necessity of reflection on motives as a necessary element in the process of self-enactment, as opposed to the reflection on outcomes or appearances which was more properly called self-disclosure, so Foucault sees the self as looking to its inner sensibility rather than external circumstances.[107] This results in an continuing project of speaking the "truth to oneself" – "making [the self] an achievement, not an initial principle."[108]

This also results therefore in a shared understanding that, as Foucault puts it, "freedom is the ontological condition of ethics."[109] Ethics is a creative endeavour, or a "style," the manner in which one shapes oneself through alignment with a self-selected *telos*. It has four distinct components: an "ethical substance," meaning intentions, motives, or feelings; the "mode of subjectivation," meaning the ideals that one chooses in relating to oneself; practices which result in changes to the self in order to become an ethical subject; and one's ends or goals in engaging in the practice overall.[110] It is therefore predicated entirely on free agency; it cannot be otherwise. There is a clear echo in this of Oakeshott's description of how reflecting on one's motives allows one to cultivate the sentiments one wishes to encourage in oneself, making this the true expression of virtue. And the end result for both thinkers is that ethics is "a product of life itself rather than a contrivance with which to judge it."[111] Ethics, or morality, is not to be assessed on the basis of outcomes, but is rather the means by which one achieves "distinctness."[112]

This has two consequences. The first is that non-instrumental individuality, or distinctness, is of critical importance: one must be able to "self-fashion" as a counterpoint to the shaping of the self by external forces (biopower, discipline, and security, for Foucault, or the mundanity of work and "doing" for Oakeshott). In other words, the self must be an endeavour to set one's own ends – to define a *telos*. And frequently this will mean acting in opposition to a governmental rationality which is forever "conducting, directing, leading, guiding, taking in hand, and manipulating [people]" in the name of a *telos* which is determined by governing "experts" embedded in institutions.

The second is that freedom cannot result from the application of ideology in order to radically remake society or civilisation. To do so would be only to impose a *telos* on others. For Foucault, this meant that there was no "point of resistance to political power other than in the relationship one has to oneself."[113] For Oakeshott, it means that the task of the moral individual is to understand the problems confronting the society within which he or she lives, and then "Set them right in his own mind – & if he is fortunate, in his own life."[114] Both conclusions can be called conservative.[115] It is perhaps more accurate to describe them as existentialist. Irrespective of that, it suggests that if political organisation is to properly respect human dignity or the process of self-enactment which is the basis of the moral/ethical life, it must be predicated on a system of law which is absent of the imposition of *telos*.

The governmentalisation of global human rights governance as an enterprise association

Having set out the relationship between law, morality, and politics in the thought of Oakeshott and Foucault, we are now able to identify a common concern at the heart of the three groups of criticisms of the managerial approach to human rights law. This is that where human beings are compulsorily put into circumstances of enterprise association, undesirable consequences naturally follow.

It will be remembered that Oakeshott's ideal of an enterprise association was that it was a voluntary one – even if voluntariness could be interpreted somewhat flexibly. To become a fire-fighter, the member of a golf club or political party, or a campaigner against this or that government policy, is a choice exercised by a free individual. It is an intelligent agent "understanding his situation and responding to it in terms of wants and choices ... and related to others ... in the cooperative pursuit of common wants."[116] And it is, of course, a necessary postulate of freedom that if that intelligent agent no longer wishes to be engaged in a cooperative pursuit in which he is previously engaged, he can dissociate from it.

This cannot be the case where the State takes on the aspect of an enterprise association. Such a model is inherently compulsory because it constitutes a relationship in which there is a common purpose for all subjects from which dissociation is not permitted, and because the managerial decisions and rules specifying how the purpose is to be pursued have absolute authority over those within the association.[117] For participation in an enterprise association to be truly voluntary and in that sense "free" on the terms previously outlined, it must be possible to dissociate oneself unilaterally. But one cannot do this in the context of the State – one can only at best "contingently escape" with permission granted through a "management decision."[118] And one must abide by the management decisions that are given in general, because to do otherwise is to hinder or subvert the purpose of the State. Indeed, in such a State, the forming by subjects of any enterprise association which does hinder or subvert the State's purpose will itself be prohibited.[119] To be living within a State conceived on the analogy of *universitas* is in short to have "surrendered choice," but to have done so compulsorily by the simple fact of living there. One cannot dissociate oneself at will, and one cannot choose not to participate in the purpose for which the State is purportedly designed.

The result is a kind of false freedom. It is the "condition of being released from every care in the world save one; namely, the care not to be idle in fulfilling one's role in the enterprise, not to inhibit or prejudice that complete mobilisation of resources which constitutes such a State." It is the replacement of the "risk of frustration of one's purposes" that stems from true free agency with the "enjoyment of assured benefits." The result is that "the member of such a State enjoys the composure of the conscript assured of his dinner." It is the freedom of "warm, compensated servility."[120]

For Oakeshott, of course, all modern European States resemble this description, not entirely but in large part. There is no State which allows subjects to dissociate at will, and there is no State which allows its subjects to act against its overriding purpose. For the people living in the modern State, "freedom" at most extends to having some limited capacity to consider desirabilities in terms of the overall purpose. They may choose between competing proposals for how to achieve that purpose. But they cannot question it, and they cannot step outside it. (This is what made distinctions between left and right, or for that matter between democracy, authoritarianism, capitalism, pluralism, and so on "totally irrelevant."[121] The State as designed by either Hayek or Lenin were in Oakeshott's view orbiting exactly the same pole.)

Yet he did not confine his comments to the State alone. He was also keenly aware that notions of "world government" which had emerged over the course of the previous three centuries had also tended to tilt towards conceiving of that government through the analogy of *universitas*.[122] And, having examined the subject matter of the previous chapters of this book, it is in fact easy to see evidence for this in the governmentalisation of global human rights governance. What is this phenomenon, indeed, if not a compulsory enterprise association from which individuals cannot freely dissociate, conceived as a *universitas*, with the common purpose of improving human well-being, with an array of institutions and technical experts whose task is to interpret that purpose and manage its pursuit through directing the actions of the associates, and with a "rule-book" of laws which justify those interpretations and allow the setting of instrumental goals?

Understanding the governmentalisation of global human rights governance in this way allows us to revisit the three potential critiques which I outlined above: those regarding the rule of law, consent, and the nature of ruling. We shall do that in turn.

The rule of law

Oakeshott's chief concern was not "the rule of law" *per se*, but rather the "type" of law which prevailed – *lex* or managerial rule-book.[123] But there is clearly a relationship between *lex* and the characteristics of the rule of law which I mentioned previously. That is, it was a given that *lex* should be clear, unconcealed, not self-contradictory, not arbitrary, predictable, and universally applicable.[124] And while he does not spell this out precisely, a system of law would be denuded these characteristics the less it resembled *lex*. That is, given that all law is an "equivocal mixture" between *lex* and managerial rule-book, there is always a tendency for the rule of law to be undermined by the mixture becoming unbalanced in favour of the latter.

This can happen in a number of ways. A concrete example Oakeshott himself gives is the doctrine of the "public interest," by which if a development is deemed likely to raise aggregate prosperity – such as a factory, bridge, railway line, etc. – then it is exempt from the ordinary common law rights versus nuisance.[125] The purpose of improving well-being, in other words, overrides prior expectations about the rules of common law and creates an exemption from their universal applicability. More abstractly, the process of adjudication is fundamentally altered when the notion creeps in that the task of the court is to achieve a managerial decision rather than to settle a dispute. In a system of *lex*, it will be recalled, adjudication is the process whereby a contingent or unique situation is examined and a decision is reached about how the norms of *lex* apply to it to achieve a resolution, with the resolution being as follows: "whether or not the action complained of was performed in the manner alleged, whether or not the defendant may be held responsible, and whether or not it constitutes the alleged infraction of the norm of conduct prescribed in *lex*."[126] A by-product of this is that the overall meaning of the relevant norms of *lex* are "amplified." But the judge's role is not to take into account considerations of policy or, as it were, to legislate. This is because to do so would be to subject the litigants, and others in positions like them, involuntarily to the imperatives of policy. It would also exclude the *cives* in general from participation in politics, properly understood as thoughtful deliberation on the nature of *respublica* and the conditions of just conduct under which they live. It would transform the civil condition into an enterprise association through the intrusion of purposiveness, and this enterprise association would inevitably be an involuntary one for reasons already set out. And it has the potential to result in abrupt and unforeseen departures from settled conditions of practice, by allowing the judge's subjective notions of appropriate policy to affect how he or she interprets the norms of *lex*.

All of this is plain from the interpretive practice of the ECtHR, of course. The decision in *Young*, for example, had all of those features. It transformed a dispute between employer and employee into an abstract question of policy, in turn putting both parties into positions not of litigants but of involuntary interlocutors for competing views on industrial relations. It severed the matter of whether compulsory trade union membership should be in principle lawful or otherwise from the political procedures by which *cives* determine the conditions under which they live, and instead put it into the hands of judges sitting outside and above those procedures. It made law the instrument of a purpose – achieving a particular "moral truth" connected to particular notions of the good – and in so doing contributed to the understanding of the State as an enterprise association with the task of improving well-being through preventing compulsion. And it made the functioning of the law unpredictable by opening it up to the judges' own subjective views on the appropriate policy for the Convention to enshrine. This had the ultimate consequence of rendering settled understandings of industrial relations uncertain. (And it might be recalled that maintaining such settled understandings was the justification for the wording of the relevant Article of the Convention in the first place.)

The process of legislation is likewise also vulnerable to corruption in this way through unbalancing matters towards the analogy of law as managerial rule-book. For Oakeshott, legislation ideally understood was an "injection" into the system of *lex* a new general norm of conduct in response to a change of belief or circumstances among *cives*.[127] It must be used sparingly, because in its too frequent use it would only be a "clumsy and hazardous invasion [of *lex*] by abrupt alteration."[128] This would render the law unstable, unpredictable, and unclear through the proliferation of new and unforeseen rules. While the practices of UN treaty- and charter-based mechanisms are generally thought not to be binding, it will be recalled that much of their work consists not only of setting out "authoritative" views on the nature of obligations deriving from rules of law, but of "setting standards" and elaborating on norms of conduct. In this respect there is not a great deal of distinction between legislation formally understood and, for example, the general comments and concluding observations of the UN treaty bodies. The chief distinction is simply the practical one that States may ignore or fail to implement the recommendations of the latter. But the potential to render prevailing legal frameworks unstable is obvious.

Consent

What is particularly dangerous about compulsory enterprise association through the State-as-*universitas*, for Oakeshott, is that it overrides the very possibility of individual self-enactment. Rather than being the result of reason, association on those terms is "caused." And hence rather than allowing individuals to acquire and confirm their autonomy, it negates it. Individuals are simply enlisted in a purported common purpose that is not their own. In effect, this means being "the property of the association, an item of its capital resources."[129] The only relevant consideration is whether they are hindering or undermining the purpose of the enterprise. If they are not, they have a certain license to act provided they stay within those bounds. But ultimately they are viewed only through the lens of the purpose which those who govern them have chosen.

This suggests that the governmentalisation of global human rights governance is, paradoxically, a process which is fundamentally opposed to individual self-enactment. As a common purpose for mankind in which no individual has made the decision to join and from which no individual may freely dissociate, it makes its project inescapable. And because that project is a programmatic and managerial one, individuals become construed only in those terms – the ends by which success is both achieved and measured. They become as a result not free agents with the capacity to cultivate their own selves as a practice of morality or ethics, but simply the tools of a morality which is determined from above.

At its simplest, this is evident from the most basic statement on which the modern system of international human rights law is founded: the Vienna Declaration's proclamation that "All human rights are universal, indivisible and interdependent and interrelated [*sic*]."[130] One cannot therefore elect not to have rights, of course. But much more importantly, because all other individuals have rights, and because the rights of all individuals are "indivisible and interdependent and interrelated," one cannot elect not to be part of the process wherein those rights are secured. One cannot be permitted to infringe upon the rights of others, it goes without saying, but more pertinently nor can one stand in the way of those rights being fulfilled or "enjoyed." Indeed, one must actively cooperate with the actors who have the obligations or responsibilities in question – not only States, but also businesses and international organisations. For Eide, this means that "The State can legitimately call on and oblige all individuals to participate in the realization of human rights."[131] For John Ruggie, it means ensuring that businesses transform themselves into active human rights monitors and enforcers throughout their supply chains and stakeholder groups, under the "Protect, Respect and Remedy" framework.[132] For Next plc, it means auditing and inspecting its suppliers and capacity building to help them "remediate risks," and carrying out human rights training for its employees.[133] For the World Health Organization (WHO) it means acting to ensure that staff have human rights "in their DNA."[134] For the OHCHR, meanwhile, it means that human rights need to be actively promoted by NHRIs so that people become engaged in the transformation of their own relationships and surroundings:

> [Promotional activities'] content and implementation should be timely and relevant, to ensure interest and maximize effect for the target audience. They should influence and convince audiences and mobilize them towards concrete action and change, both in the short and the long term. They should move audiences to transfer acquired knowledge and skills to others and to undertake integrated and sustainable action on economic, social and cultural rights. And whenever possible, they should be programme-based and part of a broader plan.[135]

And this, of course, results in the individual being conceptualised as the means by which rights are respected, protected, and fulfilled – ready to be "mobilised" for action and positive change. This means the wholesale intrusion by State and international institutions into their "life-world,"[136] with interest taken in every facet of their communal and individual lives, from the language they speak, to the media they consume, to the way they engage in the workplace, and to the way in which they raise their children.[137]

The governmentalisation of global human rights governance is practically the quintessence of Webb's aphorism, because governmentality itself is ultimately nothing other than the elaboration of processes wherein individuals find their "humble function[s] in the great social machine." They are subsumed within the statistical phenomena comprising the population, relevant not at the level of their individual self-enactment but rather because of what their lived characteristics signify at an abstract, quantitative level; what those characteristics contribute to statistical observations such as the percentage of individuals who feel safe walking home at night, the suicide rate, the prevalence of breast-feeding, the percentage of the population covered by nutritional supplement programmes, the literacy rate, and so on. They will "only be pertinent to the extent that, properly managed, maintained and encouraged, [they] will make possible what one wants to obtain at the level that is pertinent"[138] – namely, statistical evidence of improvements in well-being.

Ruling

Individuals are also transformed through this process of the abnegation (or "destruction" as Foucault put it)[139] of the self, becoming "obedient" as well as "needful." As we saw in the previous chapter, they are governed at a distance, and this involves them becoming *changed*: they are produced through mechanisms of audit and review as self-monitoring and self-governing, such that their purportedly freely chosen actions become closely aligned with the goals of those who are governing them. They become the subject of an array of "tactics" which, whether deliberately or not, have the effect of "conducting, directing, leading, guiding, taking in hand, and manipulating"[140] them not just for their own good, but for the vision of the good which has been determined for them and others.

This leads us to the final group of concerns, which were those concerning the manner of ruling. Oakeshott, as we have already seen, had a strict and conservative vision of what "politics" meant. It was considering *respublica* – which is to say *lex* and the rules concerning its creation, administration, adjudication and so on – in terms of the desirability of its conditions. From this might flow recommendations of changes to be made, which would have to be defended against alternatives or against maintaining the status quo through a process of persuasion. But that was the limit of what politics proper should be. It could never have the aim of getting others to engage in a "wished-for performance" (the domain of "policy," which he saw as distasteful); it could only consist of persuading others to agree to adopt a new or altered rule prescribing conditions of just conduct.[141]

Of all of the concepts which Oakeshott advanced in *On Human Conduct* and his other works of political philosophy, this may be the position upon which the most criticism has been heaped.[142] But it is important to re-emphasise that it, like all aspects of his "civil condition," was postulated not as an ideal in the sense of being a desirable end-state to be achieved. It was an ideal in the sense of being an abstract aid to reflection. And here, the important characteristic of his vision of politics for our purposes is that it consisted of engagement on the part of *cives* in the composition of the rules which condition their conduct, and, crucially, that its aim was not to elicit "wished-for performance" towards some substantive goal or other. It was fundamentally a matter of establishing and elaborating on a common understanding of what would be meant by just conduct within the shared practice of the *cives* and their "rulers" who enforced, adjudicated, and administered the system of *respublica* and its political processes.

As he was fond of doing, then, Oakeshott was setting up two non-existent extremes as poles within which actual human conduct could be examined and understood. On the one hand, there was what he called "politics," which was as described previously. And against it, on the other hand, was the managerial matter of policymaking and implementation; a task not of the *cives* engaging in alteration of the shared rules of just conduct, but of the ruler eliciting his or her "wished-for performance" from subjects. The former is, in other words, in keeping with what Oakeshott understood to be free agency. It stemmed from reasoned utterances and actions deriving from autonomous decision making. The latter is antagonistic towards that, because it makes human actions and utterances the result of causes – that is, managerial decisions. "Real" goings-on in the area of government will inevitably be an "equivocal mixture" of these two opposed ideals. But the further those goings-on stray away from what Oakeshott called politics and the closer therefore they drift towards policy, the less government will resemble a sphere in which free agency is respected and enshrined.

Such a drift towards policy is of course writ large across the governmentalisation of global human rights governance. It is the very thing which Koskenniemi observed, and with which this book began: the reconceptualisation of international law as a set of declarations justifying the elaboration of complex regulatory mechanisms for achieving purposes. This is visible within the sphere of human rights in particularly obvious ways, and this will be plain from what was detailed both in Chapters 1 and 5.

But it is also worth emphasising that as well as there being a drift towards the "pole" of policy in the governmentalisation of global human rights governance, there is also a strong drift away from the "pole" of what Oakeshott described as politics. There was never a strong or direct sense in which human individuals had any engagement in the content of individual rules of international human rights law. Indeed, they could never have realistically been described as *cives* within that context, and the civil condition barely even "glimpsed" there either. If anything, were the international community to be described as existing in the civil condition, it would be States who would be the analogue of *cives*. But it is at least true that, if international human rights law were to retain a resemblance to *lex* – that is, if it were to be restrained simply to declaring the shared rules of just conduct agreed to by States – then individuals would be able to undertake some very tenuous and indirect engagement in Oakeshottian "politics" in respect of rights, through democratic processes in the States in which they live. It would remain at least theoretically possible for them to carry out actions or utterances which would have the ultimate effect of enjoining changes to be made to the rules. Yet this already faint possibility diminishes almost to nothing when those laws can be interpreted teleologically in light of an overriding purpose in a manner not subject itself to rule-based restraint; when the rules themselves have given rise to a huge range of regulatory "tactics" which are not themselves rules and which can charitably be described as opaque; and when the enforcement and managerial implementation of the ends which purportedly flow from the rules are carried out not by the public institutions of the State, but by businesses and other non-State actors, and international organisations for which there are essentially no existing participatory institutions.

Pastoral power and the individual manqué

An argument presents itself that as human rights laws orient themselves away from the ideal of *lex*, they also begin to be the means by which something akin to Oakeshott's individual manqué is created. This is not to adopt Oakeshott's views on what he elsewhere called "mass man" wholesale.[143] His language in respect of this figure is contemptuous: "defeated" and "outmanoeuvred" by freedom, the individual manqué is ridden with a "self-distrust" and "natural submissiveness" that lead him to throw himself at the feet of a patron so as to be "told what to think, to ask for, and to do."[144] That he has been encouraged in this by leaders, unscrupulous or well-meaning alike, does provide some excuse, and Oakeshott also suggests that this figure is deserving of "sympathy and respect,"[145] but his view of the individual manqué is in the end entirely fatalistic. He offers no glimmer of hope for the pathetic character he depicts. Such a person is the "human postulate" of the State as *universitas*, and will encourage it eternally to "make substantive choices for those unable or indisposed to make them for themselves."[146]

Yet Oakeshott also clearly held the view that the individual manqué was ultimately the victim of circumstance. Whether morally defeated by the medieval system of enclosure or by the "conditions of modern urban life," he was still the product of *defeat* – loss, ignorance, poverty, displacement, persecution, misfortune, and so on.[147] To put it another way, the individual manqué is made, not born. And this makes it entirely natural to sympathise with him. The result is the desire to advocate his cause, to organise his life, to "formul[ate] his so-called needs in terms of 'rights' to enjoy substantive benefits."[148]

This will necessarily result in the "modification of his status as subject" (although this is never made clear to the individual manqué).[149] He is transformed, in other words, from a *cive* – an autonomous individual cultivating his own selfhood through free agency – into simply the member of a compulsory enterprise association which makes all of the relevant substantive decisions for his benefit.[150] He is thereby "infused" with self-alienation and becomes in the end merely obedient and thoughtless – interested only in getting a share of the benefits which the State directly or indirectly provides, and keen to avoid rocking the boat lest he be seen as inhibiting or prejudicing the enterprise of government.[151] In short, despite the undoubtedly "crotchety" nature of Oakeshott's description, his individual manqué is in the end to be understood not entirely as a contemptible weakling. Rather, this figure is itself better understood as an abstracted ideal – a non-existent extreme. It is held up as the postulate of a particular way of conceiving of the role of the State. For the "leaders" who Oakeshott refers to, the concept of the individual manqué is the very reason for acting. They see populations which they consider to be filled with persons who have suffered "defeat" – loss, ignorance, poverty, displacement, persecution, misfortune, and so on – and they are compelled by sympathy thereby to act. One might say indeed that they are compelled by compassion, the inability to look on while others suffer, to deploy the power of the State to act as benefactor and to organise matters accordingly. The root of the analogy of State as *universitas*, in other words, is as much a product of compassion as it is of the necessities of war or the possibilities of bureaucracy of any of the other factors Oakeshott identified. This ultimately means that the end product, so to speak, of the State conceived along those lines (an involuntary enterprise association distributing benefits to its members in the name of their well-being and denying their agency as a result) is the final consequence of operationalised compassion.

Oakeshott is far from being the only thinker in history to have expressed such concerns. For Montesquieu, of course, this came in the observation that the excess of virtue was as much to be feared as the excess of vice. And its most eloquent expression was undoubtedly that of Tocqueville, who foresaw the emergence of that "immense and tutelary power, which takes upon itself alone to secure [the populace's] gratifications, and to watch over their fate."[152] Like a "parent," willingly labouring for the happiness of the population but setting itself up as the "sole agent and the only arbiter of that happiness," it would gradually rob individuals of their agency and reduce them to an "enervate[d]" and "stupefie[d]" state, thinking of "nothing but rejoicing": a "flock of timid and industrious animals, of which the government is the shepherd."[153]

And it is helpful also to return to Foucault. The line running between pastoral power and a governmental rationality which manipulates the obedient and needful individual at every turn was absolutely clear in his work. And we see in the governmentalisation of global human rights governance the emergence of three of the dominant strands of pastoral power which he emphasised. The pastor purportedly "guides to salvation, prescribes the law, and teaches the truth."[154] But each of these strands must be problematised. First, the pastor must assure the salvation of everyone – all the individual members of the community and also hence the community itself. He must account for his sheep (the number that remain and the number that are lost), and account for their individual merits and correct their faults. The result is what Foucault describes as "the economy of faults and merits": the pastor must continually "manage the trajectories, circuits and reversals of fault and merit" amongst his flock.[155] In other words, he is not merely a guide in the sense of showing the way, but something akin to a *manager*.

Second, with respect to the law, Foucault makes clear that he does not believe that the Christian pastor is fundamentally a man of the law, because Christianity is itself not a religion of law, but one of will – that is to say, God's.[156] God's will is unique for each human individual, and therefore the pastor is not to be thought of as a judge, but rather a doctor: one who prescribes a particular cure for a particular individual in a particular case. He does not treat like cases alike as a court might, because no two cases are in fact alike. His "mode of action is individualized."[157] What this means for the sheep, on the other hand, is an expectation of submission, not to rules or laws, but to the pastor – it means entering into a relationship that is not governed by clear rules but by the nature of the participants. The sheep puts himself into his pastor's hands – subordinating himself simply because the pastor is the pastor and must be obeyed.[158] And he obeys in order to be obedient, as an end in itself. In the relationship between the pastor and the individual sheep, the latter is to continually renounce his own will and to cultivate his own complete humility – which means not merely knowing that one has committed sins, nor merely accepting orders, but "knowing that any will of one's own is a bad will."[159] It is an exercise in destruction of the self.[160]

And third, with respect to truth, Foucault begins with the natural observation that the role of the pastor is to teach his community. But this is not simply telling the members of the community what they must know and do, at least not by laying out general principles of conduct for them to follow. Far from it: it is a continual, daily modulation, requiring constant observation and supervision. "The pastor must really take charge of and observe daily life in order to form a never-ending knowledge of the behaviour and conduct of the flock."[161] This is because, of course, all of the members of the flock are individuals, with different characters and different – and constantly changing – circumstances. Moreover, because of the nature of the relationship between pastor and flock, teaching cannot simply be a matter of teaching what is true and what is not; it is much more a matter of "directing the conscience."[162] The pastor is installed as the permanent spiritual director of every sheep in the flock, with regard "to everything and for the whole of one's life."[163] This cements the relationship of subordination: spiritual direction is the exercise of examining one's conscience in order not to obtain self-mastery but to "produce a truth" which binds the sheep more closely to the pastor.

Foucault concludes that the pastorate is not, then, to be thought of as characterised by its relationship to salvation, law, and truth. Rather, it is to be thought of as a form of power which, first, creates an "entire economy and technique of the circulation, transfer and reversal of merits [and faults]"; second, establishes "a kind of exhaustive, total and permanent relationship of individual obedience"; and third, implements "a technique of ... investigation, self-examination, and the examination by others, by which a certain secret inner truth of the hidden soul, becomes the element through which the pastor's power is exercised."[164] This is what is essential to Christianity, and it is here that we see the birth of an "absolutely new form of power" – namely, pastoral power.

The contours of the critique of the governmentalisation of global human rights governance therefore present themselves. Driven by compassion, the advocates of human rights endeavour to realise a directing idea: the operationalisation, through law, of relationships of benevolent care between the powerful and the powerless. The result is a body of obligations which conceives of no limits to its purview – a solipsistic and imperialistic sphere of *teleocratic* law which expands inexorably and permeates the "life-world" everywhere, and which has nothing short of universal human well-being as its purpose. Yet because of law's ambivalence, its *nomocratic* limitations, it is insufficient in its own right to achieve that purpose, and as a consequence it becomes conceived as a set of justifications for a vast array of regulatory or managerial "tactics" or "contextual *ad hocism*" operating through governmental reason and instantiating and strengthening pastoral power of the governor over the governed – managing them, abnegating their agency, and directing their moral conduct. It is not so much, then, that compassion in this context results in what Arendt attributed to Robespierre – the "[making] light of laws."[165] It is rather that the managerial apparatuses to which human rights laws give rise come to "[cover] the surface of society with a net-work of small complicated rules, minute and uniform, through which the most original minds and the most energetic characters cannot penetrate, [so that the] will of man is not shattered, but softened, bent, and guided" in the appropriate direction.[166] It is the deployment of a pastoral power – "always a good in itself" – which reduces the individual to a powerless and subservient member of a flock.

To be governed a little less

The picture painted here, however, is incomplete. It neglects the fact that, as Michael Ignatieff has recently admitted, the human rights movement appears to have made little impact on the "ordinary virtues" which comprise the moral life of most human beings in most countries beyond the elite discourse of lawyers, advocates, victim's groups, and bureaucrats.[167]

Far from being embedded as a global ethic, they have instead become simply an "empty public discourse without traction."[168] There is a commitment to "moral community" everywhere, but it is a "contextual ... specific ... local [and] non-universal" one.[169] Nobody beyond public policy elites frames their obligations to each other in terms of abstract universal rights.

This must be read against a backdrop of malaise that contrasts with the millenarianism of much of the "human rightist" literature. We are told that human rights have reached "the end of an era."[170] While the study of international human rights is "flourishing through the academy like never before," the "utility and legitimacy" of the human rights movement is perceived to be in crisis.[171] For many people in many countries, human rights are seen as a "shell game" pushed by a cosmopolitan elite onto an unwilling population.[172] Moyn sees "depression" about the role that human rights play in the world order driving advocates towards a "more modest plan" of attempting to spread constitutional norms through a general template.[173] The implication is that this has simply made the project even less appealing.

This should hardly be surprising to anybody who is familiar with the way in which human rights are typically discussed in popular newspapers and in ordinary conversation. It has become fashionable to suggest at the time of writing that human rights (along with international law in general) are facing a "backlash."[174] But in truth the notion that ordinary men and women might place their loyalties in the human rights movement as a way of achieving their desired political settlements has never been persuasive. Put bluntly, for most people, most of the time, the phrase "human rights" is not an important source of political motivation. And the notion that people can be therefore swept up in "global civil society," "advocacy networks," or "global citizen action" in order to bring about a more just world through human rights has shown very little predictive accuracy.[175]

We are faced, then, with a very wide gap between the ambitions of the international human rights movement – the creation of an "immense and tutelary power," a pastorate of shepherds governing vast flocks with the aim of realising universal well-being – and the reality that there is a very widespread reluctance on the part of ordinary people to embrace that vision. The reaction of human rights advocates, particularly within the UN system, tends to be that more education and participation is required.[176] But in truth, it may simply be the case that a future of being "softened, bent and guided" by governmental techniques is a deeply unappealing one to the rights-holders within that purported system.

In this respect, there is something of Adam Smith's "man of system" in the way in which the human rights movement finds its expression. For Smith, this man, "wise in his own conceit," pursues his own plans and designs irrespective of the "great interests [or] strong prejudices" opposing them. He imagines that he can "arrange the different members of a great society with as much ease as the hand arranges the different pieces upon a chess-board," but he forgets that "in the great chess-board of human society, every single piece has a principle of motion of its own" – and hence that each individual is apt to pursue entirely different goals to those which are arranged.[177] The "spirit of system" thus frequently causes those advocating it to embark on flights of fancy, becoming "intoxicated with the imaginary beauty" of their plans, and failing to recognise that their game is going on "miserably" and in "disorder."[178]

But it is not only that human societies are apt to fail to respond to the schemes of those who would attempt to improve them. It is that they will often do so deliberately. Orwell, seeking to explain why Socialism had failed to capture the popular imagination, was clear that this was because there was something "inherently distasteful" about it to the very people who it was supposed to elevate.[179] This was for the most part due to the character of its bourgeois adherents, "sniffish" and "superior," for whom Socialism "mean[t] a set of reforms which 'we,' the clever ones, are going to impose upon 'them,' the Lower Orders" – with the natural reaction of ordinary people being to rebel against such a "dictatorship of the prigs."[180] Something akin to this could be said about the general unwillingness on the part of populations in developed and developing countries alike to embrace human rights as the method of their salvation. The imposition by the elite of their vision for how societies are to be improved does not merely result in people being "softened, bent and guided" into the timidity of the flock. It generates a vigorous form of what might be termed insubordination.

What Orwell put so bluntly, Foucault gave a much more rarefied air. He noted that governmentality in the sense of the "conducting of conduct" often also gives rise to "revolts" – movements whose objective is a "different form of conduct" with different leaders, different purposes and different methods, or which sought indeed to "escape direction by others" altogether so as to allow individuals to direct themselves.[181] There has in short been "resistance to power as conducting."[182] This resistance might take many forms. But a theme which Foucault returns to repeatedly is that of simple refusal. His clearest example of this is the practice of desertion. Desertion had always been present in armies everywhere, but in the modern era of conscription and national armed forces the refusal to bear arms becomes also "a refusal of civic education, of society's values, [and of] the actual political system of the nation."[183] It is no longer simply the failure to fight, but a rejection of what it means to be a good citizen, devoted to a common cause. Another such example is "medical dissent," often practiced by religious groups, which refuses modern medicine, medical institutions, and the conducting of conduct in the sphere of health *"tout court,"* or carries out certain alternative "heresies" (such as so-called traditional remedies, home-opathy, or faith healing).[184]

Wishing to come up with a new phrase to describe this desire to be conducted differently or to escape the conducting of conduct altogether, Foucault settled on the unsatisfactory coining of "counter-conduct."[185] This has very frequently since then become associated with forms of active rebellion, dissidence, or otherwise political activity in the lay sense.[186] And indeed Foucault himself at times seemed to imply this connection.[187] But it is clear elsewhere that he also meant something much broader. Counter-conduct for him did not have to be a deliberate act – or certainly not deliberately political. It could even indeed be seen in the activities of "delinquents, mad people and patients."[188] It was rather to be discerned wherever there was the desire expressed to, as he put it elsewhere, "not [be] governed quite so much."[189]

Human rights advocates are used to what might be called the standard arguments against human rights in the international sphere. Typically, these come in the form of competing conceptions of the good – cultural or moral systems which reject human rights implicitly or explicitly, or which are said to. At various times these have included, for example, Islam,[190] so-called Asian values,[191] and Marxism.[192] Apathy is a much less straightforward topic to discuss, and the response to it tends to involve platitudes or blitheness. But it may in the long term be the most serious. Orwell, with typical bluntness, thought that ultimately Socialism would fail because, as well-intentioned as its followers might be, it "smells of crankishness [and] machine-worship."[193] There is something of this in the OHCHR's carefully developed Management Plan, "facilitat[ing] dialogue between diverse stakeholders on human rights issues," "deliver[ing] human rights education," "build[ing] networks and alliances to extend human rights promotion and protection," and "enabl[ing] the functioning of the international human rights mechanisms" so as to "achieve all human rights for all."[194] It contains various diagrams, charts, and tables, stipulating "shifts," "pillars," and "organizational effectiveness action plans"; it speaks of "leverag[ing] greater human rights impact" and "scal[ing] up our human rights results";[195] it aims to expand into yet more "new frontiers."[196] Describing this as crankish "machine-worship" would be unfair, but at the same time it is hard to believe that the OHCHR's vision – which seems like Supiot's "dream of an arithmetically attainable social harmony" made flesh – will be of much appeal for an audience beyond those who are already "true believers." That the Office seems aware that "while we have been busy developing and defending human rights laws and institutions, we have allowed the public space to be occupied by negative narratives" is a sign that it partially realises this.[197] But this appears only to have strengthened its resolve to govern more.

Conclusion

One will search Oakeshott's political philosophy in vain for the advocacy of a liberal conception of human rights. But clearly there are some inferences to be drawn from his work concerning the role of rights in the civil condition – bearing in mind of course that this is an abstract, idealised portrait. First, rights in the civil condition are not "natural" (or indeed even perhaps "human") rights, but rather "positive [and] self-authenticating rules of law" – enacted by intelligent, willed human beings and recognised as such. Second, they allow free agency and postulate rights-holders to be free agents. From this, a number of further inferences follow: rights restrain any attempt to deprive free agents of their capacity to self-direct; they postulate rights-holders to be free agents who therefore themselves determine when and how their rights are to be exercised; and they do not specify substantive actions or utterances to be complied with. And third, they must be capable of being assessed in terms of their desirability and deliberately altered through what Oakeshott called "politics."

These elements, taken together, could be described as an ideal of civil rights – "considered in terms of their postulates," as Oakeshott might have put it. Thought of in this way, they ultimately reflect the underlying sentiments on which the concept of the civil condition was founded. They are predicated on that understanding of human dignity as deriving from free agency, and individual decision making as "excellen[t] simply in respect of its authenticity." And they are therefore part of the system of *lex* which ultimately realises those underlying sentiments in legal rules.

What this also suggests is that the further away one moves from that ideal within the "equivocal mixture" which real-world law will always comprise, one will move away from what those underlying sentiments express. That ideal will never exist, and hence nor will those sentiments find their full expression, but as the balance within the "equivocal mixture" moves further from it, the result will be a system of rights which resembles the aforementioned postulates less and less. And as a consequence of that, it will naturally express those underlying sentiments less and less fully.

This will take place, then, when rights are no longer primarily construed as being positive rules of law, but are rather understood as principles giving effect to opaque regulatory or governmental tactics. It will take place when rights fail to recognise rights-holders as self-directing free agents and instead renders every aspect of their lives as aggregate statistical phenomena, pertinent only in the sense of what they signify about the "human rights performance" of the State. It will take place when rights are primarily conceptualised in terms of the obligations to be performed by duty-holders towards abstract groupings such as populations or stakeholders, in the absence of self-directed claims by individual rights-holders. It will take place when in the name of protecting, respecting, and fulfilling rights, individuals are compelled by the imposition of positive obligations to engage in substantive actions or utterances. And it will take place when none of this is made sufficiently transparent or clear to be assessed by the individuals who are subject to the relevant system of law, nor amenable to alteration through politics. It might be suggested, then, that the governmentalisation of global human rights governance represents such an orientation. It might therefore also be suggested that it results in human rights law, an equivocal mixture between *lex* and managerial rule-book like any other such body of law, moving further away from an ideal of dignity as arising from free agency and the process of self-enactment – and towards, instead, one of "warm servility" and the satisfaction of wants. It is submitted that this will be a project about which it is difficult for rights-holders themselves – whose empowerment is purportedly at its core – to be enthused.

Notes

1 Amartya Sen, *Development as Freedom* (Oxford University Press, 1999), p. 3.
2 A. de Tocqueville, *Democracy in America, vol. II* [1840] (Liberty Fund, 2012; trans. J. Schleifer.), pp. 1248–1252.
3 A. Smith, *The Theory of Moral Sentiments* [6th edition, 1790] (Penguin, 2009; ed. R. Hanley), p. 275.
4 M. Foucault, in S. Lotringer (ed.), *The Politics of Truth* (Massachusetts Institute of Technology Press, 2007), p. 45.
5 G. Orwell, *The Road to Wigan Pier* [1937] (Secker & Warburg, 1980), p. 179.
6 *Ibid.*, p. 178.
7 *Ibid.*, p. 171.
8 Tocqueville, *Democracy in America.*
9 C. Coglianese and E. Mendelson, "Meta-Regulation and Self-Regulation," in R. Baldwin, M. Cave, and M. Lodge (eds), *The Oxford Handbook of Regulation* (Oxford University Press, 2010), 146.
10 See e.g., C. Tollefson, A. Zito, and F. Gale, "Conceptualising New Governance Arrangements," 90 (1), *Public Administration* (2012) 3.
11 M. Koskenniemi, "International Law: Constitutionalism, Managerialism and the Ethos of Legal Education," 1, *European Journal of Legal Studies* (2007) 1, p. 12.
12 As Tamanaha put it, "Everyone is for it, but have contrasting convictions about what it is." B. Tamanaha, *On the Rule of Law: History, Politics, Theory* (Cambridge University Press, 2004), p. 3.
13 T. Bingham, *The Rule of Law* (Penguin, 2011), p. 8.
14 *Ibid.*, pp. 37–54.

15 The phrase "intensely relaxed" is from P. Mandelson, in a speech to senior executives at Hewlett-Packard, cited in D. Wighton, "Mandelson Plans a Microchip Off the Old Block," *Financial Times*, 23rd October 1998.

16 C. Tomuschat, "International Law: Ensuring the Survival of Mankind on the Eve of a New Century," 281, *Recueil des Cours* (1999), 10, p. 161.

17 G. Letsas, *A Theory of Interpretation of the European Convention on Human Rights* (Oxford University Press, 2009), pp. 73–74.

18 See Letsas, pp. 14 and 47.

19 A. Somek, "A Bureaucratic Turn?" 22 (2), *European Journal of International Law* (2011) 345.

20 D. Archibulgi, "Principles of Cosmopolitan Democracy," in D. Archibulgi, D. Held, and M. Köhler (eds), *Re-Imagining Political Community* (Polity, 1998), 198, pp. 211–213.

21 M. Kaldor, *New and Old Wars: Organized Violence in a Global Era* (Polity, 1999), p. 120.

22 J. Galtung, "Alternative Models for Global Democracy," in B. Holden (ed.), *Global Democracy: Key Debates* (Routledge, 2000), 143, p. 155.

23 OHCHR, "Strategic Vision and Evaluation Policy," available at www.ohchr.org/Documents/AboutUs/Evaluation/EvaluationVisionPolicy.pdf (accessed 1st December 2019), p. 4.

24 *Ibid.*, p. 2.

25 Tocqueville, *Democracy in America*.

26 See Sen, *Development as Freedom*; M. Nussbaum, *Women and Human Development* (Cambridge University Press, 2000).

27 K. Dongwook, "International Nongovernmental Organisations and the Global Diffusion of National Human Rights Institutions," 67 (3), *International Organisation* (2013) 505, p. 506.

28 *Ibid.*, p. 507.

29 A. Rosga and M. Satterthwaite, "The Trust in Indicators: Measuring Human Rights," 27 (2), *Berkeley Journal of International Law* (2009) 253.

30 Y. Papadopoulos, "The Democratic Quality of Collaborative Governance," in *The OUP Handbook*, p. 515.

31 J. Gray, *Enlightenment's Wake: Politics and Culture at the Close of the Modern Age* (Routledge, 1995), p. 76.

32 M. Koskenniemi, "The Effect of Rights on Political Culture," in P. Alston (ed.), *The EU and Human Rights* (Oxford University Press, 1999), 99, p. 100.

33 *Ibid.*, p. 114.

34 B. Sokhi-Bulley, *Governing (Through) Rights* (Hart, 2016), p. 5.

35 L. Odysseos, "Human Rights, Liberal Ontogenesis and Freedom: Producing a Subject for Neoliberalism?" 38 (3), *Millennium* (2010) 747.

36 A. Supiot, *Governance by Numbers: The Making of a Legal Model of Allegiance* (Hart, 2017; trans. S. Brown).

37 *Ibid.*, p. 10.

38 *Ibid.*, pp. 13–28.

39 *Ibid.*, p. 29.

40 *Ibid.*, p. 30.
41 *Ibid.*, p. 51.
42 *Ibid.*, p. 169.
43 *Ibid.*, p. 285.
44 *Ibid.*, p. 273.
45 M. Robinson, Speech at the Launch of the AAAS Science and Human Rights Coalition, 15th January 2009, available at www.aaas.org/programs/science-and-human-rights-coalition/mary-robinson (accessed 1st December 2019).
46 M. Langford and S. Fukuda-Parr, "The Turn to Metrics," 30 (3), *Nordic Journal of Human Rights* (2012) 222, p. 223.
47 W. Espeland and M. Sauder, "Rankings and Reactivity: How Public Measures Recreate Social Worlds," 113 (1), *American Journal of Sociology* (2007) 1.
48 M. Oakeshott, *On Human Conduct* (Clarendon Press, 1975/1991), pp. 234–235.
49 *Ibid.*, p. 235.
50 J. Liddington, "Oakeshott: Freedom in a Modern European State," in Z. Pelczynski and J. Gray (eds), *Conceptions of Liberty* (St Martin's, 1984), p. 299.
51 Oakeshott, *On Human Conduct*, pp. 236–237.
52 *Ibid.*
53 *Ibid.*
54 This is not to suggest it is not present in other traditions – Chinese philosophy was of particular interest to Oakeshott (he was as likely to cite Daoist philosophers in his work as Europeans) although this interest does not appear in *On Human Conduct*. See, for example, C. Cheung, "Learning and Conversation: Oakeshott and Confucius," in W. Coats and C. Cheung (eds), *The Poetic Character of Human Activity: Collected Essays on the Thought of Michael Oakeshott* (Lexington Books, 2012), 57.
55 Oakeshott, *On Human Conduct*, p. 236.
56 *Ibid.*
57 *Ibid.*, p. 241.
58 *Ibid.*, p. 237.
59 *Ibid.*, p. 238.
60 M. Oakeshott, *Early Political Writings, 1925–1930* (Imprint Academic, 2010; ed. L. O'Sullivan), p. 112.
61 Oakeshott, *On Human Conduct*, p. 238.
62 *Ibid.*
63 *Ibid.*, p. 241 and *ibid.* at fn. 1.
64 *Ibid.*
65 *Ibid.*, p. 243.
66 *Ibid.*, p. 244.
67 *Ibid.*
68 *Ibid.*, p. 252.
69 *Ibid.*, pp. 259–260.
70 *Ibid.*, p. 261.
71 *Ibid.*, p. 261.

72 *Ibid.*, pp. 260–261.
73 M. Oakeshott, "The Tower of Babel," in M. Oakeshott, *Rationalism in Politics* (Methuen, 1962), 59.
74 Oakeshott, *On Human Conduct*, pp. 1–77.
75 *Ibid.*, p. 75.
76 *Ibid.*, p. 76.
77 *Ibid.*, p. 61.
78 M. Oakeshott, "The Masses in Representative Democracy," in M. Oakeshott, *Rationalism in Politics and Other Essays* [expanded edition] (Liberty Fund, 1991), 363, pp. 367–368.
79 I. Kant, *On the Old Saw: That Might Be Right in Theory but It Won't Work in Practice* [1793] (University of Pennsylvania Press, 1974; trans. E. Ashton), pp. 73–74.
80 I. Kant, *Groundwork of the Metaphysic of Morals* [1785] (Cambridge University Press, 2012; trans. M. Gregor).
81 "The activity of governing subsists not because it is good but because it is necessary," as he put it in M. Oakeshott, *The Politics of Faith and the Politics of Scepticism* (Yale University Press, 1996; ed. T. Fuller), p. 33.
82 *Ibid.*, p. 152.
83 Oakeshott, *On Human Conduct*, p. 182.
84 *Ibid.*, p. 317.
85 S. Webb, *Fabian Essays*, p. 54, cited in Oakeshott, *On Human Conduct*, p. 300.
86 *Ibid.*, pp. 147–148.
87 *Ibid.*, p. 148.
88 *Ibid.*, p. 150.
89 *Ibid.*, p. 164.
90 *Ibid.*, p. 152.
91 *Ibid.*, p. 152.
92 *Ibid.*, pp. 152–153.
93 *Ibid.*, p. 177.
94 *Ibid.*, p. 154.
95 *Ibid.*
96 *Ibid.*, p. 161.
97 *Ibid.*, p. 163.
98 *Ibid.*
99 *Ibid.*, p. 164.
100 *Ibid.*, pp. 163–164.
101 *Ibid.*, pp. 168–169.
102 *Ibid.*, p. 168.
103 On the "Foucauldian flavour" of Oakeshott's thought in this regard, see S. Soininen, *From a Necessary Evil to an Art of Contingency: Michael Oakeshott's Conception of Political Activity* (Imprint Academic, 2005), pp. 86–87.
104 M. Foucault, "What is Enlightenment?" in P. Rabinow (ed.), *Ethics, Subjectivity and Truth: The Essential Works of Foucault 1954–1984, Vol I* (The New Press, 1997; trans. R. Hurley et al.), pp. 315–316.

105 Oakeshott, *On Human Conduct*, p. 241.
106 M. Foucault, "The Ethics of the Concern for the Self as a Practice of Freedom," in P. Rabinow (ed.), *Ethics, Subjectivity and Truth: The Essential Works of Foucault 1954–1984, Vol I* (The New Press, 1997; trans. R. Hurley et al.), pp. 281, 284.
107 M. Foucault, *The Care of the Self: The History of Sexuality, Vol. III* (Vintage Books, 1988), p. 64.
108 T. Flynn, "Truth and Subjectivation in the Later Foucault," 82 (10), *The Journal of Philosophy* (1985) 531, p. 538.
109 Foucault, "What is Enlightenment?"
110 M. Foucault, "On the Genealogy of Ethics: An Overview of Work in Progress," in P. Rabinow (ed.), *Foucault Reader* (Pantheon, 1984), 340.
111 E. Gilson, "Ethics and the Ontology of Freedom: Problematization and Responsiveness in Foucault and Deleuze," 17, *Foucault Studies* (2014) 76, p. 79.
112 Oakeshott, *On Human Conduct*, p. 255.
113 M. Foucault, *The Hermeneutics of the Subject: Lectures at the College de France 1981–1982* (Picador, 2005; ed. F. Gros, trans. G. Burchell), p. 252.
114 M. Oakeshott, *Notebooks: 1922–86* (Imprint Academic, 2014; ed. L. O'Sullivan), p. 280.
115 Oakeshott is of course generally thought of as a conservative thinker, though he is almost as frequently described as a liberal; see e.g., J. Segal, "Freedom and Normalisation: Poststructuralism and the Liberalism of Michael Oakeshott," in 97 (3), *American Political Science Review* (2003), 447. Foucault was somewhat infamously labelled as a conservative by Jürgen Habermas in "Modernity versus Postmodernity," 22, *New German Critique* (1981) 3.
116 Oakeshott, *On Human Conduct*, p. 234.
117 *Ibid.*, p. 316.
118 *Ibid.*, p. 317.
119 *Ibid.*, p. 316.
120 *Ibid.*, p. 317.
121 *Ibid.*, p. 318.
122 *Ibid.*, p. 313, fn. 1.
123 *Ibid.*, p. 318.
124 *Ibid.*, p. 128.
125 *Ibid.*, pp. 295–296.
126 *Ibid.*, p. 132.
127 *Ibid.*, pp. 138–139.
128 *Ibid.*, p. 138.
129 *Ibid.*, p. 317.
130 Vienna Declaration and Programme of Action, World Conference on Human Rights, 25th June 1993.
131 UN Commission on Human Rights, *The New International Order and the Promotion of Human Rights: Report on the Right to Adequate Food as a Human Rights*, UN Doc. E/CN.4/Sub.2/1987/23 (1987), para. 65.

132 Human Rights Council, Protect, Respect and Remedy: A Framework for Business and Human Rights, Report of the Special Representative of the Secretary-General on the issue of human rights and transnational corporations and other business enterprises, UN Doc. A/HRC/8/5 (2008).

133 Next plc, Corporate Responsibility Report to January 2019, available at www.nextplc.co.uk/~/media/Files/N/Next-PLC-V2/documents/corporate-responsibility/cr-2019-human-rights-and-modern-slavery.pdf (accessed 1st December 2019).

134 Refer to discussion in Chapter 5.

135 OHCHR, *Economic, Social and Cultural Rights: A Handbook for National Human Rights Institutions* (2005), available at www.ohchr.org/Documents/Publications/training12en.pdf (accessed 1st December, 2019), p. 76.

136 J. Habermas, *The Theory of Communicative Action, vol. II: Lifeworld and System: A Critique of Functionalist Reason* [1981] (Beacon Press, 1987; trans. T. McCarthy).

137 References to Chapter 1.

138 M. Foucault, *Security, Territory, Population: Lectures at the Collège de France, 1977–1978* (Palgrave Macmillan, 2008; ed. M. Senellart, trans. G. Burchell), p. 42.

139 *Ibid.*, p. 180.

140 *Ibid.*, p. 165.

141 *Ibid.*, p. 163.

142 His political theory has been described, for example, as "contemporary with Noah" and "antique and irrelevant" by reviewers. See E. Corey, "The World of Michael Oakeshott," 48 (3), *Modern Age* (2006) 259.

143 Oakeshott, "The Masses in Representative Democracy."

144 Oakeshott, *On Human Conduct*, pp. 276–278.

145 *Ibid.*, p. 278.

146 *Ibid.*, p. 274.

147 *Ibid.*, p. 275.

148 *Ibid.*, pp. 277–278.

149 *Ibid.*

150 *Ibid.*, p. 274.

151 *Ibid.*, p. 317.

152 Tocqueville, *Democracy in America*.

153 *Ibid.*

154 Foucault, *Security, Territory, Population*, pp. 166–167.

155 *Ibid.*, p. 172–173.

156 *Ibid.*, p. 174.

157 *Ibid.*, p. 175.

158 *Ibid.*

159 *Ibid.*, p. 177.

160 *Ibid.*, p. 180.

161 *Ibid.*, p. 181.

162 *Ibid.*

163 *Ibid.*, p. 182.

164 *Ibid.*, p. 183.

165 H. Arendt, *On Revolution* (Viking Press, 1965), p. 86.

166 Tocqueville, *Democracy in America.*

167 M. Ignatieff, "Human Rights, Global Ethics and the Ordinary Virtues," 31 (1), *Ethics & International Affairs* (2017) 3.

168 M. Ignatieff, "Human Rights, Global Ethics and the Ordinary Virtues," 13 (1), *Journal of International Law and International Relations* (2017), 1, p. 2.

169 *Ibid.*, p. 6.

170 U. Oszu, "Neoliberalism and Human Rights: The Brandt Commission and the Struggle for a New World," 81 (4), *Law & Contemporary Problems* (2018) 139, p. 141.

171 J. Loeffler and M. Versteeg, "The Future of Human Rights Scholarship," 81 (4), *Law & Contemporary Problems* (2018) i, p. i.

172 S. Hopgood, "Fascism Rising," *Open Democracy*, 9th November 2016. The somewhat hyperventilating tone of this piece cannot completely disguise that there is a grain of truth in the notion that "human rights" have become partly associated in popular discourse with elitist projects of globalisation and global governance.

173 S. Moyn, "Beyond the Human Rights Measurement Controversy," 81 (4), *Law & Contemporary Problems* (2018) 121, pp. 128–129.

174 Much of the literature on these events is yet to be published at the time of writing. See E. Posner, "Liberal Internationalism and the Populist Backlash," at https://papers.ssrn.com/sol3/papers.cfm?abstract_id=2898357 (accessed 1st December 2019); O. Stiansen and E. Voeten, "Backlash and Judicial Restraint: Evidence from the European Court of Human Rights," at https://papers.ssrn.com/sol3/papers.cfm?abstract_id=3166110 (accessed 1st December 2019).

175 See M. Kaldor, *Global Civil Society: An Answer to War* (Polity Press, 2003); M. Keck and K. Sikkink, *Activists Beyond Borders: Advocacy Networks in International Politics* (Cornell University Press, 1998); M. Edwards and J. Gaventa (eds), *Global Citizen Action* (Earthscan, 2001).

176 Andrew Gilmour, UN Assistant Secretary-General for Human Rights, for example, in his closing remarks at the "Still Powerful: UDHR @ 70" event on Human Rights Day, 10th December 2018, said that the "starting point" for reversing the current backlash is "to make as many people as possible … aware of their rights."

177 Smith, *The Theory of Moral Sentiments*, pp. 275–276.

178 *Ibid.*

179 Orwell, *The Road to Wigan Pier*, p. 171.

180 *Ibid.*, p. 179 and p. 182.

181 Foucault, *Security, Territory, Population*, pp. 194–195.

182 *Ibid.*, p. 195.

183 *Ibid.*, p. 198.

184 *Ibid.*, pp. 199–200.

185 *Ibid.*, p. 201.

186 See, for example, the contributions to the special issue of *Global Society* on "Counter-Conduct in Global Politics: Theorising the Subjects and Practices of Contesting Conduct," 30 (2), 2016.

187 See e.g., Foucault, *Security, Territory, Population*, pp. 355–357.

188 *Ibid.*, p. 202.

189 Foucault, *The Politics of Truth*.

190 A. An-Na'im, "Human Rights in the Arab World: A Regional Perspective," 23, *Human Rights Quarterly* (2001) 701.

191 R. Peerenboom, "Human Rights and Asian Values: The Limits of Universalism," 7 (2), *China Review International* (2000) 295.

192 S. Lukes, "Can a Marxist Believe in Human Rights?" 1 (4), *Praxis International* (1984) 334.

193 G. Orwell, *The Road to Wigan Pier*, p. 215.

194 OHCHR, *UN Human Rights Management Plan 2018–2021*, available at www2.ohchr.org/english/OHCHRReport2018_2021/OHCHRManagement Plan2018-2021.pdf (accessed 1st December 2019), p. 10.

195 *Ibid.*, p. 42.

196 *Ibid.*, p. 44.

197 *Ibid.*, p. 43.

Conclusion

In the introduction to this book, reference was made to Trilling's observation that choosing to act morally did not settle all moral problems. It only displaced them. Orienting human rights law towards *teleocracy* with the aim of improving human well-being is not without its costs. In fact, the more it is turned in that direction, the more it will interfere with the freedom of individuals properly understood. This will not manifest itself in edict or command. Rather, it will appear in much more subtle form: as the deployment of a pastoral power whose interest is in improving statistically measurable phenomena, and which functions through the application of a governmental reason which indirectly shapes, manipulates, and moulds not just the conduct of individuals but their subjectivity itself. This is a vision which, were it to be fully realised, would produce them only as the self-abnegating members of a flock, obedient and needful, carefully managed by their shepherd in the name of their collective moral and physical well-being.

Yet it is very frequently argued in the literature on human rights that it *is* in fact possible to reconcile what are often called negative and positive freedoms. A prominent example of this can be found in Sandra Fredman's *Human Rights Transformed*.[1] In it, she makes the case that while the State needs to be restrained from abusing its power, "only [it] can supply what is needed for an individual to fully enjoy her rights."[2] While everybody is an end in themselves, that Kantian vision must be supplemented by Marx's insight that human beings need material resources to support them if they are to be truly empowered.[3] This is a "much richer view of freedom"[4] which is achieved through putting positive obligations on the State to secure the conditions within which individuals can exercise freedom of choice, "without imposing any particular set of choices on individuals."[5] In other words, the State must give to all individuals the material conditions in which they can "realize their own goals."[6]

For Oakeshott, the idea that such a reconciliation between negative and positive freedoms could be achieved was a myth. As his work shows us, the truth is that there is only ever a trade-off to be made between the two. One cannot act to "facilitate individuals' ability to fulfil their choices" through purposive action by the State, because to do so will necessarily result in their compulsory association in an enterprise not of their own choosing. And the consequence of this will be that they will end up being governed accordingly – free only to the extent that they do not interfere with the overriding purpose, and deprived of the conditions which permit them to act morally in their own right. The ongoing governmentalisation of global human rights governance is a stark demonstration of this.

Oakeshott's insights originate from his understanding that matters of law and political organisation are ambiguous. One cannot have a system of human rights law which embraces both negative and positive conceptions of freedom entirely. In the ideal of the civil condition, human rights would simply be conditions of *respublica*, rules of *lex* ensuring that the State functions so as to allow *cives* to pursue their own "adventure" of self-enactment alone or in cooperation with others. In opposition to this is an ideal of human rights as the legal obligations requiring States (and other powerful actors) to adopt positions of benevolent care towards those for whom they are responsible. Human rights in the real world will fall between those poles, for reasons which we have discussed, and will lean in one direction or another as circumstances and prevailing sentiments dictate. But the position of those poles is fundamentally one of opposition, not reconciliation. One can have freedom, or the "warm servility" of being subsumed into the rubric of universal well-being. In reality, one will fall somewhere in the middle of these two ideals. But they do not support one another, and one cannot have them both entire.

What Foucault's work adds to this dynamic is, of course, the observation that even purportedly negative rights may themselves take on a purposive orientation – particularly when deployed so as to deliberately encourage market activity and to produce the human individual as a market actor. This was something of which Oakeshott was well aware. Even were it possible to have a system of human rights laws which were "purely" negative, then, it would be perfectly possible for them to take on a *teleocratic* orientation. This is not to suggest, therefore, that international human rights law should only instantiate or resemble what Oakeshott called *lex*. That would be both impossible and undesirable; law will always be to some extent purposive. Much the same can be said of the role of human rights in global governance. International organisation cannot be forced into the civil condition – it would be impossible to do this, and it would indeed constitute the direct and foolish pursuit of ideals "as the crow flies" which Oakeshott so deplored.[7] Rather, it is to suggest that some "moral realism" is required.

On this point it is worth returning to Koskenniemi. It is unwise in an academic article or monograph to comment too closely on current events.

But it is difficult to ignore the fact that, as of the time of writing this book, international lawyers in general have been swept up in collective dismay about contemporary political developments. A supposed "revolt against the elites" is said to be taking place around the world.[8] This is characterised in a wide variety of ways. But it would be a mistake to describe it as a rejection of international law as such. As James Crawford and Koskenniemi both rightly point out, the basic principles of public international law – sovereignty, non-intervention, diplomatic law, *pacta sunt servanda* (which Crawford calls "necessary international law") – are not subject to challenge and appear in some ways to be stronger than ever.[9] What is being challenged instead is, in Koskenniemi's words, its "ideological ambiance."[10] It is the ambitions of *raison du monde* which are being challenged – that field of technical and economic expertise deployed through global institutions, ambivalent about if not actively hostile to national democracy, and underpinned by a particular discourse of human rights which sees a class of experts – academics, United Nations (UN) special mechanisms, non-governmental organisations, consultants, businesses, and courts – imposing a vision of what rights are on the *hoi polloi* beneath them. It is small wonder that this is a deeply unattractive image of world society to large numbers of people outside of that "expert" class. To them, global governance in general, including when it is done in the name of their human rights, is primarily thought of (when it is thought of at all) as "a kind of doom which is probably coming but must be staved off for as long as possible."[11] Their cynicism, then, is not chiefly because the expertise of the technocratic elite has been so repeatedly exposed to be wrong – although it undoubtedly has. It is rather that people who are being governed, particularly in such comprehensive and pervasive forms as they are in the modern day, will always prefer to "not be governed quite so much" – regardless of the fact that it is being done for their own supposed good. Koskenniemi's recipe for remedying the apparent crisis is to stop insisting on global governance's "truths" and instead shift to "truthfulness" – "to insist on the best available scientific – and legal – knowledge but also on its limits and its vulnerability" so as to "inject political contestation."[12] My own suggestion is that it may be best for human rights advocates to consider the possibility of, in short, simply *governing* a little less.

Notes

1 S. Fredman, *Human Rights Transformed* (Oxford University Press, 2008).
2 *Ibid.*, p. 9.
3 *Ibid.*, p. 12.

4 *Ibid.*, p. 9.
5 *Ibid.*, p. 15.
6 *Ibid.*
7 M. Oakeshott, "The Tower of Babel," in M. Oakeshott, *Rationalism in Politics and Other Essays* (Methuen, 1962), 39.
8 J. Nijman, "Foreword," in M. Koskenniemi, "International Law and the Far Right: Reflections on Law and Cynicism," *4th Annual TMC Asser Lecture* (Asser Press, 2018), p. ix. What is meant by this is typically an unreflective grouping of the election of Donald Trump; the vote by the UK electorate to leave the EU; the rise of nationalistic or "far-right" leaders in Poland, Hungary, Brazil, India, the Philippines, and elsewhere; and leftist authoritarianism in Venezuela and Bolivia, under the umbrella of "populism."
9 M. Koskenniemi, *ibid.*, p. 3, and J. Crawford, "The Current Political Discourse Concerning International Law," 81, *The Modern Law Review* (2018) 1, p. 1–22.
10 M. Koskenniemi, *ibid.*, p. 4.
11 G. Orwell, *The Road to Wigan Pier* [1937] (Secker & Walburg, 1980), p. 182.
12 Koskenniemi, "International Law and the Far Right," p. 35.

Bibliography

Table of cases and quasi-judicial decisions

Advisory Opinion OC-16/99, Inter-American Court of Human Rights, Series A no. 16 (1999)

AT v. Hungary, Comm. 2/2003, Views under Article 7, paragraph 3 of the Optional Protocol, CEDAW/C/32/D/2/2003, 26th January 2005

Austria v. Italy, App no. 788/60 (ECtHR, 1961)

Bondev Midrand (Pty) Ltd v. Mulatedzi Alton Madzhie, et al., High Court of South Africa (Gauteng Div., Pretoria) 19th December 2016

Caesar Case, Inter-American Court of Human Rights, Series C no. 123 (2005)

Case C-459/03, *Commission v. Ireland* ECR I-04635 (2006)

Case Concerning Military and Paramilitary Activities in and Against Nicaragua (Nicaragua v. USA), ICJ Reports, 1986, 14

Cox v. Canada, Comm. 539/1993, Views under Article 5, paragraph 4 of the Optional Protocol, CCPR/C/52/D/539/1993, 31st October 1994

Godinez Cruz v. Honduras, Inter-American Court of Human Rights, Series C no. 5 (1989)

Golder v. United Kingdom Series A no. 18 (1975)

Goodwin v. United Kingdom, App no. 28957/95 (ECtHR, 2002)

Griggs v. Duke Power Co., 401 US 424 (1971)

Hatton and Others v. United Kingdom, App no. 36022/97 (ECtHR, 2003)

Interpretation of the Agreement of 25 March 1951 Between the WHO and Egypt (1980), ICJ Reports, 1980, 73

Ireland v. UK, App. No. 5310/71 (ECtHR, 1978)

Judge v. Canada, Comm. 829/1998, Views under Article 5, paragraph 4 of the Optional Protocol, CCPR/C/78/D/829/1998, 5th August 2002

Kindler v. Canada, Comm. 470/1991, Views under Article 5, paragraph 4 of the Optional Protocol, CCPR/C/48/D/470/1991, 30th July 1993

Matthews v. United Kingdom, App no. 24833/94 (ECtHR, 1999)

Ng v. Canada, Comm. 469/1991, Views under Article 5, paragraph 4 of the Optional Protocol, CCPR/C/49/D/469/1991, 5th November 1993

Scotch Whisky Association and Others v. The Lord Advocate and Another (Scotland) UKSC 76 (2017)

Tyrer v. United Kingdom Series A no. 26 (1978)
Velasquez Rodriguez v. Honduras, Inter-American Court of Human Rights, Series C no. 4 (1988)
Young, James and Webster v. United Kingdom Series A no. 44 (1981)

Table of legislation and treaties

Alcohol (Minimum Pricing) (Scotland) Act 2012 [UK]
Charter of the United Nations 1945
Companies Act 2006 (Strategic Report and Directors' Report) Regulations 2013 [UK]
Convention against Torture and Other Cruel, Inhuman or Degrading Treatment or Punishment 1984
Convention on the Elimination of All Forms of Discrimination Against Women 1979
Convention on the Rights of the Child 1989
Directive 2014/95/EU of the European Parliament and of the Council of 22nd October 2014 amending Directive 2013/34/EU as regards disclosure of non-financial and diversity information by certain large undertakings and groups
Employment Act 1982 [UK]
Employment Act 1990 [UK]
Equality Act 2006 [UK]
Equality Act 2010 [UK]
International Convention on the Elimination of All Forms of Racial Discrimination 1965
International Convention on the Rights of Persons with Disabilities 2006
International Covenant on Civil and Political Rights 1966
International Covenant on Economic, Social and Cultural Rights 1966
Loi no. 2017–399 du 27 Mars 2017 relative au devoir de vigilane des sociétés mères et des enterprises donneuses d'ordre [France]
Optional Protocol to the Covenant on Economic, Social and Cultural Rights 2008
Optional Protocol to the International Covenant on Civil and Political Rights 1966
Second Optional Protocol to the International Covenant on Civil and Political Rights, aiming at the abolition of the death penalty 1989
Universal Declaration of Human Rights 1948
Vienna Convention on the Law of Treaties 1969

Select bibliography

Aaronson, S., and Higham, I., "'Re-Righting Business': John Ruggie and the Struggle to Develop International Human Rights Standards for Transnational Firms," 35 (2), *Human Rights Quarterly* (2013) 333
Afshari, R., "On Historiography of Human Rights: Reflections on Paul Gordon Lauren's *The Evolution of International Human Rights: Visions Seen*," 29, *Human Rights Quarterly* (2007) 1

Alston, P., "The International Monetary Fund and the Right to Food," 30, *Howard Law Journal* (1987) 473, p. 479

Alston, P., "Appraising the United Nations Human Rights Regime," in Alston, P. (ed.), *The United Nations and Human Rights: A Critical Appraisal* (Oxford University Press, 1992), 1

Alston, P., and Goodman, R. (eds), *International Human Rights: Text and Materials* (Oxford University Press, 2013)

Anderson, P., "The Intransigent Right at the End of the Century," 14 (18), *London Review of Books* (1992) 7

An-Na'im, A., "Human Rights in the Arab World: A Regional Perspective," 23, *Human Rights Quarterly* (2001) 701

Arambulo, K., *Strengthening the Supervision of the International Covenant on Economic, Social and Cultural Rights: Theoretical and Procedural Aspects* (Intersentia, 1999)

Archibulgi, D., "Principles of Cosmopolitan Democracy," in Archibulgi, D., Held, D., and Köhler, M. (eds), *Re-Imagining Political Community: Studies in Cosmopolitan Democracy* (Polity, 1998), 198

Archibulgi, D., "Demos and Cosmopolis," 13, *New Left Review* (2002) 24

Arendt, H., *On Revolution* (Viking Press, 1965)

Armour, L., "Michael Oakeshott – A Fish Too Big or Too Slippery?" 13 (4), *British Journal for the History of Philosophy* (2005) 779

Backman, G. et al., "Health Systems and the Right to Health: An Assessment of 194 Countries," 372 (9655), *The Lancet* (2008) 2047

Baehr, P., and Gordener, L., *The United Nations: Reality and Ideal* (Palgrave Macmillan, 2005)

Barrett, D., "The Regulatory Space of Equality and Human Rights in Britain: The Role of the Equality and Human Rights Commission," 39 (2), *Legal Studies* (2019) 247

Baxi, U., "Voices of Suffering and the Future of Human Rights," 8, *Transnational Law and Contemporary Problems* (1998) 125

Beitz, C., *The Idea of Human Rights* (Oxford University Press, 2009)

Bhuta, N., "State Failure: The US Fund for Peace Failed States Index," in Davis, K., Fisher, A., Kingsbury, B., and Engle Merry, S. (eds) *Governance by Indicators: Global Power through Quantification and Rankings* (Oxford University Press, 2012)

Bianchi, A., "Immunity versus Human Rights: The Pinochet Case," 10, *European Journal of International Law* (1999) 237

Bingham, T., *The Rule of Law* (Penguin, 2011)

Blyberg, A., "The Case of the Mislaid Allocation: Economic and Social Rights and Budget Work," 6 (11), *Sur: International Journal of Human Rights* (2009) 123

Booth, K., "Three Tyrannies," in Dunne, T., and Wheeler, N. (eds), *Human Rights in Global Politics* (Cambridge University Press, 1999), 31

Boucher, D., "Politics in a Different Mode: An Appreciation of Michael Oakeshott 1901–1990," XII (4), *History of Political Thought* (1991) 717

Brown, W., "'The Most We Can Hope For...': Human Rights and the Politics of Fatalism," 103, *South Atlantic Quarterly* (2004) 451

Butler, N., "Development of the International Mind," 9, *American Bar Association Journal* (1923) 520

Cassin, R., "L'État-Leviathan," in *La Pensée et l'Action* (F. Lalou, 1972), 63

Cata Backer, L., "Transnational Corporations' Outward Expression of Inward Self-Constitution: The Enforcement of Human Rights by Apple, Inc.," 20 (2), *Indiana Journal of Global Legal Studies* (2013) 805

Cerny, P., *Rethinking World Politics: A Theory of Transnational Pluralism* (Oxford University Press, 2009)

Chalabi, A., *National Human Rights Action Planning* (Oxford University Press, 2018)

Cheung, C., "Learning and Conversation: Oakeshott and Confucius," in Coats, W., and Cheung, C. (eds), *The Poetic Character of Human Activity: Collected Essays on the Thought of Michael Oakeshott* (Lexington Books, 2012), 57

Chevallier, P., "Michel Foucault and the Question of Right," in Golder, B. (ed.), *Re-Reading Foucault: On Law, Power and Rights* (Routledge, 2013), 171

Chimni, B. S., "International Institutions Today: An Imperial Global State in the Making," 15 (1), *European Journal of International Law* (2004) 1

Cogan, J. "The Regulatory Turn in International Law," 52, *Harvard Journal of International Law* (2011) 321

Coglianese, C., and Mendelson, E., "Meta-Regulation and Self-Regulation," in Baldwin, R., Cave, M., and Lodge, M. (eds), *The Oxford Handbook of Regulation* (Oxford University Press, 2010)

Cope, K., Crabtree, C., and Lupu, Y., "Beyond Physical Integrity," 81, *Law & Contemporary Problems* (2018) 185

Corey, E., "The World of Michael Oakeshott," 48 (3), *Modern Age* (2006) 259

Cowan, J., "Before Audit Culture: A Genealogy of International Oversight of Rights," in Muller, B. (ed.), *The Gloss of Harmony: The Politics of Policy Making in Multilateral Organisations* (Pluto Press, 2013), 103

Cowan, J., "The Universal Periodic Review as a Public Audit Ritual: An Anthropological Perspective on Emerging Practices in the Global Governance of Human Rights," in Charlesworth, H., and Larking, E. (eds), *Human Rights and the Universal Periodic Review: Rituals and Ritualism* (Cambridge University Press, 2015)

Cranston, M., "Michael Oakeshott's Politics," 28, *Encounter* (1967) 82

Crawford, J., "The Current Political Discourse Concerning International Law," 81, *The Modern Law Review* (2018) 1

Criddle, E., and Fox-Decent, E., *Fiduciaries of Humanity* (Oxford University Press, 2016)

D'Aspremont, J., "The Foundations of the International Legal Order," 18, *Finnish Yearbook of International Law* (2007) 219

Davis, S., "Human Rights and the Global Fund to Fight AIDS, Tuberculosis and Malaria," 16, *Health and Human Rights Journal* (2014) 134

de Brabandere, E., "Non-State Actors, State-Centrism and Human Rights Obligations," 22, *Leiden Journal of International Law* (2009) 191 de Londras, F., and Dzehtsariou, K., "Managing Judicial Innovation in the European Court of Human Rights," 15 (3), *Human Rights Law Review* (2015) 523

de Schutter, O., *International Human Rights Law: Cases, Materials and Commentary* (3rd edition, Cambridge University Press, 2019)

de Tocqueville, A., *Democracy in America, vol. II* [1840] (Liberty Fund, 2012; trans. Schleifer, J.)

de Vattel, E., *The Law of Nations: Or, Principles of the Law of Nature Applied to the Conduct and Affairs of Nations and Sovereigns* [1758/1797] (Liberty Fund, 2008; ed. Whatmore, R., trans. Anon.)

de Wet, E., "International Constitutional Order," 55, *International & Comparative Law Quarterly* (2006) 51

Dean, M., *Governmentality* (2nd edition, Sage, 2010)

Desierto, D., *Public Policy in International Economic Law* (Oxford University Press, 2015)

Dongwook, K., "International Nongovernmental Organisations and the Global Diffusion of National Human Rights Institutions," 67 (3), *International Organisation* (2013) 505

Donzelot, J., and Gordon, C., "Governing Liberal Societies: The Foucault Effect in the English-Speaking World," in Peters, M. et al. (eds), *Governmentality Studies in Education* (Sense, 2009), 3

Dworkin, R., "Is There a Right to Pornography?" 1, *Oxford Journal of Legal Studies* (1981) 177

Dzehtsiarou, K., "European Consensus and the Evolutive Interpretation of the European Convention on Human Rights," 12, *German Law Journal* (2011) 1730

Eckel, J., "Explaining the Human Rights Revolution of the 1970s," in Eckel, J., and Moyn, S. (eds), *The Breakthrough: Human Rights in the 1970s* (University of Pennsylvania Press, 2014), 259

Eckel, J., and Moyn, S. (eds), *The Breakthrough: Human Rights in the 1970s* (University of Pennsylvania Press, 2014)

Edwards, M., and Gaventa, J. (eds), *Global Citizen Action* (Earthscan, 2001)

Elson, D., Balakrishnan, R., and Heintz, J., "Public Finance, Maximum Available Resources and Human Rights," in Nolan, A., O'Connell, R., and Harvey, C. (eds), *Human Rights and Public Finance: Budgets and the Promotion of Economic and Social Rights* (Hart, 2013), 13

Enteman, W., *Managerialism: The Emergence of a New Ideology* (University of Wisconsin Press, 1993)

Espeland, W., and Sauder, M., "Rankings and Reactivity: How Public Measures Recreate Social Worlds," 113 (1), *American Journal of Sociology* (2007) 1

Esty, D., "Good Governance at the Supranational Scale: Globalizing Administrative Law," 116, *Yale Law Journal* (2006) 1490

Ewald, F., "Norms, Discipline and the Law," 30, *Representations* (1990) 138

Fassbender, B., "The United Nations Charter as Constitution of the International Community," 36, *Columbia Journal of Transnational Law* (1998) 529

Felner, E., "Closing the 'Escape Hatch': A Toolkit to Monitor the Progressive Realization of Economy, Social and Cultural Rights," 1 (3), *Journal of Human Rights Practice* (2009) 402

Ferrie, J., Wallace, R., and Webster, E. "Realising International Human Rights: Scotland on the World Stage," 22 (1), *The International Journal of Human Rights* (2017) 1

Fish, S., "What Makes an Interpretation Acceptable?" in Fish, S., *Is There a Text in This Class: The Authority of Interpretive Communities* (Harvard University Press, 1980), 338

Fiti Sinclair, G., *To Reform the World: International Organisations and the Making of Modern States* (Oxford University Press, 2017)

Flynn, T., "Truth and Subjectivation in the Later Foucault," 82 (10), *The Journal of Philosophy* (1985) 531

Foucault, M., "On the Genealogy of Ethics: An Overview of Work in Progress," in Rabinow, P. (ed.), *Foucault Reader* (Pantheon, 1984), 340, p. 340

Foucault, M., "Politics and Reason," in Kritzman, L. (ed.), *Michel Foucault: Philosophy, Politics, Culture – Interviews and Other Writings 1977–1984* (Routledge, 1988), 57

Foucault, M., *The Care of the Self: The History of Sexuality, Vol. III* (Vintage Books, 1988; trans. Hurley, R.)

Foucault, M., *The History of Sexuality, vol. I* [1979] (Vintage, 1990; trans. Hurley, R.)

Foucault, M., *Discipline & Punish: The Birth of the Prison* (Penguin, 1991; trans. Sheridan, A.)

Foucault, M., "The Ethics of the Concern for the Self as a Practice of Freedom," in Rabinow, P. (ed.), *Ethics, Subjectivity and Truth: The Essential Works of Foucault 1954–1984, Vol I* (The New Press, 1997; trans. Hurley, R. et al.), pp. 281, 284

Foucault, M., "What is Enlightenment?" in Rabinow, P. (ed.), *Ethics, Subjectivity and Truth: The Essential Works of Foucault 1954–1984, Vol I* (The New Press, 1997; trans. Hurley, R. et al.)

Foucault, M., "Nietzsche, Genealogy, History" in Faubion, J. (ed.), *Aesthetics, Method and Epistemology: The Essential Works of Foucault 1954–1984, Vol II* (The New Press, 1999; trans. Hurley, R. et al.)

Foucault, M., "Lemon and Milk,", in Faubion, J. (ed.), *Power: The Essential Works of Foucault 1954–1984, Vol III* (Allen Lane, 2001; trans. Hurley, R. et al.)

Foucault, M., *Society Must Be Defended: Lectures at the Collège de France 1975–1976* (Penguin, 2003; ed. Bertani, M. and Fontana, A., trans. Macey, D.)

Foucault, M., *The Hermeneutics of the Subject: Lectures at the Collège de France 1981–1982* (Picador, 2005; ed. Gros, F., trans. Burchell, G.)

Foucault, M., *The Birth of Biopolitics: Lectures at the Collège de France 1978–1979* (Palgrave Macmillan, 2008; ed. Davidson, A., trans. Burchell, G.)

Foucault, M., *Security, Territory, Population: Lectures at the Collège de France, 1977–1978* (Palgrave Macmillan, 2008; ed. Senellart, M., trans. Burchell, G.)

Franck, T., "The Emerging Right to Democratic Governance," 86, *American Journal of International Law* (1992) 46

Frankovits, A., *The Human Rights Based Approach and the United Nations System* (UNESCO, 2006)

Fredman, S., *Human Rights Transformed* (Oxford University Press, 2008)

Friedman, M., *Capitalism and Freedom* (University of Chicago Press, 1982)

Fukuda-Parr, S., Lawson-Remer, T., and Randolph, S., "An Index of Economic and Social Rights Fulfilment: Concept and Methodology," 8 (3), *Journal of Human Rights* (2009) 195

Fukuda-Parr, S., Rawson-Lemer, T., and Randolph, S., *Fulfilling Social and Economic Rights* (Oxford University Press, 2015)

Galston, W., "Oakeshott's Political Theory: Recapitulation and Criticisms," in Podoksik, E. (ed.), *The Cambridge Companion to Oakeshott* (Cambridge University Press, 2011), 222

Galtung, J., "Alternative Models for Global Democracy," in Holden, B. (ed.), *Global Democracy: Key Debates* (Routledge, 2000), 143

Ganguly Thukral, E., "Budget for Children," in A. Nolan, O'Connell, R., and Harvey, C. (eds), *Human Rights and Public Finance: Budgets and the Promotion of Economic and Social Rights* (Hart, 2013), 139

Garde, A., "Advertising Regulation and the Protection of Children-Consumers in the European Union: In the Best Interests of ... Commercial Operators?" 19, *International Journal of Children's Rights* (2011) 523

Gaskarth, J. (ed.), *China, India and the Future of the International Society* (Rowman & Littlefield, 2015)

Gilson, E., "Ethics and the Ontology of Freedom: Problematization and Responsiveness in Foucault and Deleuze," 17, *Foucault Studies* (2014) 76

Gispen, M., and Toebes, B., "The Human Rights of Children in Tobacco Control," 41 (2), *Human Rights Quarterly* (2019) 340

Glendon, M. A., *Rights Talk: The Impoverishment of Political Discourse* (Free Press, 1991)

Golder, B., and Fitzpatrick, P., *Foucault's Law* (Routledge, 2009)

Goodhart, M. (ed.), *Human Rights: Politics and Practice* (2nd edition, Oxford University Press, 2012)

Graetz, G., and Franks, D., "Incorporating Human Rights Into the Corporate Domain: Due Diligence, Impact Assessment and Integrated Risk Management," 31 (2), *Impact Assessment and Project Appraisal* (2013) 97

Gray, J., *Enlightenment's Wake: Politics and Culture at the Close of the Modern Age* (Routledge, 1995)

Green, M., "What We Talk About When We Talk About Indicators: Current Approaches to Human Rights Measurement," 23 (4), *Human Rights Quarterly* (2001) 1062

Grotius, H., *De iure belli ac pacis* [1625] (Cambridge University Press, 2012; trans. Neff, S.)

Gunther, K., "The Legacies of Injustice and Fear: A European Approach to Human Rights and Their Effects on Political Culture," in Alston, P., Bustelo, M., and Heenan, J. (eds), *The EU and Human Rights* (Oxford University Press, 1999), 117

Habermas, J., "Modernity versus Postmodernity," 22, *New German Critique* (1981) 3

Habermas, J., *The Theory of Communicative Action, vol. II: Lifeworld and System: A Critique of Functionalist Reason* [1981] (Beacon Press, 1987; trans. McCarthy, T.)

Hacking, I., *The Taming of Chance* (Cambridge University Press, 1990)

Handsley, E., Nehmy, C., Mehta, K., and Coveney, J., "A Children's Rights Perspective on Food Advertising to Children," 22, *International Journal of Children's Rights* (2014) 93

Harding, C., "Statist Assumptions, Normative Individualism, and New Forms of Personality: Evolving a Philosophy of International Law for the Twenty First Century," 1, *Non-State Actors and International Law* (2001) 107

Hauriou, M., "The Theory of the Institution and the Foundation: A Study in Social Vitalism," in Broderick, A. (ed.), *The French Institutionalists: Maurice Hauriou, Georges Renard, Joseph T Delos* (Harvard University Press, 1970), 93

Hayek, F., *The Fatal Conceit: The Errors of Socialism* (University of Chicago Press, 1988)

Henkin, L., "International Law: Politics, Values, Functions," 216, *Collected Courses of The Hague Academy of International Law* (Brill, 1989)

Hoffmann, L., "The Universality of Human Rights," 125, *Law Quarterly Review* (2009) 416

Hopgood, S., *The Endtimes of Human Rights* (Cornell University Press, 2013)

Hopgood, S., "Fascism Rising," *Open Democracy*, 9th November 2016

Hunt, L., *Inventing Human Rights: A History* (WW Norton, 2007)

Hunt, P., "Configuring the UN Human Rights System in the 'Era of Implementation': Mainland and Archipelago," 39, *Human Rights Quarterly* (2017) 489

Ignatieff, M., "Human Rights, Global Ethics and the Ordinary Virtues," 31 (1), *Ethics & International Affairs* (2017) 3

Ignatieff, M., "Human Rights, Global Ethics and the Ordinary Virtues," 13 (1), *Journal of International Law and International Relations* (2017) 1

Judt, T., *Ill Fares the Land* (Penguin, 2010)

Kacowicz, A., "Global Governance, International Order, and World Order," in Levi-Faur, D. (ed.), *The Oxford Handbook of Governance* (Oxford University Press, 2012)

Kadelbach, S., Kleinlein, T., and Roth-Isigkeit, D. (eds) *System, Order and International Law* (Oxford University Press, 2017)

Kaldor, M., *New and Old Wars: Organized Violence in a Global Era* (Polity, 1999)

Kaldor, M., *Global Civil Society: An Answer to War* (Polity Press, 2003)

Kant, I., *On the Old Saw: That Might Be Right in Theory but It Won't Work in Practice* [1793] (University of Pennsylvania Press, 1974; trans. Ashton, E.)

Kant, I., *Perpetual Peace: A Philosophical Sketch* [1795] (Hacket Classics, 2003; trans. Humphrey, T.)

Kant, I., *Groundwork of the Metaphysic of Morals* [1785] (Cambridge University Press, 2012; trans. Gregor, M.)

Kausikan, B., "Asia's Different Standard," 92, *Foreign Policy* (1993) 24

Keck, M., and Sikkink, K., *Activists Beyond Borders: Advocacy Networks in International Politics* (Cornell University Press, 1998)

Kelley, D., *A Life of One's Own: Individual Rights and the Welfare State* (Cato Institute, 1998)

Kelsen, H., *Pure Theory of Law* [2nd edition, 1960] (University of California Press, 1967; trans. Knight, M.)

Kennedy, D., "The Mystery of Global Governance," 34, *Ohio Northern University Law Review* (2008) 827

Kingsbury, B. et al., "Foreword: Global Governance as Administration – National and Transnational Approaches to Global Administrative Law," 68, *Law & Contemporary Problems* (2005) 68

Kipnis, A., "Audit Cultures: Neoliberal Governmentality, Socialist Legacy, or Technologies of Governing?" 35 (2), *American Ethnologist* (2008) 275

Klabbers, J., "Constitutionalism Lite," 1, *International Organizations Law Review* (2004) 31

Klabbers, J., "Two Concepts of International Organization," 2, *International Organizations Law Review* (2005) 277

Klabbers, J., *International Law* (2nd edition, Cambridge University Press, 2018)

Knight, W., and Egerton, F. (eds), *The Routledge Handbook of the Responsibility to Protect* (Routledge, 2014)

Koh, H. H., "Why Do Nations Obey International Law?" 106, *Yale Law Journal* (1997) 2599

Koskenniemi, M., "The Effect of Rights on Political Culture," in Alston, P. (ed.), *The EU and Human Rights* (Oxford University Press, 1999), 99

Koskenniemi, M., *From Apology to Utopia: The Structure of International Legal Argument* (reissue with new epilogue, Cambridge University Press, 2005)

Koskenniemi, M., "Constitutionalism as Mindset: Reflections on Kantian Themes About International Law and Globalization," 8 (1), *Theoretical Inquiries in Law* (2007) 9

Koskenniemi, M., "International Law: Constitutionalism, Managerialism and the Ethos of Legal Education," 1, *European Journal of Legal Studies* (2007) 1

Koskenniemi, M., "The Fate of Public International Law: Between Technique and Politics," 70 (1), *Modern Law Review* (2007) 1

Koskenniemi, M., "The Politics of International Law – 20 Years Later," 20 (1), *European Journal of International Law* (2009) 7

Koskenniemi, M., "Between Coordination and Constitution: International Law as a German Discipline," 15, *Rediscriptions* (2011) 45

Koskenniemi, M., "Law, Teleology and International Relations: An Essay in Counterdisciplinarity," 26 (1), *International Relations* (2011) 3

Koskenniemi, M., "International Law and the Far Right: Reflections on Law and Cynicism," *4th Annual TMC Asser Lecture* (Asser Press, 2018)

Krisch, N., "Global Administrative Law and the Constitutional Ambition," in Dubner, P., and Loughlin, M. (eds), *The Twilight of Constitutionalism* (Oxford University Press, 2010)

Kumm, M., "The Legitimacy of International Law: A Constitutionalist Framework Analysis," 15, *European Journal of International Law* (2006) 907

Kundera, M., *The Unbearable Lightness of Being* (Faber & Faber, 1999; trans. Heim, M.)

Kuo, M. S., "Taming Governance with Legality?" 44, *NYU Journal of International Law & Politics* (2011–2012) 55

Kuosmanen, J., "Human Rights, Public Budgets and Epistemic Challenges," 17, *Human Rights Review* (2016) 247

Kuosmanen, J., "Towards 'Human Rights Compatible' Public Budgets – An Account of Institutional Virtues," 64 (3), *Political Studies* (2016) 683

Lafont, C., "Accountability and Global Governance: Challenging the State-Centric Conception of Human Rights," 3, *Ethics & Global Politics* (2010) 193

Landman, T., "Comparative Politics and Human Rights," 24 (4), *Human Rights Quarterly* (2002) 890

Langford, M., and Fukuda-Parr, S., "The Turn to Metrics," 30 (3), *Nordic Journal of Human Rights* (2012) 222

Lauterpacht, H., *International Law and Human Rights* (Stevens & Sons, 1950)

Letsas, G., *A Theory of Interpretation of the European Convention on Human Rights* (Oxford University Press, 2007)

Liddington, J., "Oakeshott: Freedom in a Modern European State," in Pelczynski, Z., and Gray, J. (eds), *Conceptions of Liberty* (St Martin's, 1984)

Liebenberg, S., *Socio-Economic Rights: Adjudication Under a Transformative Constitution* (Oxford University Press, 2010)

Locke, R., *The Promise and Limits of Private Power: Promoting Labour Standards in a Global Economy* (Cambridge, 2013)

Loeffler, J., and Versteeg, M., "The Future of Human Rights Scholarship," 81 (4), *Law & Contemporary Problems* (2018) i

Lotringer, S. (ed.), *The Politics of Truth* (Massachusetts Institute of Technology Press, 2007)

Loughlin, M., *Political Jurisprudence* (Oxford University Press, 2010)

Luhmann, N., *Political Theory in the Welfare State* [1981] (Walter de Gruyter, 1991; trans. Bednarz Jr., J.)

Lukes, S., "Can a Marxist Believe in Human Rights?" 1 (4), *Praxis International* (1984) 334

Macklem, P., "What is International Human Rights Law? Three Applications of a Distributive Account," 52, *McGill Law Journal* (2007) 575

Manion, M., Ralston, R., Matthews, T., and Allen, I. "Budget Analysis as a Tool to Monitor Economic and Social Rights: Where the Rubber of International Commitment Meets the Road of Government Policy," 9 (1), *Journal of Human Rights Practice* (2017) 146

Marks, S., "State Centrism, International Law and the Anxieties of Influence," 19, *Leiden Journal of International Law* (2006) 339

Marks, S., "Human Rights and Root Causes," 74, *Modern Law Review* (2011) 57

Marx, K., *Capital: A Critique of Political Economy: Vol I* [1867] (Penguin, 1976; trans. Fowkes, B.)

Marx, K., *On the Jewish Question* [1844], in Waldron, J. (ed.), *Nonsense Upon Stilts: Bentham, Burke and Marx on the Rights of Man* (Routledge, 1987), 137

Mazower, M., *Governing the World: The History of an Idea* (Penguin, 2012)

Mazower, M., *No Enchanted Palace: The End of Empire and the Ideological Origins of the United Nations* (Princeton University Press, 2013)

McConnell, L., *Extracting Accountability from Non-State Actors in International Law: Assessing the Scope for Direct Regulation* (Routledge, 2017)

McCrudden, C., "Mainstreaming Equality in the Governance of Northern Ireland," 22, *Fordham International Law Journal* (1999) 1696

McCrudden, C., "A Common Law of Human Rights?: Transnational Judicial Conversations on Constitutional Rights," 20, *Oxford Journal of Legal Studies* (2000) 499

McCrudden, C., "Mainstreaming and Human Rights," in C. Harvey (ed.), *Human Rights in the Community: Rights as Agents for Change* (Hart, 2005), 9

McInnes, N., "A Sceptical Conservative," 61, *The National Interest* (2000) 82

Mechlem, K., "Treaty Bodies and the Interpretation of Human Rights," 42, *Vanderbilt Journal of Transnational Law* (2009) 905

Mégret, F. and Hoffman, F., "The UN as a Human Rights Violator? Some Reflections on the United Nations' Changing Human Rights Responsibilities," 25, *Human Rights Quarterly* (2003) 314

Meier, B., and Onzivu, W., "The Evolution of Human Rights in World Health Organization Policy and the Future of Human Rights Through Global Health Governance," 128, *Public Health* (2014) 179

Mendez, J., and Cone, C., "Human Rights Make A Difference: Lessons from Latin America," in Shelton, D. (ed.), *The Oxford Handbook of International Human Rights Law* (Oxford University Press, 2015)

Meron, T., *Human Rights and Humanitarian Norms as Customary Law* (Oxford University Press, 1989)

Merton, R., "The Unanticipated Consequences of Purposive Social Action," 1 (6), *American Sociological Review* (1936) 894

Meyer, J., and Rowan, B., "Institutionalised Organisations: Formal Structure as Myth and Ceremony," 83 (2), *American Journal of Sociology* (1977) 340

Miller, P., and Rose, N., "Governing Economic Life," 19 (1), *Economy and Society* (1990) 1

Miller, P., and Rose, N., "Governing 'Advanced' Liberal Democracies," in Barry, A., and Osborne, T. (eds), *Foucault and Political Reason: Liberalism, Neo-Liberalism and Rationalities of Government* (University College London Press, 1996)

Moka-Mubelo, W., "Human Rights and Human Dignity," in *Reconciling Law and Morality in Human Rights Discourse: Beyond the Habermasian Account of Human Rights* (Springer, 2017)

Morsink, J., *The Universal Declaration of Human Rights: Origins, Drafting and Intent* (University of Pennsylvania Press, 2000)

Moyn, S., *The Last Utopia: Human Rights in History* (Harvard University Press, 2010)

Moyn, S., *Human Rights and the Uses of History* (Verso, 2014)

Moyn, S., "A Powerless Companion: Human Rights in the Age of Neoliberalism," 77, *Law & Contemporary Problems* (2014) 147

Moyn, S., "Beyond the Human Rights Measurement Controversy," 81 (4), *Law & Contemporary Problems* (2018) 121

Moyn, S., *Not Enough: Human Rights in an Unequal World* (Belknap Press, 2018)

Muller, A., and Seidensticker, F., *The Role of National Human Rights Institutions in the United Nations Treaty Body Process* (German Institute for Human Rights, 2007), pp. 36–42

Mutua, M., "The Complexity of Universalism in Human Rights," in Sajo, A. (ed.), *Human Rights with Modesty: The Problem of Universalism* (Springer, 2004), 51

Neave, G., "On the Cultivation of Quality, Efficiency and Enterprise: An Overview of Recent Trends in Higher Education in Western Europe 1986–1988," 23 (1), *European Journal of Education* (1988) 7

Nigro, R., "From Reason of State to Liberalism: The *Coup d'État* as a Form of Government," in Lemm, V. and Vatter, M. (eds), *The Government of Life: Foucault, Biopolitics and Neoliberalism* (Fordham University Press, 2014), 127

Nijman, J., "Foreword," in Koskenniemi, M., "International Law and the Far Right: Reflections on Law and Cynicism," *4th Annual TMC Asser Lecture* (Asser Press, 2018), ix

Nolan, A., O'Connell, R., and Harvey, C. et al. (eds), *Human Rights and Public Finance: Budgets and the Promotion of Economic and Social Rights* (Hart, 2013)

Nolan, A., Lusiani, N., and Courtis, C. "Two Steps Forward, No Steps Back? Evolving Criteria on the Prohibition of Retrogression in Economic and Social Rights," in Nolan, A. (ed.), *Economic and Social Rights After the Global Financial Crisis* (Cambridge University Press, 2014), 121

Nussbaum, M., *Women and Human Development* (Cambridge University Press, 2000)

O Cathaoir, K., "Children's Right to Freedom from Obesity: Responsibilities of the Food Industry," 36 (2), *Nordic Journal of Human Rights* (2018) 109

O'Flaherty, M., "The Concluding Observations of the United Nations Human Rights Treaty Bodies," 6, *Human Rights Law Review* (2006) 27

O'Sullivan, L., "Michael Oakeshott on European Political History," 21 (1), *History of Political Thought* (2000) 132

Oakeshott, M., *Rationalism in Politics* (Methuen, 1962)

Oakeshott, M., "The Tower of Babel," in Oakeshott, M., *Rationalism in Politics* (Methuen, 1962), 59

Oakeshott, M., *On Human Conduct* (Clarendon Press, 1975/1991)

Oakeshott, M., "The Masses in Representative Democracy," in Oakeshott, M., *Rationalism in Politics and Other Essays* (expanded edition, Liberty Fund, 1991), 363

Oakeshott, M., *Morality and Politics in Modern Europe: The Harvard Lectures* (Yale University Press, 1993)

Oakeshott, M. *The Politics of Faith and the Politics of Scepticism* (Yale University Press, 1996; ed. Fuller, T.)

Oakeshott, M., *On History and Other Essays* (Liberty Fund, 1999)

Oakeshott, M., *Lectures in the History of Political Thought* (Imprint Academic, 2006; ed. O'Sullivan, L.)

Oakeshott, M., *Early Political Writings, 1925–1930* (Imprint Academic, 2010; ed. O'Sullivan, L.)

Oakeshott, M., *Notebooks: 1922–86* (Imprint Academic, 2014; ed. O'Sullivan, L.)

Oberleitner, G., "A Decade of Mainstreaming Human Rights in the UN: Achievements, Failures, Challenges," 26, *Netherlands Quarterly of Human Rights* (2008) 359

Odysseos, L., "Human Rights, Liberal Ontogenesis and Freedom: Producing a Subject for Neoliberalism?" 38 (3), *Millennium* (2010) 747

Odysseos, L., Death, C., and Malmvig, H. (eds), "Interrogating Michel Foucault's Counter-Conduct: Theorising the Subjects and Practices of Resistance in Global Politics," 30 (2), *Global Society* (2016) 151

Orwell, G., *The Road to Wigan Pier* [1937] (Secker & Warburg, 1980)

Oszu, U., "Neoliberalism and Human Rights: The Brandt Commission and the Struggle for a New World," 81 (4), *Law & Contemporary Problems* (2018), 139

Papadopoulos, Y., "The Democratic Quality of Collaborative Governance" in Levi-Faur, D. (ed.), *The Oxford Handbook of Governance* (Oxford University Press, 2012), 515

Peerenboom, R., "Human Rights and Asian Values: The Limits of Universalism," 7 (2), *China Review International* (2000) 295

Pellet, A., "Human Rightism and International Law," Gilberto Amado Memorial Lecture, 10, *Italian Yearbook of International Law* (Brill, 2000), 1

Peters, A., "Global Constitutionalism," in Gibbons, M. (ed.), *The Encyclopedia of Political Thought* (Wiley, 2015), 1484

Phelan, E., "The New International Civil Service," 11, *Foreign Affairs* (1932–1933) 307

Philpott, S., "East Timor's Double Life: Smells Like Westphalian Spirit," 27 (1), *Third World Quarterly* (2006) 135

Pitkin, H., "Inhuman Conduct and Unpolitical Theory," 4, *Political Theory* (1976) 301

Popovic, D., "Prevailing of Judicial Activism Over Self-Restraint in the Jurisprudence of the European Court of Human Rights," 42, *Creighton Law Review* (2008–2009)

Porter, T., *Trust in Numbers* (Princeton University Press, 1995)

Power, M., *The Audit Society: Rituals of Verification* (Oxford University Press, 1997)

Prashad, V., *The Darker Nations: A People's History of the Third World* (New Press, 2007)

Raz, J., *The Authority of Law: Essays on Law and Morality* (Oxford University Press, 1979)

Reinisch, A., "The Changing International Legal Framework for Dealing with Non-State Actors," in P. Alston (ed.), *Non-State Actors and Human Rights* (Oxford University Press, 2005), 37

Reisman, M., "Designing and Managing the Future of the State," 8 (3), *European Journal of International Law* (1997) 409

Rhodes, R., *Understanding Governance: Policy Networks, Governance, Reflexivity and Accountability* (Open University Press, 1997)

Roberts, A., "The So-Called 'Right' of Humanitarian Intervention," 3, *Yearbook of International Humanitarian Law* (2000) 3

Robertson, G., *Crimes Against Humanity: The Struggle for Global Justice* (Penguin, 1999)

Rose, N., "The Death of the Social? Refiguring the Territory of Government," 25 (3), *Economy and Society* (1996) 327

Rosga, A., and Satterthwaite, M., "The Trust in Indicators: Measuring Human Rights," 27 (2), *Berkeley Journal of International Law* (2009) 253

Ross, E. A., *Social Control: A Survey of the Foundations of Order* (Macmillan, 1901)

Rozakis, C., "The European Judge as Comparatist," 80, *Tulane Law Review* (2005) 257

Ruggie, J. "Commentary on the Guiding Principles on Business and Human Rights," 29 (2), *Netherlands Quarterly of Human Rights* (2011) 224

Ruggie, J., "The Social Construction of the UN Guiding Principles on Business and Human Rights," Corporate Responsibility Initiative Working Paper (June 2017)

Ruggie, J., and Sherman, J. III, "The Concept of 'Due Diligence' in the UN Guiding Principles on Business and Human Rights: A Reply to Jonathan Bonnitcha and Robert McCorquodale," 28 (3), *European Journal of International Law* (2017) 921

Schacter, O., "The Decline of the Nation-State and Its Implications for International Law," 36, *Columbia Journal of Transnational Law* (1998) 7

Scheingold, S., *The Politics of Rights: Lawyers, Public Policy and Political Change* (2nd edition, University Michigan Press, 2011)

Scheinin, M., "International Mechanisms and Procedures for Implementation," in Hanski, R. and Suksi, M. (eds), *An Introduction to the International Protection of Human Rights* (Institute for Human Rights, 1997), 369

Schwoebel, C., "Situation the Debate on Global Constitutionalism," 8, *International Journal of Constitutional Law* (2010) 611

Schwoebel, C., "The Appeal of the Project of Global Constitutionalism to Public International Lawyers," 13, *German Law Journal* (2012) 22

Segal, J., "Freedom and Normalisation: Poststructuralism and the Liberalism of Michael Oakeshott," in 97 (3), *American Political Science Review* (2003) 447

Sen, A., *Development as Freedom* (Oxford University Press, 1999)

Sepulveda, M., *The Nature of the Obligations Under the International Covenant on Economic, Social and Cultural Rights* (Intersentia, 2003)

Shamsul Alam, S. M., *Governmentality and Counter-Hegemony in Bangladesh* (Palgrave Macmillan, 2015)

Shelton, D. (ed.), *The Oxford Handbook of International Human Rights Law* (Oxford University Press, 2013)

Simma, B., "Mainstreaming Human Rights: The Contribution of the International Court of Justice," 3 (1), *Journal of International Dispute Settlement* (2012) 7

Slaughter, A. M., *A New World Order* (Princeton University Press, 2005)

Smith, A., *The Theory of Moral Sentiments* [6th edition, 1790] (Penguin, 2009; ed. Hanley, R.)

Sohn, L., "The Human Rights Law of the Charter," 12, *Texas Journal of International Law* (1977) 129

Soininen, S., *From a "Necessary Evil" to the Art of Contingency: Oakeshott's Conception of Political Activity* (Imprint Academic, 2005)

Sokhi-Bulley, B., *Governing (Through) Rights: Human Rights Law in Perspective* (Hart, 2016)

Somek, A., "Kelsen Lives," 18 (3), *European Journal of International Law* (2007) 409

Somek, A., "A Bureaucratic Turn?" 22 (2), *European Journal of International Law* (2011) 345

Strathern, M., "The Tyranny of Transparency," 26 (3), *British Educational Research Journal* (2000) 309

Supiot, A., *Governance By Numbers: The Making of a Legal Model of Allegiance* (Hart, 2017; trans. Brown, S.)

Swaine, A., "Globalising Women, Peace and Security: Trends in National Action Plans," in Aroussi, S. (ed.), *Rethinking National Action Plans on Women, Peace and Security* (IOS Publishing, 2017)

Tamanaha, B, *On the Rule of Law: History, Politics, Theory* (Cambridge University Press, 2004)

Teubner, G., "Fragmented Foundations: Social Constitutionalism Beyond the Nation State," in Dobner, P. and Loughlin, M. (eds), *The Twilight of Constitutionalism?* (Oxford University Press, 2010), 327

Teubner, G., *Constitutional Fragments: Societal Constitutionalism and Globalization* (Oxford University Press, 2012)

Thomas, C., "The Rights Revolution and America's Urban Poor: Victims or Beneficiaries?" Address Before the Federalist Society and the Manhattan Institute (16th May 1994), in 60 *Vital Speeches of the Day* (1994), 514

Thomas, R., and Magar, V., "Mainstreaming Human Rights Across the WHO," in Meier, B. and Gostin, L. (eds), *Human Rights in Global Health* (Oxford University Press, 2018), 133

Thornhill, C., "A Sociology of Constituent Power: The Political Code of Transnational Societal Constitutions," 20 (2), *Indiana Journal of Global Legal Studies* (2013) 551

Tollefson, C., Zito, A., and Gale, F., "Conceptualising New Governance Arrangements," 90 (1), *Public Administration* (2012) 3

Tomuschat, C., "Obligations Arising for States Without or Against Their Will," 241, *Recueil des Cours* (1993) 195

Tomuschat, C., "International Law: Ensuring the Survival of Mankind on the Eve of a New Century," 281 *Recueil des Cours* (1999) 10

Tonkiss, K., "Contesting Human Rights Through Institutional Reform: The Case of the UK Equality and Human Rights Commission," 20 (4), *International Journal of Human Rights* (2016) 491

Trilling, L., "Manners, Morals and The Novel," in *The Liberal Imagination: Essays on Literature and Society* (Secker & Warburg, 1951), 205

Trindade, C., *International Law for Humankind* (Brill, 2010)

Tsoukas, H., "The Tyranny of Light," 29 (9), *Futures* (1997) 827

Vandenhole, W. (ed.), *Challenging Territoriality in Human Rights Law: Building Blocks for a Plural and Diverse Duty-Bearer Regime* (Routledge, 2015)

Vatter, M., "Foucault and Hayek: Republican Law and Civil Society," in Lemm, V., and Vatter, M. (eds), *The Government of Life: Foucault, Biopolitics, and Neoliberalism* (Fordham University Press, 2014)

von Bogdandy, A., Dann, P., and Goldmann, M., "Developing the Publicness of Public International Law: Towards a Legal Framework for Global Governance Activities" in von Bogdandy, A. et al. (eds), *The Exercise of Public Authority by International Institutions: Advancing International Institutional Law* (Springer, 2010)

von Pufendorf, S., *De iure naturae et gentium* [1672] (Oceana, 1964; trans. Oldfather, W. and Oldfather, C.)

Waldron, J., "The Rule of International Law," 30, *Harvard Journal of Law & Public Policy* (2006) 15

Waldron, J., "Are Sovereigns Entitled to the Benefit of the International Rule of Law?" 22 (2), *European Journal of International Law* (2011) 315

Weissbrodt, D., and Kruger, M., "Human Rights Responsibilities of Businesses as Non-State Actors," in P. Alston, P. (ed.), *Non-State Actors and Human Rights* (Oxford University Press, 2005), 315

Welling, J., "International Indicators and Economic, Social and Cultural Rights," 30, *Human Rights Quarterly* (2008) 933

Wells, C., and Elias, J., "Catching the Conscience of the King: Corporate Players on the International Stage," in P. Alston (ed.), *Non-State Actors and Human Rights* (Oxford University Press, 2005), 141

Wheatley, S., *The Idea of International Human Rights Law* (Oxford University Press, 2019)

Wiessner, S., and Willard, A., "Policy-Oriented Jurisprudence and Human Rights Abuses in Internal Conflict: Toward a World Public Order of Human Dignity," 93, *American Journal of International Law* (1999) 316

Winter, J., and Prost, A., *Rene Cassin and Human Rights: From the Great War to the Universal Declaration* (2nd edition, Cambridge University Press, 2013)

Woods, N., "Held to Account: Governance in the World Economy," in Kuper, A. (ed.), *Global Responsibilities: Who Must Deliver on Human Rights?* (Routledge, 2012), 251

Yip, E., "Globalization and the Future of the Law of the Sovereign State," 8 (3), *International Journal of Constitutional Law* (2010) 636

Zumbansen, P., "Defining the Space of Transnational Law: Legal Theory, Global Governance and Legal Pluralism," 21 (2), *Transnational Law & Contemporary Problems* (2012) 305

Index

EU authorised representative for GPSR:
Easy Access System Europe, Mustamäe tee 50,
10621 Tallinn, Estonia
gpsr.requests@easproject.com

www.ingramcontent.com/pod-product-compliance
Lightning Source LLC
Chambersburg PA
CBHW051956270326
41929CB00015B/2673